THE CHIMERA PRINCIPLE

Hau
BOOKS

www.haubooks.com

THE CHIMERA PRINCIPLE
AN ANTHROPOLOGY OF MEMORY AND IMAGINATION

Carlo Severi

Translated by Janet Lloyd
Foreword by David Graeber

Hau Books
Chicago

Cover and layout design: Sheehan Moore
Typesetting: Prepress Plus (www.prepressplus.in)

ISBN: 978-0-9905050-5-1
LCCN: 2014953485

HAU Books
Chicago Distribution Center
11030 S. Langley
Chicago, IL 60628
www.haubooks.com

HAU Books is marketed and distributed by The University of Chicago Press. www.press.uchicago.edu

Printed and bound by CPI Group (UK) Ltd, Croydon, CR0 4YY

Haida mask, New York, American Museum of Natural History.

For Gabriella, Matteo, and Cosimo

Contents

Foreword

Concerning mental pivots and civilizations of memory

> *Fritz Saxl used to say that Warburg, in each of his articles, would write an introduction to a science that would never see the light of day.* (p. 38)

> *[E]very technique for remembering is also a technique of the imagination.* (p. 199)

It's hard to deny, these days, that many fields of anthropology have been reduced to a desultory state. These include some of those that, traditionally, have been most vital, such as the study of kinship. But nowhere is it more true than for the study of myth, ritual, cosmology—all those endeavors through which anthropologists once aspired to contribute to a broader, comparative science of meaning. It is very hard to imagine any contemporary anthropologist producing an analysis of a mythic cycle, a sacrificial ritual, or even, say, temple architecture with the richness and density we used to expect regularly from figures like Claude Lévi-Strauss, Nancy Munn, or Victor Turner.[1] The irony is not because there have been no advances in our understandings of such matters over the last several decades. To the contrary: it's precisely because there have been.

---

1. Or, if someone did, of anyone taking them seriously or paying much attention to them.

The dilemma is, as cognitive science has demonstrated, that the entire apparatus of assumptions about the nature of language, meaning, and thought on which those analyses was founded is simply false, but it has not yet provided us with the tools to create nearly as sophisticated analyses on a more sound basis. We know now that symbolic thought is not structured like a language. We understand that no synthesis of Prague school phonemics and Schleiermachian hermeneutics will ever get us even remotely close to understanding what is really happening when a man in Borneo recites a prayer over the disinterred bones of his ancestor, or a woman in Burundi tells a funny story while embroidering a piece of cloth. We know the tools we had been using were wildly inadequate. But any new tools we have are still extraordinarily crude. Cognitive science (let alone neuroscience, or allied branches of philosophy) has not come anywhere close to providing us with means to build analytical structures that could rival something like, say, Jean-Pierre Vernant's (1980) analysis of the myth of Prometheus, Lévi-Strauss' *The raw and the cooked* ([1964] 1983), let alone, to take just one example, the kind of richly beautiful ethnographic analysis we find in a book like Catherine Hugh-Jones' *From the Milk River* (1978) or Stephen Hugh-Jones' *The palm and the Pleiades* (1979).

We have, therefore, the promise of a new science of thought in front of us. We know it will someday exist. But we still don't know what it will ultimately look like.

True, the situation has, admittedly, played itself out quite differently in the English-speaking world than on the Continent. Anglophone social theorists have reacted mainly by abandoning any pretense that what they are doing has much to do with science in the first place. It's rare even to hear the term "social science" anymore, except from rational choice theorists and similar positivists. Instead, the project has been redefined as "social theory," and "theory" now refers not to hypotheses that can be tested in some way, but to ideas culled from the tradition of Continental philosophy, starting with Spinoza and ending, perhaps, with Derrida, Agamben, or Badiou. In contrast, French, German, and Italian social theorists have been reluctant to accept such a division. Many are much more willing to try to incorporate the results of cognitive science with the (largely Anglo-American) tradition of analytic philosophy that has engaged with it. They have, in other words, at least begun to undertake the painstaking and often decidedly unglamorous work of rebuilding everything from scratch.[2]

*

Carlo Severi's *The chimera principle* is, it seems to me, the first work in that latter tradition that affords us a glimpse of what this new, fully evolved science of meaning—one that does not simply do violence to what we know now about the human mind and human communication, but one that also is capable of genuinely engaging with all the big questions of myth, magic, art, ritual—might eventually look like. This is why its publication in English can be considered a landmark.

Granted, it is a first effort, a series of explorations, a throwing open of windows, each vista opening the way to another even more sweeping vision of some body of inquiry that may someday come to exist. But this is only half its charm and power. It is a work that reminds us of futures long forgotten, of days when it seemed self-evident to those drawn to the discipline that anthropology would, eventually, unlock the secrets of the human soul. Fittingly, Severi draws here on a great tradition of other such unrealized or half-realized intellectual projects from those early days: Augustus Pitt-Rivers' biology of images, Aby Warburg's Atlas of Memory, Gregory Bateson's sketch for an ethnography of the materiality of Iatmul thought, Frances Yates' (1966) work on the Medieval arts of memory and the literature that has followed in its wake.

Yates' book is an excellent example of such frustrated promises—or perhaps it just seems that way to me because I'm old enough to remember when it was (re)discovered in the anthropology department in Chicago in the 1980s. I well remember, as a graduate student, the excitement with which many of us felt, especially as we compared it with A. R. Luria's *The mind of mnemonist* (republished in 1987), and Jonathan Spence's *The memory palace of Matteo Ricci* (1985). We were convinced that something important was happening—or should be; that a new sub-discipline

---

2.   It is not of course entirely confined to the Continent—my own department, at LSE, has a significant cognitive tradition as well. But it is somewhat exceptional in this regard, and there are direct links—especially via Maurice Bloch—to the tradition of Dan Sperber and Pascal Boyer in France.

dedicated to the comparative study of mnemotechnics was in the process of formation. But it never ultimately happened. Apart from a couple pioneering, but largely ignored, works by David Napier (1987, 1996), the anticipated field failed to materialize, and everyone moved on to other things.[3] Perhaps now, in retrospect, we can understand why: the field just wasn't ready to absorb this kind of material; the intellectual tools at our disposal were simply inadequate. Now, with this book, a quarter century later, the moment seems to have finally arrived.

*

It is as a book about the arts of memory, one imagines, that *The chimera principle* is most likely to make its mark. Perhaps this is understandable: it certainly makes a very provocative intervention in this regard. Much of what we have considered "primitive art," the author argues, were not meant as self-contained objects in their own right, or even as elements in some larger performance, but as memory cues to texts—usually to be performed in some sort of ritual context—whose exact nature is, often as not, entirely lost to us. These images were never meant to exist apart from words. Yet those words were a form of artistry in and of themselves. The conclusion immediately shatters half a dozen complacent assumptions we normally bring, unthinkingly, to any analysis of comparative aesthetics: the assumption of a simple distinction between "orality" and "literacy," for example; the notion of "picture-writing"; most of our assumptions about the relationship between icon, ritual, and text. And that shattering of assumptions, in turn, proves endlessly productive. Over the course of the book it allows Severi to raise a whole series of further questions about magic, knowledge, trauma, and imagination to create a fresh technical terminology (e.g., the song-form, *nachleben*, objective and

---

3. One particularly poignant memory I have from Chicago in the 1980s was Napier delivering a Monday seminar, in which he outlined the possibility of a Yatesian anthropology of memory; then, watching as he stood awkwardly about the wine and cheese table and not a single faculty member approached him to ask any questions about it. I desperately wanted to approach him, but couldn't figure out quite what to ask.

subjective parallelism, chimera-objects, projective belief), and thus to cast even more complacent assumptions into doubt.

Still, it would be a shame if *The chimera principle* ends up being remembered simply as a book about memory techniques. True, even if that's all it were, its publication would be a landmark. But its aims are in fact much more ambitious. Severi not only builds on imaginary sciences, he also lays the groundwork for a veritable science of the imagination. It is not memory but the nature of the human imagination that the author is ultimately trying to understand. The matter is rarely stated quite as explicitly as it might be. Sometimes one almost has the sense the author feels if he were to name his quarry too explicitly, it would take heed and slip away. Still this ultimate purpose shapes every aspect of the argument: from the early evocation of Vischer and Löwy on memory images to the startling analyses of messianic and penitential cult movements with which *The chimera principle* comes to a close. The premise of the book is that there is always, everywhere, an intrinsic relation between the means by which we store and classify knowledge, and what would otherwise seem to be its opposite, "evocation, ideation, and poetic imagination," the inner resources that enable us to leap beyond the received order of things to create something radically new.

Hence the "chimera principle" itself. The central argument is that imagination is a social phenomenon, dialogic even, but crucially one that typically works itself out through the mediation of objects that are at once paradoxical, startling (in such as way as to become *imagines agentes*, "active" in the Yatesian sense), but also—and this is the crucial element others have largely ignored—to some degree unfinished, teasingly schematic in such a way as to, almost perforce, mobilize the imaginative powers of the recipient to fill in the blanks. Even what we are accustomed to thinking of as religious or magical "belief," Severi argues, is largely to be accounted for through the workings of this unstable, inherently ambiguous, endlessly imaginative process of paradox and imaginative projection.

*

A science of imagination. It's hard to imagine an intellectual project more ambitious. As much as anything that has been written in recent decades, this book really is an attempt to use the tools of anthropology to unfathom secrets of the human soul.

*

How then to celebrate a book of such ambitions? Perhaps best by simply pausing to reflect on some of the vistas it opens up. Consider, for a moment, the question of history. It was always clear that the ancient and medieval systems of "artificial memory" described by Yates (1964), Carruthers ([1990] 2008), and the rest, based on the arrangement of striking images in sequence within a fixed imaginary space, had to be rooted—however idiosyncratic they seemed—in some kind of universal human capacity. How else, for instance, could Luria's twentieth-century Russian mnemonist have come up with almost exactly the same system with, apparently, absolutely no awareness that he was doing so? So: are the various lost arts of memory described in this book also independent inventions, historically unconnected? Actually, there is one surprising piece of evidence that suggests that they are not.

For Severi, the "chimera principle" goes well beyond the mere creation of "chimera objects" such as Warburg's lightning-serpent, or actual gorgons and chimeras—that is, images created by schematizing and formalizing parts of animal or human bodies and recombining them in striking and unexpected ways. It is a much more general principle which lies at the heart of human imaginative practices everywhere. Still, it is helpful to focus for a moment on monstrous images of this sort. Because they do seem to have a specific history. They did not always exist. As archeologist David Wengrow painstakingly demonstrates in his recent monograph *The origins of monsters* (2013), in the Pleistocene, and on through the Neolithic, such figures were either extraordinarily rare or entirely nonexistent. The habit of breaking creatures up into abstract component elements and then reassembling them into strange—and usually terrifying—forms has a specific historical origin: it is the product of what he calls "the first age of mechanical reproduction," roughly corresponding to the creation of the first bureaucratic systems of governance in Mesopotamia and Egypt, whose administrative cadres were also responsible for the systematic development of systems of math and writing, and who, generally, specialized in this sort of schematization and rearrangement of aspects of the world. Odd though it may sound, chimeras were originally a bureaucratic invention.

In other words, for much of our history, some of the features we are used to identifying most closely with "primitive art" simply did not exist. At best, hybrid creatures might have popped up here and there as isolated flights of fancy, but there was nothing remotely like the systematic elaboration we've come to associate with, say, Sepik River societies of Melanesia, the Northwest coast of North America, or the nomadic kingdoms of Central Asia. And when they did appear in the bureaucratic environments of Egypt or Mesopotamia, they do not seem to have had anything to do with the kind of mnemotechnics that Severi describes. True, once they existed, the "cognitive catch" that made such images so potentially easy to fix in memory did, gradually, have its effect. Eventually, images of composite creatures spread almost everywhere, and took on a new life and new meaning as they did. Yet how this happened, and why, is something historians have hardly begun to piece together.

We don't know what really happened, but, since this is a book about imagination, perhaps it would be fitting to apply some and try to envision one possible scenario. Let us say, perhaps, there came to be a certain band of civilization, existing alongside, in opposition to, yet also intimately related to the bureaucratic urban civilizations with their writing systems. These have been referred to as heroic societies (Chadwick 1926, Wengrow 2011, Graeber 2013), but they could just as easily be referred to as "civilizations of heroic memory." Both the bureaucratic and commercial cities of the valleys, and the heroic societies of the hills, deserts, and steppes surrounding them, came to define themselves against one another. Where one valued order and administrative regularity, the other created an endlessly fluctuating world of heroic aristocrats, boasting, dueling, vying with one another in every sort of spectacular potlatch or sacrifice. Where one was held together by registers, ledgers, and accounts, the other rejected writing systems altogether, substituting either the kind of elaborate systems of oral composition that Parry (1930) and Lord ([1960] 2000) so famously described (which almost invariably were used to extemporize heroic epics that celebrated precisely this sort of heroic society), or, we can now add, the kinds of iconographic memory systems Carlo Severi documents.

Could these arts of memory have formed originally not as an alternative but as a defiant response to urbanization and written script? It's possible. In fact, in the case of the Old World, it fits the evidence quite nicely. Still, the case of the Americas renders this picture infinitely more complex. It is by no means entirely clear what relation, say, the Hopi or Bellacoola had to the large urban civilizations of the Mississippi Valley or Central Mexico. And those urban civilizations themselves had an extremely ambivalent relationship with writing. We would have to ask why the evolution of bureaucratic systems of tallies and accounts, which ultimately led to the development of Mesopotamian cuneiform and Egyptian hieroglyphics, took such a different course in the Andes—where the tallies did not lead to the emergence of a script—and Central America, where writing emerged only among the Maya and was not adopted by any of their neighbors.

In fact, it has always struck me that the latter is one of the great historical mysteries that almost no one has really attempted to explain. Mesopotamian cuneiform was widely adopted by neighboring urban civilizations, and in the process simplified into Ugaritic, and then into the Phoenician alphabet, which became the basis for an endless series of different scripts. Nothing like this happened in the Americas. Why was the Maya syllabic system never adopted by any of their neighbors? Why did the urban civilizations of Oaxaca, for example—who obviously would have known about it—instead continue to write codices using the sort of memory systems Severi describes?

Once we throw off the evolutionary shackles that still implicitly dominate our thinking on such matters, and realize that politics has always existed, such questions become far easier to address. After all, what is politics, in the final analysis, but a collection of quarrels over contrasting conceptions of what is valuable in human life? Perhaps the balance of forces in the Americas simply came out the other way. In Eurasia and Africa, bureaucratic civilization proved resilient and enduring, and heroic systems of memory where either pushed to the margins, or, as in the classical and medieval European worlds, were maintained as a kind of subculture in the shadow of the written word. Could it be that early systems of writing did emerge in a remote historical past we are now unable to reconstruct—perhaps not just in the Maya lowlands but elsewhere? And that a similar dynamic of schismogenetic mutual definition did take place, but that the political balance in this case tipped the other way? After all, if, say, the Olmecs had produced thousands of barkcloth codices, how would we really know? Perhaps the complex of values that came to be ranged against the urban, bureaucratic systems simply proved more resilient, and even in the cities, scribes came to adopt the alternative memory systems instead.

This is pure speculation. We really do not know. It's possible we never could know. Still, I think the notion of "civilizations of heroic memory" might provide a helpful starting point for a larger historical analysis—even if one that will probably have to be discarded once we develop a more nuanced understanding. If nothing else, many of the techniques described in this book seem designed to lend themselves to ostentatiously heroic feats of recall. One need think only of the extraordinary capacities of Iatmul men of knowledge, each bearing in his head lists of up to tens of thousands of totemic names. The Iatmul seem a perfect example of a society in which heroic values have been, as it were, democratized: where instead of a mass of retainers shifting allegiance between a collection of boastful feuding aristocrats, and an elite of bards or priests or druids—masters of complex, unwritten arcane lore—*all* adult males are expected to be either "men of violence" or "men of discretion," boastful warriors or guardians of totemic lore. Surely, in the endless heated men's house debates that mark Iatmul political life, feats of memory are meant to directly parallel heroic feats in war. Here, memory itself becomes an exploit.

Yet it is also—as in just about every example recounted in the book—a memory *of* exploits as well.

In no case, among the many cases Severi assembles, do we encounter the kind of lists, inventories, and accounting procedures that appear to have led to the development of writing in Mesopotamia, Egypt, the Indus Valley, or China. Math is minimal. Even the Iatmul lists of names, which might seem to bear the closest resemblance to what we have come to think of as bureaucratic procedures, really encode moments in a mythic journey that led to the gradual creation of the material and social universe. In every case the narratives these arts of memory seek to preserve involve travels, either in physical or conceptual space; almost invariably, too, these travels are punctuated by heroic feats of creation or destruction. They are memories of hunts, shamanic journeys, or military expeditions. The form, and content, of the systems of memory appears to bear a constant homology, one which itself suggests a structure of value inherently opposed to those embodied in writing as administrative technique.[4]

*

One legacy of that complex of values that has historically surrounded and supported techniques of writing is the notion of the "text." Ideally, a text, once created, is seen as floating entirely free of any concrete context of its creation or, not to mention, as a purely linguistic abstraction in no way dependent on any particularly visual element (typeface, illustrations, size, shape, design, etc.) through which it might, at any moment, be embodied or conveyed. This is the conception of text that lay behind the most influential works of interpretive anthropology (the Balinese cockfight being, of course, the most famous example)— much to the disadvantage of the hermeneutic project as a whole. But of course, this conception of text itself represents a kind of utopian ideal, in which the imaginative genius of a single, unique artist is seen to create an equally unique object destined to transcend space and time to endure forever.

That complex of values that has supported the various arts of memory has entirely different implications. In many of the cases examined in this book, the "texts," such as they are, are precisely what we no longer have. But in a way, this is a minor absence, since texts in anything like that utopian sense clearly do not exist and no one really imagines that they ought to. We are confronted instead with a series of material technologies that externalize the process of memory and imagination, making that process something intrinsically dialogic and contextual. Everything turns on a tacit complicity, whereby the author leaves the work, in effect,

---

4.   All of this leads to equally interesting questions about shamanism, which we are used to imagining as the primordial form of religion, again, on tacitly evolutionist grounds. Is it possible that shamanism—at least in the form we currently know it—was also a historical innovation that did not exist before a specific, identifiable point in time? Imagining such a thing seems particularly daunting.

half-finished so as to "capture the imagination" of the interpreter. This clearly has powerful implications for any theory of human creativity.

It seems to me it has important implications for our most basic understanding of human thought as well.

Let me conclude by explaining what I mean by this. In recent years, two philosophers of mind, Andy Clark and David Chalmers (1998), have created a great deal of stir both among analytical philosophers and cognitive scientists by challenging the assumption that the human mind must necessarily be coextensive with the brain. The assumption seems to be contradicted even by the most ordinary everyday experience. Consider, they propose, two people: one is trying to remember a colleague's name and calls it up from their memory; the other has a bad memory and turns just as automatically to their address book. Or perhaps one is doing a problem of long division in her head, and the other is working it out with a pencil and paper. If so, why is the notebook, or the pencil and paper, not, at that moment, part of that person's mind? If mind is a process of thinking, then surely the notebook, or the pencil and paper, play exactly the same role in the process as the part of their brain would have done and which otherwise would have been activated. It would be completely arbitrary to insist that the part of the woman's brain in which one is working out the long division is part of one's mind, during the moment when she is solving the problem, but that the pencil and paper is not.

This would indeed seem to be common sense; but it has enormous implications. Clark and Chalmers are more interested in human beings' relations to technology than in their relations to one another, so they devote a great deal of energy to fobbing off what any anthropologist would (I hope) consider the obvious next question: if this is true of the dynamic relation between human brains and physical technologies (abacuses, computers, rooms arranged in such a way to act as astrological calendars, etc.), then what about the relationship between brains and other brains? Cognitive science reveals that fully self-conscious thought is remarkably fleeting. Unless one practices some form of artificial mental discipline like meditation, conscious reflection rarely lasts more than a few seconds. Or, this is true of *solitary* reflection. It's obviously not the case when one is engaged in intense conversation with someone else. (This is presumably the reason so many people engage in imaginary dialogues when trying to work out a problem.) But if so, self-conscious thought generally tends to occur precisely when the difference between one mind and another is least apparent, when it might make just as much sense to speak of a single, dialogic consciousness.

The extended mind hypothesis, as it has come to be called, is one of the more dramatic philosophical breakthroughs of recent years. Yet it is riddled with gaps, contradictions, and conceptual blind spots. Its best-known exponents have almost nothing to say about creativity, cultural meaning, or social relations; sometimes they write as if they were actually unaware of them. Yet a book like this is precisely what's required to begin to turn all this around.

But consider the perspective such an approach opens up. Severi cites Vischer, Löwy, Warburg, and ultimately Boas to make a compelling case that what was then described as "primitive art" is not a crude attempt to represent the world as it reveals itself to human vision, but, rather, is a representation of mental space, of objects of memory and imagination as they reveal themselves to the human mind. Yet if he is right about the role so many of these objects played in arts of memory, and if the extended mind hypothesis is right, then we can go much further. When an archeologist unearths a series of ancient chimera-objects, she is not simply discovering a representation of the inside of an ancient mind, she is holding in her hand an object that actually *was* part of a human mind. Indeed, insofar as we think through our physical environment, we are surrounded by objects that are, in certain contexts, forms of consciousness, though merely background noise in others. But if so, the images discussed in this book are of a class of objects that plays a particularly important role in human thought because, by mobilizing imagination in such a way to link different brains, at least momentarily, contextually, into one unified process of thinking, they become pivots around which—through which—new forms of dialogic consciousness—new minds—come into being.

Armed with this understanding, would it not be possible to return to some of the foundational issues of classical social theory—e.g., Marx's fetishes, Durkheim's ritual effervescence—and see them in an entirely different light? But this time, return to them armed with a conceptual apparatus that actually reflects the findings of contemporary science? It is exciting to imagine that we are finally living in times when such things have become possible again.

DAVID GRAEBER
London, January 2015

Acknowledgments

I embarked upon the research from which this book emerged during my stay, as Getty scholar, at the Getty Institute for the Institute of Art and the Humanities in Los Angeles (1994–95). Up until then I had always focused my work on specific and localized ethnographical cases. Thanks to the, to me, stupefying range of the libraries to which I had access, I was, for the first time, able to engage in comparative anthropology, and I should now like to express all my gratitude to Salvatore Settis, who, through his friendly invitation, made this work possible. I should also like to thank all those who took part in the internal Getty seminar, which, that year, was centred on the theme "Image and Memory" and in which I presented the first results of my research work: in particular Jan Assman, Michael Baxandall, Lina Bolzoni, Mary Carruthers, Carlo Ginzburg, François Hartog, Krzysztof Pomian, Jacques Revel, Michael Roth, and Randolph Starn. In 1997 and 1998, Salvatore Settis and Michael Roth again invited me to the Getty during the summer months; and so I was able to expand my earlier results more deeply, checking them out and correcting them.

It was eight years later, in 2002–3, that an invitation made it possible for me to finish writing this book as a Fellow at the Wissenschaftskolleg in Berlin. There, I was able to make the most of the marvelous work of the librarians and the help of other friends and colleagues: Reinhardt Meyer-Kalkus, Eric Brian, and above all Wiktor Stoichita, who was kind enough to read and comment on part of my manuscript. Thanks to the friendly welcome from Peter Bolz and Viola König, the Ethnological Museum of Berlin allowed me to work on its marvelous Amerindian collections, in particular the *Dakota Bible*.

Between 1996 and 2002, a number of colleagues were kind enough to discuss my plan for an anthropology of memory, a first draft of which I am presenting in the present book. I should like to mention the seminars that, at the invitation of Jan Assman, I was able to organize, over several years, at the University of Heidelberg; the one that Claude Imbert, Jean-Philippe Antoine, and I organized at the École Normale Supérieure in the rue d'Ulm; and the one that Giovanni Careri and I set up, in 1997, at the École des Hautes Études en Sciences Sociales. Since my election in 2002 as a director of studies at the EHESS, my foremost critics have always been those who took part in my seminars devoted to the "Anthropology of Memory." My warmest thanks must therefore go to them. More recently, a number of seminars given at the Universities of Johns Hopkins (Baltimore), Venice, Mexico, and Rio de Janeiro have provided opportunities for fruitful exchanges.

David Graeber's acceptance to write a foreword to this English translation has been for me a pleasure, and an honor. Janet Lloyd has been an extremely talented, perceptive and helpful translator. I wish to thank her wholeheartedly. I would like to add a warm expression of gratitude to Giovanni Da Col, the founder of Hau Books, and to Sean Dowdy, its Managing Editor. It has been a great pleasure to share their enthusiasm, and an exceptional experience to work with them. If Social Anthropology still is an exciting crossroad of intense intellectual debates, it is thanks to passionate young researchers like them. I also wish to thank Justin Dyer, Sheehan Moore, and all the Hau Books editorial team. Without hesitation I can state that their professionalism is among the finest in academic publishing.

Other friends too have supported and helped me over all those years. I owe a great deal to Talia Pecker Berio, Maurizio Bettini, Marcel Détienne, Carlos Fausto, Françoise Héritier, Caroline Humphrey, Jean Jamin, Gilbert Lewis, Charles Malamoud, Manuela Tartari, Nathan Wachtel, and Harvey Whitehouse. My master, Claude Lévi-Strauss, followed every step of my work. To the thoughts that I confided to him in the course of a seemingly endless period of research he always responded with encouragements to persevere and rigorous critiques, tempered by a smile. Last but not least, Luciano Berio, whom I encountered much later, perceived exactly, well before I did, what an anthropology of memory might be. That opportunity to dialogue with him, brutally interrupted by his death several years ago, remains, for me, unforgettable.

CARLO SEVERI

Illustration Sources

Figure 1. Wittgenstein, Ludwig. 1963. *Philosophical investigations.* Translated by G. E. M. Anscombe. Oxford: Basil Blackwell.

Figure 2. Dampierre, Eric de. 1992. *Harpes Zandé.* Paris: Klincksieck.

Figures 3 and 4. Brincard, Marie-Thérèse. 1990. *Afrique: Formes sonores.* Catalogue de l'exposition. Paris: Musée des Arts Africains et Océaniens.

Figure 5. Photo Scala, Milan.

Figure 6. Severi, Carlo. 2003. "Warburg anthropologue, ou le déchiffrement d'une utopie: De la biologie des images à l'anthropologie de la mémoire." In *Image et anthropologie*, edited by Carlo Severi. *L'Homme* 65: 77–129.

Figure 7. Patterson, Alex. 1994. *Hopi pottery symbols.* Illustrated by Alexander M. Stephen, William Henry Holmes, and Alex Patterson. Based on the *Pottery of Tusayan.* Catalogue of the Keam Collection, 1890. Boulder, CO: Johnson Books.

Figures 8 and 9. Pitt-Rivers, Augustus H. (1874) 1979. "Principles of classification." In *The evolution of culture and other essays*, 1–19. New York: AMS Press.

Figures 10–15. Stolpe, Hjalmar. 1927. *Collected essays in ornamental art.* Stockholm: Aftonbladets Tryckeri.

Figure 16. Wassman, Jürg. 1988. *Der Gesang an das Krokodil: Die rituellen Gesänge des Dorfes Kandingei an Land und Meer, Pflanzen und Tiere (Mittelespik, Papua New Guinea).* Ethnologisches Seminar der Universität-Museum für Völkerkunde-Wepf, Basel.

Figures 17–21. Newton, Douglas. 1971. *Crocodile and cassowary: Religious art of the Upper Sepik River.* New York: Museum of Primitive Art.

Figures 22 and 23. Valadés, Diego. (1579) 1983. *Rhetorica Christiana. . . .* Translated and edited by Esteban J. Palomera. Mexico: Fondo de Cultura Economica, Universidad Nacional Autónoma de México.

Figure 24. Mallery, Garrick. (1893) 1972. *Picture-writings of the American Indians*, Vols. 1 and 2. New York: Dover.

Figure 25. Nordenskiöld, Erland. 1928. "Picture-writings and other documents." *Comparative Ethnographical Studies* 7 (2).

Figure 26. Löwy, Emanuel. (1900) 1907. *The rendering of nature in early Greek art.* Translated by John Fothergill. London: Duckworth.

Figure 27. von den Steinen, Karl. (1894) 1940. *Unter den natturvölkern Zentral-Brasiliens.* Published in Brazil as "Entre os aborigenes do Brasil Central." *Revista do Arquivo*, 34–57. São Paolo: Departamento de Cultura.

Figure 28. Löwy, Emanuel. (1900) 1907. *The rendering of nature in early Greek art.* Translated by John Fothergill. London: Duckworth.

Figures 29–35. Berlin, Staatliche Museen.

Figure 36. Wied, Maximilian zu. (1833–34) 1976. *People of the first man: Life among the Plains Indians in the final days of glory. The first account of Prince Maximilian's expedition up the Missouri River, 1833–1834.* New York: Dutton.

Figures 37 and 38. Ewers, John C. (1939) 1979. *Plains Indian painting: A description of an aboriginal American art.* New York: AMS Press.

Figure 39. Stirling, Matthew. 1938. "Three pictographic autobiographies of Sitting Bull." *Smithsonian Miscellaneous Collections* 97 (5): 1–56.

Figure 40. Berlo, Janet. 1996. *Plains Indian drawings 1865–1935: Pages of a visual history.* New York: Abrams.

Figure 41. Berlin, Staatliche Museen.

Figures 42 and 43. Petersen, Karen D. 1971. *Plains Indian art from Fort Marion.* Norman: Oklahoma University Press.

Figures 44–46. Berlin, Staatliche Museen.

Figures 47–50. Berlo, Janet. 1996. *Plains Indian drawings 1865–1935: Pages of a visual history.* New York: Abrams.

Figures 51–55. Keyser, James D. 2000. *The Five Crows Ledger: Biographic warrior art of the Flathead Indians.* Salt Lake City: University of Utah Press.

Figure 56. Mooney, James. 1896. "The *Ghost Dance* religion and the Sioux outbreak of 1890." *Annual Report of the Bureau of American Ethnology* 14 (2): 635–1136.

Figure 57. Berlo, Janet. 1996. *Plains Indian drawings 1865–1935: Pages of a visual history.* New York: Abrams.

Figure 58. Berlin, Staatliche Museen.

Figures 59–62. Bolz, Peter. 1988. "Die Berliner *Dakota-Bibler.* Ein frühes zeugnis des Ledger-Kunst bei den Lakota." *Baessler-Archiv* (Neue Folge) 36: 1–59.

Figure 63. Nordenskiöld, Erland. 1928. "Picture-writings and other documents." *Comparative Ethnographical Studies* 7 (2).

Figure 65. Severi, Carlo. 1993. *La memoria rituale: Follia e imagine del Bianco in una tradizione sciamanica amerindiana.* Florence: La Nuova Italia.

Figure 66. Severi, Carlo. 1997. "The Kuna picture-writing: A study in iconography and memory." In *The art of being Kuna: Layers of meaning among the Kuna of Panama,* edited by Mari Lyn Salvador, 245–73. Exhibition catalogue. Los Angeles: Fowler Museum.

Figure 68. Severi, Carlo. 1993. *La memoria rituale: Follia e imagine del Bianco in una tradizione sciamanica amerindiana.* Florence: La Nuova Italia.

Figure 69. Severi, Carlo. 1997. "The Kuna picture-writing: A study in iconography and memory." In *The art of being Kuna: Layers of meaning among the Kuna of Panama,* edited by Mari Lyn Salvador, 245–73. Exhibition catalogue. Los Angeles: Fowler Museum.

Figure 70. Holmer, Nils, and Henry Wassén. (1947) 1953. *The complete Mu-Igala.* Göteborg: Etnografiska Museet.

Figure 71. Severi, Carlo. 1997. "The Kuna picture-writing: A study in iconography and memory." In *The art of being Kuna: Layers of meaning among the Kuna of Panama,* edited by Mari Lyn Salvador, 245–73. Exhibition catalogue. Los Angeles: Fowler Museum.

Figures 73 and 74. Hoffman, Walter. 1895. *The Mide-wiwin, or grand society of the Ojibwa. Seventh Annual Report of the Bureau of American Ethnology.* Washington, DC:

Figures 75 and 76. Hoffman, Walter. (1891) 1975. *Graphic art of the Eskimo.* Washington, DC: AMS Press.

Figure 77. Basso, Keith, and Ned Anderson. 1975. "A Western Apache writing system." In *Linguistics and anthropology: In honor of C. F. Voegelin,* edited by D. Kinkade and K. Hale, 27–52. Lisse: The Peter de Ridder Press.

Figures 80–82. Ferg, Alan, ed. 1987. *Western Apache material culture: The Goodwin and Guenther collections.* Tucson: Arizona University Press.

Figure 83. Wallis, Michael. 1994. *En divina luz: The Penitente moradas of New Mexico.* Albuquerque: University of New Mexico Press.

Figure 84. Wroth, William. 1991. *Images of penance, images of mercy: Southwestern santos in the late nineteenth century.* Norman: University of Oklahoma Press.

Figure 85. Lummis, Charles F. (1893) 1906. *The land of poco tiempo.* New York: Scribner.

Figure 86. Shalkop, Robert. 1970. *Spanish colonial painting.* Colorado Springs: The Taylor Museum.

Figure 87. Weigle, Marta. 1976. *Brothers of light, brothers of blood: The Penitentes of the South West.* Albuquerque: University of New Mexico Press.

Figure 88. Weigle, Marta. 1977. "Ghostly flagellants and Doña Sebastiana: Two legends of the Penitente brotherhood." *Western Folklore* 36 (2): 135–47.

Figures 89–92. Wroth, William. 1991. *Images of penance, images of mercy: Southwestern santos in the late nineteenth century.* Norman: University of Oklahoma Press.

Figures 93 and 94. Stark, Louisa. 1971. "The origin of the Penitente Death Cart." *Journal of American Folklore* 84: 304–11.

Figure 95. Photo Alinari, Florence.

Figure 96. Photo Scala Ministry of Culture.

Introduction

My great-grandfather, to honor God, used to leave his house in the very early hours of the morning, at first light. He would make his way to a wood, along a path known only to him which led to a meadow lying at the foot of a hill. When he reached a spring, he would stand before a great oak tree and there, in Hebrew, he would chant a solemn, ancient, and secret prayer.

His son, my grandfather, likewise used to rise very early in the morning and follow the path that his father had indicated to him. But, being short of breath and with much on his mind, he would halt before the path reached the meadow. Here he had found a fine birch tree, close to a stream, and, standing before it, he would chant the Hebrew prayer that he had learnt as a child. It was his way of honoring God.

His eldest son, my father, had fewer memories, was less religious and more fragile in health than his father. He would go to a spot quite close to the house, in a garden where he had planted a small tree. There, to honor God, he would murmur no more than a few words of Hebrew that were often quite imprecise and ungrammatical.

I myself, who have neither memories nor time to pray, have forgotten the way to my great-grandfather's wood and now know nothing of those streams and hidden springs, nor do I know any prayer to recite. But I too rise early and will tell this story to whoever cares to listen; it is my way of honoring God.

This story, which belongs to the Hebrew tradition of the Hassidim of Eastern Europe, is less simple than it appears. At first sight, its meaning may seem banal. It is no doubt a kind of apology, a story supposed to set an example and that contains a traditional lesson: man's memory is fragile and is bound to disappear. From one generation to the next, the narrator seems to be saying, all is lost. Knowledge that is not committed to a written document (for example, a map that would fix the name of the wood close to the village, trace the path leading to the meadow at the foot of the hill and the place of the oak tree before which the grand-father's father would pray . . .) tends to disappear, as do the details of the religious hymn in honor of God that the narrator's ancestor used to chant so carefully. Everything fights against memory: words, all words, even the most solemn of them, such as those pronounced in a prayer, are lost without trace, our story seems to add.

Another meaning of this tale no doubt concerns the status of writing and the use of books, or the Book, as is natural within the Hebraic tradition and its relation to memory. Without the support of the Book, no tradition is possible, this story seems to say. So then one thinks about oral traditions: about their fragility, the way they disappear, for they depend solely on the voices of those who speak of them. Every oral memory is, inevitably, the memory of a person. And whoever tells of it is constantly assailed by the vicissitudes, often tragic ones, that characterize all human lives. Whoever tells a story (including *this story*, the narrator seems to claim) is mortal. His memory is destined to disappear into oblivion, in-comprehension, indifference. Even the narrator himself, who no longer remembers much, is living proof of this loss that is as progressive as it is ineluctable. The one telling the story, here and now, no longer knows anything. He, just like ourselves today, has lost the ritual wisdom and skill of his ancestor.

Yet—as he himself declares—that does not stop him from continu-ing to honor God. He does this in a somewhat paradoxical fashion, for he seems to wish to offer him a cult by telling of how the prayer that he might have recited has, between the time of the father and that of the son, disappeared to the point where he himself can remember only a few words of it. Here, the text no longer distinguishes simply between the spoken word and the written word. It introduces a further distinction that concerns two distinct domains of orality: a distinction between, on the one hand, what can be recounted, that is to say, stories, and, on the other, forms of speech that should be addressed, solemnly, directly to God. Some words are destined for stories. Others, more important for men's memories, are destined for prayer. But now a first contradiction appears, for the narrator of this apologia produces proof that what sticks in the memory of a tradition is narrative, not ritual chanting with all its incomprehensible words. It is only the story, and not the prayer, that persists in the memory of the narrator and allows him to celebrate the glory of God.

This first conclusion (which confirms a whole school of thought devoted to the essentially narrative nature of memory) is nevertheless far from covering the meaning of our story. There is something in this traditional apologia that is at odds with its obvious content and seems to change its meaning, scope, and internal equilibrium. Let us go back to the beginning: the narrator claims to be telling this story in order to honor God. So the narrator is praying: recounting the story—he tells us—is his way of doing so. We are to conclude that this story can certainly not be reduced to a narration, handed down from father to son, about an episode in the life of the narrator's great-grandfather. It is also something quite different: it is a recounted prayer designed to honor God. Even if the ritual recitation in honor of God here gives way to a story that now seems to have no link with the deity, this account (which turns out to be the story of a prayer that disappeared from the consciousness of the narrator) nevertheless, thanks to its ironical and ambiguous character, preserves a definite performative efficacy. If you but tell this story, it turns into a prayer.

Whoever tells the story glorifies God: the narrative and the ritual recitation—which constitute the two major branches of the oral tradition—turn out, in this apologia, to be in a relationship of reciprocal implication and this produces a state of perfect equilibrium. The story of a prayer which, even if it fades from memory, turns into pure narrative is eventually recognized to be the best of prayers. So when the narrator declares that everything gets lost, he is, on the contrary, affirming that something essential will persist.

So it is really the performative value of the prayer, the act of celebration through speech, rather than the content of the story, that persists in the tradition. It is the ritual act—and not the narrative form—that makes this story memorable. What is in play is reversed, and we discover that the surface of this apologia resembles one of those graphic illusions that contain two images simultaneously; like the crude sketch that often appears in Wittgenstein's *Philosophical investigations* and that, depending on the point of view that one adopts, shows either the head of a rabbit or else a duck with a half-open beak (Figure 1).

Figure 1. A visual illusion: the rabbit-duck.

So this story is *perfect* in that it includes the ritual register within the narrative register and vice versa, to the point where the one becomes indissociable from the other. But it also suggests that the same ambiguous relationship that is established within it between speech that recounts and speech that celebrates, between story and prayer, is reflected in the relation between memory and oblivion. The trace left by a forgotten prayer is implicitly present in a story that the narrator does not forget. According to him, it is the story, and only the story, that remains in his mind. Nevertheless, that very story may turn out to be fluid, unstable, contested, or lacunary. What remains of it, its true value here and now, lies solely in the prayer which, implicitly, lies within it.

The present book studies certain modalities of the relationship that becomes established within a culture between, on the one hand, narrative speech and ritual speech and, on the other, memory and oblivion. Our analyses will be carried out within traditions generally called "oral" and "non-Western." We shall be studying narrative's modalities of existence and the ritual use of speech within the framework of an investigation devoted to the modes of construction of what is memorable in societies which, in order to fix and formulate their knowledge, depend essentially upon the use of spoken words. This relationship between ritual, narrative, and social memory, which the Hassidim tale seemed to describe as a kind of paradoxical implication, is by no means fixed once and for all or even foreseeably within those societies that are different from our own. I shall try to show that an analysis of this relationship opens up a whole new field of study: that of the anthropology of memory, which implies starting off by reflecting upon the nature of cultural difference. In what respect are these cultures that we call "oral" different from our own?

Our daily, unconsidered, spontaneous way of thinking about cultural difference is clumsy, binary, and seemingly simple. *Us and them*. In Africa, Oceania, America, and elsewhere too, there are peoples that we no longer wish to call "primitive," social situations that we are no longer happy to call "retarded." There are cultures whose values we can no longer share yet that we can no longer hastily dismiss as "barbarian." The words used so easily barely thirty years ago to qualify all those differences today seem inadequate. One of the great merits of anthropological research has been, precisely, to make our understanding of this difference increasingly difficult.

Nevertheless, there can be no doubt of the persistence of our sense of a separation, a strong difference between our experience of social life and that which characterizes other societies, many of which, still today, are known to us no more than superficially. *Us and them; them and us*: the confrontation is enmeshed in a whole series of illusions. The first of these is, of course, a belief that this immense region outside our culture is truly *one* region that it is possible to consider as a single unit; so we set it in opposition, as a whole, to our society. But that is not simply a summary, almost rudimentary, view, but also and above all a *negative* definition: a definition that declares only what those cultures *are not*. It says pretty well nothing about what they themselves do constitute. And it is indeed this binary logic that, for the most part, dominates our daily discourse on alterity and that determines our experience of cultural difference.

One of the domains in which this logic of "*us and them*" rules almost without exception is that of writing and social memory. We no longer wish to call these peoples "primitive" but prefer to call them "peoples without writing." The absence of writing—the usual argument goes—determines a particular kind of social memory and so produces a particular type of society. This banal theory, often repeated, produces certain corollaries: the absence of writing goes hand in hand with a lack of documents, a lack of credible memories, a lack of organized knowledge, and a lack of order in tradition and thinking . . . Such reasoning, which could be described as "inferences based on a lack of *x*," is widespread. We seldom notice that these apparent banalities are founded upon negative definitions, on reasoning that always concerns a failure or absence of what we ourselves know and know that we possess. Strangely enough, it is clear that the hypnotic aspect of such reasoning stems from the fact that it rests upon observations that are generally correct. For who could deny that the use of an alphabet remained unknown in Oceania, Indian America, and much of the African continent? However, to understand such lines of reasoning, what counts is not their veracity. Rather, it is their rhetorical and psychological effects. Formulated, as they are, within the binary logic that sets "us" and "them" in opposition, they produce a limited horizon by narrowing the domain of what is possible.

Such a way of thinking (which makes understanding of cultures that are distant from our own almost impossible) is so widespread that it is probably worth pausing at this point and taking a closer look at it.

A good example, to illustrate the nature of this apparent paradox (namely, a way of interpreting a cultural difference entirely composed of irrelevant truths), is in many cases offered by the museum-space in which, in orderly fashion, we set out objects that come from cultures that are different from our own. Resorting to a procedure that some experts called "ideal experimentation," let us imagine an African Zande harp from the Congo and mentally place it in a museum, protected by the usual glass case (Figure 2). A label is provided on which we read: "Zande harp, a stringed musical instrument, African (Congo). The neck bears an anthropomorphic decoration."

That apparently perfect definition is deeply erroneous with regard to the nature of this object, in particular as regards the relation between a sound and the image that is presented. To the question, "Is this harp a musical instrument?" the reply is affirmative if, placing ourselves in what I have called the universe of inert truths, we wish to say that this is indeed a mechanism for producing sounds. But if, instead of classifying this object according to what we already know, we try to seize upon the ideas that inspire its conception (in particular the interaction between

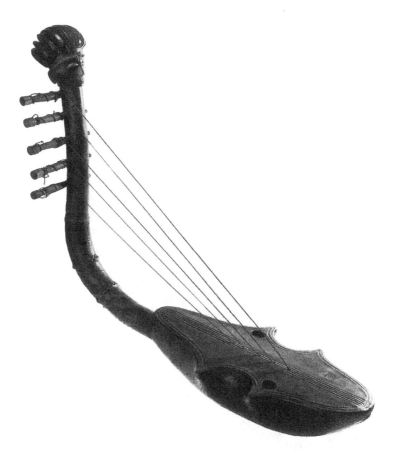

Figure 2. A Zande harp (1875).

a sonorous mechanism and an "anthropomorphic image"), the reply becomes negative. African art, in situations quite close to that of this harp, has often posed and in visual terms resolved a problem that could be formulated as follows: how does one represent a sound or a sonorous presence by a visual form? A group of Bamileke, Banum, and Luba-Shaba drums (Figures 3 and 4) presents an example that may resolve this problem. As with the label that accompanies our Zande harp, our museums customarily classify such objects in the category of musical instruments to which, by way of decoration, some image, whether anthropomorphic or not, may well be attached.

Figures 3 and 4. Luba-Shaba drums (Congo-Zaïre).

If, on the other hand, we decide to pay attention to the interarticulation between the forms and the ideas that characterize these drums, we discover that what, at first sight, appeared to be a decoration superimposed upon a function (the emission of a sound) is, in actual fact, *the idea that dominates the image*. No decoration appears upon these drums. Here, it is a matter of something quite different: the ancestor or animal that is sculpted into the wood gives *a face to the sound of the drum*. In this way it transforms the sound produced by the instrument into a voice. So the human or animal image that appears on the image is *inherent to the sound*. It qualifies the nature of the instrument by representing its voice in a specific way (which belongs to a specific idea of a *synesthesia* between visual and sonorous perception). Through this instrument there comes into being a relationship both complex and unexpected between a voice and an image: a surprising link engendered by the interaction established between two different registers of perception. It is a very close link, so close that it makes the sound and the voice of the drum indissociable. It is this link that renders the instrument capable, within the ritual context, of representing a specific situation: the presence of a now vanished being (the ancestor) or an intervention by a being against which one needs to protect oneself (a threatening spirit) (Severi 1991: 226–34). Through the very action that relates a sound to an image, a specific type of presence is established, a presence which, in both cases, is strictly associated with an absence.

Let us now return to the Zande harp. It would not, at this point, be useful to go into the entire, albeit relatively rich, ethnology concerning these instruments (see Laurenty 1960; Dampierre 1992). I shall stress only a few essential points that are connected with the relation between voice and instrument. The ethnologists who have investigated these traditions emphasize that, although there are naturally technical ways of tuning a harp (for instance, by following the set of intervals of a xylophone), any instrument of this type is, in Zande tradition, endowed with an irreducible individual existence. The reason for this absolute individuality of the African instrument (which makes it a good example of this type of thinking in the singular that Eric de Dampierre's researches [1992] have illuminated) lies in the fact that a Zande harp is always tuned to the voice of whoever plays it (Dampierre 1992: 40–41).

We should not forget that a Western musical instrument, despite certain individual features that are attributed to exceptional objects, always belongs within a mechanical and organized system of sound emissions that are common to the entire orchestra. It is accordingly always considered to be a member of a class of objects that implies the existence of a graphic system of notation, that of a particular tonal temperament. Whoever plays an instrument will, by definition, place himself within or in opposition to that system. Within this framework, the relation between voice and instrument is made possible by the fact that the voice is always that of the singer. Such voices are trained, amplified, and treated to a lengthy positioning process (in fact, the expression "the position of a voice" is actually used). In short, the training of these voices is always steered toward the instrument, whose possibilities of emission are intensified or limited within vocal music designed to be produced by an orchestra or by one or several instruments.

African tradition completely overturns that situation in which the instruments always, right from the very first chord, guide the singing. Here, it is the instrument that is "adjusted" to the voice. In fact, a Zande harp is considered to be an object that is symbolically close to the body of its player. As the musicians questioned by Eric de Dampierre (1992: 61) told him, the harp *utters the words of its player*, even as it represents his voice. Perhaps, in order to remain as faithful as possible to Zande aesthetics, we should say that the instrument *captures* the singer's voice. This is such a close link that, among the Azande, at the birth of every new instrument, a harp must *die as a body* before starting to emit sounds. So whoever wishes to play it finds himself obliged to mourn its death. And it is only after this ritually realized death that the instrument becomes able to emit sounds. It is through this gesture that leads the voice of the singer to place itself in a dying body in order to welcome it (thereby forfeiting all innate vocality of its own) that an initial identification can be established between the singer and the instrument that emits sounds. That identification is then completed or at least *intensified* by the appearance, on the instrument's body, of a symbolic image of a face. Once this has happened, when a string is plucked it utters words, thereby conveying the voice of someone, of a face whose representation is an essential part of the instrument. As in the anthropomorphic drums mentioned above (see Figures 3 and 4), the representation of a face transforms the sound that the instrument emits into a voice. It is accordingly perfectly logical that every note or sound emitted by the harp should, in the Zande language, be called *kpolo*: "voice" (Dampierre 1992: 34–35).

Now let us reflect upon the difference between the Zande and the Western situations. What do we mean when we declare that the Zande "do not have" a notation system similar or comparable to ours, or that they "think differently" about the relation between a sound and a voice? What we are doing, surely, is formulating an *inert truth*. In contrast to the European tradition, here there is neither opposition nor symmetry. Rather, there is a twofold reversal of rules. On the one hand, it is not the voice that chimes with the instrument but, on the contrary, the instrument that chimes with the voice. On the other hand, what we have here is not something that is common in our own tradition, namely an imitation or possible mimesis between the voice and the instrument. The Zande situation seems to set us in the presence of a mutual interpenetration of a voice and a sonorous object.

In this example, the cultural variation concerns not only the structure of music, but also the frontier which, within a culture, separates what is "music" from what is not, and what is considered to be an instrument from what is not. Here, an image conveys the transformation of a mechanical sound into a human voice. After its ritual death, the harp "adorned by an anthropomorphic image" becomes in reality *a ritual image of a voice*. So in this case the difference between *us* and *them* lies not only in the music but also in the nature of the object and in the type of *synesthesia* conceived and put into practice by a culture. In the Zande harp, the clear separation between vocal music and instrumental music (and the infinite possibility of imitations, references, etc.) that characterizes our own musical tradition is not present. The Zande tradition has found a way of its own to formulate the relationship.

We should therefore conclude that the harp is not an instrument superficially adorned by an anthropomorphic motif. On the contrary—if I have correctly seized upon the logic that guides its form—it now appears to us as a voice-object, itself a replica of a living body. The sculpted head, ritually associated with the death–rebirth of the instrument's body, now becomes *inherent* to the sound of the harp. It represents its iconic part that is indissociable from all the music of the Zande tradition.

A study of this example makes it possible to introduce a first distinction between two possible forms of variation. The first type is illustrated by Bach's *Goldberg variations*. A theme initially introduced with great clarity progressively engenders a great number of variations. The composition rule that guides satellite compositions of the theme, which we shall hear again right at the end, is very clear: the theme itself must reappear in each of the proposed variations. The sonorous image that results from the progressive development of the twenty-four variations is that of a marvellous rotation around a central point. It resembles the form of a sea-star, a rock-crystal, a snowflake, seen through a microscope. As in a fractal, each element recalls the center and carries it within itself. This is the very shape of ethnocentric reasoning: all that is different is organized around what is already known. All that is resistant to the schema is characterized by a kind of anamorphosis that conceals its appearance or modifies it to the point of deformation.

There is, however, another possible model for variations. Anton Webern was the first to think of it. In his *Variations for piano opus 24*, he discovered a linear and progressive way (as opposed to the traditional circular structure) to formulate variations. Once the theme has been presented together with its first variation, the second will be a variation not of the theme but of the first variation; and the third variation, for its part, will be a variation of the second, and so on. In this way, one obtains a structure that generates not only variations organized around a center but also *other centers* that can produce other variations. This model makes it possible to illustrate a way of organizing differences that does not recognize any preestablished center of epistemological priority. This is a method which, while providing us with the means to invent a comparative approach, in no way confines us to a single evolutionary path or reduces a "different" case to an exotic variation of one single case that is assumed to be the central paradigm. Such is the path that I have chosen to follow in this book.

I have spent years studying a number of oral traditions in Native America and Oceania. For a long time I focused my research on how these traditions functioned and on the specific constraints that the paths taken by the transmission of knowledge impose upon the forms and contents of shared knowledge (whether those paths involve narration or images, action or ritually delivered speech). Such work demands that close attention be paid to the examination of indigenous examples and texts and specialized literature. One works in this way, sometimes for long periods, in relative isolation, protected but at the same time severely limited by the exclusive company of specialists.

There comes a day when one feels the need to sketch in a wider horizon, think about the possibility of generalizing one's local observations about the traditions that one has studied. A shamanistic song, a ritual dance, a mask, and a myth of origins are above all complex things that need to be deciphered. But what meaning may they carry beyond the culture to which they belong? What do they suggest about the way in which they use language? What social memories do they transmit? What kind of thinking?

The first question posed naturally concerns the very concept of tradition. If I look beyond my study of specific situations in order to evaluate them within a wider perspective, I may arrive at, essentially, two conclusions. The first is that the opposition between oral traditions and written traditions, which is still current in anthropology and to which plenty of historical and linguistic traditions still refer, is, albeit not without some bases, fallacious. It may involve a number of traps, in the first place because it tends to consider the dimension of "orality" as adverse, the opposite of "written," and fails to consider its specific qualities. As a result, this opposition that appears to be so obvious proves incapable of perceiving the particular mode of existence and functioning of certain so-called "oral" traditions (and those include the patterns of utterance, typical mental representations, and discursive genres that stem from the accepted exercise of the spoken word). Secondly, this opposition hides the fact that in between the two opposite poles of an exclusive use of orality and an exclusive use of writing (even if one accepts that such traditions did exist), there are a great many intermediate situations. In those situations, neither an exclusive use of the spoken word nor that of linguistic signs dominates. When one takes the trouble to reconstruct the ways of transmitting shared knowledge, what one discovers is, rather, a particular way, used for mnemonic purposes, of combining a certain type of images with certain categories of words in the language. This happens in the case of virtual discourse, which, in the course of my researches, came to appear to be one of the essential situations that involved social practices connected with memories.

The third pitfall that underlies the seemingly commonplace opposition between the oral and the written concerns the socialization of
memory. Whereas the use of writing is necessarily a part of a series of
collective practices, "oral" cultures may, at first sight, seem to be based on
the memories of individuals. This may suggest the existence of societies
endowed with a fragile memory. But this is misleading. In fact, in such
societies, the use of memory is extremely elaborate, steered toward specific purposes and preserved as an essential asset. For these are cultures
founded upon ritual gestures and images as much as upon the use of
speech. Such cultures are part of a very rich body of iconographic traditions founded upon the use of ritual memory. One of the ethnographic
cases that I have been able to study in detail, that of the pictographs of
Native Americans, appears in this perspective in an entirely new light.
Far from being, by and large, marginal ethnographic curiosities, often
interpreted as failed attempts to invent a writing, these graphic systems
can help us to understand the modes of functioning of plenty of traditions that have discovered a path midway between orality and writing.

Another conclusion reached in my study of iconographic and oral
traditions in Oceanic and Amerindian territories concerns working
methods. As my research progressed, I came to realize that in order to
understand such graphic systems (such mnemonic uses of iconography)
and to be able to identify their basic elements and thereby generalize
the results obtained from their analysis, it was necessary to reverse the
perspective in which they have hitherto been considered. The drawings
designed to "preserve memories" in oral traditions have everywhere been
studied on the basis of more elaborated systems, the model of which
remains ideographic, syllabic, or alphabetic writings. In order to set up
comparisons, researchers have resorted to means (of a finite and coherent
nature) of representing the sounds of a language. Seen from this point of
view, pictography is bound to seem an unsuccessful attempt to invent a
type of writing. In the present book, I intend to follow a quite different
path and to consider the pictograms invented by Native Americans as
the crowning outcome of a long process that leads, starting from relatively simple models for organizing the relation between images and
words (examples of which are to be found, for instance, in a number of
Oceanic traditions), to the establishment of veritable "memory arts" in
non-Western cultures. I have accordingly chosen to analyze pictographs

starting not from very elaborate systems, but rather from more simple—sometimes infinitely simple—cases. This choice has made a new operation possible: that of sketching in a morphological scale, of mounting complexity, of iconographic traditions that are not solely "oral" but are nevertheless unconcerned with any phonetic transcription of the sounds of a language. Such a morphological scale is based upon the type of relationship that is established, case by case, between images and words within the traditional techniques of memorization.

The study of a number of apparently marginal graphic techniques has thus engendered a new intellectual project: a comparative anthropology of the arts of memory. The elaboration of this project has led me to take a new look at various different areas of knowledge hitherto kept separate, passing from a study of what is customarily called "primitive art" to a history of writing, a study of "oral" literatures, and even—for reasons that will become clear later—an anthropological study of certain thought processes.

This project of an anthropology of memory, the purpose of which was to expand the traditional concept of "the art of memory" so as to include a vast collection of techniques for constructing memorable knowledge by means of elaborating and deciphering an iconography, was fraught with difficulties.

The first difficulty was clearly the almost total absence of specialized literature on this theme. The scholarly literature certainly includes historical analyses of social memories and studies of oral traditions and also aesthetics, semiotic and sociological studies of iconographies. Anthropologists have accumulated many fine studies of non-Western arts as well as of ritual action and discourse. In those domains, research is lively and produces rich results. However, the idea of a new perspective inclined, through the interaction of particular aspects of research in these domains, to establish an anthropology of mnemonic practices in so-called "oral" cultures does not, except in a few sporadic studies, appear to have appealed to ethnologists.

On the other hand, the last fifty years have seen the appearance of a number of historical explorations into the Western traditions linked to the art of memory, ranging from the pioneering works of Paolo Rossi (1991) and Frances Yates (1966) to the more recent research work of Lina Bolzoni ([1995] 2001) and Mary Carruthers ([1990] 2008). Some of that work even recognizes that it is influenced by an anthropological approach. Mary Carruthers, for instance, considers the arts of memory not so much as practices linked purely and simply to memorization, but rather as the technical context of the *craft of thought* that, ever since late antiquity and throughout the Middle Ages, has influenced a vast collection of practices linked to memorization and mental images. A technique of memorization, together with the taxonomic organization of knowledge that this implies, should, as Carruthers rightly declares, be considered as an artifact. The only aspect that differentiates it from a work tool is the fact that, in this case, it is a mental artifact: a tool for thought.

Studies such as those of Carruthers have been of great value to my own work. However, one has to recognize that the existence of a number of different arts of memory, implying precisely a connection which, according to Paolo Rossi (1991), characterizes all *ars memorandi*, between memory, classification, and inference, on the one hand, and evocation, ideation, and poetic imagination, on the other, has been completely unnoticed by a large majority of ethnologists. According to the latter, the traditions of the peoples whom they studied might, at the most, possess just a few protowriting systems of "mnemonic supports"; but the underlying background remained orality.

The idea that a logic of memorization might influence the use of these uncertain and rudimentary drawings and that, alongside the illuminating inquiries into the mnemonic practices of the medieval West that historians were publishing, one could therefore consider reconstructing a general anthropology of these techniques of memorization seldom even crossed those scholars' minds. One of the major consequences of such a new approach remained equally unexplored: namely, the idea of considering the Western situation itself not as a universal model but, instead, simply as one possible form of an ideal series of techniques for exercising thought that were suited to the social practices of memory and could lead to the establishment of a tradition conceived as a body of shared knowledge.

Clearly, the illusion that I found myself on a truly unexplored path did not last very long. As soon as I embarked on my research, I realized that even if the project of such an anthropology had occurred to me alone, there were already numerous research studies devoted to one aspect or another of the question of memorization. If my project was to succeed, I would have to abandon at least some of the usual practices of an anthropologist in the field (an Americanist, Oceanist, Asianist, or Africanist), who would normally limit himself to one single cultural area, for my work would lead in two new directions. The first, naturally enough, led me toward comparative anthropology, to research into cases comparable to those that I had already studied. The second was equally obvious: I would have to try to gain an understanding of the historical roots of the ethnographic problem that I was posing for myself. In those very general terms, the problem could be formulated as follows: What might an iconic representation of knowledge be? That question, at once epistemological and historical, led me into a quite ill-defined area of the history of ideas, a kind of intermediary zone in between works devoted to the "origins of art" (in particular drawing) and those devoted to the history of writing. In this way, a whole tradition of studies was revealed to me, a kind of subterranean and almost forgotten layer of anthropological knowledge which underwent a remarkable intellectual development between the late eighteenth and the late nineteenth centuries. Plenty of the problems that my ethnological studies led me to consider were already formulated and debated here: How does one produce memory without writing? How can images assume and preserve meaning in a durable and not vague way? How and why does an image function as a protosign? What is a pictogram and—more importantly—what is it not? How does one cultivate a memory of images? Once I had set out along this path, I was thus led to return to an intellectual domain still somewhat vague and unexplored because it was reckoned to be a kind of cemetery of scientific ruins (Gall's phrenology, Lavater's physiognomy, and even Humboldt's obscure theory of landscapes): namely, the morphological tradition. The study of one of these half-forgotten traditions was particularly fertile for my research: this was a discipline which, between the 1840s and the early twentieth century, was practiced under the name of the biology of images or, even more specifically, the biology of ornamentation. We shall be considering its essential features a little later on.

In an essay written in 1900, the Austrian archaeologist Emanuel Löwy, who was a friend and advisor to Freud, concluded that primitive drawing is far from rudimentary: it deploys the resources of memory-images not to depict reality but another world of images that exist in our minds alone (Löwy [1900] 1907). That interpretation, formulated in the course of an illuminating analysis of archaic Greek style, really marked the outcome to an entire tradition of studies now completely forgotten. This biology of images is defined by its founder, the British general Augustus Henry Lane-Fox Pitt-Rivers, as the application of Darwin's theory of evolution to the domain of *forms* conceived by humanity and to the mental representations that those forms imply. Like animals and *like ideas*, Pitt-Rivers added, the drawings that we find in many different human cultures undergo an evolution as time passes and, like animals and ideas, these are to be found in regions of the world that favor their survival.

This intellectual tradition, elaborated in Great Britain between 1850 and 1870, is in fact composed of two major currents. The first, to a large extent, derives from German inspiration. It is linked with the synoptic perspective (for many years opposed to Darwinism) of the Goethe-style morphology founded mainly by Bastian, Humboldt, and, above all, Semper and Boas. The other current originated in England. Its founder was Pitt-Rivers, a true pioneer, whose work would lead to the formation of two great museums, the one devoted to ethnology, the other to archaeology. Among those who picked up on its intellectual heritage, which, although nowadays forgotten, was at the time surrounded by considerable prestige, were the Swedish Hjalmar Stolpe and the British Alfred Haddon and Henry Colley March. This English tradition, which developed mainly in Cambridge, in between biology and anthropology, was, through the works of Samuel Butler, to influence the work of the young Gregory Bateson. In the course of the nineteenth century it grew stronger in America, where, in intellectual circles linked to the Smithsonian Institute and in particular for those who discovered "the early writings of the Indians of America," it became a model of scientific practice. In this way, the biology of images was, between 1896 and 1898, to exert a strong influence on a young historian of art who had early on become disgusted with his chosen discipline and was ready for an ethnological adventure: he was Aby Warburg. By exploring the strange epistemological dinosaur that was the biology of ornamentation, one can discern the origin of the project of an anthropology of social memory that Warburg formulated under the title Mnemosyne. It was a project that he kept in mind throughout his life, even though he never really developed it.

I came to the conclusion that it was within this tradition that I had
to seek the bases of a new approach to the mnemonic use of images. It
was a matter of reinterpreting the point of view that this remarkable
group of researchers called *biological*. And it was not until I had explored
this unexpected field of research in which so many open problems were
posed (and so many unacceptable responses formulated) that I was able
to return to a comparative anthropology of iconographic traditions. In
this domain I applied what seemed to be an elementary methodological instruction for morphological thinking. This could be formulated as:
"Seek out the simplest case and evaluate its own complexity." While the
description of this first *Urform* is complete enough, subsequent, more
complex cases may be arranged in an orderly series, thereby (through
similarities and differences) revealing aspects thitherto unnoticed. Naturally enough, it also proved necessary to note and understand all the
reefs encountered by morphology and carefully evaluate the reasons for
its historical failure. Reversing the perspective of that tradition, it proved
necessary to pass on from an analysis of simple graphic forms (in the
manner of a scholar such as Stolpe or, today, one such as Carl Schuster)
to an analysis of the groups of relations between images and words that
became established in a tradition (or, rather, within the techniques of
memorization peculiar to a given tradition). The elementary phenomenon upon which my research is founded is thus not the material expression of so-called "primitive" graphic systems but instead the mental
link that is established between two forms of mnemonic traces, the one
iconic, the other linguistic. As we shall see, systems that seem, from the
form of the images that they employ, to be very different sometimes, seen
in this perspective, turn out to possess deep affinities.

This new anthropological approach to mnemonic forms was possible
for me to adopt not only because I had emerged from my study of the biology of images with a new set of working hypotheses, but also because,
at the same time, a surprising number of non-Western memory arts had
emerged from my research. While a number of Amerindian cases different from those that had served as my point of departure did appear, other
mnemonic procedures founded upon the use of a systematized iconography likewise emerged in Melanesia, Polynesia, Africa, and Asia. On the
basis of a number of relatively "simple" examples attested in Melanesia
(what might, somewhat imperfectly, be called minimal iconographies

linked to proper nouns, be they peoples' names or toponyms) and even far more complex cases in Native America, I was thus able to sketch in a genealogy of nonwritten, iconographic, and oral traditions founded on the types of mnemonic practices that they implied. In this way there appeared a literary form different from the narrative form—a kind of *Urform* of memory that was typical of these traditions and that I suggested calling *a song-form*. This was a form deeply linked with a ritual use of language, in which image and word carry strictly equivalent weight and dignity both from the point of view of their logic (inference, classification, etc.) and from their sometimes intensely poetic aspects.

An analysis of this form also made it possible to reach another conclusion: non-Western arts of memory are founded on at least two psychological criteria of a general kind. The first is an elaboration of a salience that is attached to counterintuitive graphic representations that one might consider to be *imagines agentes* belonging to non-Western cultures. A memorable image, in its elementary manifestation, is often a chimera. The second psychological feature of a general nature lies in the organization, equally necessary and constitutive, of memorable images into ordered sequences.

Here, as in the Middle Ages studied by Mary Carruthers ([1990] 2008), the mnemonic techniques are mental artifacts. Iconic traditions organize the images that they transcribe against a material backing (or some other form) in a manner that continues to reflect the articulation of mental images within the memory: through the salience and construction of an order. The emergence of this double criterion generally produces a mnemonic efficacy. The material image plunges its roots in a mental representation, as a pure product of ideation. Yet that is not enough. All the arts of memory that I have studied also obey another condition: they are of a ritual nature. They are always linked to a ceremonial context. For in traditions in which memorization is assigned to a particular use of iconography, the *use* of language is equally carefully controlled. An analysis of several cases has shown that these traditions apply to language the same criterion that is applied to the construction of salient iconographic representations that are deliberately designed to be counterintuitive and set apart from everyday perceptions. In the same way as mnemonic images, the type of communication that inspires the construction of something memorable within a tradition must be perceived as something particular and counterintuitive. In other words, these traditions (in America as well as in Oceania and elsewhere) propagate and preserve *counterintuitive representations by inserting them into counterintuitive situations.*

The discovery of the role played by counterintuitive contexts of communication has made it necessary to set up, alongside the analysis of mnemonic relations established by the use of an ad hoc iconography linking images and words, an elucidation of the special pragmatics that steer and orient ritual communication. The crucial part in this switch from a simple construction of counterintuitive images (such as chimeras, fantastical animals, nonhuman spirits, etc.) to the establishment of counterintuitive conditions that apply to the process of communication lies, in all the ethnographic cases that I have been able to examine, in the pragmatic definition of the status of the locutor. The image of the man or woman who speaks in the name of tradition always undergoes a transformation. In the context of communication that is ritualized, whether it be a matter of the recitation of a ritual song or of a simple performance of a danced pantomime, that image fills the publicly recognized position of an I-memory. It involves the figure of a locutor that invariably transcends the real locutor, a figure that the ritual action defines in detail. The voice of this locutor is one of the key vehicles in this symbolic identity-transformation: not only in the case of the words, whether comprehensible or obscure, that this voice pronounces, but in all its possible registers—the intonations, breathing, cries, onomatopoeias, even the rhythms marked by legato or staccato sounds . . . In traditions such as these, the voice becomes a sonorous image of the speaker and of his or her ritual transformation. As an iconic element that is essential to an iconographic tradition, the voice thus demands particular attention. It is as a result of this route imposed by an analysis of ethnographic factors that a book initially consecrated to non-Western memory arts has also turned into a book about ritual utterance and the iconic use of language.

As I understand it, what is at stake in the exercise of an art of memory is both codification and evocation. From a cognitive point of view, the practice of such an art involves, on the one hand, taxonomy and inference, and, on the other, the invention of an iconography and the establishment of a specific context, often ritualized, of communication. By use of these terms it is possible to sketch in what, in order to set it in opposition to narrative and its sequential forms, might be called iconic memory. This is an art of memory which, although unable to represent sounds, constructs around the mental representation a series of conditions affecting its vocal expression and thus, in its own way, preserves traces which, through the experience of ritual, have become part of tradition. This is the matter from which the memory of a great many traditions long described as "oral" is composed. In the present book, we shall take the concept of art of memory to consist of a series of practices which, as we shall see from certain shamanistic traditions, can constitute the context that guides inference and at the same time the persistent schema that influences evocation and therefore also, as we shall see, the source of the process which, within the context of the rite, leads to belief.

What we have here is the exercise of a complex memory in which several aspects and processes are combined. However, in the wake of Freud, it would be extremely naïve to ignore the fact that an element of forgetfulness is at work at the heart of all mnemonic traces. And it would be equally naïve not to take into account the very real fact that even such a memory, defined in Freudian terms as an internal configuration of representations and affects in which mnemonic traces and forgetfulness are indissociable, very often operates amid disorder, at the heart of social conflict and ethnic and cultural confrontation. And, finally, it is not possible to ignore the fact that a society's memory is never single. Memories are always plural and often antagonistic. Whatever the view of persistent prejudice, in this respect traditional societies (that is to say, "oral societies") are no different from others. This is why I wished to add an example, in which we find the exercise of a social memory applied to the image of an enemy. Here, within a period of confrontation between Whites and Native Americans and within a single region—lying between Arizona, New Mexico, and the north of present-day Mexico—we shall be able to follow a transformation that affects the supernatural field. On the one hand, we shall see the appearance of an Apache Christ, at once a prophet and a shaman, who becomes the founder of an ambivalent cult organized around the image of a crucified snake. On the other hand, among the Whites, who were at that time the direct antagonists of those Native Americans, we shall witness the emergence of another transformation of tradition: a Lady Sebastiana who, armed with bow and arrows, brings death to a Christ in the throes of his passion. Lady Sebastiana and the Christ of the Apache enter upon the scene to illustrate one last point. What we learn from a formal analysis (founded on the relation, on cognitive bases, between images and words) about the constitution of a tradition is by no means alien to an understanding of cultural conflict. On the contrary, the schema that emerges provides an indispensable vocabulary with which to decipher the memory of present-day conflicts, both the paradoxes within it and the consequent birth of cultural hybrids within societies that have chosen the sphere of the supernatural to represent the conflicts that set them now, as they will in the future, in opposition to the society that believes itself to be founded upon written memories: our own.

CHAPTER I

Warburg the anthropologist, or the decoding of a utopia

From the biology of images to the anthropology of memory

> *For such is the condition of the human mind that unless continuously struck by images of things rushing into it from outside, all memories can easily escape from it.*

Galileo, *Sidereus nuncius*

Why do we simply call the traditions of peoples who lack the use of writing "oral"?[1] Many ethnographers today reveal that, in many cases, these traditions are *iconographic* just as much as *oral*; they are founded on images as much as on words. In truth, the opposition between oral and written traditions is not only unrealistic—in that it pays scant attention to intermediary situations in which graphic techniques complete the exercise of speech but do not substitute for it—but it furthermore rests upon a fallacious symmetry. The fact is that there are numerous

---

1. An early version of this chapter appeared in *L'Homme, Image et Anthropologie* 65. My warmest thanks for allowing me to republish here go to its editor, Jean Jamin.

cultures in which, although the social memory seems to be based solely on spoken words, the role of images is part and parcel of the process of transmitting knowledge. So, in these circumstances, there is no symmetrical opposition between the oral and the written domains. What is contrasted to writing, in this opposition, is not simply the spoken word. A combination of words and images that forms a memory technique, particularly within the context of ritual discourse, constitutes the alternative that, in many societies, has prevailed over the practice of writing.

However, neither the simple decoding of the meaning of "aesthetic" objects nor the work of specialists in oral traditions suffices on its own to describe in detail how these relations between language and iconography become established in societies said to be without writing. As for anthropologists who set out to explore the concept of tradition itself, the critical and epistemological work that they have accomplished on the cognitive bases of cultural communication limits itself to the study of verbal exchanges and laboratory experimentation (Sperber 1975). So far it does not encompass the material offered by the anthropological terrain. Consequently, for a variety of reasons, those three approaches turn out to be incapable of defining the domain shared by iconography and the use of speech in societies that do not engage in writing, that is to say, the domain of practices and techniques linked with memorization.

I should like to show that an anthropology of memory, based on an empirical investigation of these practices, could renew this field of study in which the image seems to be one of the most powerful means used. But how should we approach thinking about the relation between images and memory? How should we regard an iconographic tradition? A whole series of studies, from Frederic Bartlett (1932) down to the present day, has linked the concept of memorization with that of narration. The salience of a narrative structure, with its sequence of actions, both for fixing a mnemonic trace and for evoking a memory, has been generally recognized by both psychologists and philosophers. Jerome Bruner (1990), for example, suggests that no memory can be imagined outside a narrative structure; according to him, any memory, even a visual one, is an account. Paul Ricoeur, for his part, defends an even more radical position,[2]

---

2. Ricoeur's position, which presents the temporal dimension as one of the
    essential elements in the concept of memory, seems still close to that of

maintaining that telling a story is a way not only of evoking it in our memory but also of reconfiguring temporal experience (Ricoeur 1988: 3).

The relation between memory and image is much less clear. Throughout his life, Aby Warburg endeavored to analyze this and to formulate a psychology of the human mind that was based on a study of social memory. A project for setting up an anthropology of the practices of memorization linked to images may therefore be sketched in, starting with some reflections on his work.

WARBURG: VISUAL SYMBOLS AND CHIMERAS

A seismograph placed along the dividing line between cultures: that is how Aby Warburg, in a text written at the end of his life, suggested describing the inspiration that guided his entire oeuvre: "When I look back on my life's journey, it seems that my function has been to serve as a seismograph . . . to be placed along the dividing lines between different cultural atmospheres and systems" (Warburg [1927] 2007: 332). With the extreme concision that characterized all his writing, that text, in just a few words, summed up the whole collection of anthropological questions upon which Warburg reflected throughout his intellectual itinerary: cultural difference and the "dividing line" that this drew between different societies in both space and time, the ritualized expression of emotions, the relation between the birth of iconographies and ritual action, and the constitution, through imagery, of a social memory.

When one considers his work as a whole, one realizes that this anthropological inspiration, which was at once fertile and incomplete, presents two aspects. The first, probably the better known, is one that greatly influenced the history of art. In a series of studies devoted to the art of the European Renaissance, Warburg revealed the need to restore

---

Aristotle, who, in *De memoria et reminiscentia*, claims that no memory is possible without a mental representation of time: "When someone is actively engaged in memory, he perceives in addition that he saw this, or heard it, or learned it earlier; and earlier and later are in time" (Aristotle 1972: 49).

to iconographic traditions all their historical and cultural complexity (Warburg [1932] 1999). Positioning himself, right from the start, somewhere in between the history of art, the history of ideas, the psychology of vision, and anthropological research, he elaborated a double strategy for the analysis of images. On the one hand, in the face of the dominant Wölfflinian formalist tradition, he inaugurated an analytical study of the meaning that works of art conveyed. On the other, that study of the meaning of iconographies was, for him, inseparable from setting the image in context, as a conveyor of social representations. The works of artists thus emerged from the museums of fine arts to become one element, among others, in a series of representations that pervade society as a whole.

Warburg's perspective can therefore not be reduced either to a perusal of style or to a simple iconological decoding of images. On the contrary, his approach opens up new ways of studying the contexts in which iconographies circulated and of analyzing the social practices that they implied, especially the ritual ones. It is from this point of view that Warburg and the researchers whom he influenced directly and profoundly modified our perception of the art and culture of the Renaissance. An analysis of iconographies indeed shows that the return of ancient art and sometimes even the cult of the Muses (Wind 1980) was a phenomenon linked with bodies of knowledge until then hardly known that ranged from representations associated with mnemotechniques (Yates 1966), to astrology, physiognomy, and other domains of magic (Walker 1958), all the way to classical and medieval tropes of rhetoric (Curtius 1953), the codified language of gestures (Barasch 1994), or the decoding of Egyptian hieroglyphs from a Neoplatonic point of view (Wittkower [1972] 1977). This was the Warburg who was best known, the one who associated the portrait of a Florentine merchant with the votive or funerary waxen masks used in Florence in the fifteenth century (Warburg [1932] 1999: 553–58); or the Warburg who, in the cycle of frescoes representing signs of the zodiac in the Este palace in Ferrara, detected the influence of an Indian astrological treatise known in Italy thanks to the intermediary of an Islamic tradition (Figure 5).

However, there is another part of Warburg's work that is far less well known, in which his anthropological ambitions are expressed in a different manner. In a collection of texts in which his remarkable account of

Figure 5. Francesco del Cossa, *The Month of March*, fresco, 1469–70, Ferrara, Palazzo Schifanoia.

his voyage among the Hopi in 1895–96 is probably the most important (Warburg [1939] 1988), we discover a Warburg who, far from limiting his scientific ambition to an analysis of European works of Renaissance art, set out, with a much wider perspective, to define the foremost elements of a " psychology of human expression" (Warburg [1923] 2007: 313), to which an analysis of images would supply the key. In these barely sketched-in texts in which a whole line of thought is concentrated into just a few statements, this art historian who was constantly seeking to transform his discipline aimed to understand the prime source of all iconography, the elementary bases of an image considered as a formal conveyor of meaning. Stimulated by the work of the earliest psychologists of visual perception (he was a psychology student in Berlin in 1891), Warburg was seeking to identify the mental operations—those particularly relevant to memory—that were implied by representation in images. Edgar Wind (1983) was the first to recognize the importance of the work of Robert Vischer for an understanding of this viewpoint of the young Warburg. What Wind called Vischer's "revolutionary little treatise" on visual empathy (Vischer [1873] 1994) marked a veritable turning point in German psychological and aesthetic nineteenth-century thought. It inspired a series of research programs in this domain, ranging from Konrad Fiedler ([1878] 1994), Heinrich Wölfflin ([1886] 1994), and Adolf Hildebrand ([1893] 1994) to Carl Einstein (1992). And for at least two generations, the concept that he was the first to formulate, that of visual empathy, was central to the European scientific debate on the notion of form (Severi 2009). As Wind saw clearly, Warburg took over this concept and made it one of the instruments of his own thinking. So it is indispensable to note some of its essential features here.

The question that Vischer posed at the start of his essay, written in a concise and not very academic style, may seem a simple one: Why is it that some visual representations are more intense than others? Why is it that the shape of a rock overlooking the sea, a cloud crossing the sky, or a rock crystal seem to us charged with particular energy? What causes the intensification of visual perception that prompts such emotion? Vischer tells us that, in order to understand this phenomenon, we need to analyze the way in which looking functions so as to understand "the structure of our imagination" (Vischer [1873] 1994). His initial intuition is that the act of looking, far from being passive, presupposes the establishment of a relation between the form of an external object and a formal, innate, and unconscious model of the perception of space, which reflects a mental image of the body. Perception thus also, and always, involves projecting an image of oneself. The idea that the very structure of the eye, in the physical sense of the term, can orient vision, is not a new one. Wundt—who believed that irregular shapes are disagreeable because they contradict or disappoint what the eye expects—had already formulated it in his *Lectures on human and animal psychology* (Wundt [1896] 2014). However, it was Scherner's *Das Leben des Traumes* that provided Vischer with a basis upon which to formulate his theory of empathy. Scherner (recognized by Freud to be, along with Maury [Freud (1900) 1976: 154–59; Ellemberger 1970: 357–60], one of the great pioneers in the study of dreams) had realized that, while dreaming, the mind always projects a symbolic representation of the body into the imagination.

For Scherner, this representation, far from being a reproduction of external images, "always implies features of the ego," which, in this way, are inscribed in or associated with the represented image. As Freud had noted in his historic chapter in *The interpretation of dreams*:

> It [the dream-imagination] does not halt, however, at the mere representation of an object; it is under an internal necessity to involve the dream-ego to a greater or lesser extent with the object and thus produce an *event*. For instance, a dream caused by a visual stimulus may represent gold coins in the street; the dreamer will pick them up delightedly and carry them off. (Freud [1900] 1976: 155–56)

Vischer deduced from Scherner's theory of dreaming that this process of the projection of an image of the body, which becomes evident in its symbolic form in the course of sleep, is in fact a constant feature of our imagination, although it is largely unconscious while we are awake. For him, all perception is a product of an unconscious relationship between the external image—or rather its form—and this ceaseless projection that is a part of visual perception. What results from this relationship that endows the image with the intensity of our own psychic life is *visual empathy*. The imagination (defined precisely as this constant production of mental images that accompanies perception) is, for Vischer, no different from the activity of dreaming:

> As in a dream, I stimulate, on the basis of simple nerve sensations, a fixed form that symbolizes my body. . . . Conversely, an objective but accidentally experienced phenomenon always provokes a related idea of the self. . . . It does not matter whether the object is imagined or actually perceived; as soon as our idea of the self is projected into it, it always becomes an imagined object, an appearance. (Vischer [1873] 1994: 101)

Indeed, like the dream image, the unconscious projection of emotions intensifies the visual representation in two ways: it links the observer intimately with the image by creating a kind of compromise between what emanates from the imagination and what is represented by perception; and it enriches the image with associative chains of ideas. The most remarkable consequence of this psychic activity is that the mental connotations, distinct from the external image, "can become entwined into an inextricable whole" in the visual experience (ibid.: 109).

Finally, it should be added that, for Vischer, this process by no means characterizes only what we call "art." On the contrary, this twofold unconscious process of liaison and association that is expressed in visual empathy is so general that it presides over any apprehension of forms. According to Vischer, this is an almost physical characteristic of every human being: "The impulse of form belongs to the human psychophysical self" (ibid.: 117). It therefore lies at the root of the creation of all cultural symbolism and, in particular, of this tendency to anthropomorphism that dominates the myths and rituals of "primitive man" (ibid.: 110).

Warburg reflected at length upon Vischer's ideas. On the one hand, by showing that the intensity of images is a phenomenon far more profound than simple aesthetic pleasure, these analyses of the process of perception presented him with the possibility of inventing a way of reading images that was radically different from that of Berenson (whom he was to detest his whole life long). On the other hand, the empathy theory enabled him to show that the study of images could lead to an elucidation of psychological phenomena of a general order, linked with man's visual thinking and not just with the history of European art. When in 1912, in his lecture in Rome, he concluded his analysis of the astrological frescoes of Ferrara, Warburg expressed this ambition very clearly: "My fellow students, I need hardly say that this lecture has not been about solving a pictorial riddle for its own sake. . . . The isolated and highly provisional experiment that I have undertaken here is intended as a plea for an extension of the methodological borders of our study of art." This experiment is justified by the fact that, "until now, a lack of adequate general evolutionary categories has impeded art history in placing its materials at the disposition of the—still unwritten—'historical psychology of human expression'" (Gombrich 1999: 270).

To understand this aspect of his thinking that Warburg himself described as *positivist*,[3] which progressively reflected his ambition to liberate the analysis of images from all ethnocentrism, we must of course turn to consider his 1895–96 ethnographic visit to the Hopi and also the whole collection of texts, both published and unpublished, in which he refers to it. For it was in the land of the Hopi that Warburg for the first time formulated his plan to observe from close up "the coining and transmission of symbols," as one of his earliest disciples put it (Saxl 1957: 326). The clearest example of this type of analysis, which we could, from this point of view, set in opposition to the representation in astrological terms of the month of March, in Ferrara, is his analysis of the Hopi lightning-snake. We know that Warburg, who had asked a group of Hopi children to illustrate a story that involved lightning, was most astonished to find that several of them had drawn a kind of snake crossing the sky (Figure 6).

In the first place, this strange representation revealed the artificial nature of the debate that had hitherto dominated studies devoted to the origin of art and that set defenders of a "realistic" origin in opposition to those who favored an "abstract and decorative" origin of graphic representation. The Hopi children's drawings were manifestly "imaginary" and

---

3.   It is Gombrich who, in his commentary on this text, mentions this unusual term, which, however, as we shall see, is most revealing. In a manuscript note that he added to the text of his lecture at the last moment, Warburg explains that the methodological argument that he wishes to defend is a positivist one: "*Ich wollte mir eine positivistisches Plaidoyer erlauben*" (cited in Gombrich 1999: 271).

Figure 6. A drawing by a Hopi child.

yet were, at the same time, created in an entirely realistic manner. In this, Warburg found striking confirmation of the ideas of the man then guiding anthropological research in the United States: Franz Boas. His work on Amerindian arts had led him to believe that, far from there being any principle of opposition between "realism" and "abstraction," there were two visual ways of representing space. One referred directly to sight and represented an object by imitating the eye, with a monofocal perspective. The other chose to represent objects not as they presented themselves to sight, but rather as they are represented by the mind. Primitive art, which in general employs the second manner, is neither naïve nor rudimentary. It chooses to construct complexity where our own eyes are accustomed to simplify. The Hopi children's representation of the lightning-snake, instead of being a simple reflection of reality, thus turned out to be charged with a number of meanings quite independent from everyday perception. As Vischer had sensed, Warburg discovered that a mental representation linked to a material trace inscribed on some kind of backing (in other words, a drawing) *can pass beyond what the image shows*. It is thanks to what Vischer had recognized to be the work of the imagination operating in association with sight that the roughly sketched snake in the sky also became a streak of lightning and was consequently charged with a particular intensity. It is not possible at this point to move on to an analysis of the drawings that Warburg collected in the land of the Hopi (even though they did play a remarkable role in the emergence of a particular concept linked to the expressionist primitivism of those children's drawings).[4] But we should note that, in studying the Hopi children's drawings, Warburg followed a path that was quite the opposite to that which he would later adopt in his studies of the painting of the Italian Renaissance. When, in Ferrara, he analyzed Roberti's fresco, Warburg was aiming above all to enrich the meaning of the iconographic representation and to restore the complexity of the visual symbolism. When, in New Mexico, he studied an apparently simpler iconography, he was trying in his analysis to identify what he called the "heraldic skeleton" of the form, the process presiding over the cultural transmission of images. In the course of this process, the visual representation (whose partially mental character he seized upon), far from becoming charged with a multiplicity of different meanings, tended to be reduced to the status of a hieroglyph: he remarked, on the subject of Hopi pottery, "It is typical of the drawing on such vessels that a kind of heraldic skeleton of natural forms is represented." A bird, for example, is decomposed into its essential parts, so that it appears as a heraldic abstraction. It changes into a hieroglyph which is composed not only to be contemplated but also to be decoded. What we have before us is "an intermediary stage between image and sign, between realistic representation and script" (Warburg [1939] 1988: 279).

Warburg was soon to recognize that this apparently simple example nevertheless possessed a complexity of its own. In fact, as the direct source of his knowledge of Hopi pottery clearly showed,[5] the sign-image

---

4. In Europe, these drawings had an interesting destiny for, after Warburg had studied them as examples of Amerindian art, they were exhibited in the first major European exhibition of children's art: *Das Kind als Kunstler* (The child as artist) in Hamburg, in 1880 (Boissel 1990).

5. This was a major catalogue of Hopi pottery, produced by Alexander Stephen. Thanks to his extraordinary familiarity with Hopi society, this Scottish engineer had been able to produce this text for the businessman William Keam at Keams Canyon. In his Journal, on April 24, 1899, Warburg wrote: "I spent the night reading Stephen's manuscript catalogue." That evening he noted that he had read "A. M. Stephen's treatise" and it had been "very useful from a theoretical point of view" (Guidi and Mann 1998: 155). It is strange that

of the Hopi bird resulted from a composition that associated *heterogeneous* elements rather than simply "parts of the body" of the bird. In order to represent supernatural beings in their pottery art, the Hopi used an iconographic schema which, like the chimera of the Greeks, associated the images of different elements within a single body. As we can see from the documents he selected from Alexander Stephen's first catalogue of Hopi pottery, the schematic representation of celestial elements (such as a cloud or a flash of lightning) could, for example, legitimately figure, among other iconographic elements endowed with a meaning, in the representation of a bird (Figure 7). So Warburg discovered that the children who represented a streak of lightning by an image of a snake in the sky were adopting exactly the same procedure of combining in one and the same body elements that designated different beings. Both the lightning-snake and the Hopi representation of the bird in the form of a hieroglyph, "an intermediary stage between image and sign," were, in reality, chimeras.

Figure 7. A Hopi snake-bird, polychrome ceramic, style D.

this connection between Warburg and the catalogue produced by Stephen (who died one year before Warburg's arrival in Arizona) was never noticed by Warburg's interpreters for, as we shall see, it was in fact crucial. Stephen's catalogue has been recently published by Alex Patterson (1994).

It was representations of this type which, for the first time, illustrated the process of a cultural transmission of symbols within the memory of a society that Warburg, developing Vischer's ideas about visual empathy, was trying to define in abstract, psychological, and general terms that lay beyond the frontiers of Western art. The problem of interpretation that faced Warburg might thus be defined as follows: How to convey the intensity of these images constructed, as he put it, around the "heraldic skeleton" of a form? How to describe the process that turned them into memorable representations? What is the meaning of this articulation between the heterogeneous elements by which they are characterized?

The historical and critical analysis of Warburg's travel notes (and of the reflections that he continued to add to them later on) effected by a number of authors, ranging from Saxl (1957) to Forster (1999), Settis (1993, 1997a), and Raulff (1998), does not suffice to supply an answer to those questions or, consequently, to define the project for an anthropology of social memory that Warburg was trying to formulate. We must therefore accept the fact that the idea of identifying the bases for an anthropology of images capable of going beyond the "dividing line" that separates the West from other cultures, or at least, to use Warburg's own words, to register the mutual influences that affected it as a "seismograph of the soul," remained, in his work, in the state of a no more than implicit or fragmentary formulation. Although notes devoted to this project appear relatively frequently in his unpublished works, none of his completed texts, not even the "Lecture on serpent ritual," explicitly formulate the terms of this new perspective. In consequence, the reconstruction of an anthropology of Warburgian inspiration, capable of identifying its bases in his work as a whole and of then, in the course of future research, developing what these indicated, inevitably implies two tasks. On the one hand, we need to rediscover the terms in which to tackle a forgotten problem that is both alien to historians of art and has, furthermore, long since disappeared from the histories of anthropology, in which the questions raised by Warburg were deeply rooted. On the other hand, we need to understand what utopian anthropology of the future with a twofold ambition to work on both the meaning of images and the mental operations that those images imply might constitute a possible development from Warburg's work.

As we have seen, the discovery of the Hopi chimera was essential for Warburg's anthropological thinking about the formation and transmission of symbols. We must therefore pay particular attention to chimerical representations and to the principle on which they are based—namely, the association within a single image of heterogeneous if not contradictory characteristics that confer a special intensity upon it and render it memorable. In order to sketch in the intellectual genealogy of this concept of a hieroglyph-image, "an intermediary stage between image and sign," let us first examine some of the intellectual roots of Warburg's oeuvre.

FORGOTTEN ROOTS, OR THE BIOLOGY OF IMAGES

Fritz Saxl used to say that Warburg, in each of his articles, would write an introduction to a science that would never see the light of day. Something similar might be said about the relation of Warburg's thought to anthropology. It is a matter that has often been raised by his interpreters.[6] A number of sources have been cited to explain his interest in anthropology. Some have drawn attention to the historian of religions Hermann Usener (Sassi 1982), whom he followed to Bonn in 1886, to Warburg's reading of the work of the Italian psychologist Vignoli (1879), which was very important for him because it coincided with and developed Vischer's thinking on empathy, or to the influence exerted upon his development by his discovery of Darwin through his famous essay "The expression of emotions in man and animals" ([1872] 1993). Others have underlined the affinity between his thinking and that of Cassirer (1955–57), who paid particular attention to mythical thought. More recently, Georges Didi-Huberman (1999) has drawn attention to the indirect influence that the anthropology of Edward B. Tylor may have had upon his thinking.

---

6.   Warburg's oeuvre has for at least forty years been studied by numerous commentators. The critical literature on him by now includes many studies which it is not possible for me to consider here. Nevertheless, here is a list of a few of the texts devoted to interpreting his thinking: Settis (1985, 1997a); Agamben (1998); Raulff (1998); Schoell-Glas (1998); Ginzburg (1990a); Forster (1999).

A reading of these studies tells us of the multiple ways in which certain major anthropological themes may have affected Warburg's ideas. However, his relationship with anthropology does not concern solely the great nineteenth-century pioneers of "armchair anthropology" or the theorists who may have influenced the anthropology of the day through philosophy or history of religions.

On the one hand, that relationship was a direct one: it was established in 1895 in the Smithsonian Institution, where the young Warburg came into contact with the ongoing work of the founders of field anthropology in the United States, who included Holmes, Powell, Cushing, Mooney, and, of course, Boas, whom Warburg repeatedly met. It was on the advice of this group of researchers, who welcomed him upon his arrival, that he set off on his journey in Arizona and, for a moment, envisaged becoming an anthropologist.

On the other hand, through this encounter with circles in the Smithsonian, Warburg came into contact with an intellectual tradition that was at that time well known in North American anthropology but that is now seldom even mentioned in anthropological handbooks. As we shall see, that tradition played an essential role in the concept that Warburg elaborated during his travels among the Hopi, about the transmission of cultural symbols through iconographies. Let us consider a few texts that date from this American period. At the point when the young Warburg was wondering about the chimerical representations of the Hopi, he had already developed the scorn for the aestheticizing contemplation of works of art that he was to retain throughout his life. We already know that what he was trying to define was the *necessity* of the image and the role that this played in the thought processes and the constitution of a tradition. Here is what he wrote in 1923, when he was reflecting upon his 1895–96 travels: "I had acquired an honest disgust of aestheticizing art history. The formal approach to the image—devoid of understanding of its biological necessity as a product between religion and art— . . . appeared to me to lead merely to barren word-mongering" (cited in Gombrich 1970: 88–89). This comment, never published, comes from a personal notebook and is clearly addressed simply to himself. It seems not so much a polemic directed against a particular kind of art history (although this is a theme that is, naturally, not absent) but, rather, a program or work plan which, although the fruit of reflection upon a path followed earlier, sketches out the terms for work in the future. So the latter is the context in which this note should be understood: Warburg is noting, for himself, the major lines along which he thinks an anthropology of images should be developed.

Warburg implies that the image is a biologically necessary product. What meaning should we ascribe to this curious expression? An initial hypothesis, no doubt close to that of his biographer, Ernst Gombrich, who was the first to publish this text (1970), might be that the word "biological" plays the role of intensifying the reference to necessity. According to Gombrich, who scarcely notices the existence of an anthropological aspect to Warburg's work,[7] it is partly in order to underline his interest in Hopi religion that Warburg uses this strange reference to biology, but also—possibly—in order to refer to Semper's (1989) materialistic ideas about the technical procedures (or "a practice of art") that constitute the essential part of artistic activities, ideas of which Gombrich was harshly critical.

Gombrich would be justified in underestimating this "biological" reference if the word appeared in this text simply as a facile reference or an isolated allusion. However, it is quite possible to show that, on the contrary, Warburg was constantly contrasting the aestheticizing approach to a dramatically opposed point of view that he was prone to describe using biological or botanical terms. The opposition between aestheticism and a "scientific" attitude, which is reminiscent of the "positivist" argument in his lecture on the Ferrara frescoes, recurs in Warburg's work on several occasions. Here, for example, is what he wrote thirty years later, in 1929, in his "Introduction" to the *Mnemosyne Atlas*:

> Hedonistic aesthetes can easily gain the cheap favours of an art-loving public when they explain this change of form by the greater sensuous appeal of far-sweeping decorative lines. May he who wants be satisfied

7. As we are bound to recognize, the anthropological aspect of Warburg's oeuvre has been mostly ignored in the tradition of studies inspired by the Warburg Institute. Not only has no-one thought to pursue the studies that Warburg himself had initiated, but the very existence of an anthropological aspect to his thought was for a long time ignored by his successors. A number of recent works by Gombrich, in which the latter, seemingly jokingly, declares himself ready "to bury Warburg, not to praise him" (Gombrich 1999: 275), are most revealing in this respect.

with a flora of the most odorous and most beautiful plants; that will never lead to a botanical physiology explaining the rising of the sap, for this will only yield its secrets to those who examine life in its subterranean roots. (Cited in Gombrich 1970: 245)

The almost poetic character of this text, in which the reference to Goethe and his *Metamorphosis of plants* is very clear, should not mislead us. Warburg is not playing on metaphors here; rather, he is referring to a precise anthropological tradition that was pursued by several generations of researchers in Germany, Sweden, and Britain and, above all, at the heart of the American Anthropological Society, thanks to which he made his first contacts with field ethnology. This branch of nineteenth-century anthropology was, for over fifty years, known as the biology of images or the biology of ornaments; and it was into this sphere of influence that Warburgian anthropology plunged its roots and from this terrain that sprang a number of notions such as *Nachleben* ("posthumous life," "return," or the transformation of an iconographic theme over a period of time). There can be no doubt about it; not only because Warburg was familiar with the works of some of these authors[8] and absorbed their ideas during his stay in the United States, but above all because the morphological thinking that developed within the biology of ornaments provided him, following the intuitions of Vischer, with a new model for thinking about images. It was at the level of its method, its way of constructing a model of iconographic tradition, and its conception of social memory seen as a process based on the construction of a series of iconographies that this tradition became one of the main references for Warburg's thinking and, for us, a precious element in our own understanding and development of his anthropological perspective.

The last history of anthropology that considered the biology of images to be a branch of our discipline was that published by Alfred Haddon in 1910. Haddon, the first professor of anthropology in Cambridge and a former embryologist, was one of the organizers of the Cambridge expedition to the Torres Strait Islands. He was the author of an important

8. Warburg had in his possession a number of important works devoted to this branch of anthropological studies, in particular those of Haddon ([1895] 1979).

work now almost completely forgotten (Urry 1993), and in the 1930s he became the teacher of Gregory Bateson, who, in 1936, dedicated his analysis of the Iatmul ritual of the Naven (Bateson [1936] 1958) to him. Along with Pitt-Rivers, Stolpe, Colley March, Holmes, and a few others, Haddon was also one of the most remarkable thinkers to have written about the biology of images. This is how, in his book *Evolution in art*, he introduces the anthropological view on art: "There are two ways in which art may be studied—the aesthetic and the scientific. The former deals with all the manifestations of art from a purely subjective point of view, and classifies objects according to certain so-called 'canons of art'" (Haddon [1895] 1979: 306).

According to Haddon, the aesthetic point of view was flawed not only because it was "subjective" but furthermore because it was too easily influenced by Western culture and was unlikely ever to succeed in liberating itself from this ethnocentric point of view. He wrote as follows: "Racial tendencies may give such a bias as to render it very difficult to treat foreign art sympathetically."[9] "Dogmatism in aesthetics is absurd, for, after all, the aesthetic sense is largely based upon personal likes and dislikes, and it is difficult to see what sure ground there can be which would be common to the majority of people." He thus concluded that "the aesthetic study of art may very well be left to professional art critics." Haddon's plan was, instead, to elaborate a "scientific treatment of art." "We will now turn to a more promising field of inquiry, and see what can be gained from a scientific treatment of art. This naturally falls into two categories, the physical and the biological" (ibid.: 306).

---

9.   Haddon's book appeared in 1895, at a time when the aesthetic ideas of Ruskin, who maintained that the non-European continents never knew of anything resembling art (Rubin 1984: 5), were widespread in British intellectual circles. So Haddon's polemic is both interesting and innovative. A few years later, the primitivist movement was to return to this critique of ethnocentrism and defend the need to formulate an aesthetic of non-Western arts (see, in particular, Carl Einstein's *Negerplastik* [1992]). Naturally enough, Haddon's point of view is very different. Although he criticized the ethnocentrism of the aesthetes, it was not in order to renew aesthetic theory but because he denied that there was any objective basis to any approach that was purely aesthetic.

Since, as Haddon put it, he was "not aware that much has been done to establish a physical basis for art" (ibid.), and all the meaning that can be attributed to works of art falls into the domain of psychology, the scientific approach to art had as its objective a study of the evolution and geographic distribution of forms in the primitive arts. This new discipline therefore fully deserved to be called the biology of art. Haddon, in the wake of Stolpe (1927), Colley March (1889), and Balfour (1889), was careful to acknowledge General Pitt-Rivers as the father of the main theories upon which this discipline was founded.

General Augustus Henry Lane-Fox Pitt-Rivers, that "splendid Victorian autocrat," who began to lay the foundations for this type of research work on art in the early 1850s, does indeed stand at the origin of all biology of the arts. He was not only a prolific author but also both a military man and a man of science. He was an ardent defender of Darwin's innovative ideas but also played an active part in his Britannic Majesty's military missions. In 1850, he particularly distinguished himself at the time of the Crimean expedition. His speciality was ballistics and his task "in the field," that is to say, in battle, was to teach his officers the most effective use of fire-arms (Thompson 1977; Bowden 1991).

His texts on the classification and the cultural evolution of objects and his great plan for an ethnographic museum, which culminated in the creation of the museum that bears his name, in Oxford, prompted the earliest attempts in the domain in the domain of the biology of images. We should therefore now turn to Pitt-Rivers and the birth of his collection in order to gain an understanding of the foundations and perspectives of this "science of forms" that emerged in England in the second half of the nineteenth century.

FORMS AND IDEAS: PITT-RIVERS AND THE PROPHECY OF THE PAST

Let us select from the quite extensive oeuvre of Pitt-Rivers a text written in 1874 entitled "Principles of classification."[10] In it, the essential

---

10. This text first became the subject of a conference organized by the Special Meeting of the Anthropological Institute of Great Britain and Ireland on

elements of his work program are formulated remarkably clearly. As Haddon was proudly to repeat, it was a matter of getting rid of all aestheticism by applying the theory of evolution, which, up until then, had been used only in the study of living organisms, to the products of the human mind. Pitt-Rivers regarded this as a way of establishing a natural history or, rather, as we shall see, a *prehistory of human thought* capable, through an analysis of forms, of shedding light on stages of evolution that went right back to periods to which writing, a relatively recent invention, could not testify.

The first stage in this research strategy was of a methodological order. It consisted in reversing the habitual point of view of a biologist. As we have seen, an anthropologist, just like a biologist, needed to refer to the Darwinian theory of evolution. However, instead of tracing the progressive stages of evolution that led from the simple to the increasingly complex, an anthropologist would seek to reconstruct the past from the traces that an evolved organism might reveal. This was, in effect, what was, in contemporary evolutionary psychology, to be known as "reverse engineering": a retrospective process that made it possible to identify the evolving stages that had led such an organism to become what it now was. Here, the ideas of Pitt-Rivers were directly inspired by another great defender of Darwin's theories, namely Thomas Henry Huxley.[11] According to Huxley, a historian of the earliest stages in the evolution of humanity should adopt what he called the Zadig method,[12] that is to say,

---

July 1, 1874, to mark the occasion of the first opening of collections of anthropological objects to the public. It was not published until the following year, when it appeared in the *Journal of the Anthropological Institute*, 1875, IV: 293–308.

11. On the use of this formula by Huxley and in Darwinian circles generally, see Ginzburg (1990b: 117) in particular.

12. As will no doubt be remembered, in Voltaire's tale (in particular in the episode called "the dog and the horse"), Zadig, "studying the properties of animals and plants," had acquired a wisdom that revealed to him "a thousand variations in visible objects that others, less curious, imagined all alike." This wisdom enabled him to recognize the queen's dog and one of her horses, by studying the tracks that the animals had left in the sand. Without ever having seen the animals, he was able to declare that the one was "a very small spaniel; she had had puppies too lately; she is a little lame on her left

the "back to front" prophetic method, based—like that of the protagonist in Voltaire's tale—upon an analysis of traces that made it possible to reconstruct the past. According to Huxley's formula, an anthropologist should invent a way of *prophesying the past* by, in total contrast to a biologist, establishing scales of decreasing complexity. This method, based on the analysis of forms, was a way of proceeding by inference from a study of what is known to knowledge of what is unknown:

> Following the orthodox scientific principle of reasoning from the known to the unknown, I have commenced my descriptive catalogue with the specimens of the art of existing savages, and have employed them, as far as possible, to illustrate the relics of primeval men, none of which, except those constructed on the more imperishable materials, such as flint and stone, have survived to our time. (Pitt-Rivers [1874] 1979: 4)

Pitt-Rivers' ethnographic collection, along—soon—with the museum that housed it, was to become the principal instrument used for this new method. From 1850 onward, the General, within the space of twenty or so years, put together a huge collection of all kinds of objects from "savage"[13] societies. In his 1874 lecture, when his work as a collector had been recognized by the British anthropological community, Pitt-Rivers presented the four major parts of his collection using terms that deserve our attention. The first and second parts in his classification of forms and objects hold few surprises. The first, which referred to physical anthropology, "consists of a small collection of 'typical skulls

---

fore foot and has long ears." The other was a horse "about five feet high, his hoofs are very small; his tail is about three feet six inches long" (Voltaire 1794: 16).

13. As a collector, Pitt-Rivers was certainly encouraged by his technical curiosity where weapons were concerned, but, furthermore, through his interest in the London Universal Exhibition of 1851, he learnt of the theories on the origins of art of another great pioneer in this field of study, namely the German Gottfried Semper, who, while exiled in London for having taken part in the 1848 Dresden Revolution, had reconstructed and exhibited a Carib hut for the exhibition (Semper 1989). However that may be, Semper's ideas about the origin of tools certainly deeply influenced the biology of images, as Boas (1927) and Haddon (1894) both attest.

and hair.'" The second, which was much larger, put together a great many weapons from existing "savage populations." The third and the fourth categories were more unexpected, for the fourth included a collection of modern forgeries, along with a number of specimens of natural forms simulating artificial forms for comparison with artificial forms. But the third was even more surprising. Among other things what it contained was "miscellaneous arts of modern savages, including pottery and substitutes for pottery; modes of navigation, clothing, textile fabrics and weaving; personal ornament; realistic art; conventionalized art; ornamentation; tools; household furniture; musical instruments; idols and religious emblems . . . money and substitutes for money; fire-arms . . . mirrors, spoons, combs, games" (Pitt-Rivers [1874] 1979: 1).

The world of objects invented by primitive peoples was thus organized into four major taxonomic categories: Skulls and Hair, Weaponry, Natural Mimetic Objects, and, so to speak, all the rest! Faced with this way of organizing the collection, one is put in mind of the fantastical Chinese taxonomy (imagined by Borges) mentioned by Foucault at the beginning of his *The order of things* and of the irresistible hilarity that it provokes: "The passage quotes 'a certain Chinese encyclopaedia' in which it is written that 'animals are divided into: (a) belonging to the Emperor, (b) embalmed, (c) tame, (d) suckling pigs, (e) sirens, (f) fabulous, (g) stray dogs, (h) included in the present classification, (i) frenzied, (j) innumerable, (k) drawn with a very fine camelhair brush, (l) *etcetera*" (Foucault 1970: xv).

Let us nevertheless attempt to identify the logic behind Pitt-Rivers' taxonomy, concentrating on the two parts that seem the strangest, namely the third and the fourth. As we have seen, the aim was to set in place a number of sequences of forms in order to reconstruct a past now lost forever. Pitt-Rivers, like Spencer, believed that all evolutions must proceed from the simple to the complex: "In the progress of life at large, as in the progress of the individual, the adjustment of inner tendencies to outer persistencies must begin with the simple and advance to the complex, seeing that, both within and without, complex relations, being made up of simple ones, cannot be established before simple ones have been established"(Pitt-Rivers [1874] 1979: 8).

This method naturally rests upon the hypothesis that it is possible to establish links between different objects once one has analyzed their forms. Here, Pitt-Rivers, who may have encountered Semper at the Universal Exhibition in London in 1851, stands as an heir to German morphological thinking of Goethean origin. He writes as follows: "Since the year 1852 I have endeavoured to supply this want from amongst the commoner class of objects which have been brought to this country, those which appeared to show *connexion of form*" (ibid.: 2). Such interrelations between forms are crucial for Pitt-Rivers' perspective, for they make it possible to reconstruct the mental operations that they imply. Every series in his collection aims to reveal "sequences of ideas," starting from the most simple examples: "[The objects] have been arranged in sequence, so as to trace, as far as practicable, the succession of ideas by which the minds of men in a primitive condition of culture have progressed from the simple to the complex and from the homogeneous to the heterogeneous" (ibid.: 2).

But in his view, it was also a matter of memory. Here, closely following in the footsteps of Herbert Spencer and his *Principles of psychology* (1855), he considers it necessary to distinguish, in the activities of the human mind, between conscious and intentional capacities and those that enable us to act without investing either will of consciousness: "We are conscious of an intellectual mind capable of reasoning upon unfamiliar occurrences, and of an automaton mind capable of acting intuitively in certain matters without effort of the will or consciousness" (Pitt-Rivers [1874] 1979: 5).

So, according to Pitt-Rivers, there is such a thing as "automatic psychism." Now, one of his major ideas, which was to be widely taken over by his successors, was that the invention of objects—and so of forms too—is deeply linked to instinctive and unconscious aspects of mental activity, which he calls *automaton mind*. This was, in fact, one of the most innovatory consequences of the application of Darwinian theory to the cultural evolution of humanity. Given that, according once again to Spencer, "*every action which is now performed by instinct, at some former period in the history of the species has been the result of conscious experience*" (ibid.: 7), by analyzing the instinctive and unconscious techniques to which present-day "savage" populations resort in order to produce forms, it is possible for us to understand the conscious actions and intellectual conquests that marked the first steps of the intellectual activity of the men of prehistory. Thanks to this constant process the effect of which is that every deliberate action that leads to a satisfying result is transferred from consciousness to the instinctual level of the mind, an analysis of man's automatic memory as expressed in the simplest of forms makes it possible to analyze the evolution of the mind in the human species.

For all these reasons, a formal analysis of objects enables great advances to be made in this "prophetic" reconstruction of the origins of humanity: much greater advances than enabled by any analysis of linguistic categories. According to Pitt-Rivers, the preeminence of form over speech is, from this point of view, beyond question: "In endeavouring to trace back prehistoric culture to its root forms, we find that in proportion as the value of language and of the ideas conveyed by language diminishes, that of ideas embodied in material forms increases in stability and permanence" (ibid.: 13).

In this respect, Pitt-Rivers shares a concept of the fragility of language that was extremely widespread in the nineteenth century but that seems astonishing to us today. For him, as for the linguist John Wesley Powell, the founder of the Smithsonian Institution, every nonwritten language is subject to constant metamorphosis. In the state of "continuous flux" of such a language, nothing remains fixed by words (Pitt-Rivers [1875] 1979: 28): "Whilst in the early phases of humanity, the names of things change with every generation if not more frequently, the things are handed down from father to son and from tribe to tribe" (Pitt-Rivers [1874] 1979: 13). If that is true, Pitt-Rivers wonders why "has language hitherto received more scientific treatment than the arts?" (ibid.). It is indeed clear that the study of what he calls "the psychology of the material arts" (ibid.) makes it possible to progress further in the exploration of the history of human thought: "In language and in all ideas communicated by word of mouth there is a hiatus between the limits of our knowledge and the origin of culture which can never be bridged over, but we may hold in our hand the first tool ever created by the hand of man" (Pitt-Rivers [1875] 1979: 31).

But, according to Pitt-Rivers, one can go even further, moving toward the animal world. If, as his collections show, forms imply mental operations and manifestly obey the laws of evolution, moving from the simple to the complex, they may legitimately be compared to living organisms. And Pitt-Rivers has no hesitation in concluding that human ideas, like animals, have a particular geographic distribution and a temporal evolution: "Human ideas, as represented by the various products of human industry, are capable of classification into genera, species and varieties, in the same manner as the products of the vegetable and animal kingdoms and in their development from the homogeneous to the heterogeneous they obey the same laws" (Pitt-Rivers [1874] 1979: 18).

The propagation of ideas is therefore in every respect comparable to that of species: "The propagation of new ideas may be said to correspond to the propagation of species. New ideas are produced by the correlation of previously existing ideas in the same manner as new individuals in a breed are produced by the union of previously existing individuals" (ibid.).

He then concludes that "progress is like a game of dominoes—like fits on to like" (ibid.: 18). The sequences of the Pitt-Rivers Museum (two examples of which are illustrated here, one of which relates to the boomerang, the other to the paddle: Figures 8 and 9), while showing how mental operations are perpetuated through time by the evolution of forms, also contributed to the construction of a zoology or botany of ideas. So this is how the expression "biology of images" may legitimately be used: this biology, based on the analysis of forms that infers the unknown from what is known, prophesies the first stages in the mental activity of humanity. It is therefore an essential chapter in a future natural history of ideas, for which the Pitt-Rivers Museum formulated a scientific program.

Two intuitions lie at the origin of this view of research, in which one is bound to recognize a number of aspects that Gregory Bateson was to develop nearly a century later in his "ecology of the mind": (1) the idea of an evolutive and almost "grammatical" sequential ordering of objects that is able to *make them speak* (as Pitt-Rivers wrote in another passage of "Principles of classification" [ibid.: 10]: "By studying the grammar [of objects], we may be able to learn to conjugate them"); and (2) the intuition that forms which enable us to read objects reflect ideas. Not one of Pitt-Rivers' successors failed to recognize his debt to the General. So Pitt-Rivers turned out to be not only a man of science but, so far as the biology of images was concerned, also an original thinker.[14] However,

---

14. Part of this work is devoted to another major project, the archaeological museum that he established in Kent. His contribution to the history of this discipline (which I cannot address in the present work) was likewise most remarkable.

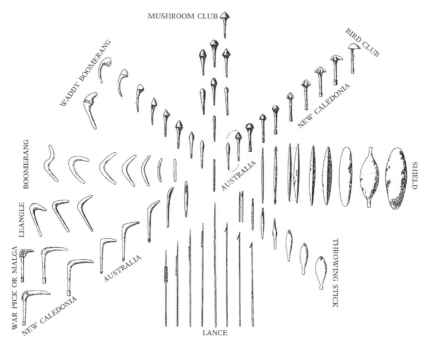

Figure 8. A morphological series showing the evolution
of the boomerang.

when he speaks of ideas linked to forms, he is mainly thinking of what
we, today, call cultural technology. He was thinking about techniques,
for which the weapons of savage populations provided the best example.
These not only constituted the majority of the artifacts classified and
preserved in the General's collections; they were also the subject of most
of his extremely technical and detailed writings on this point. After all,
his true passion, throughout his life, was that which procured him his
military successes: ballistics.

In order to pass on from such a technical and utilitarian concept of
the relation between forms, tools, and ideas to that of a veritable attribution of a religious or cosmological meaning to forms—and so to a project
for a systematic decoding of objects produced by primitive peoples—it
would be necessary to wait for another scientific figure almost all traces
of whom have disappeared from our histories of ethnology.

Figure 9. A morphological series showing the evolution of the paddle in New Ireland.

HJALMAR STOLPE: PROTOTYPES AND CRYPTOGLYPHS

As we have seen, the young Warburg considered the sign-image to be a fundamental feature of primitive drawing. He pointed out that, in primitive societies, visual representation becomes stereotyped and, as in the case of the Hopi thunderbird, resembles "an intermediary stage between image and sign." The primitive drawing thus leads to the hieroglyph. However, although based on a study of the ceramics in the Keams Canyon collection and on its catalogue produced by Alexander Stephen, this idea certainly does not go without saying. Where did it come from? At what point did primitive drawing begin to be regarded as a kind of writing?

Pictographs (Nahuatl and Maya, for example) have long since been compared to hieroglyphs. Such comparisons were already made by sixteenth-century chroniclers and, in general, by authors concerned with American proto-writings.[15] Yet such comparisons are for the most part purely rhetorical expedients and remain formulated in superficial terms. The idea that primitive drawing, up until then regarded as ornamental, constituted a veritable protowriting is one of the most striking features of the biology of images. It was Pitt-Rivers' first successor, the Swedish Hjalmar Stolpe, who, in his writings, formulated the idea in rigorous and detailed terms, at the same time describing the process that led from the earliest rudimentary but "realistic" representations to the invention of "hieroglyphs" or "pictograms."

So we need to return to Stolpe and some of his writings. In 1880–81, at the age of forty, he obtained from the Swedish government a Letterstadt grant enabling him to make a tour of the ethnological collections of Europe. Armed with thin Japanese paper and rods of black wax, the only means at his disposal for obtaining "rubbings" of the engraved or sculpted drawings that he was studying, Stolpe visited Denmark,

---

15. In this connection, see, for example, the comments of the Franciscan Diego Valadés, who was of Mexican origin, on the subject of Nahuatl pictography in the early sixteenth century: "The Mexicans, like the ancient Egyptians, had invented a method for representing abstract ideas by images." (On the history of the interpretation of Amerindian pictographs, see Taylor 1987; and Valadés [1579] 1983; see below, pp. 90–97.)

Germany, France, the Netherlands, Austria, Italy, and Switzerland. Everywhere he collected graphic patterns, decorative motifs, and, in particular, models representing the human figure. His great project was directly inspired by the writings of Pitt-Rivers and his aim was to identify, by comparison, the major graphic types of primitive iconography. After this journey, from which he brought back around six thousand impressions in the form of rubbings, Stolpe's ambition reached even further. In 1883, he embarked on a Swedish navy frigate, the *Vanadis*, and, in the course of two years, visited all the collections of objects that he could find in Rio, Santiago, Lima, Honolulu, Tokyo, Singapore, and Calcutta. He first published the conclusions from his research in an early text, "On the evolution in the ornamental art of the savage people," which aroused great interest in Swedish intellectual circles and was soon translated into English and German (1891).[16] In the opinion of Stolpe, as for Pitt-Rivers, who revolted against his colleagues' lack of interest in the art of primitive peoples, scholars were wrong not to study the drawings and ornaments of "savage populations": "*Ornament,*" he wrote, "*is not a sport with lines*" (Stolpe 1927: 69).

Stolpe's great comparative inquiry into thousands of objects enabled him to show that the drawings of these peoples were governed by two great principles. The first was that the graphic style that imposes itself within a tradition imposes an internal coherence upon forms; as a result, it is possible to identify different areas that are affected by the diffusion of graphisms. The second is that, within a particular area, a finite number of forms can be identified. Stolpe was thus in a position to pinpoint and

---

16. The research work of Stolpe (1927: 18–62), published in Vienna as early as 1892, exerted a strong influence in another domain, in which his name is very seldom cited: that of the history of art. In his *Problems of style*, published in Berlin in the following year, which deeply affected the twentieth-century history of art, Alois Riegl (1992: 38 n. 12) explicitly recognizes that he learnt a great deal from the Swedish anthropologist and from his morphological method. In particular, he mentions Stolpe's Polynesian research, including precisely the development of the first representation of the human figure and the progressive transformation of its elements, "reduced to geometrical lines" and "used as independent motifs that can be repeated and rhythmically arranged in rows": this is a subject that I shall be studying in detail later in the present work.

develop the concept of a morphological series that was introduced by Pitt-Rivers. As we know, for the latter, the major criterion that led to the construction of those series of objects was that of a *connexion of form* or a formal affinity.

On the basis of a great number of Polynesian objects, Stolpe showed that the evolution of forms is ruled by a criterion far more complex than mere affinity. He detected a process of progressive simplification that he called *conventionalization*. This evolving process, which might develop over thousands of years, obeyed geometric criteria in which the symmetry and projection of given forms played an important role. If we compare, for example, the various ways of representing the human figure in Polynesia, we find that the most realistic of them are subjected to a process of progressive conventionalization of the human form. The graphic elements of a "realistic" representation (hand, body, parted legs) undergo a double process of elaboration. Once separated out, they are first subject to a reduplication by their mirror images and are thus inserted into series of repeated elements. According to Stolpe, it is possible to follow such series of transformations step by step.

Let us consider, for example, a group of Polynesian drawings studied by Stolpe. In this body of images gathered from the decorative motifs that adorn several objects used in daily life or in ceremonial situations (paddles, clubs, plates, etc.), a relatively realistic representation of a human figure, which Stolpe calls the *prototypical representation* of the iconographic series, is progressively transformed into an increasingly simplified and abstract representation (as Figures 10, 11, and 12 clearly show). The constitutive elements of the image of a body, reduced to a symmetrical opposition of arms and parted legs, in the course of time undergoes a process of geometricization that makes them increasingly unrecognizable. The end result of this elaboration is an "ornament" the appearance of which is completely abstract (Figure 11), just as it also appears on an axe or a paddle (Figure 12). And once this sign that is apparently decorative is recognized as the ultimate term in the series of transformations that we have already considered, it appears in an altogether different light. Far from being an amusement to satisfy an aesthetic sentiment, it constitutes what Stolpe suggests calling a *cryptoglyph* or *cryptograph*, a conventional representation in "hieroglyphic form" of the prototype of the entire series: namely, a human body.

Figure 10. A prototype of the human figure in Polynesia, according to Hjalmar Stolpe.

Figure 11. Transformations of the human figure in Polynesia: from the prototype to the cryptoglyph.

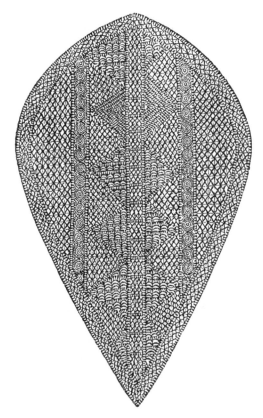

Figure 12. Polynesian paddle.

At this point, an image biologist could claim to be entering a domain which (as we have seen in Haddon's text quoted above) had hitherto been denied to him: that of the meaning attributed to images. In fact, this development in morphological analysis allowed Stolpe to take another step forward. For him, in the course of this "consecutive and regular development of a motif" (Stolpe 1927: 29), it was not, as it had been for Pitt-Rivers, simply a matter of a particular technique for controlling the environment that was perpetuating itself. If the process of the conventionalization of style pointed iconic representation in the direction of the sign, then—Stolpe argued—thanks to this graphic path, a cryptoglyph always retained the meaning of its prototype. So an apparently meaningless ornamentation such as that of a ceremonial Polynesian paddle (Figure 12) should always be interpreted as a series of representations of the human figure. To Stolpe, it hardly mattered whether or not the ornament was still understood in that way by the Polynesians of his day: "The ornament symbolizes the primitive image. It is to be considered as a cryptograph" (ibid.: 32). His conclusion was that "the conventional ornamentation of these peoples is to be considered as the very beginning of *writing*, or rather as a kind of pictograph, possessing fixed means of expression" (ibid.: 57).

Here, then, we find the bases of the very same conception of the primitive symbol as a hieroglyph and also of the compromise between iconographic representation and the sign that can be glimpsed, as on an underlying canvas, in the way that Warburg interpreted the Hopi ceramics. But that affinity goes even deeper. Stolpe's series shows that, thanks to the process of conventionalization, the Polynesian parallelogram is nothing other than the form assumed by a prototype—that of the human figure—in order to prolong its existence, generation after generation. In other words, the series that leads from a prototype to a cryptoglyph is the first abstract model of the process that Warburg was to develop, in other terms and using other examples, under the name *Nachleben*, or the "posthumous life" of iconographic representations.

In his "Studies in American ornamentation," which he published in 1896 (ibid.: vii), the perspective of Stolpe, who had meanwhile established direct links with the Smithsonian Institution, in particular with William Henry Holmes (Kubler 1988), became both more rigid and more explicit. Given that, in order to understand primitive drawing, one had to "apply the great law of evolution to ornamentation and form"

(Stolpe 1927: 62), the most natural development of Pitt-Rivers' theories is to be found in a veritable "biology of ornaments." For Stolpe, the evolution of drawing was controlled by laws as fixed as those that rule the evolution of animals. So, by analyzing the *life histories* of drawings, one can rediscover the meaning—otherwise unattainable—of the most primitive concepts of humanity. This research perspective, which is far more rigid, despite appearances, than that of Pitt-Rivers and which suffers from all the difficulties posed by conjectural history, nevertheless steers the Swedish anthropologist toward further developments of his theory of conventionalization, concerning developments involving a study of the processes of perception implied by the graphic production of primitive peoples. We should pause to dwell upon this point.

Pitt-Rivers had already understood that primitive man's first reflex was not to sketch a form on to some kind of backing, but rather to *recognize a form* in his environment. An act of looking was necessarily bound to precede any conception and realization of objects. For this reason, Pitt-Rivers considered the imitation of natural forms to be one of the principal sources of the conception of forms used to construct tools. As will be remembered, a whole section of the collections in his museum was devoted to this question; and it was precisely an object selected from those collections (Figure 13) that attracted the attention of Stolpe, who produced a very interesting commentary on it (ibid.: 82). The object in question was a Siberian ivory toggle depicting a seal. Two identical forms are interpreted in different ways: on the one hand as the shape of a wolf's head, on the other as that of an entire body (probably that of a seal). Clearly, this testifies to an act of looking that goes well beyond the simple imitation of a form. One passes on from the idea of the imitation of a natural object to that of an interpretation of a shape. The analysis of an object makes it possible to rediscover the trace of an active exercise of perception, an act of the imagination according to the principle that Vischer had called *visual empathy*.

In effect, the act of interpretation to which this object testifies indicates that "ornaments" and motifs always result from a dialogue between a gaze and a natural form. As with the Hopi chimera, which associates the features of a snake with those of a streak of lighting, an image, as a material trace, reveals the work of a mind, a series of operations that are associated with the image. The shape of the two elements of this ornament, a toggle, although ambiguous, or perhaps precisely because it is

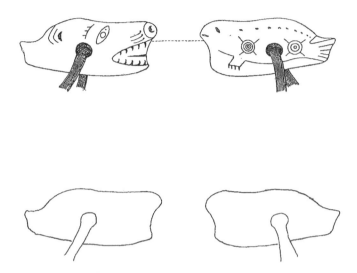

Figure 13. Ivory toggle.

ambiguous, seems to influence how it functions. We shall be returning to dwell at greater length upon this point. But for the moment we should note that the process of conventionalization discovered by Stolpe in the art of "savage" peoples, which operates both here and elsewhere by means of symmetrization and repetition, in no way attenuates the image's capacity to arouse, by projection, the chain of perceptive associations that a gaze creates when in contact with the image. On the contrary, indeed, the intensity peculiar to the conventional image seems to imply two distinct mental operations: on the one hand, it results from a selection that picks out certain particular features of the real image; on the other, that selection leads to the elaboration of a graphic model that one can subsequently replicate, possibly introducing certain variations, starting from a symmetrical axis.

It is against this kind of familiar background, obtained by the crystallization of a stereotype, that a gaze can complete or interpret an image by filling in its empty parts with a particular selection of features (and thereby obtain either the head of a wolf or else the entire body of a seal) and make implicit aspects stand out. So it is thanks to this twofold mental operation, a combination of simplification and projection, that the eye can detect, for example, a snake in a geometric schema such as that to be found on the engraved shells of Woodlands, in the United States

(Figure 14).The success of an image, testifying to both its intensity and its ability to become the prototype for a series that leads to cryptoglyphs, is thus explained by both those processes.

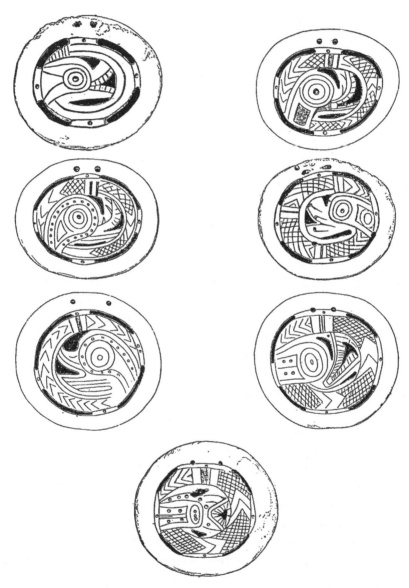

Figure 14. A conventional representation of a snake on engraved shells from the Woodlands (eastern United States, "Mississippi period," 1200–1400 AD).

Hampered by his "biological" dogmatism, Stolpe never did develop that point. His example nevertheless remains eloquent: visual thinking is at work in those acts of looking that lead to the invention of forms, and that thinking does not coincide solely with the attribution of a meaning to the object. As we shall see later, it also leads to an understanding of the intensity of the visual salience and the mnemonic aspects of the images. But let us pause again, to consider the morphological research that Stolpe devoted to "American ornaments."

A RETURN TO THE LIGHTNING-SNAKE

A sequence of representations on ceramics, established by Stolpe on the basis of material published by William Henry Holmes (one of the ethnologists whom Warburg met at the Smithsonian), provides a good illustration of the interplay of conventionalization and projection at work in this type of representations. A brief analysis of these graphisms will allows us to approach Warburg's work on the Hopi iconographs. It concerns the representation of the snake theme, using symmetry and the creation of a series (Figure 15). In his analysis of this sequence, Stolpe follows both the process of conventionalization and the geographic distribution of the theme. The sequence concerns the birth of a snake stereotype in Native American cultures from Arkansas across to the Plains region. It is at the point where this series approaches the region of the Four Corners (Arizona, Colorado, New Mexico, and Utah) that the stereotyped image of the snake progressively becomes associated with that of lightning, sometimes accompanied by a crown of feathers symbolizing a bird. In this way, the snake becomes a celestial being, resembling lightning and associated with a bird, as in Figures 14 and 15 (ibid.: 82). Here Stolpe was studying research well known to Warburg, consisting of texts by Cushing (1886), Fewkes (1892), and Holmes (1886). All the features that define the Hopi chimera studied by Warburg in 1895–96 are there: following the line taken by the research work of Stolpe, we end up at the work-desk of the young Warburg. Stolpe's model of the morphological development of forms, where the prototype is both transformed and preserved in the cryptoglyph, is illustrated here by the same materials as those upon which Warburg pondered. In fact, the first model of the idea of *Nachleben* that Warburg applied to the art of the Italian Renaissance is clearly identifiable in what Stolpe called the *life-history* of a drawing, in this case the abstract model of the evolutive morphological series the principles of which he formulated.

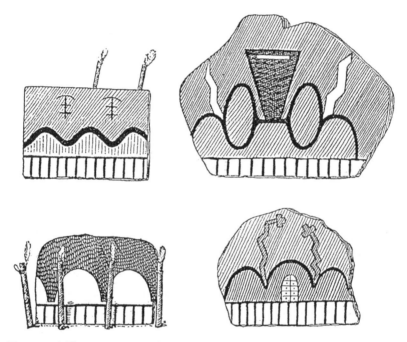

Figure 15. The association of the snake and lightning in Hopi iconography.

So when, in 1895–96, Warburg, writing his travel notes, mentions *biological necessity* in connection with art in America, he is no way resorting to vague metaphorical language. Rather, he is referring to a method of analysis which, within a positivist and Darwinian perspective, is intended to be a scientific, rather than aesthetic, study of the "decorative" arts of primitive peoples. This method is based on the hypothesis that the persistence of certain graphic motifs results from an unconscious memory or an instinctual aspect of memory that is expressed in practices that lead to the invention of forms. These are, on the one hand, analyzed as objective facts, in their evolution and geographic distribution, and, on the other hand, considered to testify to ideas or, rather, elementary mental operations. This plan for a comparative morphology of the elementary symbols imagined by human societies was conceived as a way to "prophesy," on rigorous scientific bases, the past of humanity and thereby, with a perspective directly inspired by biology, to found a study of the earliest stages of its cultural evolution.

From this inquiry into the morphological roots of Warburg's thought, we can now draw a preliminary conclusion: between, on the one hand, the thinking of the young Warburg, who sought to define the "biological necessity" of art, and, on the other, the biological study of forms practiced by Pitt-Rivers, Stolpe, and Haddon, a by no means superficial analogy may be drawn. Even if Warburg's anthropological perspective was affected by the influence of philosophers, psychologists, and historians of religions, it was nevertheless founded on the evolutionist and morphological bases that underlay the biological approach to the analysis of images. Warburg's relations with the anthropologists of the Smithsonian Institution developed from a shared intellectual heritage that was founded as much upon Darwinism as upon the German morphological tradition that led from Goethe to Semper and Boas.

WARBURG THE ANTHROPOLOGIST, OR THE DECODING OF A UTOPIA

We have seen that a reconstruction of the biological approach to a study of forms makes it possible to identify a tradition of research in which the roots of the questions that Warburg raises about the transmission of symbols are deeply embedded. Now we must try to understand how a particular utopian or future anthropology—with its twofold ambition for both critical work on the meaning of images and reflection on the mental operations involved—can become a possible development of his work. In order to make progress in our project to sketch in the earliest elements of an anthropology of memory, we must therefore now switch from historical analysis to an epistemological critique. After attempting an account of the origins and historical evolution that were followed by the concept of a biology of images, we should now examine the implications of that concept and evaluate the consequences that impinged on empirical research. This involves three questions: the bases of a comparative analysis of iconographies, the mental operations implied by forms, and the relations that may be established between images and language in traditions that we, quite wrongly, call only "oral." Where comparison is concerned it is not hard to see that the analysis of images and the establishment of sequences established by "connected forms" in accordance with their increasing complexity, as exemplified by Pitt-Rivers and Stolpe, have without doubt made a decisive contribution to the study of iconographies. Few anthropologists of art today would disagree. The cases of the other two questions require a more nuanced assessment. Let us first consider the relations between form and mental representation.

It is clear that the morphological approach that we have briefly reconstructed derives its originality from the fact that, at least where its more enlightened representatives are concerned, it aspires to pass beyond a pure taxonomy of forms in order to explore the visual thinking that lies at its origin. It is in this respect that the biology of forms constitutes a synthesis of two traditions, the one morphological (originating with Goethe), the other Darwinian. Like Goethe, in his botanical studies, initially the biologists of art were not seeking to define either causality or meaning; rather, they were concerned to describe the elementary forms of the phenomena that they studied. The Darwinian theory of evolution provided them with a way to position those elementary forms within the earliest stages of human culture by referring to the classic instruments of naturalistic thought: classification, the study of development (which Goethe still regarded as a nonevolutionary series of metamorphoses), and an analysis of geographic distribution. As we have seen, it was precisely such an ambition to carry out an analysis at two levels, the one psychological, the other formal, that conferred upon certain studies of Stolpe and Pitt-Rivers the kind of fertile ambiguity that makes them so interesting today.[17] Meanwhile morphology constituted solely by purely formal analyses of drawings and decorative motifs, making no reference to visual thinking, led the biology of art into an impasse. As can be seen from the works of some of Pitt-Rivers' successors, such as Henry Balfour's *The natural history of the musical bow* (1899), any morphology

---

17. This ambiguity between the biological and the psychological levels, already noticed by Goethe (see Severi 1988), helped Gregory Bateson to formulate the scientific program of his "ecology of the mind," as he fully recognized (Bateson 1979: 16–21).

devoid of psychological ambition becomes sterile. In works of that type, the notion of form as a basis for the transmission of knowledge progressively disappears and morphology is reduced purely to a form of classification. One is bound to conclude that, in order to be effective, morphological analysis must focus on the relation between the graphic sign and the mental operation that it presupposes.

The same applies to the third question mentioned above: that of the relation between form and language. Any analysis that seeks solely to establish a series of affinities between graphic motifs, without posing the problem of the relation between the image and verbal memorization (and, hence, tradition), is destined to revolve in a void for ever. The oeuvre of Carl Schuster, who may be considered one of the contemporary inheritors of the morphological tradition, provides a clear example. His research is at once fascinating[18] yet of little use to our project: it is fascinating because Schuster studies a considerable number of graphic materials, showing how, between them, there are "connections of form" (to use Pitt-Rivers' expression) that are sometimes informative; yet it is of little use to an understanding of the "oral and iconographic traditions" of societies without writing, because the object of the analysis is excessively reduced. In effect, what Schuster does is establish an extremely rich repertory of forms more or less endowed with meaning, instead of identifying, among specific examples, particular types of relations between forms and words. This reduced perspective leads him to produce an often uncertain exegesis of elementary visual representations, instead of seeking to understand what the images refer to. Rather than exploring how a memory becomes established in societies lacking writing, Schuster tries to establish a dictionary, by definition infinite, of possible forms and their meanings.

To avoid such a trap, one must widen one's perspective. The simplest phenomenon in the domain of traditions in which memory is based on both images and words is not a representation of an object by a typical form that imitates its appearance, but rather the relationship established between certain forms and certain words within the context of a memorization practice. As we shall see from the example from Oceania that we shall be studying, such an establishment of mnemonic relations between images and words involves, above all, proper nouns, that is, names. In the

---

18. See, for example, C. Schuster (1993).

context of techniques of memorization, such words are set out in series and treated literally as objects to be preserved. It is by no means exaggerated to consider such mnemonic series as veritable *collections* of words. On the other hand, the images that serve as props for their memorization are consulted as the bearers of meaning that has to be deciphered in order to evoke and bring to mind the name that they convey. However, the relations woven between images and names are far from simple. A form is never limited to direct imitation of the presumed meaning of a word, and each term in the relationship established between language and a visual form follows a logic of its own.

In order to switch from a classification of forms to a study of their role in the traditions of peoples "without writing," it is essential to move on from the *consecutive and regular development* of a series of forms that Stolpe engaged in to a study of the relations that the practices linked to memorization establish between images and verbal memory, for those relations contribute to the establishment of a tradition. It will therefore be necessary to retain from the morphological heritage the idea that a visual memory is certainly at work in iconographies, in order then to study how that thought functions in the context of memorization practices. With such a perspective, we shall therefore not solely study the evolution of forms but also concentrate on the mode of relation that is established within a tradition between a form considered as a material trace inscribed upon some prop and the mental operations, the acts of looking, and the types of associations that it suggests. Accordingly, instead of referring to the naïve evolutionism of the biologists, we shall return to the questions that Warburg posed in connection with the Hopi chimera and the mental operations that seem to be implied by the association of heterogeneous features by which it is characterized. This new perspective should make it possible to identify, alongside the psychological bases of any culture (as proposed by Pascal Boyer and Dan Sperber), what cognitive operations are implied by the whole collection of practices and techniques needed for the setting up and functioning of a specific tradition. Research into cognitive anthropology could in this way operate in conjunction with the findings of research in the field. But let us first pause to consider that notion of a chimera that I have so far been using in a purely intuitive way, to explain what I understand it to mean. Let us take another look at the bird-snake-lightning of the Hopi ceramics (see Figure 7, p. 36) and ask ourselves what mental operations are implied by its decoding.

I have so far described a chimera as an association, within one single image, of the heterogeneous features of a number of different beings. The Greek chimera, a monstrous body combining snake, lion, and bird, is a well-known example. However, the Hopi chimera presents the eye with far fewer visual details. By limiting the image to a small number of features, it simplifies its structure. It is on the basis of this conventionalization, the characteristics of which were noted by Stolpe, that it prompts a visual projection that actively summons up the image, at the same time completing it. Two points need to be noted here: not only does the image separate thus into two parts, the one materialized, the other mental, but the space within which it is completed is entirely mental. In the case of a Hopi ceramic, only the flat or convex basis provided by the vase provides the eye with some indication of the space within which to situate the image. Any further indication must be produced by the act of looking, which involves both projection and association. Here we discover a crucial difference between the Greek chimera and the Hopi chimera. Neither their relation to the invisible nor their manner of engendering a mental space is of the same type. The Greek chimera may be defined as an imaginary creature depicted in relatively realistic terms. As the result of an iconographic conventionalization, the Hopi chimera is a collection of abstract visual indices in which what is to be seen necessarily calls for an interpretation of what is implicit. This invisible part of the image is engendered entirely from indices given within a mental, not a realistic, space. There is a particular principle that supports the structure of these chimera-images, in which the association of heterogeneous features necessarily implies a particular articulation between the visible and the invisible. This structure "through indices" in which the condensation of the image into a few essential features always presupposes that the form is interpreted through a projection, that is to say, by filling in the parts that are lacking, has one important consequence: it confers upon the image a particular salience that distinguishes it from other visual phenomena. For this reason, that principle, which results from an interpretation of images in purely formal terms, can play a crucial role in social practices linked to memorization and the establishment of traditional knowledge.

In this new context, the force or visual salience of these images also becomes a mnemonic salience, an ability to promote and preserve meaning.

However, that salience, far from operating in a void, presupposes the elaboration of a classification, a taxonomic order of objects that underpins their decoding by triggering or upholding a memory. A brief analysis of a group of Melanesian—Iatmul and Bahinemo—objects will help to develop this hypothesis and provide an example of the kind of relationship which, in iconographic traditions, may be established between visual salience and mnemonic salience.

IMAGE-SEQUENCES AND CHIMERA-OBJECTS

The graphic memorization techniques of societies that depend on oral tradition have, up until now, been studied very little. In histories of writing, they are to be found classified as, for example, vague "figurative techniques" or "mnemotechnical props" supposedly situated "before" the invention of written linguistic signs. All types of graphism that do not represent the sounds of a language are classified as episodic and arbitrary attempts to reproduce the appearance of an object. Many authors continue to claim that what we have here is a "writing of things" as opposed to the "writing of words" (Severi 1997). Nevertheless, the real link between these images, often said to be "rudimentary," and the use of a memorizing technique has seldom been studied in detail. As soon as one passes on from the generalizations of "armchair anthropology" to the study of an actual ethnographic case, one notices that the vague idea of an "iconographic" link of resemblance that, in a universe in which the field of memory is dominated solely by the spoken word, seems to represent an isolated and sporadic attempt to fix some object in the memory is often a long way from accounting for the reality of the situation.

The example of iconographies (masks, little cords, ritual clasps) used for mnemonic purposes in the eastern Sepik region in Papua New Guinea makes it possible to illustrate this point particularly clearly. There is surely no need here to emphasize the fame of Sepik art. All studies of Oceanic art devote particular attention to it (Thomas 1995), and Western ethnological museums house a rich collection of Iatmul masks, Bahinemo clasps, Kwoma graphisms and sculpted objects, and Abelam paintings. All these objects are classified there according to principles many of which are still close to those of Pitt-Rivers (cultural zones, the evolution of morphologies, and so on). But an increasing number of studies situate these objects in their ritual or day-to-day contexts, according to their multiple significances or, more rarely, according to the criteria of indigenous aesthetics. This literature naturally constitutes an essential means for seizing upon the nature and function of each of those objects. Nevertheless, in a memorable passage in his *The way of the masks*, Claude Lévi-Strauss pointed out that a study of objects might also be carried out in accordance with a different point of view, one aimed not so much at objects considered each on their own, but at the way in which they are classified by cultures and the relations that can be established between them:

> It would be misleading to imagine, therefore, as so many ethnologists and art historians still do today, that a mask and, more generally, a sculpture or a painting may be interpreted each for itself, according to what it represents or to the aesthetic or ritual use for which it is destined. We have seen that, on the contrary, a mask does not exist in isolation; it supposes other real or potential masks always by its side, masks that might have been chosen in its stead and substituted for it. . . . I hope to have shown that a mask is not primarily what it represents but what it transforms, that is to say, what it chooses *not* to represent. (Lévi-Strauss 1982: 144)

Up until now, scant attention has been paid to the way in which Sepik societies, in particular the Iatmul, establish relations between objects or to the various ways in which they classify them. The "oeuvres" of the "great art" attributed to Sepik societies are, in fact, generally "interpreted according to what they represent or the aesthetic or ritual use for which they are destined," to use Lévi-Strauss' words. Only in rare cases has interest been shown in the functions that these objects may assume within the totemic systems of naming by which these societies are characterized. Yet within those carefully organized and preserved systems, many of those objects, in particular masks, flutes, clasps, and musical instruments, play an essential role in the memorization of names, which constitute the axis on the basis of which the whole of traditional knowledge is organized. Let us consider the case of the Iatmul.

As Gregory Bateson noticed in 1936, this people presents a particularly limpid picture of the notion of tradition, since the knowledge that the men of a patrilinear clan were expected to transmit to later generations is essentially organized and memorized on the basis of lists of names. More recent research work (Stanek 1983; Wassmann 1988; Silverman 1993) has made it possible to gain a better understanding of these lists and the way in which they are memorized. They consist of generally quite extensive collections of names (in some cases as many as several thousand[19]), which constitute the patrimony of the possible names available for patrilinear clans. These names are generally transmitted, both among the Iatmul and among other Sepik societies (such as the Karawori studied by Telban 1998), following the rule of an alternation of generations according to which those attributed to a boy and his sisters are the ones that the father of his father and his sisters possessed before him and that the son of his son (and his sisters) will receive. The names born by the sons or daughters of this masculine Ego are, on the contrary, those that his father and his sisters received, and these will be passed on to the son of his son. Specialists of Sepik culture all emphasize the importance of these veritable patrimonies of names in these societies, over and above local differences. Those lists materialize the notion of ancestorship in these societies. They define, on the one hand, social units (lineages, clan segments, and associations of patrilinear clans) and, on the other, the very concept of a person who is thus identified, by the names that he/she has received, with the ancestors who also bore them. In Sepik communities, this definition of existence by a name does not solely concern individuals and social groups: for the mythical act of the creation of the world is, among the Iatmul, largely conceived as an act of naming. Seen from this point of view, nothing can really exist, whether it be a man, an animal, or even a place, unless it has been given a name (Errington and Gewertz 1983; Silverman 1993). As Silverman (1993) has pointed out, some lists of names are interpreted as veritable *paths of ancestors*, that is to say, as lists of the names of the places that ancestors actually passed through in the course of their original migration. Jürg Wassmann, for his part, tells us that sometimes the person who bears one of these names identifies so

---

19. That is the realistic estimate of Silverman (1993). Bateson (1932), for his part, spoke, probably less cautiously, of tens of thousands of names.

closely with the ancestor who bore it that all references to real time or place may be abolished. In the remarkable study that he devoted to the Iatmul song about a Flying Fox, he describes, for instance, a man who, in the ceremonial house, claimed that he had been "the one who completed the original migration" because he bore the name of the totemic animal which, according to myth, undertook that journey (Wassmann [1982] 1991). It is worth emphasizing that, alongside the normal transmission of a name—generally a patrilinear one and only in certain cases a matrilinear one, as, for instance, among the Iatmul of Palimbei, the name of a maternal uncle passed down to a uterine nephew—there also exists a *ritual use* for a name, the purpose of which is, precisely, the establishment and periodic renewal of a complex identificatory relation to an ancestor, either matrilinear or patrilinear, which constitutes the essential function of a name. As we shall see, this ritual identificatory relationship is established within a carefully organized context. But for the moment let us simply note that it is within this dimension that the role played by certain ceremonial objects that are given names, just as human beings are, becomes crucial. It is of course not possible, here, to convey all the richness of the ethnography of the Iatmul and their neighbors. But we should note simply that two types of objects in particular are used to establish and then ritually "display" identificatory links with ancestors and thereby visually represent the names that constitute a clan's patrimony. I propose to call these types of representations image-sequences and chimera-objects.

Image-sequences

Wassmann was the first to make a detailed study of a particularly interesting mnemonic use of an image within the framework of the transmission of names (Wassmann 1988). It involves the cords bearing spaced-out knots which, among the Kandingei Iatmul but elsewhere too,[20] constitute the jealously guarded property of initiated members of a patrilinear clan (Figure 16).

---

20. Silverman (1993) collected similar objects in Tambunum and Harrison (1990) brought back very similar objects and news of similar practices among the Manambu of Atavip, the Nimhi.

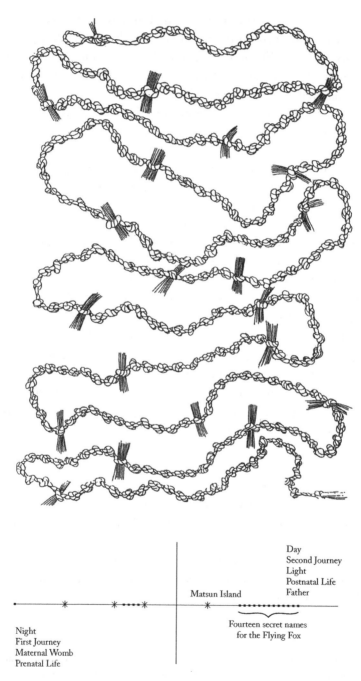

Day
Second Journey
Light
Postnatal Life
Father

Matsun Island

Fourteen secret names
for the Flying Fox

Night
First Journey
Maternal Womb
Prenatal Life

Figure 16. A Iatmul mnemonic cord and its graphic schema

Wassmann's precise and careful description reveals that, despite its relatively simple appearance, this cord is a complex visual object. Its use for mnemonic purposes operates at several levels. In the first place, the cord itself bears a name. It is "Crocodile," the very same original crocodile[21] that the Iatmul initiators represent when performing initiation rituals, by organizing lines of men all simultaneously imitating the sinuous movements of the reptile (Houseman and Severi 1998: 75). Through its name the cord is also associated with a myth of origins. From this point of view it represents the body of the crocodile which, progressively emerging from the water, was at the origin of the earth and upon which humans established their villages. This association with the first path traced in space by the clan's totemic ancestor gives rise to the two great principles that orient its interpretation. The first is that the cord, as an image of an itinerary, can only be read in one direction: from left to right. The second distinguishes two major sections of the cord and sets them in opposition: one (omitting a, so to speak, preliminary section which remains secret and about which Wassmann's ethnography, no doubt out of respect for Iatmul custom, says nothing) is called "nocturnal." Wassmann explains that it represents "the first part of the migration [the mythical voyage of the crocodile, and] is associated with darkness, the maternal womb, prenatal time and standstill." The other, in contrast, represents the day, "the second half of the primal migration[, and] is associated with brightness, post-natal time and movement in general" (Wassman [1982] 1991: 226).[22]

---

21. It comes as no surprise to find that this Crocodile here belongs to a segment of the clan that is known as *Flying Fox*. All the specialists in this field indeed emphasize that the patrimony of each clan is constantly contested by the other clans, and this provokes the addition of a great many superpositions in the totemic names that are sometimes attributed to one clan or another. Naturally enough, this rarity of names, as opposed to the great number of totemic units who lay claim to them as their own, lies at the origin of the verbal duels to establish which group controls the names that Bateson (1932, [1936] 1958) and Silverman (1993) have described among the Iatmul and Harrison (1990) has described among the Manambu.

22. Certain authors (Wassman [1982] 1991: 226–42; Telban 1998: 91–92) have provided examples of these names. However, in view of the secret

As we have seen, each knot in the cord designates a name. At this level another classificatory criterion appears. As Silverman has pointed out, all the Iatmul totemic names are organized in couples, or rather by a series of binary oppositions, as a single example from the rich corpus recorded by Wassmann suffices to show (ibid.: 227). It concerns the name of the crocodile itself, which is defined as follows:

1. Andi—Kabak—meli   1. Andi: old name for "earth"
                         Kabak: original Crocodile and "mythical
                         earth"
                         Meli (masculine suffix)

2. Kipma—Kabak—meli   2. Kipma: Earth
                         Kabak: original Crocodile and "mythical
                         earth"
                         Meli (masculine suffix)

This organization of totemic names, thanks to the alternation of constants and repetitions of the same sounds, no doubt does have a mnemonic value, which shows that, even in the Iatmul case, purely verbal techniques for learning and elaborating names must exist.[23] However, it is clear that this binary classificatory system is also illustrated by mnemonic techniques linked with the visual representation of the list of names. In the little cord that we have just analyzed, the large knots designate the toponyms of the places that, each in turn, have been visited by Crocodile in the course of the journey that led him to emerge from the waters. As for the smaller knots, they are anthroponyms designating the names of the clan ancestors. Other, more precise ordering criteria then appear within groups of large and small knots: in

---

nature of some of the totemic names, no author provides details that could lead to the identification of those who bear them.

23. Both Silverman and Wassmann also indicate the use of totemic names in the utterances of ritual, funerary, or shamanistic songs. We should note that, according to Wassmann (ibid.), this couple of totemic names of the crocodile is equivalent to the statement: "The crocodile is the original crocodile and also the earth when it was created."

each group it is possible to distinguish "elders" and "youngers." In other cases, one knot may be called the "shadow" of another. Finally, one more criterion is introduced: a distinction is drawn between "public" names that may be pronounced and "secret" names that may not. Each knot is linked with an episode relating to the life of the ancestors and each one is thus associated with the crocodile myth of origin. Since each story generally corresponds to the foundation of a village, the cord as a whole designates the general schema of Iatmul mythology: a long migration that led men and certain animals from mythical places to the spaces that they now occupy.

Returning to Figure 16, which schematizes how the cord works, we can see, for example, that the daylight part that designates the second part of Crocodile's journey begins with a "large" knot that designates a "public" toponym: that of the Matsun island. It is immediately followed by fourteen "small knots" which, for their part, are secret and feminine anthroponyms (even though they are positioned on the paternal side). These names constitute "shadows" (Wassmann calls them *shadow names*) of the public names of the men grouped in the clan segment called Flying Fox, and they are distributed within this clan as personal names (which are in all probability secret). But let us pursue our analysis of the Iatmul crocodile-cord. Its interpretation turns out to be quite complex because it reveals a large number of esoteric factors which it organizes into classes in diminishing order (the maternal or paternal nocturnal/daylight parts of the cord; large or small knots, elder or younger; feminine or masculine; public or secret, and so on). At another level, since every knot constitutes a key to or the "title" of a story, the cord also organizes the episodes of the myth into sequences (Crocodile, Flying Fox . . .).

As in other Sepik societies (Harrison 1990; Telban 1998), knowledge of these series of names organized as images by the cord furthermore implies a series of ritual rights. To know a secret name is to be able—for example by sculpting a mask or clasp—to represent the animal-ancestor of the clan or the section of the clan to which one belongs; it is to acquire rights over a place (toponym); it is also, in particular among the Iatmul, to be able, through the maternal uncle and sister's son relationship, to attach to oneself a person from another clan, by giving him a name. Every young Iatmul boy is at birth and up until his initiation given a series of "matrinames," some of which are secret. Finally, among the Iatmul as elsewhere in the region, one secret name, possibly from the maternal clan, may designate the "maternal" and therefore nocturnal, secret, and vulnerable part of a masculine Ego: so knowing that name can become a powerful magic means of attaching the boy to oneself or of attacking him. The little Iatmul mnemonic cord is clearly a powerful and precious object.

But let us pause to consider its formal aspects. Over and above its powers, it testifies to the establishment of a relation between two series of traces to be fixed in a memory: a sequence of names of persons or mythical beings (the ancestors of the clan) is interwoven with a sequence of place-names, those of the stages of the original migration, which have become so many villages. From a formal point of view, then, this is a matter of an anthroponomy interwoven with a toponomy. If one adopts a perspective close to that of the biology of images, according to which it is possible to analyze a form so as to reveal the mental operations that it implies, one may infer that, from the point of view of a mental—and therefore mnemonic—representation, the little cord makes a decisive operation possible. In the process of memorization (a linear sequence), it imprints an initial order upon minimal elements by establishing a correspondence between a spatial succession—the places visited in the mythical migra- tion—and a succession in time: the migration of the ancestors of the clan. Against the background of this initial articulation, classificatory criteria enable more specific and detailed distinctions to be introduced.

We may consider this first interaction between lists of names (which are both linked within the object yet situated within different mnemonic contexts: the physical space of inhabited villages, the stages in the original migration, and the ritual identificatory relationship with the ancestors) as a kind of paradigm that illustrates the "minimal model" of a certain type of social memorization. This model, by establishing, on the one hand, an order of images (a sequence established once and for all from left to right in a reading of Crocodile's journey) and, on the other, a regular relation between names and images (essentially anthroponyms and toponyms), may indeed develop further and throw new light upon the modalities of establishing traditional Iatmul knowledge. But it also illustrates a more general principle: any practice linked with memorization presupposes an order. We are here in a world that could not be further from the world of writing and is equally distant from the isolated, disorganized, and discontinuous character that historians of writing customarily attribute to all "mnemotechnical aids" or "the writing of things" that preceded the representation of the sounds of language. What we find, in fact, is that this first operation of memorization through images implies classification and the kind of ordering sequence that any classification presupposes.

However, although the basic elements of this taxonomic structure are certainly present in the little cord, there is no image (except that probably overgeneral one of the crocodile as a sinuous reptile) to act as a prop to memory. It is quite clear that, if it were isolated from any context, the constant order of the knots could not effectively orient the evocation of any mnemonic trace or, consequently, any memory of lists of names, which, as we should remember, may include as many as thousands of them. In effect, as all the authors who have analyzed these systems of totemic names have realized, the names are not solely concentrated in exoteric knowledge such as that illustrated by the little cord. Although they are subjected to quite strict controls covering their circulation and transmission, the names are also associated with other props. Among the Iatmul and elsewhere in Sepik territory (at least among the Manambu, the Bahinemo, and the Karawori [Newton 1971; Harrison 1990; Telban 1998]) the function of evoking a totemic name may devolve upon other types of objects that are less "abstract" than the little cord. These could be masks, musical instruments evoking the ancestors' voices, or ritual clasps registering certain features. As Nicholas Thomas has pointed out, the verb "to represent" is often quite inappropriate for conveying the relations between these objects and the image of an ancestor. He suggests that in this context "art may more productively be seen to create presences than to imitate or image something that exists elsewhere" (Thomas 1995: 34). So let us settle for a more limited but more precise function for the objects: that of making a name visible and thus present in the memory. All these objects, which are generally very carefully preserved (away from the eyes of noninitiates and, above all, of women), really do constitute so many ways of "making a name visible."[24]

---

24. According to the analysis provided by Telban (1998: 85–86), the names are called "night" or "dream" in Karawori, because a name is what makes it possible not to reveal an identity. An object, on the contrary, is a means of revealing a name or making it visible.

Chimera-objects

In order to understand this new aspect of the representation of a name by an object, we must now widen our perspective and briefly examine the rituals linked with totemic names. As well as the nonritualized modalities of transmitting names and "preserving them for others" that Wassmann ([1982] 1991: 242–47) also studied, it is possible to identify at least two ritual contexts in which names are symbolically appropriated. Throughout the Sepik region, by ritually wearing "a name-bearing object" one can either "embody" an ancestor in a ritual dance or be possessed by a spirit for warrior or hunting purposes.[25]

The first case is illustrated by the ritual dance that every young Iatmul has to perform for his mother's brother. Wearing a mask of the *mwai* type as he performs this ritual dance, the boy "embodies" the ancestor of his "matriclan," one of whose names he has been given by his mother's brother (the *wau*). Clearly, in this case the mask makes manifest the identificatory relationship with the ancestor and so becomes a visual way of representing a secret maternal name that must not be pronounced. Without referring to it directly (as by means of a sign), the mask worn by the boy indicates the ritual way of making public, and therefore visible, the association of the *laua* (the sister's son) with the ancestor. The mask *makes that relationship visible*. We may conclude from all this that, in order for plastic representations—masks or other images—to become the props of a name, it is necessary not only that their form (studied, for example, by Hauser-Schäublin 1983) be conventionalized, but also that the context in which they are used be ritually defined so that these representations are rendered clearly distinct from other, more familiar images that are less charged with meaning. It is not possible, at this point, to dwell further upon this ritual, which I have studied elsewhere as part of the Naven ritual (Houseman and Severi 1998: 73–79). Rather, let us turn to consider the other way of embodying a totemic ancestor,

---

25. The Manambu case partly confirms that these spirits are directly connected with the totemic system. Newton (1971:71) indeed points out that certain ritual clasps allow the incarnation and representation of the names, not of ancestors, but of the closest forebears who cannot yet be considered ancestors. The use of the clasp would, from that point of view, be a kind of preliminary to the mask that represents the ancestor and carries his name.

which takes the form of ritual possession by a warrior- or hunter-spirit. In many Sepik societies, the function of representing this type of spirit, which always involves the attribution of a name to the object used, has devolved upon ritual clasps. Such clasps, morphologically linked to the representation of the human figure, all of which bear names, are common throughout this region. Drawing from a whole collection of ethnographic examples, ranging from the Iatmul (among whom they embody *wagen* spirits[26]) to the Egwa, Bahinemo, and Ymar, it is possible to reconstruct a series of cases that are similar with respect to their formal elaboration[27] as well as to their ritual role. In the Iatmul case (Greub 1985: 191–92), these ritual clasps were "warmed up" or evoked by an offering of betel nuts or a chicken before the men set out on a headhunting raid or a hunting expedition. In similar situations among the Ymar and the Egwa (ibid.: 200), such clasps, which were evoked before wars or headhunting forays, represented spirits associated with the clan totems. To bring them to life, whoever owned one had to rub it with drops of blood that he squeezed from his penis (Haberland and Seyfarth 1974: 364–70; Greub 1985: 199–200).

The iconography of Bahinemo masks and clasps of a small group in the Hunstein Range is known to us thanks in particular to Douglas Newton and Meinhardt Schuster (M. Schuster 1965; Newton 1971). It is more abstract but still linked to the human figure and it helps us to gain a better understanding of the role played by images of this type, where their function of representing names is concerned. Lists of the names of Bahinemo patrilinear clans are memorized, as elsewhere, by distinguishing between, on the one hand, the incarnation of the ancestor through a ritual dance

---

26. Bateson ([1936] 1958: 233–36) had already noticed that "some ancestral spirits" can "possess" shamans among both the central Iatmul and also those of the eastern Sepik. He also seems to suggest that, from the point of view of esoteric knowledge, Mwai, who is an easily identified figure in Iatmul mythology, is in reality also a *wagan*.

27. As Greub (1985) has shown in detail, the representation of the human figure, which is relatively "realistic" in the case of the Egwa, becomes almost "abstract" among the Bahinemo, after passing through a series of intermediate transformations. Thomas (1995: 42–47) suggests extending this series to include certain Abau (Upper Sepik) shields and also certain materials made from bark in the region of Lake Sentani (Irian Jaya).

and, on the other, his incarnation by means of possession based on masks and clasps that are suspended from ropes in the men's house, like so many lists of names. But what is the relation that is established here between the memorization of a name and the perception of the visual means of representing it, whether this be by a mask or a ritual clasp? We must assume that it is a mnemonic relationship that involves a series of elementary visual operations. So let us try to define those acts of looking, or rather the stages of visual inference that the Bahinemo masks and clasps imply.

To do this, we shall adopt a morphological method and, within the Bahinemo area, set up a series of name-images, either masks or clasps, in an order of increasing complexity, so as to get "the objects to speak," as Pitt-Rivers would put it. The simplest case is that of a partial mask, collected by Newton (Figure 17). Clearly here, the elementary mental operation suggested by the form is a simple projection. What is implicitly included in this image is the part of the face that is lacking, which, in accordance with the classic image of empathy described by Vischer, the observer's gaze supplies.[28]

Figure 17. A Bahinemo partial mask.

---

28. This process is also evident in other name-objects in use in this region: for example, in the Iatmul head coverings and the *meiurr* of the Manambu (Newton 1971). Whether they consist of ceramics or head coverings, these ritual objects are also said to restore to skulls the facial features that they have lost.

As for the ritual clasps, they convey a more complex iconography for they testify to the same mental operation, namely the projection of a missing part on a specific visual pattern, the more abstract form of which constitutes, as Stolpe would say, a conventional development of a prototype of the human figure. As can be seen from the examples collected by Newton (Figure 18), every Bahinemo clasp is constructed according to a particular, easily recognized, visual model that makes it, like the Iatmul *mwai*, an exceptional object, quite separate from other objects in general use.

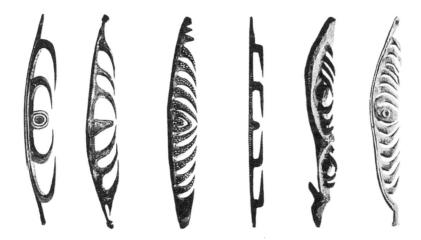

Figure 18. A series of ritual Bahinemo clasps.

This model represents the basic form of a clasp. Into this visual formula, it is possible, in order to singularize a particular object, to insert an eye in a central position (Figure 19) or add the beak of a bird (Figure 20). Two consequences follow from this insertion of a visual indicator, which is specially reserved for clasps intended for ritual purposes. On the one hand, it clearly suggests an invisible part of the image—the head of a bird or the body of a fish—which perception will then reconstruct mentally. On the other hand, the ritual clasp, initially constituted by a schematic representation of the human figure, thus becomes associated with a particular class of spirits that may be either aquatic or assimilated to birds. Once a beak or an eye is inserted into the abstract schema of the clasp, the image is marked by that reference to a bird or a fish. Through such implicit visual references, mentally elaborated as "missing parts,"

Figure 19. A ritual Bahinemo clasp: the central eye associates the form of the clasp with that of an aquatic spirit (the cat-fish).

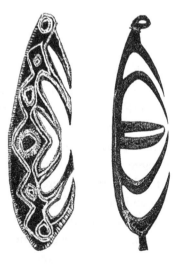

Figure 20. Ritual Bahinemo clasps. A beak is added to the eye, associating the aquatic spirit with the spirit of a bird, the *calao*.

the representation no longer refers solely to a human figure. It simultaneously refers to several bodies, of which only certain parts are visible. The ritual clasp is, in this way, transformed into a chimera.

The rudimentary "mnemonic props" to which historians of writing refer in connection with oral traditions are regularly described as attempts, often abortive, to reproduce the appearance of an object in order to fix its memory. But our brief application of the morphological method to Bahinemo ritual clasps, on the contrary, reveals that the representation of a name, far from being only triggered by an imitation of the appearance of some mythical figure or spirit, instead *follows the path of a chimerical representation*. It thus presupposes the same mental operations as those that characterize such representations elsewhere: heterogeneous features are pieced together and implicit parts are deciphered by a process of projection. Consequently, our series of clasps provides us with a regular visual *pattern* that defines a class of name-bearing objects and, by articulating a variety of visual indices, designates certain ontological transgressions—transgressions whose counterintuitive character Pascal Boyer (2000) has established. From this we can conclude that, far from just representing a human figure in "simplified" or "abstract" iconic terms, these mnemonic representations of a name are ontological transgressions translated into visual terms.

On the basis of these initial operations, we can proceed to try to interpret more complex representations. Let us consider another Bahinemo example, this time a mask (Figure 21) that also "conveys" the name of a totemic ancestor. First we should note that, as in the case of the Iatmul *mwai*, where the image of the dancer was given several simultaneous identifications, the mask here conveys a complex identity. First, we notice that the image of the ancestor is defined by means of the association of two superimposed faces. Next, we need only twist the image so as to see it in profile, to realize that this mask is, in truth, also a clasp. The representation thus associates with the two faces of the ancestor the two images implied by this clasp, which, as we have seen, may be either a fish or a bird.[29] Clearly, here again the representation conveyed by the image is constituted by heterogeneous indices that eventually produce a composite creature.

---

29. Newton (1971: 23 and 31), explains that this is cat-fish or a calao.

Figure 21. Bahinemo mask-clasp associating the beak of a bird, the eye of a
fish, and a human face.

Let us now take another step forward and re-pose our initial question: What relationship is established here between the image and the
memorization of the name? The identification of, on the one hand, the
elementary features of our iconographic series and, on the other, the
mental operations that it presupposes allows us to see that the decoding
of the image and the memory of the name both result from one and the
same operation. It is through the decoding of this complex of visual indications that the name is memorized. The mnemonic act of evoking the
name of the ancestor and the perceptive act of interpreting the implicit
parts of the image by means of a projection are thus associated in a single
mental operation. In all the cases presented in our iconographic series,
from the simplest to the most complex—which functions as a veritable
chimera, in the sense defined above—the memorization of a name coincides with the establishment of an elementary visual salience and the
emergence of a sequence of latent, associated images. The mental operation that we have illuminated by an analysis of forms and that leads to
memorization is therefore not just a passive transcription of the more or
less well-reproduced appearance of the image, but rather a combined act
of memory (an evocation) and a mental solution to a problem of visual
decoding.

We may conclude that, within the contexts studied here, the construction of memorable images rests upon two conditions: (1) that the

images, as objects belonging to a ritual context, always be recognizable as objects specially intended to be given a name (as in the cases of the little cord, the Iatmul *mwai*, and the Bahinemo clasp and mask); and (2) that those images should possess a particular visual salience, that is to say, that they prompt that singular relationship between the visible and the invisible aspects of an image which characterizes what I have defined as a chimera.

This first example shows that the memory-practices implied in an elementary iconographic tradition presuppose a group of mental operations in which the articulation of heterogeneous features both visual (clasps/beak-eye) and linguistic (the memorization of a name) operate together. As we have seen by analyzing the Iatmul cord, there can be no memorization until an ordering of what is known is established. An analysis of other forms of iconography will now make it possible to identify a second criterion that presides over the memorization of names. To borrow the technical terms used in the psychology of memory, what is necessary here is the establishment of a salience that is associated with certain images that are constructed as chimeras. Using a language closer to that of Warburg, we may describe this process as an intensification of the image's cognitive efficacy by the mobilization, through visual inferences, of its invisible parts.

The present study, carried out so as to provide an example of a possible method for analyzing chimerical iconographies, may allow us to cast a new look over a number of cultures up until now known simply as "oral." At the start of the present chapter we noted a lack of interaction between, on the one hand, research into the anthropology of art, which is devoted to the meaning and function of images, and, on the other, research in the domain of oral traditions, which is, for its part, directed toward the uses and types of the spoken word. This lack of interaction is due essentially to an inability to envisage any relationship between verbal language and visual representation other than a semiotic or aesthetic one. In short, images can be conceived only as pseudosigns or forms of decoration. The Sepik iconographic traditions that we have just considered present an example of two new ways of regarding relations between images and words: by establishing ordered sequences and by locating a visual salience. These two principles, of order and salience, introduce the possibility of what I should like to call *mnemonic relations*.

Unlike semiotic relations, these are certainly not established between a sign and its referent out in the world, as in a writing system. Rather, what we find is a collection of visual inferences, founded upon the decoding of complex images, which establish a relation between *different memories*: a spatial memory of places and a memory of words. The efficacy of practices linked to the memorization of iconographic traditions is therefore due not to a more or less successful attempt to imitate the type of reference peculiar to writing, but to a relation that they establish between different levels of mnemonic elaboration. The case of the Sepik traditions, with their two means of memorization, namely the establishment of an order and the construction of a visual salience, thus prompts a description of the unforeseen complexity of the type of mental elaboration that characterizes the way that memory is used in so-called "oral traditions." These memorizing techniques always presuppose a visual interpretation of image-sequences and chimera-objects.

I have endeavored to show that the kinds of research for a long time known as the biology of art constituted the forgotten roots of Aby Warburg's anthropological thinking. He discovered those methods in 1895–96, and the perspectives that they opened up were still stimulating his thinking in 1927, at the end of his life. On the basis of an ethnographic analysis of names in Sepik regions, I then showed that, in order to try to decode the utopia that Warburg imagined—in other words, to formulate an anthropology of social memory founded on iconographic traditions—it is necessary to turn back to consider, from a critical point of view, the morphological methods of the biology of art and its way of reconstructing the mental operations implied by the decoding of images.

A critical use of this method, which I have attempted here, requires extending the context of the study of iconographies, which the "biologists" limited to the evolution of images, to their relationship with the memory of words. Once placed within this new context, the epistemological study of the biology of art makes it possible to sketch in a study of the ways traditions establish mnemonic relations between complex images and words organized into taxonomies. This new perspective has led me to identify the role played by images in practices linked with the memorization of a body of knowledge. It involves the process of an intensification (both cognitive and mnemonic) of visual representation through a mobilization of its invisible elements. This is what I have called chimerical representation, which implies setting in place two elementary criteria that orient the practices of memorizing typical of iconographic traditions: a criterion of order and a criterion of visual salience.

There can be no doubt that much remains to be done in order to generalize this model of interpretation, which, here, it has only been possible to sketch out. However, at the end of our journey through the history and methods of a biology of images, it is perhaps possible to suggest an initial answer to the question of where Warburg's anthropology might lead us today. This anthropology, which, he wrote, is capable of introducing the study of images into the field of a "psychology of expression" (cited in Gombrich 1999: 270), might, in these non-Western so-called "oral" traditions, lead us from an analysis of the evolution of aesthetic forms to a comparative study of the arts and techniques of memory.

But let us now try progressively to apply this first approach to another example of the great so-called "oral" tradition. Here too, certain images, seemingly rudimentary, appear to assume an important role in practices linked with memorization. In this new domain, we shall encounter not only lists of names to be memorized, but also long ritual texts that constitute a coherent development from them. In anthropological literature, this new type of elementary iconography is generally, rather vaguely, called "pictography." Let us now study a few examples from the world of Native American cultures.

CHAPTER 2

An Amerindian mnemonic form
Pictography and parallelism

> *Along with the pictures that reality presents to the eye, there exists another world of images, living or coming into life in our minds alone. . . . Every primitive artist, when endeavouring to imitate nature, seeks with the spontaneity of a psychical function to reproduce merely these mental images. . . . I may say the same of the picture writings I have been able to examine.*
>
> Emanuel Löwy, *The rendering of nature in early Greek art*

There are two aspects to anthropological research as practiced here. The study of a culturally foreign phenomenon always presupposes that one sets out to accept and understand the difference, together with everything unexpected or even surprising that it implies. But such a study also obliges the researcher constantly to reconsider all that she/he has learnt and, above all, the concepts that she/he is using. Anthropological reflection implies, over and above a certain love of detailed ethnographic description, paying great attention to the use of certain words. It is through the filter of those words that much of the interpretation of foreign cultures has proceeded. When Warburg called the Hopi chimera of New

Mexico a heraldic emblem, he was borrowing the language of James Mooney. When he spoke of ornaments, he was thinking of Stolpe's theories. As we have seen in Chapter 1, when speaking of Amerindian iconographies, Warburg also used the word "hieroglyphs." But can one say that Native Americans (outside Mexico) ever possessed anything resembling writing? A definitely negative answer today seems to go without saying.[1] However, we should not forget that this was a question that for a long time remained unanswered, becoming the subject of lively debates and a whole series of imaginary projections. Once the New World was discovered, a *topos* of our view of those cultures slowly formed around that question, reducing them to the status of "oral cultures." This was a persistent idea, a rhetorical *topos* so entrenched in the thinking of the day that it seemed irrefutable. So before starting to study a few examples of Amerindian pictography within the perspective described in Chapter 1, it is important to remember how very difficult it was for Western thought to seize upon the true nature of those graphs.

The idea, now so prevalent, that Native Americans basically lacked any graphic techniques capable of preserving speech was not at all evident to the first discoverers of the American continent. Nor was it immediately accepted by the authors who, from the first decades of the sixteenth century onward, began writing the history of the discovery of the New World. On the contrary, for quite a few of them it seemed perfectly natural to assume that the autochthonous peoples of America had always possessed a technique for the preservation of knowledge and that they were familiar, if not with the letters of an alphabet, at least with signs that could be deciphered, parchments covered by texts, or even whole books. Throughout the sixteenth century, attempts were made to identify the first pictographs to emerge from Mexico with some early form of writing, in particular Egyptian hieroglyphs, the *hieroglyphica* that aroused such interest among Italian humanist groups ranging from Pier Valeriano (1556) to Michele Mercati (1598).[2] One of these attempts deserves our attention.

---

1. On this, see Diringer (1937: 559–61); Gelb (1952); Cohen (1958: Vol. I, 30, Vol. II, 45); and DeFrancis (1990).
2. In his description of the obelisks of Rome (1589), Mercati already established a comparison between Egyptian hieroglyphs and the "usages of

In Perugia, in 1579, Diego Valadés, a Franciscan brother of Mexican origin (he was born in Tlaxcala in 1533, the natural son of a conquistador serving under Cortés and a Nahuatl mother), published a treatise on Christian rhetoric in which he added a section based on "examples drawn from the traditions of the Indians of America"[3] (Figure 22). Valadés, who on the face of it seems to be harking back to the already well-established comparison between pictographs and Egyptian hieroglyphs, in reality defends a most unusual thesis. According to him, the ancient Americans had always used, if not a veritable form of writing, at least something very similar to what Valadés' contemporaries called an art of memory. In several passages of this extremely rich book, Valadés even seems to suggest that the efficacy of classic methods of the art of memory (knowledge of which he, like so many others, derived mainly from Aristotle's *De memoria* and the pseudo-Cicero's *Rhetoric for Herennius*) was *proved by* the discovery that Native Americans had made of them, in a manner completely independent of the European tradition. For example, in a chapter of his *Rhetoric* entitled "*Indorum exemplis artificialis memoria probatur*," Valadés wrote as follows: "The Indians who did not know our letters and the alphabet, could nevertheless communicate between one another with the help of certain images that they drew on tissues or on sheets of porous paper that they obtained from the leaves of trees" (Valadés [1579] 1983).[4] He then added, "These images served to remind them of what they wished to communicate, either openly or secretly; as a result, with the aid of a few images, some of them could sustain a dialogue for as long as one hour." Here Valadés' thesis, which was possibly referring to ceremonial dialogues, draws an important comparison with what was, at that time, believed about Egyptian hieroglyphs:

---

peoples in the New World who do not use the letters of the alphabet" (Mercati 1598: 82–83, cited by Prosperi 2000: 463). On Pier Valeriano, also mentioned by Prosperi (2000), see *Hieroglyphica seu de sacris Aegyptiorum literis* (1556). On the question of hieroglyphs in the Renaissance, see Rossi (1969) and Basile (1979). On the European interpretation of Amerindian pictographs, see Browne (1981).

3.   My warmest thanks go to Lina Bolzoni, who allowed me to reproduce her copy of Valadés' *Rhetorica Christiana*. On Valadés, see, above all, Palomera (1963); also Taylor (1987) and Bolzoni ([1995] 2001).

4.   I have also consulted the Mexican edition, translated into Spanish, and with a commentary by Esteban Palomera.

Figure 22. Diego Valadés, frontispiece of the *Rhetorica Christiana*, 1579.

The Indians shared in common with the ancient Egyptians a method for expressing ideas through images. Thus, swiftness was represented by the image of a falcon, vigilance by that of a crocodile. . . . The image of a bee expressed the authority of the king because he, in the exercise of justice, likewise had to use the sting, which represented severity, and honey which, for its part, represented clemency. (Valadés [1579] 1983: 233 and 239)[5]

5.   See Taylor (1987: 53–54).

Valadés was, without doubt, a figure of great intellectual and political stature. He was "the first mixed-race theologian" (ibid.: 15–21) to hold a post of authority within the hierarchy of the Catholic Church. In 1575, he became procurator general of the Order in the Curia of Rome, following over twenty years of militant preaching in the New World. Thanks to his Tlaxcal origins (they were one of the seven Nahuatl groups), he was probably the first author capable of setting up a comparison based on a twofold cultural competence, that of the Nahuatl tradition together with that of the European tradition. So it is not hard to understand the very great interest aroused by his comparison between the Mexican pictographs and the European art of memory. There were at least two reasons for that interest. In the first place, Valadés was the first to have imported into the New World the use of the art of memory derived from classical and medieval sources. In his *Rhetorica Christiana*, Diego demonstrates his absolute mastery of the memorization techniques of the Western tradition. He always knows how to choose a mental *topos* for fixing a memory and how to get it to live on in the memory by means of an appropriate *imago agens*. His treatise testifies to his great familiarity with the traditional themes of the *ars memorandi*. But he furthermore declared most solemnly, in Spain, before the Council for the Indies, that he had invented an updated and adapted version of that technique, a new version that the Franciscan Order was to use with great success throughout Mexico. These new techniques were designed in particular to assist preaching and the conversion of the Amerindian peoples (Figure 23). Valadés was explicit on this point: "We ourselves are the ones who discovered this new art and we managed to do so after fasting and long watches spent on our knees, praying that our Lord God would deign to show us the best adapted means for the conversion of these people" (ibid.: 237). He then went on to say: "For this reason, this method was presented before the Council for the Indies, so that this Council might confirm its use by men of the cloth . . . and we claim this honor as our right, as can easily be seen in the engravings that appear in my book."

Indeed, Valadés was not only a writer and preacher; he was also a painter, or rather an engraver. In the art of drawing, as in many other things, he was a pupil of Peter of Ghent, who, in Mexico, had taught art and other graphic techniques to a whole generation of young aristocrats. This group of young men, who went on to form the earliest ruling

Figure 23. Diego Valadés, crucifixion, engraving from the *Rhetorica Christiana*, 1579.

class in Mexico, quite exceptionally included Diego, but only thanks to a stratagem that enabled him to conceal his mixed origin. For we should remember that not only was he the natural son of Valadés the conquistador, he was also half-Indian, a fact that would normally have excluded him from an ecclesiastical training and career. We find echoes of his origin, which Valadés does not here attempt to conceal, in a passage of his *Rhetorica Christiana*, in which he declares that the reason why he has been able to invent such a novel and effective art of memory is that he has deliberately drawn a comparison with Nahuatl pictographic art. Other, crucial, pages in his book contain a rigorous argument based on a comparison between the Old and New Worlds.

> Just as the Ancients had sages, philosophers, kings, and princes who were able to invent many different ways in which to send messages to very distant places and to transmit all that they needed to communicate without recourse to alphabetic letters—similarly, our Indians (even though they may sometimes seem to include ignorant and uneducated persons) confided their secrets by a variety of means . . . without using alphabetic letters, but rather with the aid of signs and figures, in fact by using a kind of *polygraphy*. (Valadés [1579] 1983: 235)[6]

These pages testify to a cultural universalism which at that time was very rare. In effect, from this comparison between the Old and the New Worlds, Valadés concluded that "what follows from our considerations is that the artifice of memory"—what we today would call its exercise guided by a conscious technique—"is constituted by places and images duly set out in an order. What becomes clear is that these elements, places, and images constitute the very essence of this art" (ibid.: 235).

Here Diego expresses himself with great clarity: places and images, as he sees it, designate the essence of *all* memorization techniques, whether they be European or American. This shows not only that, by using the *ars memorandi* that he has perfected, one could preach the Catholic message to the Indians with effective results, but also that those who read his *Doctrina* (and remember that we are, here, in Perugia in 1572) "will be able to exercise and extend their memory by cultivating it *in the manner invented by the Indians*" (ibid.: 239).

It is no doubt reasonable to compare the individualism of Valadés to other great defenders of the Indians, such as Bartholomé de las Casas (Palomera 1963). Nevertheless, if one thinks of his ability to welcome on the same intellectual level images of the Nahuatl tradition along with

---

6.   The Latin term used by Valadés is *polygraphia* (my italics).

those of the memory arts of the European Renaissance (not forgetting the extraordinary engravings on which he worked for so long in order to illustrate his *Doctrina*), it is probably to Dürer that he should be compared. As is well known, Dürer looked at the American objects that had been brought to Charles V from the new territories of America with an extraordinarily free eye and judgment. As can be seen from a few pages in his *Journal*, he considered them to be "marvelous works" that testified to impressive genius: "I have seen the things brought to the king from the new golden land: a sun, wholly of gold . . . also a moon, wholly of silver. . . . I have seen their wonders of art and have marveled at the subtle *ingenia* of people in far-off lands" (cited in Panofsky 1955: 209).

As we shall later see, the comparison proposed by Valadés between American pictography and the European art of memory was not without foundation.[7] Nevertheless, his great intuition remained isolated and has been virtually unrepeated down to the present day. It is true that that audacious hypothesis was formulated by a member of a religious Order who, with his courageous defense of the rights of the Indians, very soon provoked the hostility of the powerful Council for the Indies, the Roman Curia, and part of the Order to which he himself belonged. Later, Valadés was even bold enough to oppose some of the rules imposed by Philip II, the King of Spain (Taylor 1987: 52). We should, of course, bear in mind that the very act of referring to the Nahuatl tradition (about which Diego spoke with informed respect) constituted a transgression against the total censure that Philip II had decreed in respect of the customs of his new Western subjects.

Nevertheless, when Valadés compared the Mexican pictographs to ancient writings, in particular Egyptian hieroglyphs, he was far from isolated. The comparison of pictographs with hieroglyphs had preceded him. It was a *topos* that early on became widespread and very persistent. (As we have seen, Warburg himself, when faced with the Hopi bird-chimera, was still using the term "hieroglyph.") The success of this

---

7.   Seeking a model for interpreting the Kuna pictographs and totally unaware of Valadés' book, twenty or so years ago I myself referred to an analogy with the arts of memory. See "Penser par séquences, penser par territoires: Cosmologie et art de la mémoire dans la pictographie des Indiens Kuna" (reproduced in Severi 1993c: 175–200).

idea was general throughout Renaissance Europe. Some authors represented the Indians as being deeply occupied by the task of noting down their archaic traditions in hieroglyphic writing. Others pushed the comparison as far as to represent the amazement with which the Indians discovered the existence of writing among the Whites.

Pietro Martire, a Milanese navigator and humanist, was the first, in 1530, to publish a history of the discovery of the New World. His *De rebus oceanis et novo orbe* (Martire 1577)[8] was reprinted several times, was translated into Italian, and enjoyed an extraordinary success among the cultivated European public. Pietro, who, having sailed from Hispaniola on the coast of the present-day Panama and Colombia all the way to the Uraba gulf, knew the recently conquered lands, recounts the following story. One day, in Santa María de Darién (the town founded by the Spaniards on the continent in between the present-day Panama and Columbia, which had become the first bishopric in America), a certain Corrales, a Darién magistrate (*"legum peritus quidam,"* as Pietro puts it [ibid.: 316]), received an Indian who, having been thrown out of a village in the interior, was seeking refuge in the town. After an initial period during which the Spaniards had assumed that controlling the local people would be as trouble-free as in Hispaniola, requests for asylum had multiplied in Santa María. The peoples of the Darién interior (the Cuevas, the Sinu, and possibly also the Kuna) had soon perceived the true intentions of the newcomers: between the coast and the Darién forest, war was raging everywhere. In Santa María, a group of Spaniards, who were thus paying the price for their violent behavior, were putting up a desperate resistance to the besieging Indians, "clenching their souls between their teeth, to prevent them from escaping from their bodies," as Pietro put it. Among the Indians, those who, out of self-interest or naïvety, had allied themselves with the Whites were now seeking refuge in a town which, as Pietro again writes, was no longer defended by anything but "the mass of mud of the marshes that surrounded it." When this Indian was brought before the magistrate, he saw Corrales reading his great law books. He jumped in amazement and begged the interpreter to translate a series of questions: "Have you Whites also got books? Do you too know the art of using signs that allow those who are absent to understand you?"

---

8.   See also Pagden (1982).

Next, still according to Pietro, the Indian asked to be shown the books, thinking that he would find in them the signs with which he was familiar. But once he was placed before a page in one of Corrales' books, his enthusiasm died away. The *patrias litteras* that he thought, by some miracle, to have come upon again in the dwelling of the magistrate were totally incomprehensible to him. As Pietro soberly wrote, "*Dissimiles reperit eas esse.*" All the absurd hopes that were entertained on both sides, and naturally enough especially by the reader of *De rebus oceanis et novo orbe*, that despite the differences of language, culture, and history, there would be immediate mutual comprehension, were now definitively dashed. We should, of course, be wary of taking literally the story told by Pietro, the Milanese humanist who would later become chaplain to Queen Isabella, an influential member of the Council for the Indies, and a personal friend of quite a few navigators (ibid.: 316).[9] The Indian described by Pietro is probably too knowledgeable and too close to Western concepts of writing for us to take his account literally. In the story, this native of the Darién forests presents precisely the qualities attributed to writing by a long European tradition. They are the very same as those that Galileo would enumerate in a memorable passage in his *Dialogue on the great world systems*. To his mind, writing made it possible to speak to those far away, not only in the sense of "those momentarily absent" but also "those that are not yet born."

> What sublimity of mind (*l'eminenza di mente*) must have been his who conceived how to communicate his most secret thoughts to any other person, though very far distant either in time or place, speaking with those who are in the Indies; speaking to those who are not yet born, nor shall be this thousand or ten thousand years? And with no greater difficulty than the various collocation of twenty little characters upon a paper? (Galilei [1632] 1953: 116–17)

The Milanese humanist was, of course, addressing his public. Through the anecdote that he was telling, he wished also to set on stage the great

---

9.   This passage is also mentioned by Nordenskiöld (1928: 13–14). A slightly modified résumé can be found in Ramusio (1985: 181–82). For other commentaries, see Severi (1994).

adventure of the Discovery of the New World, and to make it interesting from a literary point of view, morally acceptable, and politically justifiable. All the same, the story was neither isolated nor exceptional. Its particularity consisted only in the fact that it reversed one of the current *topoi* of the chronicles of the Discovery. It ascribed to an unknown Indian what many European travelers had believed and, in some cases, described in detail. Ever since Martín Fernández de Enciso, who in 1519 declared that Native Americans had not only gold and pearls, but also books, and that "they read and wrote them just as we do,"[10] down to Lehmann, who in 1920 was still dreaming of parchments painted by the inhabitants of the Pacific coast of Nicaragua,[11] there had been a long list of authors who believed in the existence of veritable writings, painted on animal skins or engraved on rocks.[12] Admittedly, for those early chroniclers, as for the scholars of the seventeenth to the nineteenth centuries, that writing remained mysterious. In default of documents of a kind to testify to its existence, the strange paintings of Indians were generally considered to be fragmentary traces of ancient writing, now probably gone for ever. This notion of pictography as a remnant of a now lost writing was one that was long to persist.[13]

---

10. "In this part of the Southern Seas there are many islands. According to the Indians, those islands contain much gold and many pearls as well as silver. Also according to the Indians, those lands are populated by peoples who possess books and who, just like ourselves, know how to read and write" (Enciso [1519] 1857: xxx, cited in Nordenskiöld 1928: 14).

11. According to Walter Lehmann, the Indian mentioned by Pietro Martire was probably a Mangua from Nicaragua (see Lehmann 1920).

12. Among the sixteenth-century authors, Oviedo, at least, deserves a mention, for he writes of "parchments covered in red and black figures" among the Niocarao people (Oviedo y Valdes 1851–55: 36), as does Pedro Simón, who describes "cloaks covered with hieroglyphs" worn by the Catio: "The Catio were people of genius who had clothing and wrote down their stories, using hieroglyphs that they painted on to their cloaks" (Simón 1882).

13. For other examples of the dominant interpretation of American writings in the eighteenth century, see Sangro (1982). An example similar to that provided by Martire is that of the Chibcha pictography, a few examples of which may be found in Triana (1921: 205–22). Triana's interpretations are discussed further by Diringer (1937: 559–61).

When the Spanish Jesuit Leonardo Gassó (the first missionary to settle among the Kuna of the San Blas archipelago[14] in order to undertake their difficult Christianization) reported a current and widespread use of pictographs, he regarded the Indians' writing according to the same perspective. On the one hand, he had no doubt at all that it was a vestige from the past, a practice of years gone by: "*In the past*, these Indians knew of writing," he noted in 1910, referring to a practice there before his very eyes and one which, it is worth pointing out, continues to exist to this day.

On the other hand, for Gassó, as for Enciso or Oviedo, the pictographs were "hieroglyphs" in every way comparable, in their functions, to our own systems of noting down language. Yet everything about these graphisms eluded him: their ritual functions, the techniques for executing them, and even the appearance of the pictographs remained completely mysterious to the missionary (Gassó 1910–14). Clearly, these projections, this mirror-play between Whites and Indians, could only proceed in the absence of the real documents. The first genuine texts "written by the Indians of America" were eventually located, around the mid-nineteenth century, in the northern United States, a very long way from Panama and its tropical forests. Among the discoverers who collected such evidence, Hoffman, Schoolcraft, and Mallery were probably the most active (Figure 24). Not one of them was really a theorist. Many of these discoverers of a new kind were military men, as Hoffman and Mallery were, or else they worked among the Indians as agents for the United States government, as did Schoolcraft. They were all men working in the field, collecting documents but leaving all speculation to others. Their ideas

---

14. The Kuna (a group of tropical farmers consisting of between twenty-seven thousand and thirty thousand people, according to recent calculations) today live mostly on the San Blas archipelago, opposite the Atlantic coast of Panama. They speak a language that is traditionally associated by linguists with the Chibcha family of languages (Holmer 1947). David Stout, the only author to have studied the history of the Kuna, has suggested that in the sixteenth century this Amerindian group, probably one of the first to come into contact with the Whites, constituted a society that was heavily stratified and divided into four classes: leaders, nobles, citizens, and slaves (Stout 1947). On Kuna society today, see Sherzer (1983); Howe (1986); Severi (1993b).

were a far cry from those of the seekers of fabulous lost writings. Mallery, to whom we owe a rich corpus of Amerindian pictographs (Mallery [1893] 1972), was a colonel in the American army and he saw these drawings with a completely new eye. As William Powell, then director of the Bureau of American Ethnology wrote: "There was in him no bias toward a mystic interpretation, or any predetermination to discover an occult significance in pictographs. . . . The probability appeared, from his actual experience, that the interpretation was a simple and direct, not a mysterious and involved process" (cited in Hinsley 1994: 170).

Figure 24. Ojibwa pictographs collected by Hoffman.

Mallery himself expressed this new spirit, which was at once ethical, scientific, and military, in a very revealing poetic composition (cited in ibid.: 170):

> *But now the cosmological drama's o'er.*
> *Mithra's a myth,*
> *Great Pan pans out no more*
> *Our world gives little scope to doctrine mystic*
> *'Tis wary, doubting, stern and realistic*
> *Takes every axiom on strict probation*
> *And calls for propter hoc and demonstration.*

It was probably after reading and consulting the works of these authors that Erland Nordenskiöld began collecting the first pictographic documents from the Kuna territory. These no doubt consisted of documents similar to those that the missionary Leonardo Gassó had seen. Nordenskiöld visited the Kuna for the first time in 1927. Like Mallery, Hoffman, and Schoolcraft, he was a field worker. However, unlike his American predecessors, he did not limit himself to collecting images accompanied only by vague comments or a few random words. He worked with young Indians and began to collect veritable pictographic texts that were recited by chiefs and shamans. They consisted of incantations, shamans' songs, and real pictographic texts. The work involved was of course tricky, made uncertain by Nordenskiöld's inadequate grasp of the Kuna language. The first results of that research work were published in 1927 and reappeared ten years later in a posthumous edition. Unfortunately, Nordenskiöld's premature death, in 1932, interrupted this work. In the fieldwork notes that he left in the Göteborg Ethnographic Museum,[15] many of the images lacked commentaries and many texts remained incomplete. Nevertheless, the documents published by Nordenskiöld and by his successors were in many respects exceptional. For the first time, it was no longer a matter, as in Mallery's work, of seeing a few—for the most part very few—vague signs set out on a single page

---

15. My warmest thanks go to the Fyssen Foundation, which funded my mission to Göteborg in 1985, and also to Sven Erik Isaksson, who was then the director of the American department of the museum.

and accompanied by no more than scattered and lacunary comments. Thanks to Nordenskiöld's earliest studies, the usage of an American pictography was clearly revealed and in a manner that was neither uncertain nor isolated nor rudimentary. The Indians visited by Nordenskiöld seemed, miraculously, to confirm the Indian invented by Pietro Martire (and, interestingly enough, in the very same area: the Uraba gulf and its surrounding region). They scrupulously filled page after page of the little notebooks that the Swedish ethnologist had brought them. In this way, a whole repertory of texts was revealed: stories about the origins of certain mythical beings associated with the sun or the moon; invocations to magical crystals or the spirits of snakes or birds; shamanistic and funerary songs. Other songs, many of them linked with initiation rituals, a recitation of which could last for hours, were recorded in long sequences of pictograms (Figure 25).

Nordenskiöld revealed two important details concerning the material backings of these writings and their internal organization. In the first place, he noticed that the pictographs were traditionally on planks of balsa wood (several examples of which he collected; they are now preserved in the Göteborg Ethnographic Museum). And secondly, he discovered that a particular order of the signs, generally working up from the bottom to the top, in a boustrophedon, was respected. As can be imagined, historians of writing reacted extremely reticently to this new evidence, which became known between 1930 and 1938 and upon which Nordenskiöld's work had hardly commented. The question of writing, to which the men of the Renaissance had paid so little attention, was crucial to these scholars, who, in an evolutionist and positivist spirit, were bent upon establishing a synoptic and chronological tableau of the inventions of humanity. What had seemed natural to the humanists and navigators of the sixteenth century had become unbelievable. We should not forget that since Ferguson's great work on the history of Civil Society, which appeared in 1767, the Indians of America had been considered not as primitives, but rather as *barbarians*. In Ferguson's view (which, through Morgan, greatly influenced Engels and Marxism), the fact that several Amerindian tribes were composed of hunter-gatherers definitively attested to their character, which was not "primitive" but *decadent* (Ferguson [1767] 1971). With such a view, the societies of the Indians of America were not considered as primitive or rudimentary civilizations

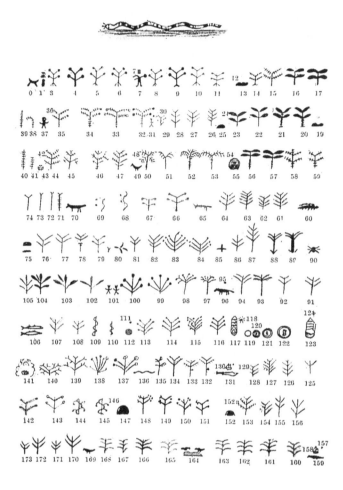

Figure 25. Kuna pictographs collected by Nordenskiöld

that might well develop further. Rather, their "customs" were regarded as scattered and static testimony to a finished history with no future. In a spirit close to the philosophy of Hume, the materialist thinking of Ferguson attempted to reconstruct "a natural history of man in a savage state and through the successive stages of stock-raising, agriculture and commerce."[16] To this, Schoolcraft added an extremely American biblical

---

16. See the entry "Ferguson" in the *Encyclopedia of Social Sciences*.

reference. In his report on the Amerindian peoples of the United States (a text to which I shall have occasion to return), he wrote as follows:

> History, as viewed in the earliest and most authentic record, namely the Pentateuch, represents man as having been created, not in the savage, but in the industrial and civilized state. . . . Commencing his career as a horticulturalist, the highest form of the agricultural type, he is next presented to our view as a shepherd and grain-grower or a "tiller of the ground." If these views are correct . . . then it may be declared, that the hunter state is a declension from the industrial, and that barbarism assumes its character, not only as the antagonistical point to civilization, but as a falling from it, and a direct consequence as the neglect of its higher and sublime principles. (Schoolcraft 1851: 44)[17]

Now, if the presence of writing was the sign of a stage of evolution which the Indians of America, blocked as they were in a state of barbarism, had never attained, the question was: How should the strange drawings discovered by Nordenskiöld be interpreted? Where should the pictographs be slotted into the scale of man's technical evolution? It was not an easy question to answer, particularly since a certain strand of Western rhetoric was far from being unconcerned by the problem. For example, in the eyes of David Diringer, who published a large work on such questions in Fascist Italy in the 1930s, the evolution of writing went hand-in-hand with the civilizing work of Rome and the religion of Christ. "Should I be wrong to affirm that the path of the alphabet coincides perfectly with that of the Christian religion?," he asked himself rhetorically. His answer was clear: "Born in the Holy Land and developed in Ancient Greece, writing then became almost universal thanks to the expansion of the Roman Empire" (Diringer 1937: 4). Although he recognized the astonishing similarity of the Kuna pictographs to the Ojibwa pictograms, Diringer reckoned that the evidence published by Nordenskiöld resulted from a recent invention (ibid.: 605). As a true "armchair anthropologist," he regarded the Kuna pictographs as a belated result of an acculturation

---

17. Schoolcraft then remarks that "an ethological study of the Indians of America no doubt makes it possible to reconstruct the age of Noah" (ibid.: 45–46).

that he assumed to be completed but which, at the time of the publication of his book, had barely begun. From being a mysterious trace of a
perfect but unrecognized writing (a *palaeography* such as the missionary
Gassó considered it to be), the Kuna pictography became the result of an
imitation of the Whites and thereby testified to the strength of the one
group and the weakness of the other. Diringer's conclusion seemed to be
that those who did not attain their own writing had only one choice left
to them, that of clumsily aping ours. According to such a view, only a system of symbols of a phonetic type capable of transcribing the sounds of a
language in a coherent manner could provide a solid basis for communication and hence for a social memory. All other attempts were doomed to
failure. The use of drawing in order to represent knowledge and communicate it remained arbitrary, naïvely linked with an imperfect representation of reality, and it led, as Gelb and DeFrancis later put it, to a *dead-end
symbolism.*[18] Such symbolism was incapable of evolving, just as was the

---

18. For Gelb, "What we normally understand as pictures . . . do not fall under the category of writing. [However,] writing had its origin in simple
pictures. The case could be paralleled, for example, by calling steam the
first stage in a chart showing the development of the steam-engine. Steam
. . . is in itself not a steam-engine, but it is the element around which the
successive stages had to build in order to reach the ultimate development"
(Gelb 1952: 190). Since then, Gelb's verdict on the nature of pictography
has hardly been questioned. DeFrancis (1990), in his book about writings,
definitely classifies pictograms among the *dead-end symbols*. In a whole
series of works, Goody has developed an idea of orality that corresponds
perfectly to the image of writing sketched in by Gelb. The illusion of the
grammatologist, who seeks to base his science of writing on a study of the
internal properties of systems of signs, thus corresponds to an idea of the
oral tradition that is still defined negatively in relation to writing. The position adopted by Goody and Watt perhaps illustrates better than any other
how those two positions interact: the one jealous of the autonomy of the
sign in relation to the forms of utterance; the other jealous of the autonomy
of speech in relation to all material supports such as objects and images and
so on. According to those two authors, societies without writing can lay
claim neither to a hierarchy nor to any clear distinction in traditional forms
of knowledge. Knowledge circulates freely in such societies, unaffected by
obstacles or rules, since speech is by definition unstable and hard to control. In such a situation, all knowledge responds directly to the homeostatic
exigencies of the social organism. As a result, as in African societies in

"barbarian" state in which the Indians found themselves. The technical literature devoted to non-Western writings indeed seems to rest upon a tirelessly repeated kind of rhetorical question. How could one imagine that a system of symbols composed of uncertain and variable signs would be able to retranscribe all the words of a language? That question naturally contains an implicit answer: before the birth of alphabetic writing there was nothing that could fix, and so perpetuate, knowledge. The old Latin adage *verba volant* applied. As we have already seen in the Introduction, such a perspective leads to a negative way of classifying phenomena that do not belong to our own culture. As we shall now see from numerous examples of Amerindian pictographs, the supposed semiotic weakness of those systems is completely unfounded.

However, I cannot conclude this rapid examination of the literature devoted to Native American pictographs[19] without pointing out that, except for Nordenskiöld, who established facts but almost invariably desisted from producing a commentary, no technical study of the American protowritings has ever been attempted. No author has tried to interpret either the iconographies as such or their relation to the spoken word. From the epistemological point of view, certain aspects of which we have noted, Amerindian pictography has, up until now, been considered from two points of view: either as just drawing, the function of which is, in an arbitrary and individual way, to illustrate a certain number of texts; or as a failed attempt to invent writing—a rudimentary and very early stage in the long process of evolution that culminated in what it has become customary, at least ever since Marcel Cohen, to call "the great invention of writing."

Such an approach does not make it possible to understand either how Native American pictography functions or its logical nature. As soon as one considers a sufficiently complex example, drawn from materials

---

which genealogical depth is so feeble that any past event is attributed to the third generation preceding Ego, no memory has any chance of being preserved. This echoes a longstanding idea: namely, that societies that have not invented writing can neither represent the past nor have any sense of historicity (see Goody 1987).

19. I am here taking into consideration no more than a few of the major tendencies characteristic of this field of studies. For a more detailed discussion, see Severi (1994).

collected in the field and with due respect for the facts, it becomes evident that this technique is guided by coherent usage and totally explicit and precise rules of apprenticeship that are linked both to oral apprenticeship and to graphism. We shall in fact see that a study of pictography opens up the path to an analysis of the processes for the transmission of knowledge that are linked with images within societies that are traditionally described as "oral." This study will thus lead us to a first inkling of the typical way of "making memory" invented by Native Americans.

We have already noted the brilliant but isolated genius of Diego Valadés, who was bold enough to compare Nahuatl pictography to the arts of memory of the Western tradition. However, Valadés was not alone in accurately noting the nature of this way of constructing memory without resorting to writing. As an introduction to our inquiry into pictography, we can refer to two observations made by two seemingly very different isolated authors who nevertheless shared in common a keen interest in such materials and in the theoretical questions that they implied. The first observation came from Schoolcraft. This veritable pioneer of nineteenth-century American ethnography spent twenty years of his life in an Ojibwa village. There he carried out the political, military, philanthropic, scientific, and administrative functions that characterized the United States government in the early decades of the nineteenth century. As we cannot, here, examine his personality and life in depth, suffice it to say that Schoolcraft was an American of the William Henry Thoreau or Charles Ives type. He had the generous and contradictory soul of an American pioneer. As a commissioner to the Indians appointed by Congress, he was at the same time moved by a real enthusiasm for democracy and an indestructible conviction that he was always right. As a man of politics he wished to liberate, and of course dominate, the Indians whom he protected and whom, in his own way, he admired. Inspired by an extraordinary ideal of universality, he aspired to be at once an artist, a politician, and a scientist. He produced dictionaries of the Indian languages and sketches of their grammars. He transcribed Ojibwa texts, adapting them in the form of legends or even fables for children. At the same time he organized the administration of the Indian villages surrounding the frontier-post of Sainte-Marie, between Lakes Michigan and Huron, where he engaged in a furious battle against the diffusion of alcohol among the inhabitants. With close relations with the government, he returned to Washington, where he entered into the discussion of politics, natural sciences, and literature in influential circles. But later he returned among the Native Americans, married a Chippewa girl, and lived there in isolation for years. In 1847, thanks to an official appointment made by the United States Congress, he became the author of the monumental American ethnographic work of the nineteenth century, entitled *Historical and statistical information respecting the history, condition, and prospects of the Indian tribes of the United States* (Schoolcraft 1851).[20] In the eleventh part of the book, he noted that "the Indians possess *certain signs that represent certain key-words in the compositions that they learn by heart*" (ibid.: 221–22).[21]

Here, for the first time, we find reasoning that is different from that which, tirelessly, has directed the rhetoric of historians of writing. For them, as we have seen, either peoples practiced the exercise of simple oral memory and produced fragile and uncertain traditions; or else they invented techniques for the transcription of language and opened up a path to writing. But here Schoolcraft intuited a point that was essential. In reality, the Amerindian cultures eluded that opposition. Among these peoples, the oral exercise of memory and the use of graphic signs did not seem dissociated. On the contrary, the Ojibwa had invented a systematic method of using them together. In the text produced by Schoolcraft, we find no more than a rapid observation, completely lacking any claims for the genius of the Indians such as those that had been so important to the mixed-race Valadés. Schoolcraft simply notes down this observation, almost without comment, and immediately passes on to other matters. For those of us who today study these practices—which, happily, are alive and well, for example among the Kuna of Panama, to whom we shall be returning—that intuition cannot fail to arouse admiration. For the observation made by Schoolcraft, which appears to contain no more than a passing intuition, in effect implies a radical change in perspective. In order to understand how Ojibwa legends or the magic texts of the Kuna are committed to memory, it would no longer be necessary to seek out a long-lost writing or to identify an imperfect arbitrary symbolism limited to an individual domain. It would be more useful to try to understand *what relation between a figure and a memory* is established by the Amerindian

---

20. On the personality of Schoolcraft, see Hays (1958).
21. This passage concerns Dakota in particular.

way of constructing a tradition that we obstinately persist in believing to be founded on speech, meanwhile reducing their images to some kind of vague decoration. As we shall see, Schoolcraft's observation indicates the right way to understand pictography. By following that path, we shall be able not only to interpret facts established by today's ethnography, but also to return, in a critical fashion, to the isolated and mostly ignored remarks of Valadés. For we should remember that he too had seen Indians who, on the basis of perusing a very limited number of images, were able, as he put it in his *Rhetorica Christiana*, to "speak and dialogue for hours."[22]

A few years later, the Austrian archaeologist Emanuel Löwy, linked in various ways with the work and persona of Warburg, made an altogether unexpected intervention in the discussion about pictographs and the origins of writing. Löwy, who taught at the University of Rome from 1899 to 1915, published a brief but very dense essay in which the problem of the logical nature of pictography was considered in relation to the origin of archaic Greek art (Löwy [1900] 1907).[23] The Austrian archaeologist's argumentation went as follows: if one studies the origin of drawing from a comparative point of view, one is inevitably struck by "an independence of the real appearance of objects, an independence that not seldom amounts to open opposition" (ibid. 7). Archaic Greek drawing, as epitomized for instance in the Dipylon preserved in the Museum of Athens (Figure 26), is always simplified, schematic, indifferent to real space. To understand that indifference, Löwy believed it necessary to step outside the Greek context and work back to the general question of the origins of drawing. In his own words, one has to go back to "the genesis of the figurative expression of humans " (ibid.). This was a matter that was then the subject of a great debate in both Europe and North America and, over roughly fifty years, it miraculously brought together ethnographers, art historians, and classicists in a common research program. In this context, Löwy was not afraid, as

---

22. "When our western Indians spoke among themselves, they drew figures about which they could speak and dialogue for hours" (Valadés [1579] 1983: 233).

23. On Löwy (who was a friend of Freud's and advised him with regard to his archaeological collection), see in particular Gombrich (1984) and Donato (1993).

one might be today, to compare the archaic Greek style of the Dipylon to that of the Brazilian drawings that Karl von den Steinen had collected in the Xingu and published in a book which, toward the end of the nineteenth century, had circulated in many European universities (Figure 27).[24]

Figure 26. Figures in chariots on a Greek vase in the Dipylon style.

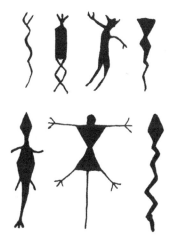

Figure 27. Drawings by the Indians of the Brazilian Xingu

24. On von den Steinen (1894), I have consulted the Brazilian version ("Entre os aborigenes do Brasil Central," 1940). On the remarkable diffusion of the material collected by von den Steinen and on his ideas, see Nordenskiöld's (1930) comments in the *Journal de la Société des américanistes*: "Von den Steinen's travels among the Xingu were definitely a geographical success. . . . In many cases, just a few lines written by this genius of a man have inspired whole treatises."

Löwy had two questions in mind: What is the origin of the simplest forms of drawing, the *decorations* that (as Hjalmar Stolpe put it) seem to function as the conveyors of meaning in all so-called "primitive" cultures and that lead us directly to the origins of art in situations in which not only does writing not yet exist but even the use of oral language seems unstable, linked as it is to the caprices of a spoken language? Why do these drawings that come from the Brazilian Amazon, archaic Greece, or even from the hands of children[25] (Figure 28) all resemble one another in style?

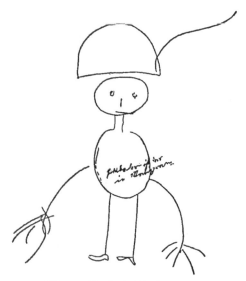

Figure 28. A child's drawing.

25. A reference to children's drawings is already to be found in Löwy (ibid.: 15–17). Comparisons of children's drawings to the graphic techniques of "primitives" can be traced back at least to the work of the historian of Italian art Corrado Ricci (1887), whose early works engendered an abundant body of literature between 1880 and 1914. On this subject as a whole, see Boissel (1990). In this domain, which is clearly very close to primitivism, I cannot pass over the decisive contributions made by the artists of the *Blaue Reiter*, chief among them Marc and Kandinsky. The latter seems particularly close to Löwy when he compares the "unconscious, enormous power" that characterizes the drawings of children as it does those of "primitives" (Kandinsky [1912] 1982: 251).

Löwy was in no doubt as to the fact that the extraordinarily widespread character of this form of primitive drawing excluded not only influence passing from one culture to another but also any deliberate intentionality. For him, the universality of this manner of drawing results from its unconscious character, for Löwy did indeed write: "We should rule out, in the first instance, the usual explanation of the above peculiarities as being conventional" (ibid.: 8).

Löwy was a powerful and ambitious thinker. Through the analysis of the style of "primitive drawings" he wanted to elucidate the "psychic process" that lay at the origin of any art. To this end he carefully constructed a precise line of argument based on a detailed analysis of the drawings. Before suggesting an explanation for the extraordinary series of resemblances that appear to lie along an altogether traditional axis leading from children's art to primitive art and archaic art, he sets out to provide a detailed description of this "basic model" of primitive drawing. He detects seven essential features that seem to him common to primitive Greek drawings (to which Greek art was to remain faithful "up until the mid-sixth century BC") and to the Native American graphisms that he found in von den Steinen's book:

1. The structure and movement of the figures are always described with the aid of a limited number of typical graphic schemas.
2. The shapes are always stylized. They are reduced to images that are linear and regular or that tend to be regular.
3. The representation of a form depends on its outline. This may either preserve the character of independent lines or else, in a case in which it assumes the same color as the inner surface, it may melt in with that color, thereby forming a flat *silhouette*.
4. When color is used, it is always unvaried and homogenous. No notice is ever taken of naturalistic nuances of light.
5. As a general rule, the figures are presented to the observer in such a way that every part is seen in accordance with a particular modality that we may call "the widest view."
6. With very few exceptions, the figures that make up a composition follow on from one to the next on the surface so that the most important parts neither cross over one another nor are superimposed.

Things which, in natural space, are to be found one behind another, are always presented next to each other.

7. Any representation of the location in which the action is taking place is partially or even wholly neglected (cf. ibid.: 5–6).

I have reproduced the gist of this passage from Löwy's text not only because it is extremely useful when it comes to understanding the pictographic documents that we shall be studying, but also because it testifies to an attitude completely different from that of the historians of writing. Where, for example, Diringer (to take an author who is practically Löwy's contemporary and is likewise a German from Italy) limits himself to emphasizing the rudimentary aspect of the Indians' drawing, Löwy carefully analyzes their style in the greatest detail. If we consider the few examples of Amerindian pictography that I have mentioned so far (Figures 24 to 27), even before embarking on a detailed analysis, we recognize that every figure that we have obeys, from a strictly graphic point of view, the characteristics that Löwy was able to list. His view therefore helps us to perceive these graphisms more clearly, noting their regular and constant features even better than in any particular realization, for such are sometimes uncertain or clumsy. A purely graphic reading of the style leads to a better comprehension of these drawings that is far more remarkable than one might suppose.

So why do all drawings by children or "primitives" or that stem from an archaic style resemble one another? Löwy's answer is that, far from aiming clumsily to reproduce real space, such figures always transcribe series of mental images and, in particular, images as they are fixed by memory. His thesis is as clear as it is revolutionary. *Primitive drawing is not rudimentary, it is mnemonic.* It is indifferent to space, does not describe any real scene, and registers almost exclusively the contour of figures because the images do not appear situated virtually in some external landscape, but are always perceived mentally and, so to speak, organized with closed eyes, in the empty and abstract space of consciousness. "The principle upon which mental images are built up is that the elements, viz., the spontaneous single memory-pictures as explained above, . . . are set up one beside the other in the order in which they happen to follow one another into consciousness (ibid.: 14). Löwy goes on to say that the images are schematic and are reduced to outline for another reason too.

Memory selects a number of them and reduces their basic elements in order to be able to fix them more easily. The Austrian archaeologist calls the result of this process "the widest view." Again, these iconographic schemas should be understood in a cognitive context. Later in his text, Löwy explains:

> The aspect which is selected by the memory is that which shows the form with the property that differentiates it from other forms, makes it thereby most easily distinguishable, and presents it in the greatest possible clearness and completeness of its constituent parts; this aspect will certainly be found in almost every case to be coincident with the form's greatest expansion. (Löwy [1907] 1946: 12)

These figures that appear to be so simple are the way they are because memory *makes them typical*. The images are conceived and intended for the inner eye, the one that does not describe reality but evokes some mnemonic trace of it. So these graphic representations are spontaneously situated within the mental process, not in external reality. "Along with the pictures that reality presents to the eye, there exists another world of images, living or coming into life in one's mind alone. . . . Every primitive artist, when endeavouring to imitate nature, seeks with the spontaneity of a psychical function to reproduce merely these mental images." Then Löwy adds an important remark: "I may say the same of the picture writings I have been able to examine" (ibid.: 18).

Pictography or figurative writing: a drawing with a mnemonic value, graphic style with "the spontaneity of a psychical function." There can be no doubt that Löwy's contribution helps us, as few others do, to understand the meaning of the word "pictography."

A DECODING OF PICTOGRAPHY: THE *DAKOTA BIBLE*

All the same, "pictography" does remain a strange word, the meaning of which really is not easy to seize upon. The *Oxford Dictionary* defines it as a pictorial symbol representing a word or phrase. Pictorial symbol is here implicitly opposed to a sign or a letter of the alphabet, which represents an individual sound. Unfortunately, though, this familiar opposition between a drawing and a sign barely helps us to understand what a pictograph is. All that it really indicates is precisely what a pictograph is not. As soon as we try to define a pictograph in positive terms, a swarm of questions and even conceptual confusions appear. What is it exactly that distinguishes a graphic symbol from a drawing, and in what context? In fact, if that definition does enable us to distinguish between a graphic symbol and a drawing, how can we distinguish between different pictographs? Or should we assume that a pictograph, at the heart of any tradition, always has the same appearance?

As a result of all these uncertainties, the word "pictograph"—even if we do not accept the reductive view of a linguist such as Gelb, who regarded it as no more than "steam"—turns out to be used in the most heterogeneous of contexts. An affirmation that an image is "pictographic" may in fact mean that it is intended to be associated with a prehistoric drawing on a rock. Or it may mean that it has a resemblance to certain "iconic" aspects of Egyptian hieroglyphs. Or else that it seems to present analogies with graphisms, examples of which have been found among the Nahuatl of Central America, the Inuit of Alaska, or even in the Naxi tradition in southern China. "Pictographic" may also be applied to a cryptoglyph hidden inside a Polynesian ornament, as Stolpe claimed. Nor does the plurality of contexts stop there. Some art historians have even regarded as pictography the secret symbolic and strictly individual visual language that a painter such as Hieronymus Bosch developed (Bax 1979). Nor should we forget that other iconographic systems, such as that of medieval heraldry, have been considered to be close to pictography. So what can be the meaning of this word in Native American cultures, a few aspects of which we shall now study? There can be no doubt that the only way to form a clear idea of it must be to study one precise example. Let us concentrate on a document discovered round about the 1870s in a Sioux village in the Great Lakes region, now preserved in Berlin's Dahlem Museum.[26]

Specialists call it the *Dakota Bible*. This little book contains a series of drawings in which a man on horseback, in many cases brandishing a

---

26. Its director, Viola King, and Peter Bolz, the curator of the American department, offered me their precious help and allowed me to profit from all their skills. I thank them most warmly.

spear or a bow, appears several times, his body leaning forward. The image of the horse is seized upon as it races forward and is drawn in pencil with an extraordinarily fine and precise line (Figure 29).

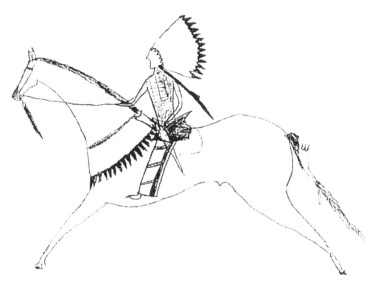

Figure 29. The figure of a horseman (*Dakota Bible*, Berlin, 1860).

One almost gains the impression of recognizing in one drawing after another the same warrior figure crowned with his eagle-feathered headgear (Figures 30 and 31). However, it is not his face that conveys this impression. His features are always quite vague, almost neutral; the artist seems to have had no interest in them. It is the entire figure of the man and the horse, in every case facing left, that in drawing after drawing and in the same stereotyped position seems to have concentrated the artist's full attention. This recurrent, regular, strongly coherent image of an Amerindian horseman seems to obey a constant and precise schema. The horseman sits upright in the saddle, grasping a spear or a bow, and always leaning slightly forward toward his horse's neck.

A few pages further on in this series of drawings the horse appears alone. But its position, as it dashes to the left of the visual field, remains the same. Elsewhere, a long series of drawings represents the running of a deer, an antelope, and an elk. A few pages later, the schematic figure of the rider reappears in his crown of eagle feathers. A final scene,

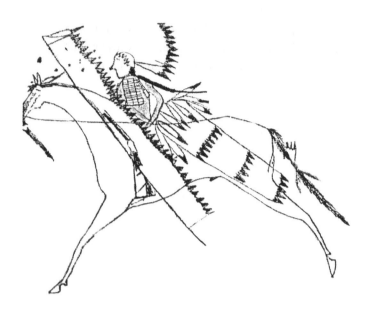

Figure 30. The figure of a horseman wearing a plumed headdress (*Dakota Bible*, Berlin, 1860).

Figure 31. Warrior armed with a bow (*Dakota Bible*, Berlin, 1860).

representing a duel with another warrior, who is fighting on foot, brings the *Dakota Bible* to a close. In all, it contains fifty-seven drawings. The warrior-horseman is probably a Plains Indian, as all the indications suggest: the headdress of eagle feathers, the bow, the spear, the saddle decorations, the way of drawing the horse. To be more precise, he is from the Lakota tribe, a Sioux-Teton group of nomadic hunters who, around 1860, when the stream of Anglo-American colonizers was becoming unstoppable, lived in the Great Lakes region. So it is possible to situate these drawings in both space and time; and that represents a first, essential step toward interpreting them. Yet, as soon as we seek a better understanding of these images, the earliest interpreters of which emphasized that they were drawn using pencils and colors of Western origin (Bolz 1988), they arouse hesitation and surprise. It is true that we are not familiar with the historical and, in particular, iconographic sources concerning the Natives of North America and, moreover, these drawings are by no means recent. They were executed around 1872–73. It was Walter James Hoffman, a medical officer in the American army, who collected them. Hoffman, like Mallery, was at that time particularly interested in the graphic arts of the Indians. We shall be returning to discuss his research work and his view of these pictographs. But for the moment I must confess that it is not just the yellowing paper of the *Dakota Bible* that attracts our attention. Undeniably, these drawings are very fine: the precise lines and the elegance with which space looms up around the figures constitute these drawings as a unique kind of evidence (Figures 32–34). Hoffman perceived this immediately. He reckoned they were precious, so precious that, a few years later, he sent them to the German ambassador in Washington so that the latter could, on his behalf, offer them to the Ethnological Museum of Berlin. The ambassador recognized that they were "created in a very intelligent manner and were, without doubt, in a style far superior to the normal style of pictographic evidence."[27] On May 26, 1894, he delivered them to Adolf Bastian, who was then the museum's director.

Twenty years after they were executed, these drawings that provided evidence of Native American graphic art had already found a place in a famous museum. The work of the anonymous warrior who had drawn

---

27. This letter was, in part, published in Bolz 1988.

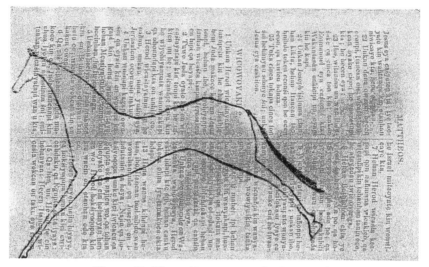

Figure 32. Horse (*Dakota Bible*, Berlin, 1860).

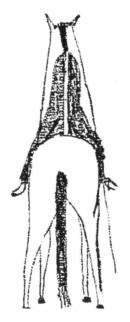

Figure 33. Horse and rider, seen back view (*Dakota Bible*, Berlin, 1860).

Figure 34. Nocturnal scene: masked elk and owl (*Dakota Bible*, Berlin, 1860).

them thus received the recognition that was due to its value. However, it was not solely the beauty of these drawings that justified their being sent to Berlin. As Hoffman saw it, they constituted very important evidence and even, perhaps, a document that was unique. These beautiful drawings had not been produced on a white backing or on the kind of neutral backing generally used for drawings. Although the artist appeared to be extremely attentive to details, he seemed to have totally ignored the nature of the material on which he worked. For he had drawn almost all these pictures on the printed pages of a small book: a bible published in 1866 in the Dakota language by the American Biblical Society.[28] In 1878, Hoffman, who had been sent to the Sioux-Teton territory as an agent of the United States government, had come across this little book

---

28. This is a copy of the New Testament translated into the Dakotan language "from the original Greek" by Stephen R. Reggs, together with a Genesis and a Book of Proverbs, both translated from the Hebrew (the Dakota text calls this "the language of Solomon") by Thomas Williamson. Reggs and Williamson had both worked as missionaries among the Ucpapa (one of the seven Teton-Sioux or Lakota groups) in a small reserve called Standing Rock.

in altogether singular circumstances. In a letter to Bastian, the German ambassador summed up the nature of this exceptional document: "It is with great pleasure that I pass on to you a curious and interesting relic that used to be the property of a Sioux chieftain. It is a New Testament in the Dakota language which contains a pictorial story of the hunting and warrior exploits of the owner of the book . . ." (cited in Bolz 1988: 1). In his reply, dated June 26, 1894, Bastian thanked Hoffman for the extraordinary gift and added a detail that is important to us. This was not only a book with strange illustrations, but also an object associated with a funerary ritual. Just as if it also contained a spiritual testament of the Indian chieftain who had owned it, the little bible had been placed on his tomb. Bastian wrote to say that it was a "Dakotan New Testament in which the owner had inscribed his own story up until his death. The little book had been placed on the scaffolding that protected its author's tomb, on top of the dead man's body and had been found there several years later . . ." (cited in ibid.).

To sum up: in this case, the first that I have described in reasonable detail, the term "pictograph" corresponds among Native Americans to a cycle of drawings, most of them very similar, drawn on the already printed pages of a bible, and linked to the story of a particular person. According to the earliest information, this series of drawings represented a "pictorial history" of his life and was ritually deposited on his tomb. We have come a long way both from the dictionary's vague descriptions and also from the speculations of historians of writing. The pictographic symbolism, which, from their point of view, was bound to be unstable, episodic, individual, and incapable of expressing any more than a few isolated notions, seems here to be used in a systematic and deliberate manner. In this new context, we are therefore justified in raising a number of questions. The first of these concerns what then seemed the absolute originality of this little book. Was it really, as Bastian believed, a "unique document"—a kind of private journal set out in images that only the Sioux warrior who had produced them was capable of interpreting? Today we know that Bastian was mistaken and was justified only by the lack, in Europe, of any similar documents. Regarding the creator of these drawings as an exceptional man (as Bastian did) hardly allayed the uncertainty that was—and still is today—aroused by the strange imagistic biography of this warrior. But above all such a perspective reflected one of the most persistent prejudices regarding Native American pictographs. It was often thought then, and this view persists, that the pictographs were private drawings, imagistic monologues that only one individual, their creator, could decipher, without anyone else being able to understand them. But in that case, how could the evident stylist coherence of the *Dakota Bible* be accounted for? What was the explanation for the recurrent appearance of certain images and the perfect stylistic mastery to which the creator of these drawings testifies?

In the first place, it has to be recognized that certain aspects of this strange graphic object have still not yet been interpreted. It is true that we do possess a detailed commentary on the *Dakota Bible,* meticulously drawn up by a specialist of Native American art (Bolz 1988). However, the interpretation provided by Bolz is extremely prudent. On the basis of an analysis of techniques and, in part, a study of the graphic style, he proposes to associate the *Dakota Bible* with a quite unusual and now long forgotten artistic activity known in Americanist literature by the name of "Ledger-Book Art." We do, it is true, know of a few examples of this form of art produced by the Plains Indians. In histories of the Amerindian arts, it is often described as a late attempt by Native Americans to learn drawing and its techniques, making use of the new means that Westerners sometimes placed at their disposal: a few colored crayons and a few little notebooks, for example. Seen in this perspective, the Dakota New Testament seemed to Bolz to be a kind of notebook of sketches to which the anonymous author had consigned a few isolated exercises in drawing. However, this German anthropologist, who had no doubt carefully analyzed the details of this document, understood its nature not at all. The notion of pictography, along with, of course, that of "Ledger-Book paintings," was too ambiguous to steer his interpretation in the right direction. As a result, the label which, still today, accompanies this document in the Dahlem Museum refers, somewhat absurdly, to "a bible used as a sketchbook" by an anonymous Sioux chieftain. Why were these drawings made on the pages of a quite modest book that was sacred to the Whites? Why did this notebook then become a ritual object linked with a warrior's burial? Why are so many similar figures, schemas, and graphic formulae repeated so often? In Bolz's commentary, such questions remain unanswered.

Our uncertainty in the face of the admittedly rather rudimentary notion of pictography now found expression in a retrospective series of questions. What kind of document would be connected with a cycle of images of this type? What is the nature of the drawings contained in the *Dakota Bible*? There are fifty-seven plates designed to give an account of the life of a warrior. As Hoffman declared, this Sioux chieftain had certainly been an exceptional man and he may have wished to leave some trace of himself and also of his style and skill in telling a story by means of images. But why did he then request that this little book be deposited on his tomb, thereby committing it to the most absolute oblivion—oblivion from which only Hoffman's interest had rescued it?

Over the past century, research work has made great progress, despite being dispersed across separate fields of knowledge, ranging from the study of colonial art to linguistics, archaeology, and a study of contemporary Native American art. From the point of view of the collection of evidence, we today know far more than Adolf Bastian did in 1894. We can therefore attempt to analyze our example of pictography within a new perspective. Accordingly, I shall try to account for the great complexity of a term (namely, "pictography") that seems so very simple. Today, our closest element for comparison is provided by a corpus of drawings produced by another Sioux chieftain also known to Hoffman. He was a warrior known by the name Running Antelope, who, at the time when Hoffman was working in the Dakota territory, was the chief of the Ucpapa community of Little Rock. According to Hoffman (cited in Bolz 1988: 4, n. 11), Running Antelope was at this time "a well-known orator for the Sioux nation" and "was one of the best indigenous artists." His drawings, some of which are also to be found in the Dahlem Museum, reproduce with astonishing fidelity the schema that organized those of the anonymous artist of the bible: a man on horseback, always facing in the same direction, to the left, who is repeated at least a dozen times, is represented in a series of plates drawn using crayons. As in the *Dakota Bible*, we are faced with a series of almost identical drawings.

Through this sequence of images, Running Antelope, too, has left us a biography in pictures. So the *Dakota Bible* is not a unique case, an isolated and solitary invention. Thanks to the work of a few exceptional anthropologists interested in these documents, chief among them certainly John Canfield Ewers ([1939] 1979), we are now able to compare these two examples to other Amerindian instances of pictographic autobiography. The practice of drawing "the pictorial history" of a life is attested quite early, according to the standards of the conquest of these regions of North America. The bison skins magnificently turned into historical documents by the Mandan chieftain Four-Bears, collected by the German Prince Maximilian zu Wied in 1833–34 (Wied [1833–34] 1976) in the course of his expedition to the north of the Great Lakes, represent one of the oldest historical documents available. These skins display a narrative in images of the exploits of the warrior Mato Tope, the brother of Four-Bears, who died heroically in battle (Figure 35). Chief Four-Bears would proudly wear this bison-skin coat, as can be seen from a memorable water-colour painting by Bodmer (Figure 36). The meaning of these paintings was clearly incomprehensible to those early explorers, who, incidentally, were accompanied by at least two artists, the painter George Catlin and the sketcher employed by the prince, Karl Bodmer. In his journal recording this mission of his, the prince noted, on the subject of these paintings on bison skins, that they consisted in general of "parallel black lines, interspersed with other rudimentary figures, often decorated with arrow-heads or other arabesques" (cited in Ewers [1939] 1979: 2).

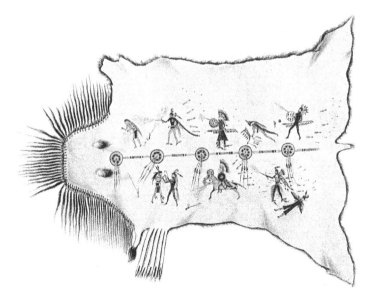

Figure 35. Bison skin painted by the Mandan chieftain Four-Bears.

Figure 36. A Plains Warrior dressed in a bison-skin, drawn by Karl Bodmer.

John Canfield Ewers was the first to realize that, on the contrary, this tradition of the Plains Indians throughout the nineteenth century manifested a strong unity of iconographic styles and themes that were illustrated by a regular diffusion of typical and coherent graphic schemas such as those of the horse, a human head, and certain weapons and details of the images of a horse (Figures 37 and 38). Ewers also showed that a "pictorial history" of a warrior, along with calendars (*Winter Counts*) was one of the typical iconographic genres of this culture:

> In the old days the surest way for a Plains Indian to win the admiration and respect of his fellows was by the performance of brave deeds in war. The successful warrior was rewarded for his bravery, not with medals, but with the right to wear certain kinds of ornaments, to recount his deeds on special occasions, and to picture on his buffalo robe or tepee his outstanding achievements, so that all who saw him might know that he was a brave and important man. (Ewers [1939] 1979: 17)

Ewers' text contains two crucial remarks. The first is that, ever since it was first noticed in the field, this kind of painting has been associated with an occasion involving public eloquence that is linked with the interpretation of the images. In this instance it is clear that the painted ornaments constitute a means for the warrior "to recount his deeds on special [public] occasions." Ewers emphasizes this point. The second important remark that we need to take note of is that the people who elaborated and developed this kind of pictography were, precisely, the Teton-Sioux group, from which the *Dakota Bible* came. Ewers proposed distinguishing, amid the general productions of the Plains Indians, one particular style, which he called "late-Siouan" (ibid.: 60). These Teton-Dakota paintings, he declares, constitute "the highest achievement of the Plains Indians painter" (ibid.: 62).

Thanks to Ewers' pioneering work, we can make some progress in our attempt to understand the *Dakota Bible* and its pictography. We have already noted the extraordinary elegance and lightness of its creator's drawing in his depiction of horses, bears, elks, and antelopes. We can now, if not explain, at least understand that this beauty and this drawing skill are not only the fruit of the particular talent of the warrior buried

Figures 37 and 38. Horses and warriors, in the graphic style of the Plains Indians.

at Standing Rock but also result from an autochthonous tradition that managed to invent a graphic style and develop it in a masterly, coherent, and original fashion. Clearly, the creator of that bible was familiar with a well-established graphic language and used it with great skill. There is no trace of uncertainty in the drawings of the *Dakota Bible*.

Secondly, we can now see that the tradition to which the anonymous artist of that bible refers, far from being an individual and anonymous way of drawing, was constituted by a perfectly coherent iconography; and this, even if not reducible to a veritable dictionary of symbols, was without doubt focused around a limited number of central themes, described by means of recurrent graphic schemas. The pictorial autobiography of the warrior thus turns out to be a specific iconographic genre that, as the *Dakota Bible* shows, invariably implies the evocation of the central figure of a horseman and an account of his exploits as a warrior and a hunter. It is therefore natural that a major part of this cycle of drawings should represent the central figure of the horseman, who becomes a kind of schema-figure that organizes the entire sequence. The creator of the drawings in this bible, and Running Antelope a few years later, simply took over an iconographic tradition attested at least from the time of the Mandan bison skins collected by Prince Maximilian in 1833.

From this we may conclude that among the Plains Indians pictography did not result from a clumsy and individual technique of graphic representation, but was a kind of drawing that certainly presupposes an iconographic tradition. As we shall now see, with these pictographs it was not just a matter of learning to draw and repeating schematic figures. It was also a matter of using a particular glyph to transcribe one particular word: the name of the warrior. In the Amerindian context, there are many instances of such a pictographic transcription of a warrior's name. A remarkable example of this way to designate a name is to be found in the three pictographic autobiographies of Sitting Bull that remain to us, which were published in 1936 by Matthew Stirling, together with a brief commentary. Here too, we find long sequences of apparently repetitive drawings in which the figure of a warrior on horseback is shown several times, all in different situations. Here too, it is a matter of hunting and fighting. Alongside the schematic figure of the warrior, the artist never omits to draw an image of a bull, the symbol of his own name. The bull is then linked by a pencil line to the head of the warrior (Figure 39).[29] Such a graphic transcription of a name is, as is suggested above, extremely widespread, and numerous cases of this are attested among many tribes of Plains Indians (see, for example, Figure 40). Just such a transcription is to be found in the *Dakota Bible*, where the glyphs of the warrior's name appear in two cases. One represents a figure that we may call Bison's Head; the other refers to a warrior whose name was no doubt Bow-decorated-by-feathers (Figure 41). We then find the same convention, associating the name with the schematic figure of the horseman, in the drawings that Running Antelope made at Hoffman's request. From all this we may conclude that the creator of the *Dakota Bible* was not simply demonstrating his skill and talent as an artist. He was also following a number of graphic conventions.

Figure 39. Glyph of the name "Sitting Bull."

---

29. This mention of his name was so important to Sitting Bull that he later denied that he was the author of a drawing in which the symbol for his name did not appear (on this point, see Stirling 1938).

Figure 40. Arapaho examples of name glyphs.

Figure 41. The "Bow-decorated-by-feathers" glyph (*Dakota Bible*, Berlin, 1860).

So we discover that neither the creator of the *Dakota Bible* nor Running Antelope invented this kind of testimony. Clearly, neither was a professional artist. For them, as for any Plains Indian, drawing was "a part of daily life" (Petersen 1971: ix). However, this attempt to decode the basic features of this iconography may lead even further. A comparison with a series of other documents, in particular the evidence collected and studied by Petersen (ibid.), reveals the existence, also in documents from Plains hunter peoples, of a rich and regular iconographic code. In this code, stylistic features and symbolical aspects are combined in a package characterized by a surprising coherence. It is, alas, a telling fact that, in the complex history of the pictographs of North America, one of the richest sources of such documents should be a prison. Between 1873 and 1875 about seventy warriors from several Plains tribes were imprisoned in Fort Marion, in Florida. Twenty-six of them, some of whom appear in an old group photograph (Figure 42), produced numerous drawings, with the encouragement of the prison Director, who was keen for them to supply curiosities that could be sold to visitors. Eight hundred and forty-seven of the drawings produced in this remarkable situation are still available for study today. Let us try to compare them to the pictographs of the Berlin *Dakota Bible*. A comparison (never before attempted) between, on the one hand, the pictographic collection compiled by Petersen from the large collection of drawings in Fort Marion and, on the other, the iconography of the *Dakota Bible* is both fertile and surprising. An entire iconographic tradition constituted by "rigorously prescribed conventions"(ibid.: x) is clearly revealed.

First let us note that the graphic representation of a horseman's name, to which I have referred above, is to be found everywhere in the Fort Marion materials. One of the drawings collected by Petersen shows that a Kiowa warrior imprisoned in Fort Marion presented the name of a horseman, "White Horse," in exactly the same manner as the sources that we have already examined: the *Dakota Bible* artist for the character known as "Bison-Head", Running Antelope in the drawings dating from 1882, and, finally, Sitting Bull in a number of pictographic autobiographies. In the case of the Kiowa warrior, we find a small figure of a horse that is connected by a line to the head of the horseman. This confirms the unity of this iconographic tradition despite the fact that it was shared by peoples speaking different languages. But let us now continue

Figure 42. Plains Indians imprisoned in Fort Marion.

our comparative examination of the iconography of Fort Marion and that of the *Dakota Bible*. How are a horse, a bear, and an antelope drawn in this tradition? According to a pictographic repertory that Petersen drew up from his study of the 847 pages in Fort Marion, a drawing of a horse should always possess five features: a small head; a long curved neck; a very long body; front and back legs extended in the act of running; and hooves and hoof imprints that are not cloven.[30] In the case of a horse, an extra distinction was later introduced between a domesticated horse and a wild one. The wild horse had a supernatural, particularly funerary connotation and was always represented with a black tail and a black mane.

As for the pictographic representation of a bear, this was marked by six characteristic features: small ears; short, thick tail; teeth always

---

30. It is interesting to compare this analysis with that produced by Ewers, who, almost forty years before Petersen, had noted that "the feet, hoofs, eye and phallus" of the horse were always represented in the same manner. Furthermore, the horse's body always seemed to be "distorted by a horizontal elongation." (see Ewers [1939] 1979: 19–20).

visible; a dark or black body; long, curved claws, and paw-imprints. That of an antelope included at least five typical features: curved horns; a chest marked by zig-zag stripes; a very short tail; a white rump; and cloven hooves (Figure 43).

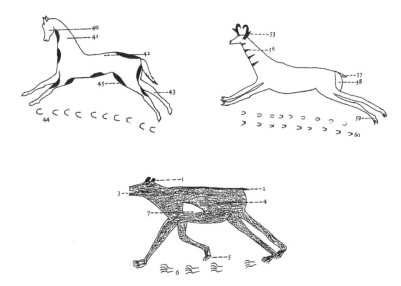

Figure 43. Horse, antelope, and bear iconographic schemas from the drawings of the Indians in Fort Marion.

Even a rapid look at the *Dakota Bible* (for the horse, see Figure 32; for the bear, Figure 44, for the antelope, Figure 45) shows clearly that the artist, with great talent but also great coherence, follows the kind of iconographic handbook that Petersen reconstructed from his perusal of the paintings of the Plains Indians. But a comparative examination of these two iconographic series can lead us still further: it also allows us to interpret a number of details that characterize the schematic figure of the horseman. The clothing, the position of the warrior, his headgear, the use of feathers, and the type of saddle: all these features possess a specific significance within this context. By comparing the Fort Marion documents with the *Dakota Bible*, we can read the figure of the horseman who appears there on page after page, almost feature for feature. Not only is the warrior's name transcribed by a drawing, but what could be called his epithets and some of the actions that he has performed also figure in the

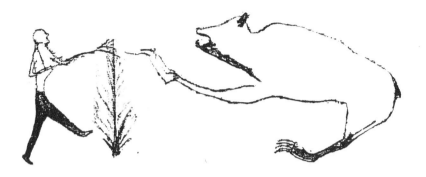

Figure 44. Bear, hunting scene (*Dakota Bible*, Berlin, 1860).

Figure 45. Antelope (*Dakota Bible*, Berlin, 1860).

pictographic image. The feathered crown (and likewise the figure's costume, presented in a heraldic manner) is shown either positioned on the horseman's head or lying flat along his back (Figure 46); and it always designates "a warrior of great courage (Petersen 1971: 28). The shape of the saddle always indicates whether this is a war-like action or just a journey. The timing and sequential dynamic of the warrior's exploits are also represented in the pictographic image: the presence of a trail of hoof-prints, grouped in a sequence, as, for example, in Figure 41, is

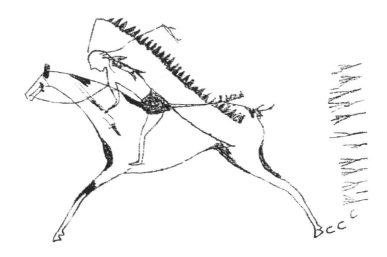

Figure 46. Horseman (*Dakota Bible*, Berlin, 1860).

always—both in the *Dakota Bible* and in the Fort Marion documents—
a way of indicating that the action took place in the past. We find this
same convention in the formidable representation of the hunting of an
elk, which was drawn by the Cheyenne warrior Making Medicine in
Fort Marion (Figure 47).

We can thus make some progress in our understanding of the term
"pictography." Among the Plains Indians, the word designates a coherent, even relatively closed iconographic system. In the cases that we have
studied, we find a code focused on a specific theme, an account of exploits
in hunting or warfare and constituted by an iconographic vocabulary that
spread throughout an extremely vast cultural area inhabited by peoples
speaking very different languages. As Ewers was the first to notice, this
iconographic tradition was always linked with particular public occasions
in the course of which the Indian warrior could give a public account of
his exploits. This system of iconographic indications was so coherent that
the earliest ethnologists were tempted to compare it to writing. We shall
be studying this question in detail. But for the moment it is worth pointing out that in the *Dakota Bible*, as in the little ledgers in which so many
of these drawings were produced, writing, in the Western sense, is *already*
present. As we have already had occasion to note, in the *Dakota Bible*, the
great majority of pictures were drawn directly on to a printed text.

Killing an Elk

Figure 47. Making Medicine (Cheyenne), "Killing an Elk" (the elk hunt).

So far, our comparison has made it possible to associate the *Dakota Bible* with the genre of a Plains Indian's pictorial history and, at the same time, with a specific style in this iconographic tradition. Our document leaves behind its apparent isolation. It can no longer be thought to be unique and exceptional, as it was by Bastian. All the same, the analysis provided above does not fully explain how these drawings were, so to speak, "read" within these cultures. We should therefore now examine the relation between pictography and the spoken language. A plate from the Henderson Ledger represents precisely the kind of public recitation that was based on an interpretation of pictographic images. The drawing shows a warrior on horseback as he gives a public account of his exploits, to a rhythmic accompaniment of drums. Around him the women and men of his tribe listen to his song (Figure 48). The position adopted by the horseman, no doubt peculiar to such a ritual address, the feathered headdress falling right to the ground, the marks painted on the rider's trousers, signaling his membership of a warrior society, and the horse's decoration—all suggest that this is no simple narration. There can be no doubt that this representation, like the image of Chief Four-Bears clad in his decorated bison skin (Figure 36), indicates an exceptional context that includes a rhythmic rendition of a ritual song. We should also assume that the regularity of the iconographic code, as reflected, for example, by the regular transcription of the horseman's name and the force and coherence of this conventional scene, corresponded to the regular structure of a ritual declaration. The presence of drums in this picture suggests that the pictographs drawn on the jacket worn by the warrior perhaps corresponded to the words of his song.

Figure 48. A warrior publicly recounting his feats
(Henderson Ledger)

Let us now return to the *Dakota Bible*. We know that it was placed on the tomb of a Sioux warrior who had chosen it as a novel means of conveying the pictorial account of his life. We may well think that this represented a new way of using pictography in a funerary context. Nevertheless, the choice of a book, instead of an animal skin, is by no means neutral. From the 1870s onward, when the war against the Whites was increasingly clearly indicating the inevitability of defeat for the Indian tribes, many Plains warriors "drew pictorial histories in small books [often the ledgers in which the officers of the American army kept their accounts] which they wore on their persons when going off to battle in a miniaturization of their age-old convention of wrapping themselves in autobiographical hide robes" (Berlo and Philips 1998: 28).

What was the anonymous Teton-Sioux warrior trying to do when he used a bible to carry a pictorial history of his life? Did he wish to indicate a conversion to Christianity? Did he wish magically to appropriate a symbol belonging to the Whites, who would soon become the conquerors in this conflict? We have no way of knowing. We can do no more than note that, by this gesture, he replaced the traditional bison skin by a book-relic. But what makes his gesture unique and remarkably intense is that he decided to use not just any army ledger, as he might have done, but instead a bible.

What Americanist literature today calls "ledger painting" is a quite exceptional form of graphic expression. The first thing that strikes one is that the naming of this art picks out the material *prop* or backing upon which it is inscribed, even before the existence of any coherent iconography and style to match. Of course, as many authors have acquired the habit of repeating, Native Americans, at this time, very rarely had at their disposal the indispensable materials—crayons, paintbrushes, and sheets of paper—necessary for them to produce their pictographs. So they procured paper wherever they could. Nevertheless, Native Americans had been "drawing" for several centuries and were aware of many possible traditional materials: the sides of rocks, tepees, clothing, everyday utensils, some of which were painted, and—above all—a bison-skin cloak, which, for a warrior, constituted an unfailing source of pride and glory. So why did the they choose to use those ledgers? Historians of art in the Warburg tradition have been studying other examples of these hybrid objects that can reflect the clash of hostile cultures. We should recall the classic cameos that are to be found inserted into some barbarian buckles or even the pagan columns that the late Middle Ages reused in the construction of their Christian cathedrals. Through the insertion of such easily identifiable elements into a space that is foreign to them, we may perhaps read into the object not only the memory of a long-lost past but also a kind of declaration of victory.

The ledgers used by the military, covered in pictographic stories created by the Plains Indians (from almost all the tribes: Arapaho, Kiowa, Ojibwa, Cheyenne, Lakota . . .) from the 1840s onward, constitute documents of this type, in which the clash between enemy cultures finds a way, both singular and intense, of expressing itself. In effect, during this period there developed among the Native Americans a kind of cult of books, seen as objects of power that could be used as a means of protection or an offensive weapon. The ethnography of the period registered its appearance.

We know that a number of famous warriors, such as the Cheyenne Old-Bear and the Lakota George Bushotter, had jealously preserved collections of books; and more recently it has gradually been discovered that these little books became included amongst the magic objects that a Native American warrior carried upon his person on the battlefield, frequently fighting against the American army. That discovery clearly reveals the meaning behind this. Janet Berlo has seized upon what is essentially involved in this appropriation of cash-registers:

> Books held a valued place in the lives both of incarcerated warriors . . . and of those still fighting for their lands in the West. . . . Some of this regard for the power of books was transferred from white culture, but some was grounded in an indigenous Aboriginal belief in the power of history and of images, now combined in a belief in the power of the written word. (Berlo 1996: 16)

"Ledger Art" ("an art for intercultural exchange", as Janet Berlo somewhat euphemistically puts it) thus expresses in explicit terms the conflict between two openly hostile cultures. For the Native American warriors, these little books replaced the bison skins of their fathers and, at the same time, represented objects that were potent, endowed with a magic power precisely because they combined a graphic memory of traditional iconography and a partial imitation of the customs of their adversary. In appropriating objects that marked out the symbolic frontier between two cultural universes, the Plains warrior was endeavoring to preserve his own categories even as he used materials provided by his enemy. In the context, it will come as no surprise to learn that many of the documents available to us today were collected on battlefields by the victors, in a cruel despoiling of the warriors who had fallen in battle that some, not without cynicism, have called "battlefield tourism." Clearly, the American soldiers considered these little books as war trophies and *spolia*, as Berlo continues to call them, which, beneath their appearance of souvenirs to be taken home to surprise their families, friends, and colleagues, in effect testify explicitly to the victory over the Native Americans.

This transitional character of the ledgers painted by the Native Americans perhaps explains the fascination that they exert today upon contemporary sensibilities and also the interest that they now arouse among historians of art and anthropologists. We should, however, bear in mind that this interest was only shown after a very long silence interrupted solely by the pioneering work of Petersen and Ewers. That ambivalence may also explain the very different kinds of studies that these documents have prompted. On the one hand, there are the authors who have considered these drawings to be precursors of present-day Native American art. With this point of view, they have studied the developments in this iconography over a period of roughly seventy years, up until the 1930s, which, alongside the decadence in the pictographic nature of such images, witnessed a veritable American modernism. Within this context, we see the typical stages that the Western discourse on art presupposes in the transformation of an ethnographic object into an art object. Faced with a drawing, such discourse always tries first to identify its author, evaluating his personality in comparison to the traditional style. Next, it endeavors precisely to situate in time the evolution of styles as they succeed from one artist to another. In this way, through the writings and the exhibitions organized by Berlo, Szabo, Maurer, and Greene, it has been possible to establish a historical sequence characterized by different styles, in which a Four Horns period (the 1870s) precedes the Red Horse, Black Hawk, and Sinte periods (the 1880s), those of Bone Shirt and Bad Heart Bull (approximately between 1890 and 1910), and finally the Two Horns and White Bull periods. Each Indian warrior thus becomes an *author* and each period of this art is defined on the basis of a style that is at once archaic and new, Western and Indian, and which he seems to have invented. It was probably the period when warriors were imprisoned in Fort Marion that produced the most impressive results of this work of graphic elaboration, a compound of assimilation and synthesis and of revolt and invention. We can gain some idea of the coexistence of the different worlds and styles that characterize "Ledger Art" by comparing, on the one hand, certain of the magnificent drawings by Howling Wolf (Szabo 1994), in which the detention in Fort Marion is recounted with an implacable precision (Figure 49) and, on the other, the drawings so similar yet so different from the Henderson Ledger, in which strictly biographical themes linked with pictorial history and initiatory visions still occupy center stage (Figure 50).[31]

---

31. A remarkable exception is constituted by the research work of Dawn Wong, who tried to understand the essentially autobiographical nature of these

Figure 49. Howling Wolf, "A class in the Fort Marion school."

drawings. In particular, Wong drew a parallel between the appearance of these graphic techniques and that of autobiographical narratives in the Indian oral tradition. On these themes and the appearance of autobiography as a "literary genre of ethnography," see Severi (1990); Wong (1992).

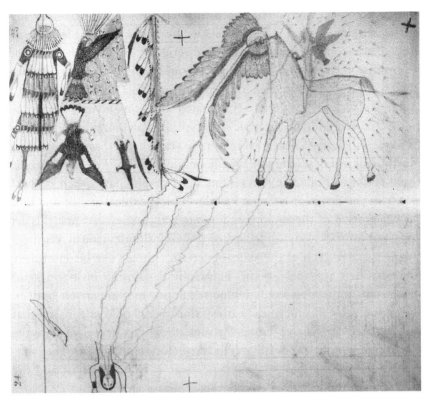

Figure 50. The initiatory vision of a young warrior
(Henderson Ledger).

Other authors have considered the ledgers from an exclusively archaeological point of view, seeing them as documents that contain not
only dramatic traces of a conflict between cultures, but also evidence
of a past that preceded the Whites' conquest. Seen in this perspective,
the drawings in the ledgers become the veritable "Rosetta Stone" of
the northern Amerindian pictographs and seem to indicate a tradition that goes a very long way back in time, even as far as the rock
engravings frequently attested in territories long ago inhabited by Native Americans . The earliest examples of this rock art go back to the
thirteenth century. Let us now follow this path that leads from the
"Ledger Art" of the second half of the nineteenth century as far back as
the most ancient rock engravings, and so to an iconographic tradition
that precedes contact with the Whites by several centuries. This view

of archaeological analysis has been instilled with remarkable new life by the work of a group of researchers led by James Keyser. He has succeeded in reconstructing a progressive series of graphic schemas that lead retrospectively from the earliest examples of "Ledger Art" in our possession right back to American prehistory. This research work into American rock art eventually culminated in a convincing reconstruction of the evolution of a graphic style typical of pictography. According to Keyser, the early fourteenth century (or even earlier) saw the birth in North America of a ceremonial iconography that was linked to specific ritual actions or shamanistic visions. This graphic style then evolved slowly in the direction of what he calls "a biographical art" linked with the celebration of the exploits of hunters and warriors. At first this art appeared on rock walls and then, or possibly simultaneously, on more fragile surfaces such as the skins of certain animals like bison or deer. The very first examples of this biographical painting on bison skins display an impressive iconographic regularity in comparison both to the earlier rock art and to the earliest documents of "Ledger Art" that can be dated. As Keyser wrote: "As such, these [art items] validate the evolutionary sequence of Biographic Art" (Keyser 2000: 16). They thus constitute an important intermediate stage between rock art and the later style of the ledgers.

It was on the basis of this twofold temporal relationship that Keyser, in the morphological and sequential spirit of a Pitt-Rivers, but using far more trustworthy modern methods of verification, was able to construct a sequence between Ceremonial Rock Art (late-American prehistory)— a protobiographical style (characterized by the use of a rock surface, the rigid form of its figures, and the absence of any representation of action) which can be dated to between 1600 and 1750 (Figure 51b)—and a biographical style (on a rock surface or an animal skin) characterized by an iconographic transformation in which Keyser distinguishes an "early" period from 1750 to 1835 (Figure 51c); followed by a style that he calls "mature" (Figure 51d), which emerged from 1835 on, when one begins to detect a Western influence, for example in the presence of perspective of a rudimentary nature. According to Keyser, it is from the beginning of the development of a "mature" style onward that there developed the typically hybrid iconography in continuous metamorphosis of the so-called "ledgers" style.

Figure 51. A succession of rock art styles: an example of the human figure.

To demonstrate the validity of this historical sequence, which—it must be said—seems very solid, Keyser analyzed an exceptional document found in the archives of the Missouri Jesuit Mission. This was the *Five Crows Ledger*, a sequence of very early drawings collected already in the early 1840s, in which we recognize many of the conventions registered by Petersen in Fort Marion almost thirty years later. One has only to note the manner in which one of the authors of this little notebook draws the human figure and then to compare it with the sequence depicting that figure in a series of different temporal phases identified by Keyser (Figure 51) to recognize that not only is the resemblance between them very clear, but so too is the evolution from one form to another.

Where we are dealing with the representation of warriors clashing in combat, which is more complex from a graphic point of view, the evolving nature of the sequence between the *Five Crows Ledger* and that of more ancient documents (Figures 51 and 52) emerges with equal clarity.

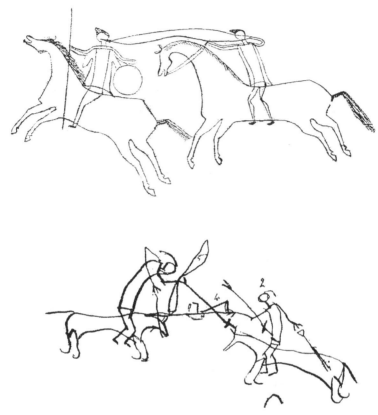

Figure 52. Two horsemen, one on a Cheyenne bison hide dating to 1845, the
other in the *Five Crows Ledger*.

Within that ledger, it is possible to move beyond a study of figures
that are either isolated or in a very simple relationship with others. In
the simple cases, the relation between the figures seems to be oriented
only by a right-to-left axis, in which, for example, the direction of the
charge of a horseman is indicated by the horse's hoof-prints, as in Figure 53. In other cases, we find a simple repetition of the same graphic
structure, for example an area roughly represented as circular in which
conventional figures alternate, as in Figure 54, representing fortifica-
tions. Let us now address a slightly more complex case. In Figure 55,
the series of confrontational scenes between battling warriors is organized in a spiral sequence. In connection with this, Keyser notes that it
is one of the very earliest cases in which the sequence of figures makes

it possible to link the various scenes together. Figure 55 does indeed testify to the representation of a temporal order of images—to a before and an after—which it is possible to identify simply by resorting to an interpretation of the iconography. It is, I think, worth adding that this spiral order imposed upon the succession of images is identical to that of all the calendars known as "Winter Counts" (Figure 56). However that may be, this example clearly shows the transference of an ancient ceremonial art, essentially composed of isolated figures, to a more complex iconography that is linked to a sequential description of the action. In this way, the *Five Crows Ledger* shows that the particularly pictographic character of this iconography originated in the early biographic style (Keyser 2000: 13).

Figure 53. The way of indicating a horse's route. *Five Crows Ledger.*

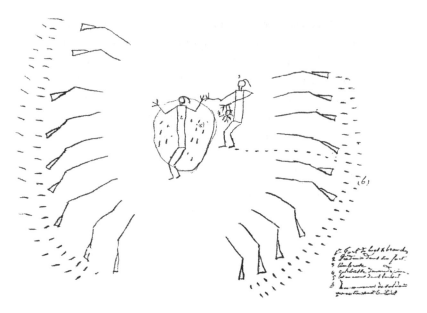

Figure 54. Typical graphic representation of the "Biographical Style,"
Five Crows Ledger.

Figure 55. A narrative composed in a spiral sequence,
Five Crows Ledger.

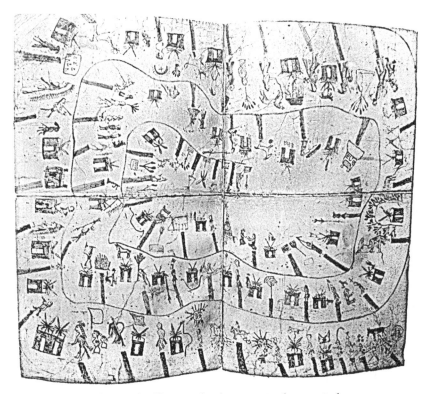

Figure 56. Kiowa calendar organized as a spiral.

Let me now try to give a more precise account of this new notion of pictography and its relationship with language by comparing one of the battle scenes drawn by Ambrose, a Flathead Indian, in the *Five Crows Ledger* to the commentary that the Jesuit Father De Smet, following the indications of its author, appended to the graphic representation. Look again at Figure 53. To this drawing which, for Keyser, is an excellent example of "Protobiographic Art" (Keyser 2000: 33), Father De Smet, who was present when Ambrose executed his drawings, added the following commentary:

Ambrose discovered his Blackfoot enemy at daybreak near the mission of Saint Mary. He pursued him at full speed on horseback. The horse of the Blackfoot fell and threw his rider. Ambrose tried to shoot, but his gun misfired. The Blackfoot rose up and ran away, Ambrose pursued him, jumped down from his horse and knocked the Blackfoot to the ground with the butt-end of his gun and climbed astride his enemy's back—another Flathead who had been following closely shot two arrows into the body of the Blackfoot which Ambrose pushed deeper into his body until he was dead. (Cited in Keyser 2000: 33)

From an iconographic point of view, there can be no doubt that the style adopted by Ambrose in his drawing possesses a certain coherence. The Mission, represented by a square containing six crayon strokes ("persons," who are in this way registered graphically, even though they are not pertinent to the telling of the story), the two horses, the hoof marks that they leave on the ground, and, above all, the two human figures all follow the rules of the iconographic tradition in an almost rigid fashion. So in Ambrose's drawing virtually nothing graphically arbitrary is introduced either into this representation of the constituent elements of the image (the house, the mission, human figures, etc.) or into anything that he sets out to recount visually. On the contrary, Ambrose's drawing shows that the figures retain a stable form and that, for the relationship between the narrative and the visual representation of a story, there exists a process of *coherent selection*.

On the one hand, the drawing *does not transcribe* the entire content of the story of the battle between the two warriors, as it is related in the commentary added by the Jesuit. On the other, it also turns out that the image, although much simplified, *always adds* aspects of the action that neither the commentary nor the story registers. We may conclude from this that here the pictography aims not for a realistic representation of the scene but rather for a certain crosscutting between what is said and what is drawn: a certain sequential manner of orienting the memory of an episode on the basis of a few graphic indications (not many, certainly, but recurrent).

An analysis of these particularly "early" documents reveals that Indian America had a primitive or even prehistoric way of constructing memories by using images. It also suggests that these techniques based on pictographic representation went through an evolution completely ignored by historians of writing. In histories of writing, indeed, there is only one kind of evolution possible: a graphic form is progressively simplified, becoming less iconic, and eventually and definitively assumes a conventional form and a stable phonetic value. A study of the *Five Crows Ledger* reveals, on the contrary, an iconography that develops in an entirely different direction. The evolution in the use of the pictogram, the form of which remains iconic, leads to the establishment of a specific relationship between a sequence of images and the sequence of actions that are represented. I shall be returning to dwell at length on this point, but right now, already, it is important to point out that, although the iconography of the *Five Crows Ledger* remains quite rudimentary, it nevertheless marks a decisive turning point in the evolution of pictography: the sequence of images always makes a *selection* from the number of facts to be represented.

This discovery of the selective character of the pictographic symbolism, as compared to a linguistic formulation of a story, once again radically changes the notion of pictography. As I have had occasion to remark, historians of writing, from Gelb to DeFrancis, have always described pictography as an unstable semiotic medium, dependent on an individual's free will and, in consequence, incomprehensible to others and invariably leading to a dead end. In fact, though, we discover that pictography provides an eloquent example of what, in the Introduction to the present work, I called a process of *negative definition* of everything that is found in unknown cultures. Within such a perspective, pictography comes to be defined only by the absence of the features that characterize writing. However, if we now compare the analysis of the *Five Crows Ledger* to what we have noticed about the *Dakota Bible* and the drawings collected in Fort Marion, we can see that the pictography of the American Indians is, on the contrary, definable in entirely positive terms. This iconic tradition is characterized by the following features:

1. *Conventional*: Each "author" follows a recognizable conventional style.
2. *Closed*: In the universe of discourse that pictography is capable of describing, only a certain number of predefined scenes are drawn, and they are always, at least in the examples studied here, linked to the "pictorial autobiography" of the warrior. For example, this iconographic genre sets out to describe in detail the clash between two adversaries but, except in easily identifiable cases, it never has any way of providing information about the context in which this scene takes

place. The persons, although present at the scene of combat, are not considered pertinent to the description of the fight and so are never drawn as complete figures by the author of a pictographic notebook. In a ledger, their presence may be indicated by no more than a rapid pencil stroke.

3. *Selective*: The man who draws the pictographs uses simple graphic conventions to suggest complex images. The use of these graphic schemas, which Keyser appositely calls "conventional short-hands," enables the drawing to select, from within the real image, just a limited number of features. The schema that designates a fortification, for instance, will always be represented by a circle surrounding a single warrior figure, and this applies as much to the *Five Crows Ledger* as it does to the *Dakota Bible*.

4. *Redundant*: The pictographic iconography always adds a number of details to the linguistic description of the scene or episode described in the drawings, as can be seen, for example, in the context of the *Five Crows Ledger* by comparing the pictographic image and the description provided by the Jesuit father who tried to transcribe what the Indian informant told him.

5. *Sequential*: While some plates in the *Five Crows Ledger* follow the rule for reading or decoding the drawings by reading from right to left, others suggest the establishment of a truly organized sequence. An arrangement such as that in Figure 55 would be completely undecipherable if it did not follow the spiriform order that the author has imposed on the narrative.

6. *Persistent in time*: Although we are not obliged to accept all Keyser's hypotheses, what does emerge clearly from his research among the Plains Indians is that a unified iconography developed following a linear evolution over the course of at least two or three centuries.

7. *Widely spread*: The presence of the kind of pictographs studied here is attested at least from the Great Lakes region (northern United States) all the way down to southern Texas; and, as we shall soon see, it is now possible to extend this geographic area both northward and southward. Right now, though, we should note that within this great geographic and cultural area, pictography appears to be a system that is independent of any particular language. In this respect it seems analogous to the sign language known to the Plains Indians. In a code

such as this it is only possible to express a limited number of meanings. All the same, it is possible to do so throughout a vast territory and in many different languages that are mutually incomprehensible.

8. *Evolutionary*: The negative view of pictography circulated by the historians of writing is essentially based on the argument that pictography is a sterile symbolism, incapable of developing because it is constituted by countless individual, incomplete attempts to transmit information. Seen from this point of view, writing appears not to have developed from pictography but simply to have bypassed it, starting from quite different principles, in particular that of representing the sounds of language. The discoveries made by Keyser, once combined with our present analysis of pictographic drawings such as those in the *Five Crows Ledger* and the *Dakota Bible*, indicate, on the contrary, that the pictograph may well have followed a coherent and autonomous evolution.

The work of Keyser and his collaborators is very important for our understanding of these aspects of pictography. However, once we begin to consider how pictography might relate to a text or to traditional autobiographical story-telling, those analyses cease to be useful. Keyser does not neglect the possibility that pictographs may have been used as "auxiliaries for memory." It is indeed a possibility that is compatible with his hypothesis of a late birth for a truly pictographic style, within the iconography peculiar to the Plains Indians. All the same, the total lack of any connection with their oral traditions makes his argumentation extremely fragile. Even if, from the point of view of an anthropology of memory, the documents analyzed by Keyser provide good indications of an *iconographic codification* of information, he provides no solution to another problem: that of the nature of mnemonic evocation, or rather of the decoding of these drawings. The readings that he, in his studies, suggests for the pictographic images are just paraphrases of the drawings. As he just worked on the archaeological evidence, he could not do otherwise. Nevertheless, we shall see that fieldwork, focusing on living pictographic systems, shows that where pictography follows a systematic evolution and has therefore been able to establish a link with language, the decipherment of pictographic images relates not to the daily use of speech, but rather to a perfectly identifiable kind of oral tradition.

Wherever we have been able to establish the details of such a link, the pictograph operates within the context of ritual discourse . This is an essential aspect in the definition of pictography. We have already established that the world of pictographic discourse (the whole collection of things that can be designated by pictograms) is limited. We also know that the graphic style is always regular and recognizable. A study of the terrain in which pictography is used on a daily basis makes it possible to add that the linguistic form that guides the decoding of images is, equally, established by tradition. Within this framework, we shall see that a comparison between the "early" biographical style (around 1840), the ledgers (1870–90), and present-day pictography (in two contemporary cases: Kuna and Western Apache) presents not only a way of constructing what is memorable that is different from writing, but also a type of evolution that is radically different from that described by historians of writing. We find a progression which, instead of leading the pictogram to the phonogram through a process of progressive stylization, instead develops a mnemonic relationship between, on the one hand, certain sequences of images, either realistic or conventional, and, on the other, certain sequences of words that are ritually enunciated and memorized in a specific form. As we shall see, it is by undergoing a process such as this that the pictogram became the principal instrument for memorizing Amerindian ritual songs.

Traces of this process, which, little by little, linked pictography with the singing of a ritual song, are already identifiable in the *Dakota Bible*. Following our initial analysis, we now know that this represents a late-Sioux example of "Ledger Art" and also an "early" biographical style. This little book found on a warrior's tomb now appears to be a symbolic equivalent of the animal skin in which a traditional warrior would wrap himself. We may presume that, when he set off for war, the author of these pictographs would take this little book with him, as a powerful kind of talisman. We also know the subject of this sequence of drawings: in its own particular style, it aimed to transform the image of a man into an incarnation of the traditional glorious warrior-figure amid scenes of war or hunting.

But let us try to progress a little further. A number of historians and anthropologists, faced with documents of this type, have wondered what stories these pictographs "narrated." Just as Keyser himself often did, those researchers wanted to understand the nature of those stories and of the collective facts that made it possible to reconstruct the history of the Indians before the arrival of the Whites, a history that was entrusted to this pictographic evidence. But very few authors have wondered *how* these stories were told. Apart from producing commentaries on the series of pictures in this Indian iconography, almost nobody tried to reconstruct the way in which these pictographs constructed a narrative. We should bear in mind, in this connection, that one of the characteristics that seemed the least comprehensible to those researchers was the repetitive nature of the pictographic images. Indeed, it seemed so puzzling that, as we have seen above, they suggested that the images were clumsy attempts that the Indians made with a view to perfecting their drawing abilities. Now we know that that was nonsense. So let us try to move on a bit and understand the manner in which the pictographic figures are organized in space and to see if it is possible to get an idea of the linguistic form implied by the images that we already know to have been linked with the performance of a song.

With this new aim, let us return to the figure-schema that we have seen repeated many times in the *Dakota Bible*. As will be remembered, the drawing shows a warrior on horseback, always turned toward the left. An examination of this configuration in the various traditions of "Ledger Art"—Cheyenne,[32] Kiowa, or Arapaho, for example—reveals that the figure of the horseman nearly always implies an initial elementary organization of the space, in which the right side is always more important than the left and in which every movement is directed from right to left (or from the right toward the center of the image). As Candace Greene spotted, the figure situated to the right always represents the active subject of the action; the one situated to the left represents the passive object of the action. That is so very much the case that if a warrior, usually drawn on the right, is felled by the blows of an enemy, thereby becoming the passive victim of the action (Berlo 1996: 30), he is always placed on the left. We find an identical convention in most of the ledgers, particularly in the *Collins Drawings*, a notebook containing the drawings of a Lakota warrior who signs his name as "His Fight." When

---

32. Candace Greene, in Berlo (1996). The development that follows is based on Greene's analysis.

this warrior represents himself as wounded and surrounded by a great number of Crow warriors, he sets his own image to the left. The same thing happens when a hunter is attacked and brought to the ground by an animal, as in Figure 57. If, in certain drawings, a group of women appear in the right-hand side of the image and therefore seemingly in the dominant position, there is, in accordance with the same principle, good reason to suppose that they are men in disguise, *berdache*. In short, these examples testify to the existence, in this iconographic tradition, of a conventional organization of space, which is always conceived as being composed of two symmetrical and opposed sections.

Figure 57. Cheyenne art: a young bison attacks a hunter.

In this schema, each part of the space is thus endowed with a specific semantic value. The next thing to be noticed is that within this schema only two types of variation are possible. Either one multiplies each term in the opposition (A1, A2, A3, A4 . . . /B1, B2, B3, B4 . . .) within a single scene or theme (hunting, warfare, etc.); or else one constructs a series of identical oppositions on the formal plan, that is to say, constructed on the basis of a symmetrical axis, but associated with different themes. On the basis of such a formal homology, a hunting scene will thus become "analogous" to a scene of warfare or seduction. And this visual schema constitutes a faithful transcription, at the graphic level, of the structure of the verbal organization that we have recognized as "parallelist." Given such spatial organizational rules that are established implicitly, it is therefore not possible to draw just any image. Within this space, which is, so to speak, organized in advance and functions as a symbolic equivalent of a world of discourse established by convention, it is only possible to draw series of variations with two constant features: the section on the right, which is active and dominant, and the section on the left, which is passive and dominated. Virtually every image and every figure constitutes a confirmation or a transgression of the order that here governs graphic representation, just as, elsewhere, it governs the ritual expression of words.

In this way, in this kind of iconography, the figures, far from being independent of one another, find themselves defined by one another. Candace Greene has pointed out that we are faced here with a graphic style of great coherence, in which the observer's attention is always drawn toward some specific aspect of a figure through the contrast that it presents to the figure facing it (ibid.: 28). I should add that this is equally true when, instead of a symmetrical structure in which the images confront one another, we find a linear sequence in which each figure precedes or follows another. In other words, the reciprocal definition of images which constitutes an essential aspect of the pictographic style may be engendered not only by a comparison established on the basis of a symmetrical axis, but equally by a linear sequence. To clarify this point, let us consider the series of three images that represent the horseman of the *Dakota Bible* (Figure 58).

In all probability, these three images that follow on from one another all represent the same horseman. Each representation emphasizes or shows particular characteristics within the same iconographic schema. In this way a series of different features is presented, each image creating a contrast to those that precede or follow it. In Figure 58a, the image of the horseman is entirely hidden by a covering; only the "heraldic" blazon, alongside the saddle and no doubt also the visible pattern on his trousers, makes it possible to identify him. Those are markings that indicate that the horseman belongs to a society of warriors. Next, in Figure 58b, the same horseman uncovers his head; but his position, the pattern on his trousers, and the spear held in his hand remain the same. In Figure 58c, which follows on immediately, the horseman appears without any covering and still with the same pattern on his trousers. The decisive detail is

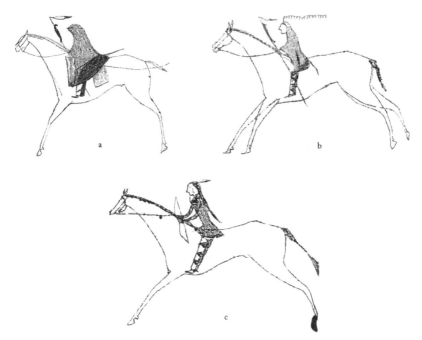

Figure 58. Parallelist sequence from the *Dakota Bible* (Berlin, 1860).

that the weapon in his hand is no longer a spear but a bow; this difference, which may appear negligible, is on the contrary crucial because it leads to a regular consequence in the organization of the iconography.

The fact is that, in the *Dakota Bible*, whenever the horseman holds a bow in his hand, his face is marked by war-decorations. The feather that appeared earlier on his spear now adorns the head of the horseman figure. To those who regard these drawings as "free artistic expressions," this detail may appear to be of minor importance. But from our present point of view it is, on the contrary, crucial since it indicates a sequential mode of organization that is typical of all these drawings. If we consider the whole narrative sequence of the *Dakota Bible* from which this detail is drawn, we find that the entire story of the warrior on horseback is told by starting with a constant iconographic figure and regularly alternating on this pattern a series of variations that are only apparently minor. In this way, the figure of the horseman seems at once recognizable yet, in each image, endowed with different attributes.

The discovery of this inherent consistency in the elaboration of graphic sequences will help us to understand how picture-writing has become, among Native Americans, the principal means of memorizing ritual discourses. Let us now examine a complete episode in the *Dakota Bible* (Bolz 1988) and attempt a faithful translation of this sequence of statements, trying hard not to omit or add anything at all (Figure 59).

- *Figure 59a*: A few rays of light, indicating spiritual strength, appear (announcing the appearance of an image).
- *Figure 59b*: The Sioux horseman (facing left, so the active subject in the story), enveloped in a covering, holds in his hand a spear adorned by a feather. He leads a horse with its mane and tail adorned with feathers.
- *Figure 59c*: The Sioux horseman, enveloped in a covering, grasps a spear adorned by a feather, from which hangs a scalp.
- *Figure 59d*: A few rays of light appear above the head of the Sioux horseman. With his head now uncovered, he holds in his hand a spear adorned by a feather, from which hangs a scalp.

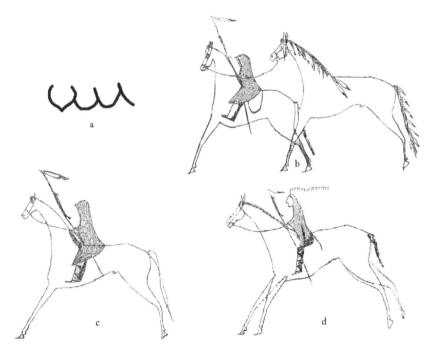

Figure 59. Parallelist sequence produced in the Berlin *Dakota Bible*: (a) cosmic rays; (b) horseman with concealed face leading another horse; (c) horseman with concealed face; (d) horseman with uncovered face.

- *Figure 60a*: This long-haired Sioux horseman, with head uncovered and painted face, holds a bow. A feather adorns his head. He wears a loin-cloth and grasps a quiver for his arrows.
- *Figure 60b*: The Sioux horseman, wrapped in a covering, grasps a spear decorated by a feather, from which a scalp hangs. The tail of his horse is adorned by a feather.
- *Figure 60c*: The long-haired Sioux horseman with a painted face, his head uncovered and adorned by a feather, holds a bow; his chest is also decorated, as are his trousers. In front of him is a woman.

Figure 60. Parallelist sequence in the *Dakota Bible*, continued:
(a) horseman with uncovered face, holding a bow; (b) horseman with covered face; (c) horseman, holding a bow, with a woman.

- *Figure 61a*: The long-haired Sioux horseman with a painted face, his head bare and adorned by a feather, grasps a bow. He wears only a loin-cloth and also holds a spear, this, too, decorated by two feathers.
- *Figure 61b*: The Sioux horseman holds a bow, wears decorated trousers and decorations on his chest. He wears a magnificent feathered headdress, indicating that he is a courageous warrior.

- *Figure 61c:* An increasingly triumphal picture of the warrior: holding a spear adorned by a feather, with a decorated chest and a painted face, he sports the feathered crown that designates "courageous warriors"(Petersen 1971: Bolz 1988).

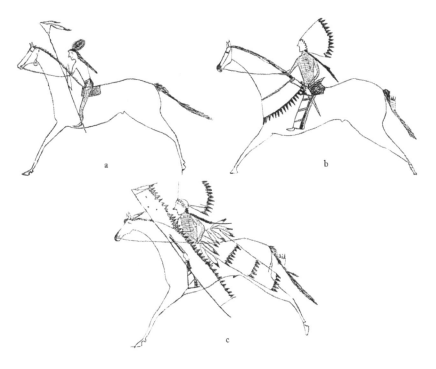

Figure 61. Parallelist sequence completed: (a) horseman; (b) horseman wearing a crown of feathers; (c) horseman wearing a crown of feathers, a cloak, and warrior decorations.

It is clear that in this mosaic construction of a series of representations of the horseman, every image is composed of a large number of identical items or epithets. Each figure reflects a particular distribution of the pieces of the mosaic that are no doubt finite in number. But at the same time, within a parallelist sequence such as this, each figure constitutes a transformation of another that either precedes or follows it.

This little experiment in decoding the pictographs of the *Dakota Bible* can easily be repeated with other parts of the text. Let us now consider a different sequence, for example one that concerns the representation of a horse.

- *Figure 62a*: Rays of light (spiritual force) appear and a horse is suddenly there.
- *Figure 62b*: A wild horse appears (as is indicated by the blackness of its tail).
- *Figure 62c*: This is a wild horse, as can be seen from its straight black tail, its small ears, and its cloven hooves.
- *Figure 62d*: The wild horse with its straight black tail and its small ears now races forward.
- *Figure 62e*: The wild horse with its long curved tail, cloven hooves, and tiny ears now rears up on its hind legs.
- *Figure 62f*: The wild horse with its very long, curved black tail and cloven hooves races forward.

And so the text continues up to:

- *Figure 62i*: The figure of the horse is joined by that of the warrior, whose name (Bison Head) is explicitly mentioned. The Sioux warrior (Bison Head, situated on the right), who mounts a horse with an ornate saddle, a long curved tail, tiny ears, and cloven hooves, triumphs over an enemy warrior (situated on the left). The latter holds a bow and fights on foot.

The above analysis confirms the hypothesis formulated in connection with the organization of the images: each figure of a warrior (or even of a horse) is indissociable from that which precedes it and that which follows it. These image sequences are perfectly suited to fulfill the task assumed by the iconography: namely, to represent a succession of facts and to enumerate and at the same time distinguish between persons and between situations (and eventually—as we shall see—represent their transformations).[33] This initial decoding process reveals a formal aspect

---

33. It should be noted that this mode of sequential organization is not recent but fits perfectly into the chronology suggested by Keyser.

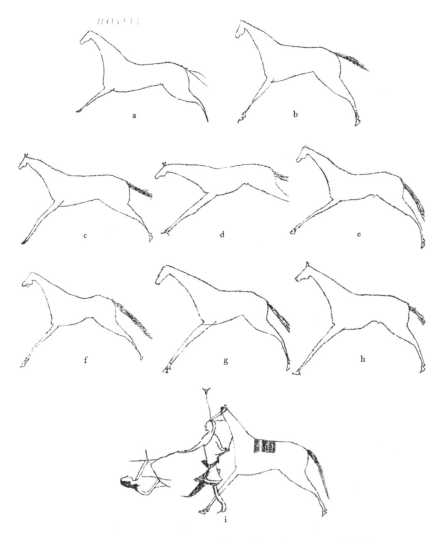

Figure 62. Parallelist sequences focused on the image of the horse.

of the pictography that is to my mind of the greatest interest: the "scenes of hunting and warfare" that appear in the *Dakota Bible* are always represented in a strictly parallelist form. This suggests that they are most probably a transcription in the visual register of a form that is dominant in Amerindian oral literature linked to ritual singing.

This form and manner of imposing order upon knowledge that should be committed to memory are expressed in the *Dakota Bible* through a sequential organization of images. This clearly reflects the succession of repeated yet subtly varied formulae that is typical of the singing-form throughout Indian America. We know that, upon returning from an expedition, the Sioux warriors would gather together in order to give a public account of their hunting and warfare exploits, each one relating the part that he had played. It would seem that no traces remain of those songs. However, an analysis of the iconography allows us to suppose that the songs were rhythmic, parallelist structures. The sequential organization of the drawings indicates, with reasonable certainty, that the "mnemonic codification" that the graphic style implied was directed at adopting a parallelist form. In the *Dakota Bible*, pictography and parallelism turn out to be closely linked.

PICTOGRAPHY AND SHAMANISTIC SINGING: THE KUNA CASE

Let me summarize what we have discovered so far. An analysis of the research of archaeologists, art historians, and ethnologists who have worked on oral traditions has enabled us to enrich our knowledge of the context in which Amerindian pictography was practiced. Two aspects on which we have concentrated in the preceding section of this chapter have not sufficiently attracted the attention of anthropologists. The first of these is the parallelist structure that organizes the process of memorization implied by the use of pictography. That is certainly true from the period of the "early biographical style" down to the present day. The second overlooked aspect that we have identified is the link between pictographic representation and language, which has allowed us to understand the type of evocation that this iconographic codification of mnemonic traces implied.

We shall now see that it is precisely those two aspects that orient the evolution of pictography when this is applied, in America, to more complex situations. The shamanistic traditions of the Kuna today constitute one of the richest examples of these situations. In cases of this kind, the evolution of pictography has implied a progressive regularization that affects not only parallelist iconography but also the relationship that is established between two different parallelist elaborations: that which affects iconography and that which organizes ritual discourse. So let us move on from the analysis of archival documents to a direct reading of a number of more complex pictographic examples drawn from material that I have collected during my fieldwork among the Kuna of the Comarca de San Blas (Panama),[34] as well as from the group of documents collected by Nordenskiöld and his students from the 1920s onward.

We have already mentioned Nordenskiöld's discovery of the Kuna pictography and the mistrust that it triggered among historians of writing in the 1930s. But, when examined closely, how does a Kuna pictographic document function? Let us examine a first example (Figure 63). This is a pictographic plate now preserved in the Göteborg Ethnographic Museum and it describes the evolution in the sky of the "moon canoe." Around this canoe is depicted a whole group of spirits and mythological beings who accompany the moon on its nocturnal journey. So this is a *list*, accompanied by a description of a celestial *journey*.

Figure 63. Moon canoe, Kuna pictography.

---

34. I have already cited these early examples in my book *La memoria rituale* (Severi 1993c: 177–78).

When we try to understand how a Kuna shaman interprets a document of this type, we can be guided by the numbering transcribed on to the plate. We discover that two principles of classification are used simultaneously for these images. Alongside an enumeration of the mythological spirits associated with the moon (the details of which are irrelevant here), by means of a list (organized on either a vertical axis or a horizontal one), we discover that this image also conveys a spatial classification operated by *territories*.

Sequences of pictograms are regrouped according to the three regions of space that structure this pictographic plate, namely the sea, the horizon, and the sky. Thanks to this horizon, which cuts the plate into two distinct territories, we are able to distinguish not only different persons but also groups that could be called "sea spirits," "sky spirits or ones that belong to the celestial dimension, and "spirits situated along the line of the horizon." This organization of the figures has at least two functions. On the one hand, it provides an extra connotation for the images of the spirits, which are described here in a very summary manner. On the other, it enables one to make a list of names (the series of the names of mythological beings that need to be memorized) within a spatial order already known: the sky, the sea, the earth.

While directly representing the moon's journey through the night sky, accompanied by all the spirits, just as any drawing would, the pictographic plate that we have just "read" thus becomes a memory prop in which images representing proper names are organized simultaneously in accordance with two principles: a classification "by linear successions" and a classification "by territories." As we shall see, the articulation between those two criteria plays an important role in the Kuna pictographic tradition.

But let us dwell a little longer on this example, which seems so simple. In what sense can we speak of a mnemotechnique here? Are we presented with a series of quite rudimentary drawings that the Kuna shaman or chieftain has produced, simply guided by his talent and imagination? Are these images perhaps sketched rapidly for his own use, comprehensible to him alone? Or should we rather believe that these pictograms constitute a coherent and conventional notation that, as such, can be learnt and then taught by *any* Kuna specialist?[35]

---

35. These two hypotheses recur frequently in literature devoted to the Kuna: see Holmer (1947); Herrera and Cardale y de Schrimpff (1974).

That last hypothesis, which provisionally ascribes to Kuna pictography phonetic characters similar to those of Maya pictographs, was indeed considered but then definitively rejected by the Swedish linguist Nils Holmer (1952). And indeed, there can be no doubt that the documents today available do not in any way confirm that hypothesis. All the same, a few years spent studying the Kuna pictographs have convinced me of the hasty, slapdash character and in the end of the extreme weakness of an interpretation that set out to reduce the impact of this pictographic symbolism solely to the domain of an individual imagination. Many of the Kuna pictographic texts at our disposal,[36] ranging from those collected by Nordenskiöld in the 1920s to texts of the present day, even though they were found at different times and by researchers quite independent of one another, reveal that, as in the case of the Plains Indians, they share a surprising stylistic homogeneity. They all respect a number of rules concerning the graphic representation of objects: the succession of the pictograms follows a preestablished order (almost always from right to left, starting from the lower part of the plate and moving upward in a boustrophedon manner); and a remarkable number of pictograms, recognizable as such, are regularly borrowed from evidence and documents of a widely differing nature.

The problem that needs to be resolved may thus be formulated as follows: If the pictography of the Kuna is neither a phonetic notation of words nor an arbitrary drawing of objects, what is its function in the transmission of knowledge within the shamanistic tradition, and, consequently, what is the explanation for its internal coherence and its temporal persistence? In this connection, it may be useful to provide a brief description of the empirical modalities for learning a Kuna shamanistic song.

A Kuna shaman's pupil spends lengthy days in his master's hut. He is expected to be respectful and obedient. Nearly every day, he brings his master presents and he may work for him for many years. In exchange, his master welcomes his pupil into his home and passes his knowledge on to him. This teaching is based on two forms of apprenticeship: the first, which is purely verbal, appeals to the apprentice's memory of sounds. The

---

36. A good bibliography of these texts may be found in Kramer (1970). The following works are also worth recalling: Nordenskiöld (1928, 1938); Holmer and Wassén ([1947] 1953).

master recites a passage from a song that is to be memorized and gets the disciple to repeat it until he knows it by heart. The text is treated as a "relic," as Dennis Tedlock (1983) appositely put it. In the course of this first phase of the apprenticeship, the pupil in many cases learns only brief texts, the meaning of which completely escapes him.

The second apprenticeship technique used by Kuna specialists is based on pictograms. The master begins by showing his young pupil a few images that represent important figures in shamanistic narratives. These might include, for example, a sick person in a hammock, a ritual brazier with escaping smoke, supernatural "villages" inhabited by animal spirits, or a Celestial Jaguar, one of the great protagonists of Kuna mythology. The pupil must then register these images in his memory and learn to copy them carefully. He will be told that these drawings play an indispensable role in memorization, which can attain to remarkable precision in traditional shamanistic songs, some of which are very long.

This twofold organization of shamanistic teaching may seem simple, but in reality it leaves nothing to chance. It corresponds closely to the specific structure of Kuna songs, which, as in many Amerindian literatures, are generally constituted by verbal formulae endlessly repeated with slight variations. Without dwelling upon analyses that are developed elsewhere (Severi 1982, 1994, 1997), it is worth repeating here one general condition for the practice of pictography. The pictographs apply, albeit in different contexts at the heart of tradition, exclusively to texts constructed according to this parallelist pattern. Pictographic symbolism is only used coherently and significantly in cases where the structure of the text to be memorized is parallelist. This rule, which I have emphasized elsewhere (Severi 1994), emerges particularly clearly in the Kuna case. Let us consider another example, this time taken from *The Song of the Demon*:[37]

In the distance, where the sun canoe rises, another village appears.
The village of *monkeys* appears.
The village reveals its *monkeys*.
[...]

---

37. This is the Nia Igala, the Kuna song devoted to the therapy for madness (see Holmer and Wassén [1947] 1953, 1958; Severi 1993b).

In the distance, where the sun canoe rises, another village appears, the village of threads [i.e., snakes] appears.
The village that rolls up like a thread appears
The village that rolls up like a thread shows itself.
The village that rolls up like a thread and the village of monkeys unite, like two canoes in the sea they crash together.
Far, far away, the two villages unite, they seem to touch.
In the distance, where the sun canoe rises, another village appears.
[. . .]
The village of the *skirt* appears. The village shows its skirt.
[. . .]
Far away, where the sun canoe rises, even further away, another village appears, the village of *lianas* appears.
The village of lianas appears.
The village shows its lianas.

The pictogram transcription of this text (the part of which that concerns us is reproduced in Figure 65) translates into images *only* the list of *variations* (the *names* of the villages: monkey, thread [or rather snake], skirt, liana) in the text that is sung. The basic formula of the shamanistic narrative—"far away, where the sun canoe rises, a village appears"—is never translated by the pictographic image. So learning this depends solely on the oral mnemotechnique (Figure 64).

Constant graphic formula	Translated variations	Constant verbal formulation
	monkeys	Far away,
	skirts	where the sun canoe rises,
	lianas	a village appears
	...	

Figure 64. The mnemotechnique of Figure 65.

Meanwhile the graphic representation of the "village of spirits," using the shape of a triangle, seems quite separate from the text. Although the text sometimes provides precise information about the spatial site of the village ("where the sun canoe rises" naturally signifies "toward the east"),

Figure 65. Kuna pictograph from *The Song of the Demon*: the villages of the monkeys, snakes, skirts, and lianas.

it never describes the *shape* of a village. Conversely, the representation of a "village of spirits" by a triangle appears to be completely independent of the textual indications and to possess an autonomous meaning. For example, in Figure 66, a Kuna specialist will immediately recognize the pictographic rendering of a whole set of "villages of spirits." In this plate, in which a series of triangles is positioned within a larger triangle, we can spot a first trace of the recursiveness that is typical of Kuna graphic techniques and that we shall later find again in a much more developed form. The two paths of shamanistic apprenticeship thus imply three distinct elements: a verbal formula, a relatively recurrent graphic formula that is quite independent from the verbal formula, and a series of *variations of the text translated into images* (Figure 64).

This schema gives us a preliminary, albeit simplified and schematic, idea of the interdependent relationship that the pictography establishes between images and oral statements in a Kuna ritual chant. This

Figure 66. A series of Kuna spirits' villages.

preliminary system is enough to show that the usages of the present-day Kuna, far from being (as Diringer [1937] claimed) nothing but a clumsy imitation of the writings introduced by the Whites, on the contrary obey a system of organizing images and "rhythmic" texts that closely resembles the "stanzas" that Schoolcraft (1851) briefly described among the Ojibwa of Sainte Marie, in the nineteenth century. What the Kuna do is match certain drawings to certain (parallelist) "rhythmic texts." They then organize these representations of objects into complex sequences without (as Löwy [(1900) 1907] pointed out) bothering to situate them in realistic-looking space or establishing any relationship between the pictograms and a representation of the sounds of the language.

However, the example that we have just analyzed is still relatively simple. In principle, a systematic relation between figures drawn in accordance with a mnemonic style (Löwy) and then organized so as to function as an aid for the memorization of certain texts (Schoolcraft) can be applied to more complex examples. In such new situations, a somewhat more subtle technique is necessary. As we shall see, it will be a matter not just of perfecting a purely graphic technique, but rather of setting up a complex mental technique designed to establish a mnemonic organization of pictograms in a person's mind. We shall discover that such principles, which we have already noted at work in the *Dakota Bible*, apply not only to the case of the Kuna tradition that I have taken as an example, but also to other Amerindian traditions.

For the moment, let us proceed with our study of the Kuna picto-grams. When the shaman needs to transmit to his pupil a description of great supernatural villages inhabited by a whole series of animal spirits with characteristics that the song enumerates, he adopts not a different graphic technique (for his visual style remains faithful to the schematic criteria described by Löwy), but instead a more complex criterion for classifying and organizing figures in space. Here is another example, a description, also in *The Song of the Demon*,[38] of the "village of dances," a mythical place in which humans and animals perform a dance in which they are said to court one another:

> There where the sun canoe rises, another village of spirits appeared.
> The village of spirits reveals itself.
> "All the spirits of this village line up to begin to dance," says Balsa, the old diviner.
> Close to the Ettoro river, they begin to dance.
> Close to the Ettoro river, they begin to move.
> Close to the Ettoro river, they move to and fro.
> Close to the Ettoro river, the spirits move forward.
> Close to the Ettoro river, they move backward.
> Close to the Ettoro river, the spirits, masters of this place, feel happy.
> The Nia-women dance with the thin spirits.
> The Nia-women dance with the bird-men (*urkukku*).
> The bird-men begin to move.
> The bird-men move to and fro.
> The bird-men move forward.
> The bird-men move backward.
> The bird-men, masters of this place, feel happy.
> The Nia-Women dance with the bird-men (*sipleleka*).

---

38. In his admirable analysis of Zuni literature, Tedlock writes as follows: "Or-dinary talk not only has words in it, in the sense of strings of consonants and vowels, but it has patterns of stress, of emphasis, of pitch, of tone, of pauses or stops that can move somewhat independently of the sheer words and make the same words mean quite different things. . . . To fix a text without making visible marks is to bring stress and pitch and pause into a fixed relationship to the words. The Zuni call this technique 'raising it right up'; we would call it 'chant'" (Tedlock 1983: 234).

These bird-men begin to move.

These bird-men move to and fro.

These bird-men move forward.

These bird-men move backward.

These bird-men, masters of this place, feel happy.

The Nia-women wear their blue clothes; now, in this part of the village, they line up, they prepare to dance.

Their clothes become a light blue-green, the spirit masters of this part of the village line up and prepare to dance.

Their clothes become bright red, the master-spirits of this part of the village line up and prepare to dance.

The Nia-women have donned red clothes like the ikkwi-bird, they line up to begin to dance.

The Nia-women, who wear red skirts like the ikkwi-bird, line up to begin to dance in this part of the village.

The Nia-women wear yellow skirts and now prepare to dance.

Their clothes become powerful in this part of the village.

The Nia-women dance with deer-men, the Nia-women dance with deer-men.

The deer-men begin to move.

The deer-men move to and fro.

The deer-men move forward.

The deer-men move backward, masters of this place, they feel happy.

The Nia-women now dance with the deer-men.

The deer-men begin to move.

The deer-men, with interlaced horns, are the masters of this part of the village, they shout "me-me."

The Nia-women who live in this part of the village wave their hats, they toss up their red hats and line up, preparing to dance. (Severi 1993c: 183–84)

Let us examine this text from the point of view of oral memory and focus our attention upon the order in which the sequences of names appear: that is to say, the mnemonic variations translated into images that it contains. In this text, a description of the list of spirits living in the village is inserted into the general schema of the journey of the spirits that is recounted by the shaman, the account of which was, up until now, based on the formula of presenting a list of "villages of spirits." From the point of view of the structure of the text, we now have at the village of dances a list of the names of the spirits, which appears within the more general sequence of the names of the supernatural villages (Figure 67).

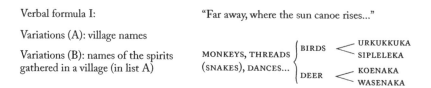

Figure 67. The mnemotechnique of Figure 68: the constant formulae and variations in the "village of dances."

In the pictographic plate that corresponds to this text (Figure 68, in which the passage that we are studying is inscribed), the pictography translates this new complexity of the textual structure by changing the spatial distribution of the figures. The pictography aligns the spirits according to what we might call a "linear process." The spirits thus find themselves *situated in the village* (just as the moon spirits found themselves grouped in different spaces in the mythical organization: sky, sea, horizon) and, at the same time, arranged in a linear sequence and a pre-established order. In this way, each pictogram is restored to its mental place in the textual memory. At the same time, given the place that it occupies in a specific sequence, it makes the general structure apprehensible. The space that is drawn and the mental space, both organized according to mnemonic criteria, thus tend to coincide. Löwy's idea that primitive drawing is of a mnemonic nature is entirely verified by the relevant fieldwork.

A study of the above examples now allows us to distinguish between two pictographic procedures that, each in its own way, develop the logical possibilities that we detected in our first Kuna example (see Figure 63). The first procedure organizes the pictograms "village by village," distributing or regrouping them in a given geographic space. The second superposes upon this first order a series of lines that organize the pictograms into linear successions. Thanks to this interaction between a temporal order and a spatial one, the description of a large village such as the "village of dances" in *The Song of the Demon* can appear as a veritable

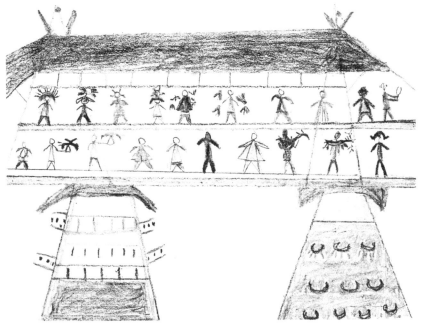

Figure 68. The "village of dances."

"pictographic page." Behind this graphic representation we can glimpse a cognitive schema made up of fixed places and identified in linear sequences. The technical exercise of memory is organized on the basis of this schema.

The principle of inserting lists of names into other lists of names, which technically constitutes an art of memory more highly developed but still founded upon the same principle as the "pictorial autobiographies" attested among the Plains Indians, is, in the Kuna tradition, able to develop even further and to engender more complex configurations. Instead of simply including one list within another (such as a list of spirit names in a list of village names), one could, for example, include a further group of variants, specifying, for instance, the sex, the species, and the color of the spirits. Or indeed, instead of including one list inside another, one could alternate them. Here are a few more examples.

This first is again drawn from *The Song of the Demon*. It comes at the start of the first part, the title of which is "In the shaman's hut," and I collected it in the Kuna village of Mulatupu, in 1982 (Severi 1997). The second is drawn from another Kuna song, the Mu Igala (*The Way of Mu*), devoted to the therapy for a difficult childbirth, collected and published by Holmer and Wassén in 1953. Our third example comes from *The Song of the Rock Crystal*, a Kuna text discovered probably at Ustupu by Nordenskiöld in 1927.

In our first example, at the start of *The Song of the Demon*, the text describes the shaman seated on a "golden seat" facing the sea. A storm is approaching. The trunks of the palm trees are bending in the violent wind. The sea is rough, the waves white with foam. Here is how the song, in its double pictographic (Figure 69) and oral version (as sung by the shaman, Enrique Gomez from Mulatupu, Panama), describes the situation:

1. The wind bringing harm is blowing, the shaman sits in his hut. He is seated on his little golden seat and looks all about him.
2. The wind bringing harm is whistling, the shaman sits in his hut, he is seated on his little golden seat and looks all about him. The wind bringing harm whips up eddies.
3. The shaman sits in his hut. He is seated on his little golden seat and looks all about him.
4. The wind bringing harm blows, whistles. The shaman sits in his hut. He is seated on his little golden seat and looks all about him
5. The trunks of the palm trees close to the sea bend in the wind. The shaman sits in his hut. He is seated on his little golden seat and looks all about him.
6. The palm trees close to the sea bend. The shaman sits in his hut. He is seated on his little golden seat and looks all about him.
7. The leaves of the palm trees close to the sea are changing. They are becoming yellow, they are as dazzling as gold. The shaman sits in his hut. He is seated on his little golden seat and looks all about him.
8. The leaves of the palm trees close to the sea are still. The shaman sits in his hut. He is seated on his little golden seat and looks all about him.
9. The leaves of the palm trees are now becoming green and blue. The shaman sits in his hut. He is seated on his little golden seat and looks all about him.
10. The leaves of the palm trees rustle. The shaman sits in his hut. He is seated on his little golden seat and looks all about him.

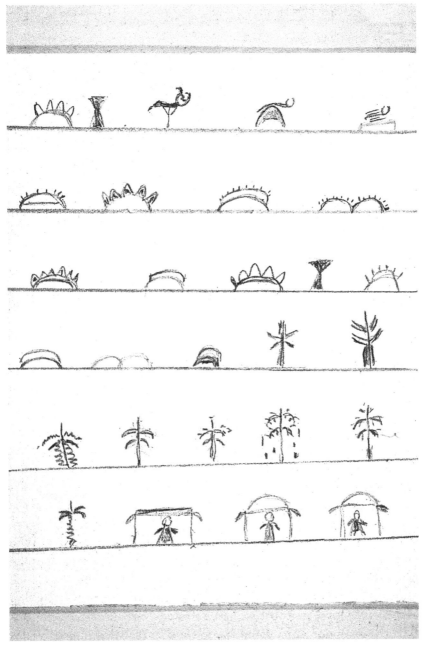

Figure 69. The first page of *The Song of the Demon* (Kuna).

11.   The branches of the palm trees close to the sea whistle. The shaman sits in his hut. He is seated on his little golden seat and looks all about him.

12.   The branches of the palm trees close to the sea become blue and green. The shaman sits in his hut. He is seated on his little golden seat and looks all about him.

13.   The waves of the sea rise up toward the sky. The shaman sits in his hut. He is seated on his little golden seat and looks all about him.

14.   The waves of the sea chase one another. The shaman sits in his hut. He is seated on his little golden seat and looks all about him.

15.   The waves of the sea catch one another, they chase one another.

16.   The waves of the sea are chased.

17.   The waves of the sea begin to speak.

18.   The waves of the sea pursue one another.

19.   The waves of the sea become white.

20.   The waves of the sea are white now.

21.   The waves of the sea pursue one another.

22.   The waves of the sea catch one another, they have caught one another.

23.   The waves of the sea begin to speak.

24.   The waves of the sea become white.

25.   The waves of the sea appear in their whiteness.

If we compare this text with the corresponding plate, it immediately becomes clear that the shaman has translated into images only part of this splendid description of an approaching storm (in which the transformation of the palm trees into trees "as dazzling as gold" introduces a theme that is dominant in much of the Kuna shamanistic tradition, the theme of metamorphosis). In the first series of pictograms, at the bottom, on the right, we recognize the graphic transcription of part of the first four lines of the text, that is to say, the description of the singer sitting in his hut on his ceremonial seat, attentively watching the sea. One might think that the shaman has, exceptionally, drawn not the variation in the text, but the part that we have called the verbal constant. But this apparent exception is probably due to the fact that it is impossible for the wind, which is the true subject of this passage, to be represented graphically. In fact, the text does then return immediately to the rule of an alternation between a constant, only stated verbally, and a variant that is translated in the pictography. The pictogram and the verbal formula again swap roles: the initial passage is not repeated again in the graphic part and becomes the verbal formula that is constantly repeated in the rest of the text. From the fifth line onward, we thus return to a situation that has become familiar: a verbal formula that is not transcribed graphically is now associated with the translation of a list of variations into drawings.

From a mnemotechnical point of view, we have up to now considered cases in which the song was composed exclusively by a graphic formula that was independent from the text (for example, the graphic triangle that represents a "village of spirits") together with a verbal formula never translated into images and a variant that is transcribed in pictograms. Now we can see that this structure can be used in a more subtle manner without modifying its essential features. In this case, a verbal formula, introduced in the first lines of the text, is first translated in pictograms but is then *used as a constant* in the following passage. The technique of mental representation that directs the memorization of the text also makes possible a first alternation between a constant and a variation and between a part transcribed in drawings and a part stated orally. This technique may undergo further developments. Here is an example in an extract from the Mu Igala (Holmer and Wassén [1947] 1953: 79–91):

79. Under the hammock of the sick woman, I put you, *nelegan*.[39]
80. Under the hammock of the sick woman, I gather you, *nelegan*.
81. Under the hammock of the sick woman, I raise you up, *nelegan*.
82. Along the extremity of Muu Puklip's[40] road the *nelegan* rise.
83. The shaman summons the master-spirits of the plants. They run up to call for other *nelegan*.
84. In the east, he calls Nele Uluburwigwalele, Nele Binaisegwalele.
85. They arrive, bringing clothes that steam with blood.
86. They arrive, bringing hats that steam with blood.
87. They arrive, bringing pearls of glass that steam with blood.

39. The *nelegan* are the spirit assistants of the Kuna shaman.
40. The spirit that presides over the female genital function.

88.   Under the hammock of the sick woman, I place you, *nelegan.*
89.   Under the hammock of the sick woman, I gather you, *nelegan.*
90.   Under the hammock of the sick woman, I raise you up, *nelegan.*
91.   At the extremity of Muu Puklip's road they rise.

This text starts with a sequence of four statements, to which the same sequence of pictograms always corresponds. We should note that here the variation always concerns the verbs (*urbiali*, to put; *odiali*, to gather; *odilamakali*, to raise up). This variation is always transcribed for mnemonic purposes, using different colors for the same image. An analogous structure in the text corresponds to this microvariation (which is implicit and internal to the verbal formula). In this part of the song, this formula often alternates with passages in which, as in statements 84–87, the drawings explicitly assume their customary function of transcribing a variant within the text. Here, it is a matter of clothing or material, represented by flags, hats (which constitute a metaphor of spiritual power; see Severi 1997), and glass beads. It is also worth noting that the textual expression "the shaman summons the master-spirits of the plants" is always transcribed by the same image of a standing figure raising his arms to the sky (Figure 70).

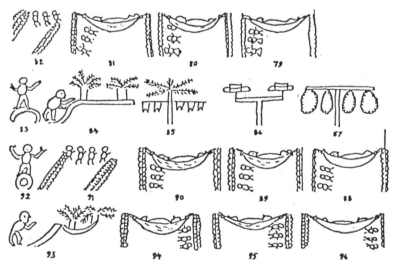

Figure 70. Pictographic page from the Kuna song about a difficult birth.

Among the material collected by Nordenskiöld in 1927, we find other examples of this way of proceeding. Let us consider the third example, from *The Song of the Rock Crystal* (*Akwanele igar*) (Nordenskiöld 1938: 559–60). In the Kuna shamanistic tradition, rock crystals are considered to be clairvoyants, and shamans often include them among their spirit-helpers. Here, as in *The Way of Mu*, the shaman alternates cosmological references to places occupied by crystals in the underground world with a description of the offering which rises up in smoke from the ceremonial brazier: for Kuna spirits feed on the smoke provided by a variety of leaves (tobacco, coconuts, etc.) and derive part of their strength from this. This smoke that they breathe in induces a state of inebriation that makes them particularly powerful.

At the river's mouth the first God placed your dwelling
Nele-nusa-Kalele, Akwalele, Kunakalele,[41] I am speaking to you
[Burning] the Innakiklipa herb, I speak to you, burning the Innakikipla herb, I speak to you.
Burning cocoa, I speak to you, burning tobacco, I speak to you,
Burning tobacco, I speak to you, Nele-nusa-kalele, Akwalele, Kunakalele,
It is for you that the first God established shelters.
It is for you that the first god established palisades,
Nele-nusa-kalele, Akwalele, Kunakalele.

If we compare the text and the image (Figure 71), once more we see that the pictographic transcription always operates in accordance with the principle of representing variants within the verbal formulae that one learns by heart. In this last case, however, instead of a list of names inserted into another list, we have a succession of formulae that alternate in the text. Finally, we should note that the same series of pictographic images always transcribes the same statements and so ends by producing, as in the *Dakota Bible*, a perfect *visual equivalent* of the parallelist structure that organizes the text. This last point yet again underlines the coherence and efficacy of pictography used for memorization (Figure 72).

---

41. These are ritual names for the rock crystal.

PLATE VII.

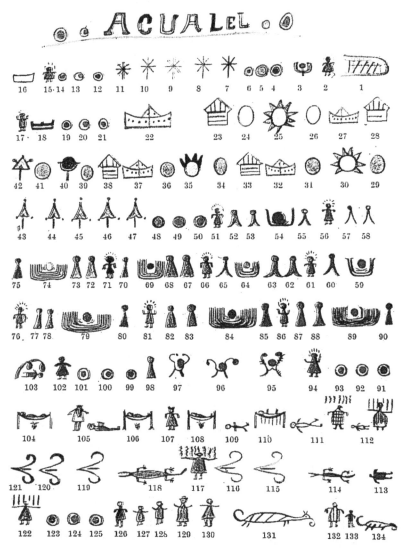

Figure 71. *The Song of the Rock Crystal.*

A B C D E F G H I L M D E F N O D E F ...

Figure 72. Parallelist schema of *The Song of the Rock Crystal.*

A FEW MORE AMERINDIAN CASES

The Kuna case thus, in a very complex context, develops a number of fundamental features that are characteristic of the iconographies of the Plains Indians. To complete the present demonstration let us now see how the Kuna case relates to other examples of the practice of pictography among Amerindians. Our most significant evidence comes from the Inuit, the Ojibwa shamanistic tradition, and the Western Apache.

As we have seen, the first discoveries and analyses of Amerindian pictographs took place very far away from the Kuna and in an altogether different context. If we read the accounts of those studies of the second half of the nineteenth century, the "graphic arts" of the Indians—as they were called at that time—seem very different from the cases that we have so far studied here. A large number of rudimentary figures are transcribed, one after another, often accompanied by commentaries as detailed as they are imprecise, which, it was then thought, were designed to guide the reader's understanding of those first attempts by the "Aborigenes of America to represent ideas graphically" (Hoffman 1898: 1). We have by now acquired enough familiarity with the world of pictographs to be able, over and above the commentaries produced by the earliest collectors of this evidence, to recognize indications that may lead to their correct interpretation.

Let us consider a first example drawn from the studies that Hoffman devoted to Inuit pictographs in 1895. The schema of interpretation that guides the presentation of the pictograms seems very simple, if not banal. Hoffman's method consisted in carefully setting out numbered sequences of figures, as he does with this "account of a hunt" that he found in 1882 in the possession of the Alaskan Commercial Company of San Francisco (Figure 73). Hoffman adds to this numbered series of figures "an explanation of the figures involved," which he attributes to his preferred informant, Vladimir Naomoff. Let us now read this text and compare it to the series of numbered figurines.

Figure 73. An account of an Inuit hunt.

1. The speaker, with the right hand indicating himself and with the left pointing in the direction taken.
2. Holding a boat paddle, *going by boat* (Hoffman's italics).
3. The speaker holding the right hand to the side of his head, to denote sleep, and the left elevated with one finger erect to signify one night.
4. A circle with two marks in the middle, signifying an island with huts upon it.
5. The same statement as in 1.
6. A circle to denote another island where they touched.
7. Similar to 3, with an additional finger elevated, signifying two nights or sleeps.
8. The speaker with his harpoon, with the left hand making a gesture to denote the sea-lion.
9. The sea-lion, which the hunter
10. Secured by shooting with bow and arrow.
11. The boat with two persons in it.
12. The winter habitation of the speaker. (Hoffman 1895: 904–905)

This series of "translations" of the Inuit signs leads Hoffman to conclude that the pictograms can neither transcribe nor represent a text coherently. To his mind, they constitute an episodic and approximate indication that refers vaguely to a daily occurrence such as, in the example just seen, a hunting expedition. Seen in this way, this example of pictography, like hundreds of others collected by Hoffman, seems rudimentary in many respects: the drawing, the type of communication, the signs' relation to language, appear, in this example, no more than vaguely sketched in. The type of memorization that a document such as this can prompt seems extremely fragile, inevitably linked to a measure of good will on the part of whoever is addressed by the message. The latter appears to have to extend the meaning, starting from a little animal-figure, a rough sketch of a tree or a small hut, without being offered the technical means to fix a memory firmly. This account of an Inuit hunting expedition clearly illustrates a concept of the origin of writing that was much favored by linguists such as Gelb and DeFrancis: here, the pictograph seems a shapeless, episodic, unstable, and individual kind of symbolism. Yet if we are willing to look more closely, we gradually discover that the point of view adopted by Hoffman's interpretation is definitely oriented by a set of initial prejudices. His demonstration method follows a stable schema repeated so tirelessly that it sometimes tries the patience of the reader. After a summary account of the purely graphic aspect of the drawings (what he calls their "decorative" character), he appends a text that he calls "an interpretation of the characters" (ibid.: 925), "the meaning of the illustrations" (ibid.: 884), "a description of the drawings," or even "a free translation of the pictographs." Only much later does the reader discover that the interpretation of the pictographs is *never* based on the words that the Inuit themselves apply, case by case, to the drawings. The fact is that Hoffman almost never interprets the pictograms on the basis of the mnemonic associations that they prompt in Inuit tradition. He depends on the interpretation or even the "free translation" that he himself has constructed. In this way, the impression created is that of a pictography that relates only imprecisely and in a rudimentary manner to the meaning that is expressed verbally.

However, the whole situation changes when Hoffman, who remains a researcher of great honesty, mentions, alongside his "illustration of the characters," another type of document that he often calls a "dialect translation" of the pictographs. He does so in the case of the Inuit hunt that we have examined above. The "dialect translation" of this pictographic document appears not in the book that I have so far cited and that dates from 1895, but in an article published a few years later (Hoffman 1898) which is devoted to a comparison between the Inuit pictographs and those of other "aboriginal peoples" of America. So let us take a look at the English "literal translation" of Figure 73 that Hoffman set alongside the Inuit text:

I there (to that place) go (by boat)
That island one sleep (night) there.
Then I go to another island
There two sleeps (nights).
I catch one then return to place mine. (Hoffman 1898: 6)

Any reader who has followed my study of the pictographs of the Plains Indians and also those, more complex, of the Kuna tradition will immediately recognize the nature of this text. Although remarkably simple, it is definitely formulated in parallelist terms. Three aspects of this document deserve our attention: the structure of the text, that of the drawing, and the implied distribution between words and drawings. The message here seems quite unexceptional: it is a simple account of a hunt. But as soon as we manage to hear the voice of Hoffman's informant who deciphers and comments on the drawings without his interpretation being covered over by Hoffman's "free translation," the structure of the text to which the images refer conveys a meaning of its own. Clearly, the narrative here develops in a purely parallelist style, where the same words alternate:

> I there go that island, one night
> I go to another island, two nights . . .

The drawing has an analogous structure in which a single figure, a representation of the speaker, when repeated several times, comes to constitute the guiding thread throughout the series. I should add that this double series, which is both verbal and graphic, does not effect a complete coincidence between the message—the hunt narrative—and the drawings that ought to transcribe it completely. On the contrary, as in the earliest examples of "Ledger Art" (such as the *Five Crows Ledger* studied above), the information that the drawing provides and that conveyed by words coincide only partially. The simplest example of the additions that the images supply to the text, of which we have already noted many examples, is that of the hunt itself, which is represented in the drawings by the harpoon and the arrows but about which the text says nothing. Other details, such as the huts represented in the first line, are not mentioned at all in the "literal translation" provided by Hoffman. Finally, as is certainly obvious, in the last part of the series—the canoe's return to the place where the narrator lives—many details (the canoe, the number of rowers, the number of oars, the structure of the narrator's home . . .) are totally ignored in the oral version of the narrative provided by the informant. Typically, for pictography, the relation of meaning to symbolism, even in such a simple case, is based on a textual structure in which the information is distributed between what is repeated, as a verbal formula, and what is transcribed in images. From this we may conclude that Hoffman, given his need, for evident ideological reasons, to show the incomplete and rudimentary nature of pictography, played down pictographical symbolism without analyzing its structure, thereby transforming these examples of Inuit pictography into what seem to be proofs of a particular concept of the origin of writing that is as erroneous as it is taken for granted.

An analysis of the earliest ledgers, the pictorial autobiographies of the Plains Indians, and of the Kuna case, combined with a study of our earliest Oceanic examples, enable us, on the contrary, to understand that even within this elementary sequence of figurines, it is possible to identify the basic characteristics of a mnemotechnique: order and salience. On the one hand, an order is clearly imposed on this sequence of images for, as we have seen, the Inuit pictography is organized through an alternating repetition of the same figures; furthermore, the direction in which they should be read is clearly indicated. On the other hand, this way of organizing the pictographs also produces a particular salience since, starting with the same basic figure, one can always operate variations and so engender a new meaning, for example by modifying a hand gesture. I should add that this first graphic configuration is placed in a regular relationship with a text that possesses a structure of its own. The reading supplied by Vladimir Naomoff, Hoffman's Inuit informant, is certainly set out in a parallelist form, which implies that a fundamental relationship of reciprocity is established between the stated words and the image.

Another example, taken from Hoffman's work, enables us to proceed further with our analysis. Again, it concerns "an account of a hunt," but this time it is slightly more complex (Figure 74) (Hoffman 1895: 880).

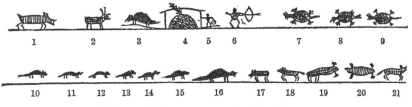

Figure 74. An account of an Inuit hunt.

As always, Hoffman starts by setting out his interpretation of the characters" (ibid.: 880–81):

1 and 2 represent deer.
3.   is the outline of a porcupine, next to which is the habitation of the hunter.
4.   Smoke is seen issuing from the roof of the hut, while
5.   at the door of the hut is the hunter's wife with a vessel.
6.   The outline of the hunter in the attitude of shooting an arrow.
7, 8, 9 are beavers.
10 to 14 are martens.
15.   is a vessel, according to the interpretation given by Naomoff.
16.   A land otter.
17.   A bear.
18.   A fox.
19.   A walrus.
20.   A seal.
21.   A wolf.

However, in this case too, Hoffman's honesty as an ethnographer impelled him to transcribe what he calls a "literal translation," which was provided by his informant (ibid.: 881–82):

I, from my place
I went hunting for skins
Martens five
Weasel one
Land otter one, I caught

Wolf one
Deer two, I killed
Beavers three
Porcupine one, I caught none.

Seal, I caught none
Walrus, I caught none
Fox, I caught none
Bear, I caught none.

In this brief "account of a hunt," in which we immediately recognize alternating repetitions and variations, the distribution of the meaning between the words pronounced and the drawings is even closer than what we have seen in the most simple Kuna examples. The list of prey is, in effect, just a list of animal names that the pictographic text regularly transcribes as a variant to the oral text. Here too, the text is composed of repeated verbal formulae. We recognize the type of relationship between the constant and the variant that we have already found in numerous examples. But in this "account of a hunt" there is something else too. The images do not transcribe only variants to the formulations of the text; they also enrich the meaning. As Hoffman writes, transcribing the words of his informant: "[T]he animals are all indicated; those with the heads turned toward the hunter were secured, while those with their heads turned away from him were observed, but not secured by him" (ibid.: 881).

It is not hard to recognize the structure of one of the first Kuna examples that we have studied above: the plate found by Nordenskiöld, in which a horizon line drawn on the representation of a list of names concerned spirits that took their places on the moon canoe. This enabled us to distinguish between three classes of spirits: those of the sky, those of the earth, and those that moved in both dimensions (see Figure 63). There too, a simple graphic intervention, an inversion of the image, constituted an elementary but effective way to establish a visual commentary and thereby to formulate new information about an ordered series of images. We may conclude from this that, despite their differences in graphic style and the great cultural distance between them, the pictographic systems practiced by the Plains Indians, the Inuit iconography, and the Kuna pictographic tradition all obey common criteria from the point of view of the mental operations implied by the drawings.

Similar conclusions are prompted by other Amerindian cases. At the end of his study of Inuit (Eskimo) graphic art, Hoffman writes:

> Although the Eskimo are extremely superstitious, and numbers of them are recognized shamans of ability, yet there seems to be a general scarcity of pictographic matter pertaining thereto. This is strange, too, as among some peoples the records are almost entirely devoted to shamanistic ceremonies, and in several instances, as among the Ojibwa, the mnemonic and hunting records—all shamanistic—are the only relics of pictography at this day. (Hoffman 1895: 912)

Following on from the Plains Indians, our sources thus lead us in the direction of the peoples of northeastern America. They suggest that, in parallel to the "autobiographical" tradition linked with a warrior figure, northern America, too, was familiar with a pictographic tradition linked with shamanism. For a long time, these documents, to which Hoffman devoted an impressive study, seemed obscure and hard to understand. But if we return to this shamanistic material that Hoffman himself associates with the Inuit findings, we are bound to see that much of the documents' obscurity was his own creation. His working method, even on this new material, did not change. In the detailed descriptions produced in 1891 of the *Mnemonic Songs* used by the initiatory Midewiwin Ojibwa society, long sequences of "elementary" drawings are followed by the ethnologist's own "interpretations of the characters." All that is different here is that this interpretation is sometimes given in the original Ojibwa language, which inevitably suggests to the reader that this is an actual transcription that the Indians spontaneously associated with the drawings. But nothing could be further from the truth: the text that corresponded to the pictograms of the shamanistic song has, in this case, been irremediably lost; replacing it, we find a commentary that is full of gaps and is quite imprecise. As Hoffman sees it, this is just an inevitable simplification of ritual texts which, as he notes with a certain impatience, for the most part consist "purely and simply" of repetitions: "The greater number of the songs are mere repetitions of short phrases, and frequently but single words . . . repeated *ad libitum* in direct proportion to the degree of inspiration which the singer imagines himself to have attained" (Hoffman [1891] 1975: 192).

We are already familiar with the meaning of these verbal repetitions, which, here as elsewhere, are a feature of the parallelist technique of Amerindian ritual songs. But in the case of the Ojibwa songs it is actually Hoffman's own honesty as an ethnographer that enables us to use the pictographic evidence that he collected the better to refute his ideas. In the long work that he devoted to the Ojibwa initiatory societies, Hoffman, as in his essay on the Inuit, sometimes draws a distinction between what he calls "an interpretation of the characters" and the Ojibwa text "as it is sung by the Indians." He adds that in this case he is recording "the phraseology of the text, as the Indians sing it." Then he adds a transcription of the music. All that, for us, remains to be done is to look again at some of his text transcriptions linked with the music in order to see that what we have here is a mnemotechnic strategy that establishes a relationship between the drawing and the uttered text—a strategy with which we are by now familiar. For example, a first hint of the interdependency between the two registers, which is less commonplace than Hoffman's interpretation suggests, emerges when we come upon a pictographic text that sets up a correspondence between, on the one hand, the following two utterances:

I give you medicine, and a lodge, also
I am flying to my lodge,

both of which start with the word "I," and, on the other, two picto-grams (Figures 75a and 75b) that correspond to two different animals. These drawings represent two distinct incarnations of the original spirit (Manído) who is evoked by the text. It is clear that in this case the pic-togram indicates a change in the speaker, about which the verbal text says nothing.[42] An analogous situation is detectable in another exam-ple, in which the verbal interpretation of the pictogram that we see in Figure 75c—"My Migis spirit, that is why I am stronger than you"—makes no mention of the fact, recorded in visual terms, that there are three signs of the presence of Migis spirits (which penetrate the body of the initiate in order to give him strength).

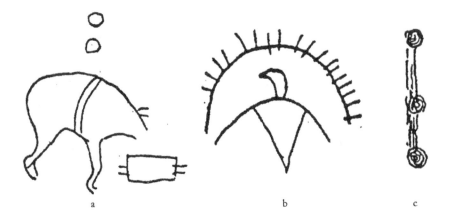

a   b   c

Figure 75. Ojibwa pictographs: bear, thunder-bird, and a pictographic indication, absent from the chanted text, of the intervention of spirits.

---

42. It is nevertheless worth noting that the word "bear" appears in the Ojibwa text (*ma'kwin*) (see Piggott and Grafstein 1983).

This distribution of the meaning between the drawings and the words ritually spoken becomes particularly noticeable when a literal translation (accompanied by a melody picked up on a pentagram) follows the graphic representation of the pictograms. It describes a phase in the initiation into the Ojibwa Mide Wiwin society. In this phase, the initiation candidate, whose ritual action establishes a relationship with the spirits of the initiated (here given material expression by a metaphorical meal shared in the hut where the ritual is celebrated), is symbolized by the image of a "plate" surrounded by the arms of the spirits (Figure 76a).

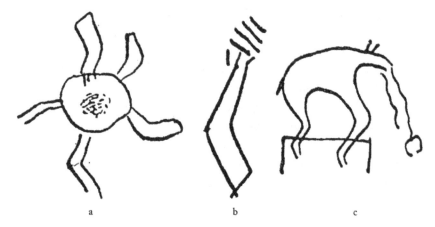

a   b   c

Figure 76. Ojibwa pictographs: (a) the symbol of the initiate, (b) arm, (c) the Manído-bear.

In the next part of the ritual song, the pictogram reflects the young candidate's identification with the ritual plate itself. If we follow what Hoffman calls "an explanation of the graphic characters," the correspondence seems immediate. For the following commentary corresponds to Figure 76a: "My plate, at midday I prepare my plate" (Hoffman [1891] 1975: 267). However, if we compare the pictogram with the song "as sung by the Indians," we find that the metaphorical plate that represents the candidate is inserted into a very precise parallelist structure that organizes the text. In this context, the repetition of an isolated name is not senseless but instead corresponds to an intentional elaboration of the text. The drawing, as in other Kuna examples (for example, the one in *The Song of the Demon*), seems here to refer only to the repeated part of the text, even if it already includes a redundant character, given that it identifies the speaker with the candidate for initiation who is engaged in the process of turning himself ritually into a spirit. However, the text, precisely, makes no mention of that transformation. Nevertheless, in the next part of the initiatory song we rediscover the structure that we have identified in our Kuna pictographs, since the graphic transcription of the variant returns regularly. The two pictograms 76b and 76c are what the identical verbal formulae in the text refer to.

I am a spirit (Manído)
I am a spirit
I am a spirit
I am a spirit, my body is made of fire

I am a spirit (Manído)
I am a spirit
I am a spirit
I am a spirit, my body is made of fire

One difference, only, separates those two formulae: the identity of the locutor. He is represented, the first time, by one of the hands that hold the ritual plate in Figure 76a; the second time by a bear standing in the *wigwam* (the ceremonial hut) in which the ritual is celebrated. Here again the pictogram transcribes the variation in the text (namely, the identity of the "supernatural" locutor)—a variation that Hoffman regarded as simply "a useless repetition" (ibid.: 266). We can now see clearly that here, as in the Kuna and the Inuit cases, the function of the pictogram is not only to transcribe the text, but also to enrich its meaning.

If we bear in mind the facts that the original of the initiatory document known as the Ojibwa *Mnemonic Songs*, which Hoffman collected, was already in use in Thousand Lakes (Minnesota) in 1825 and that, as Hoffman added (ibid.: 259), in that case it already took the form of a copy of an earlier document, we can form a clear idea of longevity possessed by a graphic code founded on the bases designed to activate memory that have been described so far. Hoffman's idea of a "fragile" pictographic symbolism constituted by inadequate attempts to represent elementary ideas graphically thus seems singularly weak in the light of the above analysis of this type of document.

In 1906, a young Apache in the West, by the name of Silas John, had a vision. John, like other young Apaches, had long yearned for such an experience. So he had followed the procedure designed for any young warrior who aspired to become a shaman. Up to a point this involved a customary training that included taking drugs and long periods of living alone in the forests. John naturally also followed the teaching of an experienced shaman, in his case his own father. As was traditionally expected, this apprenticeship of shamanistic learning led to a "direct" experience of the supernatural world.

However, there was also an exceptional aspect to John's vision, and it immediately became well known in the Apache villages of San Carlos and then in all the Apache reserves from White Mountain right across to Mescalero and Jicarilla. On his return from his experience, John told how the supernatural spirit with whom he entered into contact did more than just teach him a few ritual songs designed to cure a number of illnesses, as he did other young men aspiring to become shamans. He also revealed to him an "alphabet" that enabled him to transcribe those songs and fix them in his memory. The last chapter of the present book will discuss at length Silas John's shamanistic apprenticeship, which constituted an altogether exemplary experience and was to engender one of the most intense and violent messianic movements among the indigenous peoples of North America. For now, though, let us take a preliminary look at his strange invention—produced, he claimed, in a dream of a pictography linked to a collection of ritual songs. John's invention and the path followed by his imagination are, in fact, very close to the pictographic traditions of other American peoples that we have already examined.

Naturally, that certainly does not mean that the figures and the basic elements of this dreamed pictography resemble the pictographs that we have seen used among the Inuit, the Ojibwa, the Lakota, and the Kuna. If the analyses already carried out teach us anything from the point of view of method, it is precisely that the nature of a pictographic system is by no means determined by the graphic style of the drawings, but rather by the type of relationship established between, on the one hand, the structure of a text regularly declaimed in a parallelist mode and, on the other, the intervention of pictograms that convey a mnemonic trace of the words to be spoken. A comparison between different pictographic systems should therefore be organized around an analysis of the relationship that they set up between the visual and the verbal registers. In every case that we have managed to analyze, that relationship is independent from the iconographic style.

Within these traditions, the graphic style may be realistic or conventional, or, in some cases, may even include a number of characters borrowed from Western alphabetic writing. But these variations in no way modify the structure of the distribution of meaning between the visual and the verbal, which seems to characterize the exercise of pictography. The morphology upon which the comparative analyses carried out here are founded is based on an analysis of relations, not on a comparison of elementary graphic forms, such as a Carl Schuster might have envisaged. As is stated in Chapter 1, the perspective that I have chosen leads to a study of the mental operations implied by the establishment of those relations rather than to the evolution of any particular graphic character. Adopting this perspective, let us now consider the structure of one of the "prayers" that Silas John claims to have learnt in a dream (Figure 77):

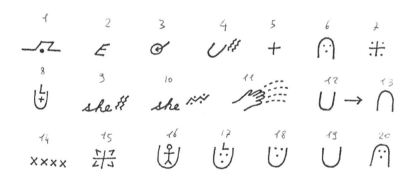

Figure 77. Pictographic transcription of Silas John's prayer.

1. THE EARTH when it was created for the first time
2. THE SKY when it was created for first time
3. At the centre, when everything began
4. The SACRED POLLEN of God

5. A CROSS of SACRED POLLEN
6. The SACRED POLLEN, alive
7. A CROSS of SACRED POLLEN breathes in all four directions
8. THE SACRED POLLEN of God is alive
9. My POLLEN, my SACRED POLLEN
[. . .]

The selective, redundant, and parallelist relation between text and image, which is typical of Amerindian pictography, is clearly present in this document. The dream of the young Apache prophet undeniably observes the rules of a tradition that spread throughout a vast region of America, ranging from the Alaska of the Inuit as far as the Darién of Panama. As for a formal analysis of the symbolism that he used to fix these ritual songs in his memory, Silas John's visions testify to a strict respect for the Amerindian pictographic tradition.

PICTOGRAPHY AND MNEMONIC REPRESENTATION

In conclusion, let us note a number of essential points in our analysis. Over and above the variations that may characterize particular local traditions, the principles that direct the exercise of pictography in a number of Amerindian cultures have clearly emerged. A narrative theme (a journey, a scene of meditation close to the sea, a dialogue between spirits, a warrior expedition or an account of a hunt . . .) is expressed in a song, initially through the imposition of an *order of words* that always follows a parallelist structure. This order transforms a narrative sequence into an alternation between formulae that are constantly repeated and a series of variations that are introduced one after another. Within this block of words organized in a mnemonic form, several examples of which we have noted, the function of a pictographic image is to confer salience upon the variations. A pictogram thus makes it possible to memorize lists of names that may be very long. Order and salience, the two principles that we have noticed shaping the earliest representations of lists of names in the Sepik cultures of New Guinea, are thus also at work, albeit in a different manner, in Amerindian pictography.

This pictography is an iconic tradition (in some cases more complex than the Sepik totemic lists of names) in which an image has the power to fix in one's memory actual texts that may, as in the Kuna case, become very long, at the same time acquiring a great poetic richness. Such a result is the fruit of an altogether unexpected evolution in the history of writing. Out of an early basic iconography of prehistoric origin,[43] linked with ritual actions and shamanistic visions, examples of which have been noted in rock art, there developed in America a coherent and virtually closed symbolism. Within this system, the problem of representing a name (which, as we have seen, likewise arose in Oceania) received a specific solution that emerged in parallel to an indication of a number of temporal features, for example through a succession of marks that might precede or follow an image.

At the heart of the "biographical style," instances of which are first to be found in rock art and, later, in the decoration of deer and bison pelts (AD 1600–1800, according to Keyser), this symbolism was linked—particularly among the Plains Indians—to a specific kind of ritual speech that consisted of narratives describing the exploits of hunters or warriors.

At the heart of this iconographic tradition there emerged a new way of presenting ordered sequences of figures, for example by setting up an opposition between the right and the left on a flat surface (as in the Cheyenne case), or a spiral organization (among the Flathead Indians, as can be seen from a section of the *Five Crows Ledger*), or even a purely linear sequence. In many documents, particularly those that reflect a remarkable evolution in graphic style, such as the *Dakota Bible*, this sequential organization corresponds to a mnemonic codification of a parallelist type. In this way there developed the style composed of varied sequences of figure-schemes that characterizes many documents of the so-called "late" period of American pictography. These early developments unfolded entirely within the context of great shamanistic traditions, for example that of the Kuna, in which the relation between pictography and parallelism gave birth to a veritable literature based on the form of ritual song.

By studying a number of ethnographic cases, it is thus possible to detect the emergence of a new model of interpretation. Seen in this new

---

43. That is, dating from American prehistory (AD 1000–1300).

perspective, the pictographies of the Native Americans can no longer be interpreted as what they are not, that is to say, as arbitrary drawings or even phonetic writings. I have tried to identify the nature of this symbolism by, on the one hand, studying the "Ledger Art" tradition and, on the other, by analyzing practices that can be observed, in the field, in an Amerindian tradition. I have also compared this system of representations, particularly where the mental operations that they imply are concerned, with the principles that direct *more simple* systems of mnemonic images, such as those we have studied in the Sepik region.

We may conclude that the social memory of an Amerindian tradition is founded neither on a practice analogous to alphabetic writing, nor on a tradition vaguely defined as "oral." Rather, it is based on a figurative mnemotechnique the essential nature of which may be identified in the relation established between a relatively stable iconography and a rigorously structured use of ritual speech, that is to say, between memorization and an iconography organized in a parallelist form. As Amerindian pictography appears from this ethnographic study, it is certainly not an unfulfilled harbinger of alphabetic writing. On the contrary, it is a particularly subtle and sophisticated art of memory. To put that more precisely, pictograms translate the figurative part of a mnemotechnique that essentially stems, albeit upon new bases, from the two criteria that orient the mental representation of the graphic transcription of the lists of totemic names that characterize Sepik societies: salience and order are here inserted into a context of complexities that are *different but comparable*.

Amerindian pictographs, the unexpected extension, logical coherence, and even unforeseen beauty of which we have assessed for the first time, no longer appear as incomplete attempts to invent a writing, but now provide us with the key to a new understanding of the social practices linked with memory and the construction of a tradition that is both "oral" and iconographic.

CHAPTER 3

Memory, projection, belief
Or, the metamorphoses of the locutor

Native American pictography is not a rudimentary, individual, or arbitrary system of writing. It is the graphic part of a memory technique: parallelism. It can represent a text by reflecting its structure. In the documents that we have analyzed, the parallelist structure of the text, composed of variants and constants, always corresponds to a clear distinction between the pictograms, which translate the variations in the text, and the words, which are not represented by an image. The visual register offers no support at all to the part of the text that is made up by constant verbal formulae. Seen from this point of view, the pictography may appear to us as a schema of parallelist organization transferred into the domain of images. This schema organizes images in a way that echoes the way in which words are organized in the text. The mnemotechnical character and efficacy of this technique for organizing words and images have by now been demonstrated.

All the same, every technique for remembering is also a technique of the imagination, and that is certainly the case of the pictography of Native Americans. This means that the pictography possesses a form that is typical of an art of memory and implies an association between two kinds of phenomena: on the one hand, the fixing of a mnemonic trace, together with the classification and chains of inferences that it implies, and, on the other hand, a process involving evocation, ideation, and also poetic imagination. Even as it fixes upon a specific word chosen from an order established by the oral tradition, a pictogram always makes it possible to add details or visual variations that are provided by the image and that enrich the information.

This balance between freedom and coherence that is characteristic of pictography no doubt depends on the fact that, at a deeper level, there is a parallelist cognitive organizing force at work, directing the very exercise of memory. This is an organizing technique that leads one to manipulate linguistic features and iconic features in the same fashion, like pieces in a mosaic. It may articulate them in ways that differ, but those modalities are always ruled by a common logic. At this juncture, a first point needs to be made: the song-form transcribed in pictograms in American traditions is not primarily based on sequential developments in a narrative. It does not depend upon the interplay peculiar to a narrative style that consists in setting up an expectation in the mind of the listener, progressively working toward its resolution, and finally fulfilling it. Instead, the form of a ritual song depends on a parallelist organization of the mental representation itself. This iconic manner of representing words proceeds in a series of parallels. The particular way of accompanying a text by conjuring up images, which is typical of narration, does remain present. But whereas within the framework of a narrative it conjured up mental images, in the transcription of a ritual song into pictograms that process is objectivized in real images transcribed on to a material backing and in accordance with a preestablished code. A mnemonic representation, as a purely mental process, is thus very close to this graphic technique.

It is also necessary to point out that, like anything to do with memory, this process does not solely concern the acquisition of a mechanical ability to nail down information on to a passive background of "memories." It also involves a mental reconstruction that is a feature of any endeavor of evocation and hence of the very exercise of thinking or of mental representation. All the theoretical, experimental, and historical literature devoted to memory stresses the link that connects inference and the work of evocation. Seen in this perspective, mental parallelism can thus become not only a way of preserving the structure of a text, but also a means of deducing from a text and later representing and applying to other contexts concepts and schemas of organization or even *creatures* that are typical of the world that one wishes to represent.

If we now return to the Kuna example, we shall find that the shamanistic songs are not just composed of sequences of words organized in a parallelist way. They are also peopled by creatures which, thanks to the parallelist handling, are composed of heterogeneous features. Through one's growing familiarity with the songs, these creatures come to play an active part in both memories and thoughts. To put that another way, these songs, which generally represent journeys in an invisible dimension of the world, are peopled with *chimeras*. The most simple example is the Celestial Jaguar, a veritable Kuna version of the Greek model of a chimera: a bird that roars like a jaguar and a jaguar that sings like a bird, an inextricable mosaic figure produced by shifting into the field of ontological imagining the technique of organizing the groups of words that a shaman's pupil learns in order to memorize ritual texts. In my book (Severi 1993c), I made a study of this figure from Kuna mythology. Right now, suffice it to recall just one passage from *The Song of the Demon*, namely the description of the "village of darkness," where, in the middle of a violent storm, "the celestial jaguars" make an appearance.

> The village is covered by clouds, the village is invaded by fog, in the village rivers form, the village resounds with the noise of falling rain, the village is full of puddles of water, over there, in the dark village.
> The jaguars of the sky appear in the air, the jaguars of the sky hang there in the sky, crying out *swa-swa*.
> This part of the village resounds, the village resounds (with their cry), the village can be heard from afar.
> From end to end in the village, the Golden Disk descends; suspended from a-cord-to-accompany-the-dead, the Golden Disk descends: over there, in the village.[1]

---

1.   The Golden Disk is one of the ritual names of the Jaguar of the Sky. The name refers to the jaguar's identification with the sun. As for the cord mentioned here in the shaman's song, this is the *kwilogar*, the cord that the Kuna place upon the bodies of the dead before their burial. It is said to accompany the body on its voyage in the subterranean world.

The teeth of the Jaguar of the Sky are red, they are the color of mageb,[2]
the blue Golden Disk descends over there, in the dark village.
Hanging from an umbilical cord, the bird cries out, hanging from an
umbilical cord, just like a jaguar, the bird is crying out.
The jaguar sings like a bird, its teeth are the color of mageb, its claws are
the color of mageb.
Over there, where the dark village is to be found, the village resounds,
the village trembles; from far away, one can hear it, over there, where the
dark village is to be found. (Cited in Severi 1993c: 127–28)

In this passage, the process of transformation that turns the jaguar
into a creature with the voice of a bird is constructed according to
a parallelist model. So we may conclude that the term "parallelism"
has two meanings: a straightforward one that designates a technique
that enables one to organize a text and learn it by heart; and a less
commonplace meaning that leads one to detect, at the very heart of
this memorizing technique, a way of orienting the imagination. To be
more precise, this is a process, probably inherent in the very exercise
of the spoken word (whether within the framework of a narrative or
within that of a ritual discourse), which establishes what might be
called *a link through a mental image* between the locutors and their
listeners. It is also worth noting that through the introduction of a
chimera (which, through its surprising or counterintuitive character,
becomes the salient point in the mnemonic sequence, thereby assuming the functions of a veritable *imago agens*), a first link (elementary
but crucial) is established between perception and memory at the
heart of this practice.

The technique of a parallelist use of memory thus implies the construction of cosmological schemas of order and even of traditional figures represented and learnt in accordance with this form. In the course
of learning a Kuna song, one learns not only a technique but also a cosmology. A mnemonic form thus becomes the starting point for a specific
style of representation. So far we have focused our attention upon one

---

2.   This is a dark red color, composed of *Bixa irellana*, which both Kuna men
     and Kuna women use as make-up.

single aspect of the exercise of memory that is typical of ritual parallelism: namely, the codification of texts, a codification that now seems far more effective and solid than a mistaken view might have suggested. But the time has come to explore another aspect of memory that implies not only the evocation of certain texts but also the margins of variation allowed by the parallelist technique, and even, as we shall see, a purposeful creation of new images.

In a series of studies devoted to the relation between social memory and history, Krzysztof Pomian has produced a very clear description of the traditional concept of the kind of social memory that is characteristic of so-called "oral" societies. For him, in a society where only an oral tradition exists, "memory is always the memory of a specific individual" (Pomian 1999: 270). It is only with the invention of writing "that the full objectivation of the contents of social memory becomes possible" (ibid.: 280).[3] Anthropologists have objected in various ways to this conception, which is, nevertheless, still widely accepted among certain historians and specialists in the social sciences. One of the most frequent arguments opposed to this point of view runs as follows: if the social memory of these societies was so exposed to the arbitrary will of individuals, we should expect to find the category of common knowledge in so-called "oral" societies in a state of constant instability and disorder. However, it has been shown many times that that is by no means the case. On the contrary, fieldwork has revealed very clearly that the transmission of common knowledge in oral societies is never left in the hands of a single person. What makes an individual representation part of a tradition is, above all, the form in which that representation is expressed. Shared knowledge is everywhere transmitted following preestablished forms. One of those forms consists in narration itself, or rather a group of stories arranged in sequences or genres endlessly revised and repeatedly told from one generation to another. Furthermore, although they are subject to a constant process of variation, these stories are, almost without exception, based upon a limited number of exemplary narrative schemas: typical sequences and characteristic models and styles that even Jack Goody (1987), an author always attentive to the variation and instability

---

3. However, it should be noted that Pomian's idea of historical memory is far more complex and should certainly not be reduced to this aspect.

of oral knowledge, has recognized as being "typical scenarios" or "plots" in African oral traditions. In the course of time, it is not the stories as such but rather these "typical scenarios" that acquire a certain stability. In this way they preserve both a relative liberty for the narrator and also the general identity of a tradition. From Vladimir Propp ([1946] 1983) down to the present day, specialists have shown, for instance, that a number of structures of this type are characteristic of European folklore. These "typical fables," which always, to a certain extent, tolerate individual variations, are neither unstable nor reducible purely to decisions made by a narrator. On the contrary, one of the particular characteristics of these stories is, precisely, that they remain relatively independent of the identity of the narrator. From the whole body of stories preserved in the folklore tradition, a story can be told by anyone without losing its character or impact. One can trust or distrust this particular way of transmitting common knowledge, but it is indisputable that a certain form of cultural memory, that is, one that is independent of any individual will, is operating in this domain.

All the same, even if we can rebut such objections where narrative traditions are concerned, that task certainly becomes more difficult when common knowledge is not formulated in narrative terms. What happens when a tradition is expressed in the form of ritual recitations? The situation that we have so far been analyzing seems closer to that described by Pomian. It is well known that in ritual ceremonies, and in particular within the framework of a ritual use of language as it is expressed in shamanistic songs, individual improvisation may play an important role. In this respect, the Amerindian tradition of shamanistic songs implies many different kinds of situations. A tradition may, of course, as in the case of the Kuna (Severi and Gomez 1983) or the Zuni case, imply a recitation of extremely long texts learnt by heart. However, the memory of a song may likewise, among Native Americans, imply a relatively free use of a small group of esoteric metaphors. That is generally the situation with Amazonian traditions (in particular, Yaminahua, Arawete, Parakana, etc.) (Viveiros de Castro 1989; Townsley 1993; Fausto [2001] 2012). In other cases, it seems that the recitation of a song may be reduced to the emission of meaningless sounds, for instance among the Guajiros of Venezuela (Perrin 1976).

However that may be, it is clear that in all these shamanistic traditions, narrative forms are quite rare. Even when present, they do not seem to constitute an essential element in the elaboration of traditional knowledge, for this seems, in general, to follow what we have called a "song-form." So how should we describe a model of cultural memory that characterizes the transmission of common knowledge in these traditions? How should we describe the process through which a certain number of representations are preserved in time and are perceived as being part of the tradition? How should we respond to the perplexity expressed by Pomian when faced with an oral transmission that seems to obey no rule and to be entirely dependent on the will of a single individual?

As in the case of European folklore, an initial response can be based on empirical factors. Even when a measure of improvisation is present, an Amerindian shamanistic song always results from learning a particular utterance technique, of which parallelism is but one example. In almost all Amerindian shamanistic traditions, improvisation is, in truth, but *one* of the rules that apply to ritual recitation. Many ethnographers have described the recitation of ritual songs in which a certain balance is always maintained between, on the one hand, what is subject to variations and, on the other, a number of passages in the text (which one might, in an analogy with vision, call the *foci* of ritual recitation) in which improvisation plays a minor role. In cases of this kind, which are frequently attested in Amazonia, learning a shamanistic song does not necessarily imply learning by heart all the details of a fixed text. But it does always imply learning a particular technique, typical of recitation, that may range from simply working on one's breathing and modulating one's voice, which needs to sound somewhat different from in daily conversation, to mastering a specific linguistic form that guides the singer-shaman in the formulation of a sequence of verbal images based on alternating fixed formulae and variations. As Graham Townsley has explained in connection with the Yaminahua of Peruvian Amazonia: "Learning to be a shaman is learning to sing, to intone the powerful chant rhythms, to carefully thread together verbal images couched in the abstruse metaphorical language of shamanic songs, and follow them" (Townsley 1993: 457).

A number of forms of ritual recitation (alternating dialogues, the enumeration of lists, the use of animal onomatopoeia, etc.), all of which are linked to parallelism, are widespread in Amerindian shamanistic traditions. However, it is not the use of one particular linguistic form that turns them into specifically ritual contexts of communication. As Albert B. Lord's remarkable research on Serbo-Croatian narrative traditions has long since shown, the citation of dialogues, the singing technique, and parallelist structures may themselves be used in nonritual contexts. So there is no reason to consider these techniques to be inherent in or constitutive of the ritual communication that characterizes shamanistic traditions throughout America.

For there is another reason why these traditions are never left to chance and cannot depend on the arbitrary will of any individual: they are shaped by the particular context of ritual interaction and communication, which, by virtue of its formal characteristics as well as its content, is always considered distinct from ordinary daily communication. For an Amerindian shaman, "singing" always signifies to perform an action, not to narrate a story. All shamanistic power, whether aimed at therapy or at pathogenic aggression, is founded upon the idea that, through a specific transformation of the "normal" use of language—what in native language may be called the use of a "twisted language" (Yaminahua) or "raising his words right" (Zuni)—the shaman becomes able to *understand, see, and name* the things of the world in an exceptional fashion. The simple fact, attested virtually everywhere, that the recitations are hardly ever fully understood by nonspecialists is enough to show that the type of communication that these traditions employ is not at all the same as ordinary communication. Of course, in order to understand its nature it is not enough simply to declare that a "special form of speech" is used in such cases or simply to note that shamanistic songs "are almost totally incomprehensible" because they are addressed to "non-human *yoshi* [spirits]," as Townsley, for instance, does (ibid.: 459). Nor can we depend upon some fine description of the metaphorical language used by the shaman in order to formulate an adequate definition of the specific formal context that confers upon the ritual communication its internal coherence. In order to understand the bases upon which this type of memory is founded, we shall have to pose some new questions. How is this specific context of communication constructed? Under what conditions does it operate? How does it influence or modify ordinary forms of communication? Until we find satisfactory answers to these questions, we shall not discover a good solution to the problem of the individuality of memory posed by Krzysztof Pomian. In order truly to understand what particular kind of cultural memory operates in such a context, we need not only to describe the linguistic forms used in the shamanistic song, but also to propose in formal terms an interpretation of the relational context that characterizes ritual communication in such cases.

A COMPLEX LOCUTOR

In a book devoted to the study of ritual action, *Naven or the other self* (Houseman and Severi 1998), Michael Houseman and I claimed that one of the crucial features of ritual communication lies in the way in which, through the establishment of a particular form of symbolic interaction, a specific identity for the participants is constructed. In the example that we analyzed, the Naven, a transvestite ritual celebrated among the Iatmul of New Guinea (already discussed above, in Chapter 1), our study of the interaction of a maternal uncle, who *acts as* a mother *and* a wife, in relation to a sister's son, who *acts as* a son *and* a husband, led us to examine a series of rituals involving larger and larger social groups, where the competition between men of the maternal side and women on the paternal side of Ego played a central role. One of our conclusions was that the identity of each of the participants is constructed, in the ritual context, from a series of contradictory connotations. For example, in that context one person will simultaneously assume the roles of mother and of son, another assumes the roles of sister's son and wife, and so on. The process of symbolic transformation realized through the ritual action, which we called a "ritual condensation," gives to the context of the communication a particular form that distinguishes it from the ordinary interactions of daily life.

My study of Native American shamanistic traditions and of the particular type of memory that they imply prompts me to extend that approach, which, hitherto, has been based almost entirely on an analysis of actions. So now I shall examine ritual situations in which action seems to play a minor role and is replaced by a special use of language. There can be no doubt that Amerindian shamanism also implies not only a particular utterance technique (ranging from a familiarity with collections of metaphors to mastery of a certain way of singing) but also a particular kind of transformation of the identity of the singer. He or, more rarely, she is never regarded as similar to everybody else. Through what he/she does, he/she becomes a kind of representative of the tradition—what one might call an "I-memory," rather than an ordinary individual. So the question that we shall be attempting to resolve will be: How, in this new context in which the only "ritual action" seems reduced to the utterance of a song, is it possible to bring about the identity-transformation that characterizes ritual interaction and to establish the specific context of communication on which this depends?

In the anthropological study of symbolism, great attention has been paid to the various ways in which language, in the course of the celebration of a ritual, transforms the participant's vision of the world, thereby constructing a universe of truth of its own. One typical way of obtaining this result, in Amerindian shamanism, consists in establishing a metaphorical link or a collection of mystical relations between ritual objects and living beings. The Celestial Jaguar in the song about madness, which managed to bring together in a single being cords used for funerary purposes, birds' voices, paintings to decorate faces, and ritual representations of the sun, provides one illustration of this way of proceeding. Another example is to be found in *The Way of Mu*, the Kuna song devoted to the therapy of difficult childbirth (Holmer and Wassén [1947] 1953). In this song, the child due to emerge from the mother's body is gradually transformed into a hybrid being with a number of heterogeneous features, which the text eventually, at the end of a long development, ends up calling "the bead from which blood drips." Let us briefly pick out the phases within the text that lead to this definition of the child. Throughout the first part of the text, the mother's body is gradually changed into a tree. After giving a very realistic description of the birthing scene and the mother's suffering, the song begins to refer to "the roots of the mother's body":

> Your stems grow.
> In the pure golden stratum of the earth . . . your root supports you. . . .
> As far as the golden stratum of earth your root stands firmly planted.
> The animals climb every single one of (your) spotted branches, every single one of your spotted branches emits juices, they drip all like blood.

This description is followed by a passage in which the suffering body of the patient is represented as a tree the branches of which bend in the wild blast of a stormy wind.

> When the north wind blows through you
> Your branches bend down with the wind . . . they are inclining in the wind. . . .

> Toward the East your silver branches are spreading . . . . (Cited in Holmer and Wassén [1947] 1953: 56–57, ll. 184–88)[4]

From this point on, the shaman-singer begins to refer, on the one hand, to the mother as a "bleeding tree" and, on the other, to the child as the "fruit" that is "coming out" from the tree. The shaman sings:

> Every single one of your spotted branches
> emits juices, they drip all like blood. (Cited in Holmer and Wassén [1947] 1953: l. 184)

This series of transformations (itself founded upon a double analogy between the body of the mother and the tree and also between the child and the fruit) is here followed by another series constructed through the implicit establishment of another analogy, based on the axis fruit/glass beads. Thus, having mentioned a "fruit from which blood drips," as a symbolic equivalent of the child, the song ends this series of transformations by speaking of a "bead from which blood drips." By following this process it will be possible, later in the song, to find statements such as the following one, in which a similar child/bleeding fruit/glass pearl axis is later developed:

> Your striped necklace beads open up inside, all red.
> Your necklace beads are all reeking with blood. (Cited in Holmer and Wassén [1947] 1953: 59, l. 227–28)

---

4. See also ibid.: 58, l. 213. I have revised and checked all the translations of the Kuna text.

Even without carrying this analysis of the text further, we can say that the equivalence established between the fruit and the child at this point already suggests a series of "implicit thoughts" that could be summarized as follows:

- The mother is a tree.
- The baby is a fruit.
- The body of the mother bleeds.
- The tree is bleeding.
- The fruit of the tree is bleeding.
- The fruit is a ritual bead.
- The bead (that is to say, the baby) is bleeding.

Through a progressive extension of this way of transferring groups of analogical connotations to various objects and living beings, the Kuna shamanistic tradition effects an entire ritual transformation of the universe. The linguistic instrument that serves to bring out these transformations is the same as that used by shamans to memorize songs and pictographic images. Again, the technique is parallelism, that way of "carefully thread[ing] together verbal images," as Townsley has put it (Townsley 1993: 457), which the Kuna practice with extraordinary skill. At this point it is quite clear that parallelism is not just a technique of recitation. When applied to a description of suffering, as in this case, this technique also becomes a way to construct a supernatural dimension, regarded as an invisible double or at least a possible world that exists in parallel to the real world. For example, in this context, the shaman who speaks of a "fruit from which blood drips" is referring both to the real experience of a mother and to a Tree-Woman who engenders human fruits. It is at the heart of this process of evocation linked with the recitation of songs organized in sequences of constants and variants that the ambiguous beings in continual metamorphosis that I have called "parallelist creatures" are born. An organized exercise of a technique for remembering thus also directs the type of imagination that is at work within traditional knowledge.

But let us go further. As we have noted, the shamanistic tradition of songs is not characterized solely by the exercise of a mnemonic technique founded on parallelism. Throughout America, these traditions also presuppose a certain transformation of the image of the locutor. At the same time as being an ordinary individual (as Pomian wished to see him), he always assumes the role of a representative of the tradition. His voice becomes the voice of common knowledge. So a conscious transformation of speech that is ritually uttered entails a transformation of the image of the locutor. How does this process come about? As we shall see, the same instrument of transformation that I have so far described as a means of transforming the image of the exterior world can also be used, *in a reflexive form*, in order to transform the image of the locutor. It is by means of this crucial switch from an objective use to the reflexive use of the parallelist technique that, in the case of American shamanistic traditions, the context characteristic of ritual communication is established. As we shall see, it is within this context that a more specific mnemonic effect is produced: the creation of a belief.

But now let us return to the Kuna song devoted to therapy for a difficult birth and continue our analysis. As in many other songs in the Kuna tradition, *The Way of Mu* begins with an introduction that contains a detailed evocation of the ritual gestures and procedures that are necessary for the utterance of a song. In the preliminary section, we find the shaman in his hut, asking his wife to prepare him a meal of boiled plantains. We see him go off to the river to wash, then, sitting on his ceremonial seat, in dead silence, starting to burn cocoa seeds in the brazier placed before him. He then gathers together the statuettes that will attend the utterance of the ritual song, sits down again, and finally begins to sing. In *The Way of Mu*, a text to which we shall soon be returning and which Claude Lévi-Strauss (1963) mentioned in a famous article ("The effectiveness of symbols"), this section occupies much of the transcription of the song published by Holmer and Wassén in 1953. It precedes a description that is more familiar to specialists in shamanism, that of the adventures of a soul ravished by spirits whose absence prompts the pathology. But let us take a closer look at a passage from this "introduction":

> The midwife opens the door of the hut.
> The door of the medicine man's hut creaks.
> The midwife is about to enter the medicine man's door.
> The medicine man is lying down in the hammock in front of her.
> The (chief) wife of the medicine man is also about to lie down beside the medicine man.

The midwife comes to address the medicine man.

The medicine man asks: "Why have you come before me?"

The medicine man asks: "Why have you come to see me?"

The midwife answers . . . "My (sick) woman feels that she is being dressed in the hot garment of the disease."

The medicine man says (to the midwife): "Your (sick) woman says she is being dressed in the hot garment of the disease, I also hear."

The medicine man asks (the midwife): "For how many days has your woman suffer the hot garment of the disease?"

The midwife answers (the medicine man): "For two days my (sick) woman feels that she is being dressed in the hot garment of the disease."

The medicine man says (to the midwife): "For two days your (sick) woman feels that she is being dressed in the hot garment of the disease."

The medicine man says (to the midwife): "Having (then) no lights to see by, I shall enter into the dark inner place."

The midwife puts forth her foot (to go).

The midwife touches the ground with her foot.

The midwife puts her other foot forward.

The midwife is about to leave the medicine man's door.

The midwife puts forth her foot (to go).

The midwife touches the ground with her foot.

The midwife puts her other foot forward.

The midwife is about to enter the (sick) woman's door.

The medicine man lowers his leg from the hammock.

The medicine man rises to his feet from the hammock.

The medicine man takes hold of (his) staff.

The medicine man turns about in the hut.

The midwife puts forth her foot (to go).

The midwife touches the ground with her foot.

The midwife puts her other foot forward.

The medicine man arrives at the door of his hut.

The medicine man pushes the door of his hut open.

The door of the medicine man's hut creaks.

Outside his place the medicine man stands looking about in confusion.

The medicine man turns his steps toward the path of the woman's hut.

The medicine man puts forth his foot on the path to the woman's hut.

The medicine man puts down his foot on the path to the woman's hut.

The medicine man is about to enter the (sick) woman's door.
A small golden seat is put under the hammock of the (sick) woman.
The medicine man sits down on the small golden seat.
Under the woman's hammock there is put a brazier, the brazier being concave.
The medicine man looks for cocoa beans.
The medicine man puts the cocoa beans into the hollow of the brazier.
The cocoa beans are being burned.
The cocoa beans are healing.
The (smoke of the) cocoa beans fill up the hut.

In order to understand the paradox implied by a description of this type, we need to bear in mind that, in this passage of the song, all that the shaman is describing (the dialogue with the midwife, the meeting with the woman, and finally the preparation of the brazier, which is fundamental to the therapeutic rite) *has already taken place* when the singer begins his song. In other words, if we change the perspective and move from a simple reading of the text to a description of the conditions in which the utterance of the ritual recitation takes place, we discover that the shaman always uses the third-person singular to refer to himself. In this way a kind of *regressus ad infinitum* is produced: a shaman, sitting by his brazier beneath the hammock containing the sick woman, speaks of a shaman sitting by his brazier beneath a hammock containing the sick woman, . . . and so on. Before starting to sing, the shaman describes himself in the act of starting to sing.

This is not the first time that I have analyzed this situation at the start of a Kuna ritual recitation (see Severi 1993c). But for a long time I thought that this passage in the song just reflected a quite simple mnemonic strategy. As an example of the many "ways of speaking" that characterize Kuna society (Sherzer 1983), *The Way of Mu* includes a description of its own conditions of utterance. In view of the importance that Kuna shamans attach to the circumstances in which a song is uttered, it seemed to me quite natural that the tradition should expect to transmit not only the content of its songs but also its "instructions for use" in the ritual utterance. The simplest way of transmitting those instructions had to be to put them into words and turn them into a kind of "introductory section" of the text.

Now, though, I can see that that interpretation explained only one superficial aspect of ritual utterance; and I think that it is possible to go further. As we have already seen, the act of singing, by describing "someone who is about to begin to sing," entails at least one consequence. The action introduces a paradox regarding the timing of the action. If we bear in mind that, almost without exception, the only tense used in this part of the text is the present, this will be quite clear. We have already noted that, in the passage in question, the locutor declares that he is approaching the ritual seat, the hammock, the door, and then the path leading to the woman's hut, and so on, at a moment when he has already performed those actions. He finds himself sitting, as tradition dictates, facing "in the direction of the East" and "toward the sea." The immediate consequence that follows from this timeless description is that all that is expressed here in the present tense in fact refers to the past. This perspective, which is paradoxical from the point of view of time, affects the ritual situation in a number of ways. One of these is particularly important for an understanding of the definition of the identity of the locutor. When this present tense, which really refers to the past and is here a feature of speech ritually delivered, meets with the real present—that is to say, when the fictitious description of the situation becomes a realistic description of the conditions in which the utterance occurs (with the shaman now truly seated on the ceremonial seat and in reality beginning to sing), a paradoxical situation arises, one absolutely impossible in daily life, where "someone is speaking about someone actually speaking." In such a case, we should not forget one essential point: it is precisely when this description of the position of the locutor is produced that "the particular mode of communication" peculiar to ritual singing is achieved. Once this part of the song has been correctly uttered, the shaman's journey in the supernatural world can begin. It is at this moment that the song becomes an effective therapeutic instrument. A simple narrative about a journey in the beyond would, in the eyes of the Kuna, have no therapeutic effect at all.

So why does this strange "utterance of an utterance" turn out to be necessary here? What is changed by this apparently paradoxical description by the locutor? This definition of the shaman as "a locutor designating a locutor" ceases to be paradoxical once we understand that what is involved here is another use of that same parallelism that has already engendered chimerical figures in a state of perpetual transformation, such as the Celestial Jaguar or the Tree-Woman. In order to define himself as a shaman, the singer of *The Way of Mu* resorts to the same technique as that which we have seen used in the text when the child is progressively transformed into a "fruit from which blood drips." This technique for transforming a body, a real person, into a supernatural presence, which is described by the song, in this instance applies to the locutor himself. The transformation is never explicitly described in the text itself, as it is in the case of the mother in *The Way of Mu*, who gradually becomes a tree, or in the case of the child who becomes a fruit. Nevertheless, from the moment when the singer starts to speak of a singer who recites a song, from the point of view of the definition of the identity of that locutor, an entirely new situation is created. Two locutors have appeared, the one being a parallel image of the other. There is, on the one hand, the locutor described as belonging to the faraway world (in the supernatural scene described by the song, preparing for a journey in quest of a lost soul) and, on the other, another locutor who is here, in the real hut, beneath the hammock in which the ailing woman lies. In his song, the latter locutor describes the one who is elsewhere.

This first, still quite elementary model of the process of constructing a plural locutor constitutes neither an episodic detail nor an exception. On the contrary, this way of "doubling the presence" of the singer by introducing a temporal paradox in the image conveyed by the song illustrates but one of the simplest ways of defining a ritual and plural locutor in shamanistic literature. As we shall see, this process may assume extremely elaborate forms in Amerindian shamanistic traditions. Furthermore, this initial analysis may help us to find an answer to the question asked above relating to the context of ritual communication in the case of Amerindian shamanism.

I have mentioned the hypothesis[5] that a context of communication becomes ritual (and therefore more subject to improvisation than a narrative form but nevertheless extremely memorable) when there is a transformation of the identity of participants, founded on the simultaneous presence of contradictory connotations. I have also added that in the Iatmul case, this analysis was made easier by the fact that in the transvestite ritual that I had been studying, the ritual interaction was almost entirely expressed by actions. But how is it possible to construct

---

5.   This hypothesis was formulated in Houseman and Severi (1998).

a ritual identity of that kind in a situation in which, as in the traditions of Amerindian shamanistic songs, only a recitation of ritual speech is present, in which actions may be described but not carried out?

The elementary process described above seems to offer an initial ritual way of multiplying the identities of the locutor. Now let us look more closely into the relational context in which such a transformation, which will lead to the construction of a particularly complex image of the locutor, can come about and be developed.

It would certainly not be useful at this point to examine all the recent literature devoted to Amerindian shamanism. So let us focus first upon just one point. Shamanistic "therapy" is, in almost the whole of America, represented as the result of a confrontation between two rivals. On the one hand, we find the pathogenic spirit (often embodied in the image of a predatory animal such as a jaguar or an anaconda), on the other, the shaman, aided by his spirit-assistant, which is often imagined (as in the Kuna case) as a spirit of a vegetal nature that possesses the power to cure. This kind of ritual intervention has long been considered as analogous to the Siberian model. According to the latter, the aim of the shaman's intervention is to reintegrate into the body of the patient a soul or a spiritual principle that is missing. For this reason, many scholars, rather in the wake of Mircea Eliade ([1951] 1989), continue to repeat that the symbolism of shamanistic ritual is based on the idea of a "cosmological journey" that the shaman undertakes in order to retrieve the spirit that has "stolen" a soul. Numerous ethnographic studies today[6] enable us to see clearly that, while that approach may account partially for the indigenous discourse about the activities of a shaman, it provides no explanation for the complexity of the ritual practices acted out by Amerindian shamans. To put that another way, this perspective perhaps explains what the shamans, when they offer an ethnologist a commentary on their activities, *say they are doing*. But it throws no light at all upon what they are really doing when performing a ritual, nor does it explain the texts that

---

6.   For the Amerindian area, see, for example, Crocker (1985); Descola and Taylor (1993); Severi (1993c, 2001a); Townsley (1993); Wilbert (1993); Descola (1996); Carneiro de Cunha (1998). In Asia, see in particular, Sales (1991); Humphrey (1996).

they actually recite in their songs, in which they always tackle the theme of a "journey" in an unexpected, complex, and specific way.

Researchers more attentive to the ethnographic reality have accordingly turned toward the performative aspect of shamanistic songs, paying renewed attention to the way in which a series of symbolic transformations take place through a special use of speech. Some of them (for example, Tedlock 1983; Tambiah 1985) have certainly understood that this aspect is just as important as the narrative aspect of the shaman's song, if not more so.

In the light of this new approach, an understanding of shamanism is not simply a matter of describing the underlying categories of shamanistic discourse. It also involves understanding what is concretely taking place on the ritual stage, which is conveyed by an absolutely specific use of the modalities of vocal expression that may affect many aspects of speech, ranging from a purely sonorous modulation of the voice to the use of a special language. Edmund Leach has pointed out that in ritual language, "it is not the case that the words are one thing, and the rite another. The uttering of the words is itself a ritual" (Leach 1966: 407). That is certainly true of Amerindian shamanistic traditions.

More recently, it has been recognized that Amerindian shamanistic ritual includes two essential aspects: a specific process of metamorphosis that is implied by the model of a journey, and the idea of a symbolic predation that the shaman engages in against a pathogenic animal spirit. One may conclude from this that "singing in order to heal" is the equivalent of setting off to hunt the most dangerous hunters of humans, frequently represented, as noted above, by a supernatural animal that may be a mythical jaguar or anaconda. In this context, the illness appears not as a relatively indefinite "external malady," but as a crisis in one's relationship to oneself.

These new approaches have shed considerable fresh light upon our understanding of shamanistic traditions: ritual speech is no longer regarded as an isolated fragment of what is in many cases an imaginary discourse concerning Native Americans' idea of the origin or nature of the universe; rather, it is seen as the instrument of an act of symbolic predation (Descola 1996). This new view of a shaman, no longer seen as an isolated figure but instead as the end result of a complex web of relations (such as those represented by the model of symbolic predation), certainly constitutes progress. Nevertheless, the nature of the relationship that is established, in the course of the ritual, between the shaman and his supernatural rival still remains very inadequately understood, as does the relationship that links the shaman to the sick person.

It is clear that the ritual identity assumed by the shaman in the course of the ritual cannot be reduced purely to an inversion of the image of his supernatural adversary. Significantly enough, in cases where the ethnography is able to provide a detailed picture of the activity of a shaman, the figure of the shaman becomes increasingly paradoxical. True, he may be represented as the principal enemy of a jaguar or an anaconda. But often enough he is represented *also as a possible incarnation* of those animal spirits. As a result, the ritual identity of the shaman may oscillate between the image of a therapeutic and beneficent spirit and the threatening image of a symbolic predator (Crocker 1985; Viveiros de Castro 1989). The most gripping example of that ambivalence, almost always presented in a latent form, is probably that of the Achuar of Equadorian Amazonia, where it is believed that every case of sickness tended by a shaman has in reality been provoked by another shaman (Descola 1996).

This ambivalence deserves our full attention. Almost everywhere in America, one crucial—but little-studied—aspect emerges clearly: becoming the adversary of a supernatural being is never a process that can lead to a permanent symbolic status or a stable social function. Regardless of whether the shaman's function is therapeutic or divinatory, either it is always so widely generalized that any member of the group may assume the function, or else it is extremely unstable. To be able to act as a shaman and effect a cure, for example, is a very special and temporary state of body and mind. It is a state that must be reacquired each time one celebrates a therapeutic ritual. To be able to chase away a supernatural predator, it is necessary for the shaman to undergo a specific transformation every time he celebrates a ritual. His symbolic state and the identity that implies his power are thus *inherent in the ritual action.* Ritually constructed and often linked to the use of hallucinogenic drugs, this state threatens to disappear once the ritual is over. It is on account of this that the paradoxical representation of the shaman is not reduced solely to an ambiguous concept of his powers. That ambiguity has a form of its own.

Considered from the point of view of the relations that it implies, the ritual identity of the shaman, which in fact makes him both a predator and an antipredator, is in reality founded upon a collection of contradictory connotations. So it assumes the full complexity that is characteristic of all ritual relations (Houseman and Severi 1998). It is when seen from this angle that the construction of the identity of the shaman as a complex or plural locutor, an example of which we have found in *The Way of Mu*, reveals its real meaning. Furthermore, this is by no means an isolated case. *The Song of the Demon*, the Nia Igala, a song used to cure what the Kuna today call *locura*, madness, presents a particularly elaborate example of such a construction of the ritual identity of the shaman-singer. The notion upon which the ritual recitation is based is well known: the Celestial Jaguar has attacked a human being; in consequence, that person finds himself (or herself) obliged to imitate the behavior of the supernatural predator and may, at any moment, himself (or herself) become a predator, in Kuna terms "a hunter of men."[7] As indigenous peoples see it, the sick person may penetrate the dreams and thoughts of others and in this way provoke other anxieties and bouts of madness. In the shamanistic tradition, this contagious state is described as a progressive imitation of an animal spirit. Such a process, set off by the appearance of occasional behavior-crises, may lead to total identification with the supernatural jaguar. At this stage in the pathology, the person affected by what the Kuna call "madness" is definitely regarded as the incarnation of a pathogenic spirit. The logic of the model of interpretation linked with the idea of symbolic predation that I have mentioned above would normally lead us to expect a direct confrontation between, on the one hand, a therapeutic spirit of a vegetal nature, allied to human beings, and, on the other, a pathogenic spirit of an animal nature. The jaguar's act of hunting would in this way be balanced by a reciprocal attack in the form of a symbolical hunt aimed against it.

In the Kuna song about madness, as in many other cases, the situation is far more complicated. In the first place, the jaguar that the shaman must confront is not an animal like any other; it is always represented as a creature of a quite exceptional nature that possesses a hybrid

---

7. The Kuna term is *tulekintaked*. (In this connection, see Severi 1993c: 49–69.)

ontological status very different from that of the predators that one may come across in real life. As we have seen, the Celestial Jaguar is always represented as a double being. When it appears in a song, it is never altogether itself: it may appear either as a bird that roars like a jaguar or as a jaguar with the singing voice of a bird. This double nature of the jaguar is represented by means of a perfect application of the parallelist technique, which, as we have seen, makes it possible to construct veritable mosaics of words (Severi 1993c: 126–29).

As a threatening incarnation of death and madness, the Celestial Jaguar is defined here as an animal in a state of perpetual metamorphosis. Indeed, it is precisely this partial ontological coincidence, this intersection of two animal species, a bird and a jaguar, that traditionally conveys its supernatural status (Severi 2001a, 2002b).

Secondly, we should not forget that this double being is always represented as being invisible. Its presence is manifested solely by sound. The sole images capable of representing it appear either through dazzling sunlight or else as dream-images that can only be seen by closed eyes. Furthermore, the presence of the Jaguar cannot be perceived through its own voice, but only through a series of cries from other animals. When the Jaguar passes through the forest, it manifests its presence by provoking a characteristic series of animal cries. In such a situation, a hunter passing through the forest will hear the cry of a bird or a monkey, the grunting of a wild boar, or the cry of a deer, but he will never be able to see any of those animals. The Jaguar, trapped in a ceaseless series of metamorphoses and endowed with multiple identities, will manifest itself through a *series* of animal cries.

In order to do battle with such an exceptional animal, the shaman must be able to experience an analogous transformation. He must change into a multiple being endowed, like the Jaguar, with a plural identity. This symbolic transformation takes place, in the ritual, through the establishment of a complex relationship between the celebrant and the animal predator. Adopting the Jaguar's form of existence, a form that is realized mainly in sounds, the shaman, in order to conquer that multiple identity, must acquire what one might call a *complex voice*: a voice within which a whole collection of different creatures, potential enemies, can be evoked.

Conversely in the Kuna tradition, the madness of a patient is, right from the start, interpreted in acoustic terms: madness indicates the presence of the Jaguar within the body of the sick person. The latter accepts the Jaguar in his thoughts and his dreams and is thereby forced to "speak its language." A Kuna shaman has two means of battling against this emergence of animal speech within the voice of a human being. In the first part of his song he explores the supernatural path that leads to the place where the missing soul, the *purpa* that presides over the exercise of thought, has been hidden by the spirits. As he does so, he begins to speak "the language of the vegetal spirits," the language in which Kuna shamanistic songs are transmitted. The shaman-singer identifies thus with a seer spirit of the forest, in particular the balsa tree, represented as an aged diviner who acts as an auxiliary spirit. In this way, the shaman embodies two powers, the power to heal and the power to see what is not visible to the profane. This first transformation is linked to the doubling of his identity, as both the singer and the song's protagonist, as has been mentioned above. Now, when he pronounces the word "shaman" (designating himself in the third person), the celebrant will be referring to *the me that belongs to the song*, as a diviner spirit of a vegetal nature.

This is but the first stage in the definition of the shaman's ritual identity. In the narration of his shamanistic journey, once he has reached the place where the lost soul is located, the symbolic relationship that links him to the patient undergoes a radical change. At this point the shaman must not only embody the vegetal seer-spirit but also represent the animal spirits residing in the patient's body, or rather he must lend them his voice. As soon as he starts to describe the village in which these spirits live, as the song requires him to do, he begins to emit long series of animal cries. These are the "hunting cries" shouted by the animal spirits, the *nias* into which the Jaguar transforms itself, one by one. Now a bird is heard, then a monkey, a boar, a deer, and so on. Here is the text:

> Here the *nias* (spirits) turn into peccaries, the peccaries are there, with their black clothes. They cry "ya-ya-ya-ya."
> The peccaries are now changed into *nias*, they are transformed into *nias*, the *nias* are transformed.
> They are transformed into lords of animals with the striped fur; above the trees, the *nias* with the striped fur cry "turku-turku."

The animals with the striped fur are now changed into deer, the *nias* are there, at the foot of the tree, with their black clothes, with their antlers intertwined, with their great pointed antlers, they cry "me-me."
The young deer now change into *nias*, the *nias* are transformed [. . .]
Into monkeys the *nias* are transformed; up there, above the trees, the *nias* now cry "ti-ti-ti-ti," . . . "uli-uli," . . . "uma-uma." (Cited in Severi 1993c: 138–40, l. 251)

Thus, in this crucial section of *The Song of the Demon*, the shaman sings not only as a vegetal spirit of the forest but also, and—so to speak—simultaneously, as an animal spirit. Through the sequence of animal cries in this phase of the ritual recitation, what is present is the multiple voice of the Celestial Jaguar. In this way the shaman becomes a unique and unexpected species of locutor, constituted by a series of connotations that at the same time indicate both allied spirits and enemy ones and both vegetal and animal ones, the divine sage represented by the balsa tree and also the Celestial Jaguar.

This reflexive use of the parallelist technique which—as we have seen—characterizes the locutor of *The Way of Mu*, in which the shaman starts to sing by describing himself in the act of singing, was thus just an introduction to the process, which, at this point, produces spectacular results. In the sequence of *The Song of the Demon*, analyzed above, a whole crowd of contradictory connotations (on the temporal, spatial, and generally symbolic planes) are heaped upon the figure of the locutor of the song. The shaman becomes a complex locutor, able to lend his voice to a series of different invisible beings. What, in *The Way of Mu*, was just a relatively simple means of doubling the presence of the locutor here develops into a wider process that ends up by concentrating upon the singer a whole series of contradictory identities. You could say that the shaman's voice receives the *echo* of the cries of the animal spirits.

We may thus conclude that the native discourse on shamanistic therapy (a discourse that constitutes an *ideology*) is founded, in Amerindian shamanism, upon the symbolic opposition of two terms: on the one hand, the patient seen as an animal spirit; on the other, the therapist considered as a spirit of a vegetal nature. However, from a relational point of view, we have to recognize that the shaman's identity, as realized on the ritual stage, is very much more complex. It is based on a cumulative process through which the features characteristic of one of the poles of the patient–Jaguar opposition are gradually drawn into the sphere of influence of the other pole (the vegetal shaman). The ritual identity of the shaman in this way, through the sonorous manifestation of the different voices that appear in the locutor's own voice, thus takes on a logical status comparable to that which is attributed to the supernatural Jaguar, by subsuming a series of contradictory connotations situated at different logical levels (Figure 78).

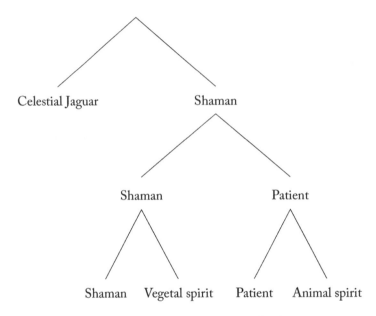

Figure 78. The complex identity of a shaman.

We should not forget, however, that the only means of bringing about this transformation lies in the context of the ritual recitation. No gestures accompany that recitation: Kuna shamans remain completely still throughout the ritual. All the same, the speech pronounced is not treated solely as a means of describing or even of transforming an image of the world—as it is in the case of the Tree-Woman or the child "bead from which blood drips" in *The Way of Mu*. Here the recitation is used, above all, as a means of designating the identity of a voice, a complex voice which, in its turn, indicates the exceptional nature of its locutor. Through the appearance of animal cries within the "vegetal language of songs," the supernatural predator and his human adversary become perceptible simultaneously. There they become present on the ritual stage.

Let us conclude this analysis of the Kuna case by formulating the hypothesis that it is precisely this specific use of language—relatively distinct from the actual meaning of the texts—that characterizes the song-form as it is attested in Amerindian shamanistic traditions. Here the language is used not only as a way of engendering meaning or as a "magic" way of bringing about a therapeutic act, but above all as an *acoustic mask*: a reflexive means of engendering the ritual identity of the locutor.

So now we can reply to the question posed at the start of this chapter: namely, how, in formal terms, to describe this specific context that turns ritual communication (in our case, within the shamanistic song-form) into a way of communicating that is radically different from ordinary communication. The answer is that the ritual context, as illustrated here, is distinct from ordinary communication in that, over and above the meaning of the words, it highlights certain pragmatic aspects of communication and subjects them to an unexpected elaboration founded upon a reflexive and parallelist definition of the locutor. This is a locutor to whom there will always be attributed speech unlike any other kind of speech, not only with regard to the style or the kind of metaphors employed, but also and above all on account of this complex construction of a figure quite distinct from the real locutor, a figure that I suggest calling an "I-memory."

Let us now aim for a deeper understanding of the context of the utterance of ritual speech and ask what mental states are implied by it. From this point of view, there can be no doubt that one of the mental states characteristic of a ritual performance (as compared, for example, to a simple narrative and to the feeling of expectation, the act of listening with one's eyes that every successful narrative instills in the listener) is the establishment of a belief. It is natural enough to think that a representation that is the object of a belief becomes relatively stable in a society's memory. Such a representation is crystallized at the heart of shared beliefs and thereby becomes "memorable" for the members of that society. Belief is certainly also a way of fixing certain particular representations amid the flood of those that are possible. In such a case the constitution of a social memory is no longer based solely on the source of the representation but, on the contrary, on its recipient, who, even as he/she believes, also generates memories.

It has been noted several times that ritual fosters a paradoxical relationship with belief. On the one hand, rituals, in that they are made up of sequences of symbolic actions, have frequently been described as attempts to create belief in the supernatural world. Pierre Smith is convincing enough when he suggests that the establishment of a belief is a good criterion for distinguishing "true rituals" from other, vaguer, contexts of social interaction that merely resemble them: for example, festivals, dances, and other profane celebrations (Smith [1979] 1982). At the same time, it is quite clear that the kind of beliefs that a ritual seems able to instill is never really dissociated from doubt and uncertainty. One group of young anthropologists (Højbjerg, Rubow, and Sjørslev 1999) has pointed out, with considerable subtlety, that rituals never fail to provoke commentaries on what they constitute or what they may achieve. This means not only that traditional societies, both in Europe and elsewhere, are far from being societies of believers, but also that a reflexive attitude, linked to the very nature of the ceremonial action, is seldom absent from the performance of a ritual.

Rituals do not exist solely to affirm the existence of a supernatural world. They also exist in order to defy that world to reveal itself in order publicly to demonstrate its existence and its efficacy. Unlike a story that is told, a ritual does not only aim to engender adhesion, an immediate belief that is provisional yet spontaneous and that results simply from listening to the story. Instead, it arouses a sense of doubt, a need for proof. If that is true, then the existence of doubt in the context of ritual cannot be limited to a commentary concerning the present circumstances surrounding the celebration of a ceremony. Doubt can even become a constitutive element in the ritual act itself (Severi 2002a). A particular kind of uncertainty, the nature of which I shall try to illuminate, in this way changes from being an external element into being one of the basic features of ritual actions.

We have considered ritual speech, as characterized by a particular type of communication. Then we have managed to define, more precisely, the conditions of such communication, from the point of view of its locutor. We have seen that what is transformed in this type of communication is the premise upon which all utterance depends: the very identity of the locutor. Now we can try to pin down the consequences that this particular type of utterance wreaks upon its listeners. To put that another way, in order to delve more deeply into the ways of constituting a ritual memory, we must now seek to understand the aspect which, in speech act theory, is known as the *perlocutionary effect* of such speech.[8]

Let us try to grasp what effect upon a listener might result from this multiple definition of the locutor, as formulated in shamanistic songs. We already know that ritual speech engenders not only a simple state of belief but also a mental state the definition of which is more complex: a particular tension between doubt and belief that appears typical of a ritual performance. Let us consider one particular aspect of this situation: the fictitious nature of the locutor and the possible modes in which he might be represented. As we have seen, an Amerindian shaman transcends his ordinary identity and acquires a new one, which results from a series of metamorphoses that are invariably fragile and are linked solely to the ritual performance. We can now compare this mode of defining a locutor with other types of interactive situations in which a definition of a locutor's fictitious or special identity may emerge.

A familiar situation in which a "special" identity of the locutor is produced is a theatrical performance. Suppose, for example, that in a performance of Christopher Marlowe's magnificent *Tamburlaine the Great*, an actor playing the role of the cruel emperor declaims the following words:

I hold the Fates bound fast in iron chains
And with my hands turn Fortune's wheel about,
And sooner shall the sun fall from his sphere
Than Tamburlaine be slain or overcome.
Draw forth thy sword, thou mighty man-at-arms,
Intending but to raze my charmed skin
And Jove himself will stretch his hand from heaven
To ward the blow and shield me safe from harm. (Marlowe [1590] 1950: Act I, Scene II)

Now let us consider the actor's intervention on stage from a formal point of view, that which we adopted in our analysis of the shamanistic

---

8. Austin (1962), later followed by Searle (1969), uses the word "perlocutionary" to express the effect produced on a subject by the formulation of a speech act.

song. Given that, by definition, the public considers that the actor is just playing the role of Tamburlaine, the identities of the emperor and the actor are mutually exclusive. The actor, the image of the character who appears on stage, may be identified *either* as "Tamburlaine the emperor" while he expresses his defiance, *or else* as Mr. X, the famous Elizabethan actor. The emotions and thoughts that he expresses and even some of his physical features, such as the *charmed skin* that he claims to possess, are, naturally, attributed to the emperor, not to the person interpreting the role of Tamburlaine. On stage, in the theater, those two identities are bound to alternate, because the context allows no confusion and keeps them in a relationship of reciprocal exclusion. When I *believe in* Tamburlaine, I do not recognize the actor, and vice versa. The perlocutionary effect of this situation is clear: during even the most successful interpretation of the dramatic character, no confusion as to the identity of the locutor on stage is possible, for when we enter the theater we accept without difficulty the type of relationship to the fiction that this kind of representation implies.

Now let us return to the case of the Amerindian shaman reciting a ritual song, standing outside his hut, and let us compare it to the representation of Marlowe's drama. The first difference is of a formal nature. The two locutors, the actor and the shaman, possess a different identity as soon as they set foot on stage or begin to recite a song. However, the shaman, unlike the actor, *does not alternate* different definitions of his identity that are mutually exclusive. Indeed, on the contrary, he progressively accumulates on his own image as a locutor (a figure that he himself designates: "the shaman is now entering the hut . . .") a whole series of contradictory but not exclusive identities: first as a vegetal spirit, then as a deer, a monkey, a peccary, a boar, and so on.

So his definition as locutor, like that of the actor playing the role of Tamburlaine, is different from that of everyday life. However, the type of fiction implied by this type of communication is, despite appearances, radically different from that seen on the theater stage. And this first formal difference (the construction of a cumulative identity instead of the constitution of an alternate actor/stage character-identity) gives rise to a second important difference that concerns the creation of the perlocutionary effect of the shamanistic recitation. By heaping upon his own image as locutor a whole series of contradictory yet not exclusive identities, the figure of the shaman arouses and maintains doubt as to his precise transformation into other identities that are at once latent and indecipherable. As the recitation proceeds, his image progressively becomes a paradoxical figure. As such, this figure of the shaman prompts questions that remain *impossible to answer*: Has he *really* become a vegetal or animal spirit? Has he become a boar, a monkey, a deer, a jaguar? Has he really been transformed in the course of the recitation of his song? Will he really be capable, as he claims, of transforming himself yet again, every time this turns out to be necessary?

Here, the ritual action constructs a specific kind of fiction, a special context of communication in which *any* response, whether positive or negative, implies doubt, uncertainty. Everyone has to believe but no-one is truly convinced. If we bear in mind Pierre Smith's suggestion—to consider as "true rituals" only ceremonies that engender belief in the supernatural—we can make more headway in our demonstration. Linguistic communication becomes ritual when a particular mode of elaborating a complex image of the locutor is constructed in such a way as to create the specific tension between doubt and belief that defines the effect of ritual action. As we have seen, in Amerindian shamanistic traditions, constructing what is memorable means not only acquiring a codification technique linked with a specific linguistic form (parallelism), but also decoding verbal and graphic images. Now we can add that that memory is further sustained by a reflexive elaboration of the figure of the locutor—an image entirely constructed by a special use of uttered speech—as well as by its perlocutionary effect: that tension between doubt and acceptance which, in its deepest nature, characterizes the very act of belief.

PROJECTION AND BELIEF

> *It would be convenient to dismiss these difficulties by declaring that we are dealing with psychological cures. But this term will remain meaningless unless one can explain how specific psychological representations are invoked to combat equally specific physiological disturbances.*
>
> Lévi-Strauss, "The effectiveness of symbols"

Our analysis should lead us to reflect not only upon the situation that arises, within a tradition, between the processes of memorization and the establishment of belief, but also upon the very nature of the latter concept. We should not forget that the Kuna case prompted the formulation of a theory that has exerted considerable influence upon the way that belief operates in shamanistic traditions. Of course, this involves what Claude Lévi-Strauss called the theory of symbolic efficacy. Let us return to thinking about belief as a means of constructing a common memory, taking as our starting point a brief rereading of Lévi-Strauss' "The effectiveness of symbols" (1963). More than fifty years on from its first publication, this essay retains all the qualities that made it such a memorable text. The style is limpid, the analysis of facts is brilliant, and the comparison between the case of shamanism and the psychoanalysis of those years is rigorous and founded on first-hand knowledge. The central idea that organizes the text as a whole deserves, still today, to be reread and discussed. For Lévi-Strauss, the Freudian unconscious was part of a more extensive group of the functions of human symbolism. These lead from organic processes to conscious inferences, in accordance with a model derived from Bernard Russell's theory of types, later also adopted by Gregory Bateson.

As is well known, the subject of Lévi-Strauss' study is *The Way of Mu*, the Kuna song, discussed above, that is devoted to therapy for difficult instances of childbirth. In this text, the spirits that have set off in search of the lost soul, the absence of which has provoked the suffering of the woman in labor, "visit" a mysterious mythical landscape. As Lévi-Strauss shows, this supernatural universe represents the suffering body of the woman. In the course of the narrative telling of the itinerary of the shaman's spirits, "palpitating mountains" thus appear, along with "rivers of blood" and strange monsters which, caught in the act of biting and attacking, symbolically represent the pain felt by the woman. Through the sung recitation, what Lévi-Strauss calls "an affective geography" is thus progressively engendered. The supernatural landscape evoked by the shaman is based in the living body of the mother who is in such pain.

In the Kuna shamanistic tradition, the classic journey of the shaman thus becomes the means of a remarkable operation that Lévi-Strauss calls a "psychological manipulation" of physical pain. The story told in the song becomes a means of constructing a sequence of representations in which the pain, at first impossible to formulate in its terrible intensity, *becomes expressible through a suitable symbolism*. Lévi-Strauss' principal thesis is that the shaman in this way performs an operation analogous to that of psychoanalytical therapy, the aim of which is, precisely, to reconstruct *in a new language* what, because of the repression of unconscious conflicts, may have disappeared from the patient's conscious experience. The shaman of a so-called "primitive" society and the Western psychoanalyst thus find themselves for the first time—and despite the enormous cultural differences that separate them—compared to each other.

Although relatively brief, "The effectiveness of symbols" is probably one of Lévi-Strauss' most ambitious texts. Seldom was he to set out the problem of the relation of anthropology to Freudian thought with such clarity. Where might the Freudian idea of the unconscious lead us: Toward a cultural concept of psychic life, to which certain passages in the essay seem to refer? Or toward the disappearance of the very description of neurotic or psychotic symptoms in psychological terms? The master of structural anthropology wonders whether this kind of psychological description is destined one day to be replaced by a physiological or even biochemical concept of mental disorders. That question, like so many others that concern the relation between anthropology and psychoanalysis, is raised without any answer being explicitly formulated.

Faced with the vast amplitude of Lévi-Strauss' thesis, many anthropologists have hesitated to comment on this text and discuss it point by point. Furthermore, even the purely empirical aspect of his analysis has seemed exceptionally difficult to evaluate. After the work of Holmer and Wassén, the two main sources for Lévi-Strauss at the point when he was writing his essay (1947), fieldwork among the Kuna experienced a lengthy hiatus. No doubt on account of the crisis that hit the Swedish School of Anthropology founded by Nordenskiöld, it was not until the 1970s that more was discovered about the Kuna shamanistic tradition.

In truth, the real difficulty about the problem posed by Lévi-Strauss lay in the tricky issue of relating a study of the Kuna facts—the functioning of a therapy, in particular conditions, within a particular framework of concepts, with particular results and some specific failures—to a problem that was not really psychological but, rather, of a *metapsychological* nature, in the Freudian sense of that term. For it was really a matter—well beyond what Lévi-Strauss had called a "psychological manipulation" of the ailing organ—of the very nature of unconscious psychic elaborations and of how they *related* to the biochemical functioning of the organism. When critically examined, both the terms in that interarticulation, namely the "empirical" term and the "metapsychological" term, had reasons of their own for collapsing or resisting. It was, on the one hand, the twofold fragility of the thesis of *symbolic efficacy* and, on the other, the twofold risk that Lévi-Strauss took in his essay that gave rise to the difficulty of *discussing* a text that depended upon the existence of their relationship. Basically, there were two questions (presented in the essay in a symmetrical fashion, as if they were two halves of a sea-shell) and it is important to keep them quite distinct. The first question is: Does Kuna shamanistic therapy function in accordance with the logic sketched out by Lévi-Strauss in his essay? The second is: Can we conceive of a way in which unconscious representations operate in conjunction with somatic pathologies?

The empirical aspect linked with Kuna shamanistic therapy poses problems to which a solution can only be provided by observation in the course of fieldwork. Here, on the basis of my first months of work in the Kuna village of Mulatupu (in 1977), I soon perceived the solution. Kuna songs are formulated in a special language that can only be learnt in the course of a lengthy initiation. No patient can fully understand this language. The state of intense suffering of the pregnant woman in *The Way of Mu* can, in this respect, constitute nothing but an aggravating circumstance. It is therefore not possible to accept the idea that, as Lévi-Strauss believed, thanks to the text he pronounced, the shaman can, for the patient, become the protagonist in a mythical journey that is progressively identified with the surge and development of physical suffering that the woman is experiencing. It is not possible to believe that, when the shaman speaks of an encounter with certain monstrous animals, the woman in labor can, as Lévi-Strauss supposed, react psychologically to the text by finding in it the language in which it is possible to symbolize the extreme situation of agony in which she finds herself, making it comply with a mental order and eventually be consciously overcome.

What this direct observation in the field rules out is, of course, one particular passage in Lévi-Strauss' argument. This passage tells us that "once the sick woman understands, however, she does more than resign herself; she gets well. But no such thing happens to our sick when the causes of their diseases have been explained to them in terms of secretions, germs, or viruses" (ibid.: 197).

Lévi-Strauss then explains that the reason for this difference is that microbes possess an objective existence in the outside world. Monsters, on the other hand, do not exist in reality, but do arise within our consciousness. They are objects of belief and, precisely on that account, they are lodged in our thoughts and *function as signs* of the unconscious states of our psychic lives.

> The relationship between germ and disease is external to the mind of the patient, for it is a cause-and-effect relationship; whereas the relationship between monster and disease is internal to his mind, whether conscious or unconscious: it is a relationship between symbol and thing symbolized, or, to use the terminology of linguists, between sign and meaning. The shaman provides the sick woman with a *language*, by means of which unexpressed, and otherwise inexpressible, psychic states can be immediately expressed. (Lévi-Strauss 1963: 197–98)

In the crude light of direct observation, that relationship, which is here postulated entirely upon one's understanding of the text, turns out to depend purely upon one's perception of a partially incomprehensible sound. The language spoken by the shaman, in which the inexpressible states provoked by physical pain ought to find immediate expression and thereby have a therapeutic effect, turns out to be an inaccessible language reserved for specialists in the tradition, the meaning of which is impenetrable. The song formulated by the shaman, the story supposed to be capable of interpreting the pain, is, for the suffering woman, a lengthy and monotonous sequence of incomprehensible sounds, possibly punctuated only by a ceaseless repetition of fixed verbal forms. The unavoidable conclusion has to be that the entire part of Lévi-Strauss' empirical argument about the therapeutic efficacy of Kuna songs—which rested upon the premise of a transmission of meaning between the shaman and the sick woman—is, according to the present state of the facts, without foundation. The effect of research is sometimes not only to develop our thoughts, but also to oblige us to arrest their flow, increase our caution and prudence, and even force us into silence. The Lévi-Straussian idea of therapy as a construction of an internal and maybe unconscious language in which pain could find expression was certainly seductive, but impracticable. I have long felt it to be inevitable, from a strictly empirical point of view, that we should give up pursuing such a line any further.

I am now reopening this case for two reasons. The first concerns the *nature of belief*, which seems to me particularly badly defined in Lévi-Strauss' essay and, in general today, in the domain of anthropological studies. The second relates to the emergence, in contemporary psychoanalytic research, of a new type of therapeutic communication founded on the sound of language and not just on its meaning. Recent research suggests a new interpretation of the Kuna data. But it is also clear that these two subjects—the nature of belief and the relation between meaning and sound—constitute the very basis of Lévi-Strauss' argument. To continue to study them from the starting point of new thinking may perhaps lead to making some progress along the path that he opened up almost fifty years ago.

The concept of belief has been discussed at length in anthropology. The positions held by Needham (1972), Pouillon (1983), and Tambiah (1985), to mention but a few examples, are well known. Some focus their attention on the language that the believer uses to state what he or she believes; others concentrate instead on the ritual acts that constitute the context; yet others study the way in which the concept of belief may vary from one culture to another. However, there is one point upon which those differing perspectives seem to converge: belief is always seen as *the act of believing possible, likely, or true a particular declaration regarding the state of affairs that exists in the outside world.* To put that another way, belief is always considered by anthropologists to be an element in a conception of the world. If, for example, a Miraña of Colombian Amazonia declares that "a ray is a fish, but also one of the stars in the constellation of Orion,"[9] generally the anthropologist will seek out other, complementary statements that will eventually enable him or her to reconstruct a vision of the world as a whole, whether that vision concerns the sky, aquatic species, mythology, or kinship relations. While suspending the question of the truth of this or that declaration, the anthropologist will work to construct a network of analogous, symmetrical, or complementary connotations in the indigenous account. The attention of a researcher in the field very seldom strays from a representation of those contents (and their

---

9.   On the ethnoastronomy of the Miranas, see Karadimas (1999).

possible relation to other indigenous representations) to the psychological processes that lead to the establishment of belief. It is sometimes said that those processes are the business of a psychologist and in no way concern an anthropologist studying symbolic systems. I believe that, in that hasty conclusion, there is a serious risk of distorting the facts. From the point of view of understanding cultural phenomena, it is well worth accepting the risk and undertaking to consider belief from a psychological perspective. The fact is that the concept of belief, as normally used in anthropology, contains a latent paradox that rarely emerges as clearly as it should. If "to believe" merely signifies adhering to this or that conception of the world, then the very meaning of the word "believe" should designate very different mental states from one culture to another. The relativist objection concerning symbolic systems in which belief operates ought to concern the very act of believing (over and above the problems with the term "believe" or its indigenous synonym). However, it is precisely that line of argument, mainly upheld by Needham, according to which a "belief," in itself, does not exist and should be dissolved into a concept peculiar to each culture, that turns out to be rather unconvincing. In fact, the very examples Needham studied appear, on the contrary, to prove that such a thing as "the action of believing" seems resistant to cultural variation. It is impossible not to recognize that in many anthropological analyses of belief devoted, for example, to belief in magic, this latent paradox arouses a feeling of dissatisfaction. Belief always appears to be something too strongly rooted in personal psychic processes to be possible to describe simply as an intimate adherence to some conception of the world. The act of believing seems too rooted in an individual's flesh and blood to be able to be reduced purely to "a theory about the state of the world" or a "profession of faith."

Furthermore, any anthropologist working in the field knows that traditional societies, whether European or non-European, are by no means composed of believers. Incredulity is present in traditional societies just as much as belief is. So the problem is not whether one believes or does not believe; it is more a matter of understanding how a particular representation spreads within a culture's space of common knowledge, and how that propagation comes about. To put that another way, when a representation becomes an object of belief, the problem that we should focus on is not simply how beliefs that exist alongside one another are organized, but also how the *specific link* that is established between a representation and the person who claims to believe in it functions. From this point of view, belief *indicates a relationship*, and an anthropologist should certainly consider it as such.

As expressed in these new terms, belief, in particular with regard to ritual situations, will have to be conceived as a projective process that leads to the establishment of a particularly complex type of social link.

Accordingly, let me formulate the hypothesis that, at least in ritual situations, one is led to believe something not because one shares a common patrimony (a "culture") but, on the contrary, because much of the content of the belief results from a private projection effected by the one who believes. In truth, an analysis of the sources of belief, whether it be a matter of ritual or of narrative, does not point us toward any persuasive discourse aimed at bringing about ideological adhesion. Far more often, the conducive means leading to belief are constituted by projected or reinterpreted images (even if these are formulated by words). Belief is very often a matter of discourse interwoven with images that, far from imposing themselves as rules that should be obeyed, offer themselves up to personal interpretation suggested by a ritual context.

Let us now consider an empirical example to pinpoint this perspective of an analysis of the process that leads to the establishment of a belief. The historian Carlo Ginzburg's masterly analysis of witchcraft in the Friuli region between the sixteenth and the seventeenth centuries (Ginzburg [1966] 1983) is particularly useful from this point of view. Ginzburg showed in particular how the collection of beliefs that characterized the Benandanti (literally "good walkers," a Friulian fertility cult) were progressively associated with a number of central themes: namely, appearances or returns of the dead; the idea (which he describes as "shamanistic") of a mobile soul that may at any moment leave the body; a nocturnal battle between rival supernatural powers; and, finally, a demonic Sabbath. In the course of the two centuries that Ginzburg studied, this collection of beliefs developed essentially in two directions. One part of the tradition was progressively associated with a group of funerary rituals; another part, which was propagated in parallel, seems, on the contrary, to have been linked with rituals that peasants celebrated in order to ensure the fertility of the crops in their fields.

The pages that Ginzburg devoted to this popular tradition present a particularly clear example of the way in which a given collection of beliefs can be propagated in a particular place and at a particular time. The magico-ritual idea of nocturnal hunts, of the witchcraft of the Friuli area, was not propagated throughout the rural society in this region of Italy (and also in central and eastern Europe) as an explicitly formulated theory surrounded by specific cults and beliefs. It is, on the contrary, symptomatic that, as soon as a Benandante summoned to appear before some ecclesiastical tribunal attempted a description of a specific cult or deity, the picture immediately became confused. Sometimes there were mentions of a mysterious female deity, for example a certain Frau Selga (whose mysterious double, Perchta, appears in a more recent work by Ginzburg 1989 [1991][10]). On other occasions, the peasant summoned to the tribunal would evoke "a certain woman called the abbess, seated in majesty on the edge of a well" (Ginzburg [1966] 1983: 54).

A reader of Ginzburg's book soon notices that the peasants know very little about these supernatural creatures. As we study the agrarian cults of the sixteenth-century Friuli peasants we do not find any return to a famous pagan culture handed down from antiquity, complete with its systems of deities and rituals. The belief in the existence of witches seems, rather, to be propagated in a much less systematic way, as a *forest of resemblances*, a subtle interplay of analogies between one event and another. In many of the cases mentioned and discussed by Ginzburg, the man or woman who is beginning to believe in the existence of witchcraft does not really profess a faith any different from that of Catholicism. Rather, he or she turns out to be struck by some intense image (for example, by the appearance of a strange animal in the courtyard or by the unusual brightness of a light at night . . .). Such an image is generally associated with a traumatic experience that the future believer cannot interpret. From a psychological point of view, instead of an act of affirmation of the truth or the apparent truth of the state of affairs that characterizes the external world (what one might call a *credo*), we find a believer filled with great hesitancy and distress, in an agony of suspended judgment. This subjective aspect is reflected in the manner in which belief in the nocturnal Sabbath is propagated. The constant

10. For a commentary, see Severi (1992b).

variation, almost from one person to another, in the collection of beliefs (which, however, are always contained within the two main branches: the funerary one and the one linked with the fertility of the fields) is not associated only with particular individual cases. This kind of cultural variation and uncertainty and the lack of any real doctrinal development that this implies seem, on the contrary, to be typical of this type of uncodified representations. Even as Ginzburg pursues his aim as a historian, which is to shed new light on the comparison between peasant culture and the official doctrine of the Inquisition, he shows clearly that the Benandanti of the Friuli region do not constitute a homogeneous group of people who share the same view of the world, dominated by particular ritual representations. The fact is that the Benandanti never did become such a group, nor would they be regarded as a coherent heretical one until such time as those representations were classified as belonging to the model of witchcraft elaborated by the church. The coherence of the Benandante system of beliefs—which defined it as a negation of Catholic doctrine—originated *outside* this peasant culture. That coherence was in truth completely foreign to these traditions. Until the church intervened, the propagation of beliefs was, it could be said, confined, rather, to the narration of fabulous tales, the benevolent or malevolent speculations of individuals, the expression of general fears, or mere gossip.

Belief, we may conclude, can be unsystematic.

It would therefore be pointless to seek for an overall collection of similar cultural features in the series of resemblances linking the individual cases or episodes reported to the church authorities. From the evidence studied by Ginzburg what, instead, emerges with unexpected regularity are certain details that at first sight may seem minor. In many cases it is simply a matter of the stylistic features that characterize the narratives of this episode and, Ginzburg would say, confer upon them a certain family resemblance. Let us now examine one of these curious details. Perhaps this will help us to identify one of the factors that serve to support the propagation of belief, or even one of its typical modes of functioning. In plenty of the sources mentioned by Ginzburg, the witnesses maintain that when a Benandante gets up and goes off to celebrate a Sabbath with witches, his body remains motionless in his bed, apparently fast asleep. Almost all the witnesses insist that, at such a moment, one should take care *not to alter the position of his body*. If the body did happen to be moved, the soul of the Benandante, which is absent, in many cases assuming the form of an animal in a faraway forest, would, upon its return the next morning, no longer be able to find an opening—the mouth, for example—through which to reenter the body. A great misfortune would follow, for the Benandante would in that case die. From the numerous statements from witnesses, let me select, for instance, that made by Chonradt Stöcklin, a thirty-seven-year-old shepherd who was tried for heresy and then perished at the stake in Oberstdorf in 1586. Commenting on what happened at that trial, Ginzburg writes as follows:

> The journeying of "the nocturnal band" took place during the Ember Days, on Fridays and Saturdays, almost always at night. Prior to setting out one fell into a swoon and remained in an inert state: it was the soul (at least so he [Stöcklin] supposed) which departed, leaving the body behind immobile and lifeless for an hour or a little more. *Woe, however, if the body, meanwhile, be turned over, because that would make the re-entry of the soul painful and difficult.* (Ginzburg [1966] 1983: 53, my italics)

"Woe, however, if the body, meanwhile, be turned over. . . ." We should pause to consider this detail. The first point to note is that this warning is not really part of the belief concerning the nocturnal rituals of the Sabbath. The remark that is formulated in connection with the sleeping body—which is here more or less observed from the outside—lies, so to speak, at the threshold to belief. It is situated both within the space of belief (the nocturnal field and the distant forest where the secret rituals may take place) and outside, in the familiar space of the house where the others, the nonprotagonists, remain, those who are preparing to be believers but are not so yet. Indeed, when someone says, "Take care, do not move the body of the one [him or her] who sleeps at your side," that person is certainly speaking not of an invisible elsewhere where secret rituals are performed, but rather of a familiar detail, a situation that may arise any day or any night. Through this relationship established between two images situated in very different spaces yet at the same time regarded as communicating, a tension is established between the here-and-now dimension (what I can see at this very moment) and the dimension of a distant elsewhere (which I cannot see but that seems

to be secretly linked with what I can see right now, as one of its latent aspects). It is from this specific tension that the representation of the Benandante seems to draw its force and to engender a belief. The force of the image seems to lie precisely in the projection of a familiar and daily experience (sleeping alongside one's spouse) into a completely invisible context. Such a projection is certainly far more intense than any description of bizarre or frightening details that a popular legend may attribute to some secret ritual or other.

To make that point more forcefully, let us consider an analogous example. One of the popular legends most widely known in the Lozère region of France is famously dominated by the monstrous figure of a particularly cruel wolf known as the Beast of Gévaudan. Robert Louis Stevenson mentions this monstrous creature in his *Travels with a donkey in the Cévennes* ([1879] 2004). According to popular legend, the Beast of Gévaudan spreads irresistible terror around it. Although it looks exactly like a wolf, it is not at all the same as other wolves. It feeds exclusively on human flesh and can appear in two different places at the same time and at any moment. As the legend goes on to suggest, the magic Beast of Gévaudan is probably immortal. This story, which is particularly long-lived, still appears to be well known even today. Richard Holmes, an English writer who recently followed in Stevenson's footsteps through the Cévennes, undertook a little inquiry about the Beast as it appears now in local legends. Among the common explanations, then as now, for this fearful behavior on the part of the Beast, Holmes notes one. It consists in assuming that a group belonging to a particular species of wolves, composed of only three specimens, once tasted human flesh and could no longer do without it (R. Holmes 1984).[11]

That explanation for the belief may provide us with a few leads as to its efficacy and hence its tenacious persistence in peasant society's memory. The fact that this is a specific species explains the particularly savage behavior of the Beast: it performs unparalleled actions because it belongs to an altogether extraordinary group of animals. Furthermore, the fact that the species is made up of more than one individual *explains*,

---

11. For an initial commentary on this text, see Houseman and Severi (1998: 240).

within the system of beliefs, why the Beast is reputed to be in two places at once. But there remains another crucial point: because it always
mentions *three* wolves, not just two, the explanation always implies a
member of this pseudospecies about which nothing is known. This third
individual, which remains strictly unknown but might at any time be
found in the vicinity of a pasture or a farm (the animal *still unaccounted
for*, as Holmes rightly puts it), can always be used to explain any new,
even incomprehensible, exploit of the legendary Beast. The legend's
"third wolf" not only offers a narrator and whoever is listening to him
a solution to the difficulty of explaining enigmatic situations; it also
and above all presents a neutral point, a lacuna in the story, which will
always make a later interpretation possible. Whoever wants to understand the legend will fill that lacuna in his or her own way, on his or
her own initiative. The existence of such a story in the popular tradition
turns out to be linked to a series of peripeteiai in the narrative (which
sustain in the listener to any story a particular kind of *expectation*, as in
fairy-tales[12]). However, at the heart of such stories, it is also possible
to detect another mechanism: the appearance of some isolated lacuna,
some commonplace or unknown detail that, in its own way, attracts attention. Such a process does not imply a torrent of details, as would, on
the contrary, a description of some fabulous, unexpected, and mysterious manifestation. In fact, it implies precisely the reverse: the lack of
a connotation. What appears to be absolutely unknown, or, quite the
opposite, totally commonplace, arouses in the listener other images that
will then become confused with those that are explicitly evoked. In this
way, the frontier between that which is recounted (which does unfold
within the narrative sequence) and that which the story encourages one
to imagine becomes particularly uncertain. The existence of the immortal wolf, in the form of the Beast of Gévaudan slips out of the narrative
framework and acquires a sort of presence, indeed a quite unusual mental presence. Any story told as part of a tradition of this kind affects that
frontier line, which accordingly becomes more distant or closer each
time a story is told.

If we now return to the warning that accompanies the Benandante's
evidence—"*Woe, however, if the body, meanwhile, be turned over, because*

---

12. On this subject, see Severi (1999b).

that would make the re-entry of the soul painful and difficult"—we discover that it too, in the same way as the "third wolf" of the Beast of Gévaudan, assumes *the function of indicating the frontier* between that which is actually formulated in the Benandante's evidence and that which such stories bring into existence in the imagination of believers. The only difference is that in this new context that frontier limit applies no longer to the story that is told, but to the actual formulation of belief in the Sabbath. In the evidence relating to witchcraft in the Friuli region, *a run-of-the-mill image* (seldom noted) *melts into the image of something fabulous* (the ritual that is celebrated in secret) through the spontaneous projective interpretation of a point that is left empty. That empty point seems to be perfectly unexceptional and so confers upon the existence of witches a verisimilitude and everyday normality that is associated with the body sleeping next to one.

It is now possible to formulate a first conclusion: in the act of believing, it is its *possible banality* that gives it the force of a representation, not its strangeness. Caught up in this tension, the banal detail opens up a kind of gap in the description of the imagined witchcraft scene; and it is a gap into which the subjective imagination of a believer can slip. This particular configuration gives rise to the typical form in which belief manifests itself: namely, doubt. Typically enough, it is never a certainty that something is true that produces the strength of a belief. Except in extreme or exceptional cases, such certainty never exists in a believer. What does almost always exist, though, is *an absence of certainty* that this or that phenomenon or state of affairs that is declared through the belief is actually false. This ambiguous state of the image in which one believes can never be described correctly as a decision to believe; rather, it is a *reticence not to believe.* The only link with the image of a witch is established through a refusal, or rather an inability, not to believe in her existence.[13] This "negative" way of fixing belief can be explained from the point of view that I have proposed above. The fact is that the link that is established between the person and the representation (which I have suggested calling the psychological aspect of belief), a link both

---

13. I should also point out that on the whole the Kuna shamanistic beliefs are based on a use of negatively defined concepts such as "soul," "spirit," "invisible power," and so on (Severi 1993c: 221–49).

distressing and persistent from the affective point of view and fragile from the logical point of view, is always generated by projection. That *link, established through doubt*, has none of the serenity of a profession of faith. A characteristic feature of all the witnesses' statements regarding witchcraft in the Friuli region is that they approach the subject in an extremely prudent or even insidious fashion. The witness will not start off by saying either "I know that witches do not exist" or "I know that they do exist." Almost always he or she will say, "*I do not know if witches exist*," an expression of doubt that is found shocking not because, as the feigned humility of the believer would like to have it believed, it is possible to believe in the existence of a witch or a sorcerer. In fact what is so scandalous—including in the eyes of the Inquisitors—is not the fact that the peasant "believes" in the actual existence of one or another aspect of the witches' ritual. In his *Ecstasies* ([1989] 1991), Ginzburg has shown, for instance, the imagined sexual contact with an animal being (which lay at the heart of the "belief" in the Sabbath) was for a long time considered by a Catholic confessor as a pure fruit of the imagination about which the church need not worry too much. What so shocked and disturbed the Inquisition judges was the fact that, among the peasants who had become Benandanti and their disciples, *faith did not extinguish* doubt as to the existence of witches. This *not knowing whether* witches exist thus became, not an absolute negation of the Christian faith, but rather what might be called *a perhaps belief*, a way of admitting the existence of supernatural beings but at the same locating them in an ambiguous space somewhere in between belief and nonbelief.

So now we can reformulate our hypothesis regarding the nature of belief. This mental state is better described, in connection with both the propagation of a collection of beliefs within the social body and also an individual's adhesion to a patrimony of common representations, by a doubtful *not knowing whether* rather than an affirmative *knowing that*. This "not knowing whether" results from a process that leads to the establishment of two parallel spaces composed of features both commonplace and mysterious. Through this process, a specific mental state is constructed in which any feature that stands out in one's memory also becomes a key factor in the establishment of belief. It is within that space that belief must be situated. The attitude of a peasant who believes in the existence of the Sabbath is characterized not by the force of contradicting the official doctrine of the church, but rather by the weakness of an acceptance of some rare exception. His mental state is far better defined by his inability not to believe in an imaginary situation in which, through some projection, he feels that he is involved, than by an explicit negation of what the church declares.

From these considerations, we may draw a general conclusion on belief. Believing and projecting seem to be two psychological phenomena that are closely linked. In order to understand belief, anthropologists must distance themselves from the "propositional" view of this concept (the one that has led them to speak of a system of beliefs and a conception of the world) and draw closer to the point of view of psychologists. In this perspective, belief appears as a specific type of projection, prompted by an interpretation of an incomplete constellation of indications. This brief examination of the witchcraft studied by Ginzburg has thus furthered our understanding of belief as a specific mental state. It has also led me to formulate some new hypotheses about the way in which certain representations can propagate themselves (as in what Dan Sperber [1996] has called an "epidemiology of representations") within a particular community. However, these analyses tell us nothing about belief, when such a mental state establishes itself, as in the Kuna case, in the presence of pain. In this respect, we can still conclude nothing about its possible role in the therapeutic act as practiced in the Kuna shamanistic tradition. In order to gain a better understanding of this aspect, which will lead us to a new approach to the *effectiveness of symbols*, let us now study the work of an Italian psychoanalyst, Gaetano Roi, on the subject of communication in a community of young autistic people.[14]

---

14. I am here using the definition of the term "autistic" originally formulated by Bleuer and later by Asperger. In this perspective, "autistic" is applied to a subject lacking the ability to establish an affective contact with someone else. In many cases, this inability is indicated by great difficulties in the use of language.

SOUND AND SENSE: A MUSICAL WAY OF LISTENING

> *Even if they are painted without eyes, figures must give the impression that they are looking; and painted without ears, they must give the impression that they are listening. There are things that ten thousand strokes of the brush cannot represent but that can be seized upon with a single precise stroke. That is the true way of representing the invisible.*
>
> Lao Zi, *The Dao of painting*

Voices, sonorous rhythms, words unspoken, condensed, or deformed: Gaetano Roi's therapeutic researches explore and reveal an extremely unusual way of communicating that seems to challenge our current ideas about linguistic exchange. In his works he describes and analyzes a large number of cases that it would be impractical, here, to examine one by one (Roi 1998). Instead, let us follow just one of the paths taken by this remarkable psychoanalyst working among therapeutic communities of autistic adolescents. The first step, only seemingly paradoxical, taken by Roi is his decision to limit himself (apart from his attentive interpretation of everything that can make sense of his patients' behavior) to a *musical way of listening* to their language.

A reader of Roi's works progressively discovers that, in the communicative situations that he studies, other elements of utterance, generally considered to be accidental or even obstacles to communication, in fact play a crucial role. Fulvio, Ornella, Umberto, and the other young autistic patients observed by Roi seem to entrust the expression of their thoughts not so much to words, but rather to certain particular sounds, gobbledegooks, or else to truncated or amalgamated linguistic expressions. Guided by Roi's analyses, we learn to listen attentively to voice-tones, exclamations, apparent monologues, or even reproachful asides deflected from their natural interlocutors. Next, the reader begins to realize that these sounds, these distortions of normal communication, are organized according to a logic that is as rigorous as it is unexpected. The adolescents studied by Roi are clearly not able to use words to which other people resort every day. Nevertheless, by changing the conditions of speech and submitting words to a different order of communication, they manage to express or to translate into words an intense suffering. One of them, Fulvio, at a certain point referred to this way of using one's voice and words as "the other way of saying." What does such a use of language consist of? How does it manage to communicate anything? What is the relation, here, of sound and sense or meaning?

Roi, who is a psychoanalyst endowed with extraordinary sensitivity, has explored in depth the clinical aspects of this speech that had, up until then, remained largely unnoticed. I could add nothing to his account of its clinical aspects and therefore simply refer the reader to his own works. All the same, I should like to suggest that an example of a cultural nature might help us to gain a better understanding of this specific form of communication, in which the customary balance between meaning and form is profoundly modified.

Clearly, the closest thing to what young Fulvio calls "the other way of saying" is poetry, and that is so for two reasons: the first is that in poetry, sound, or rather the sonorous form of words, is more intense than in customary communication. But this *word-music* is far from being a matter of chance. On the contrary, this music is perceptible only thanks to a specific organization of the sounds, which establishes a double register of resonances, the one between sounds and meanings, the other between sequences of pure sounds. This may put one in mind of one of Jakobson's great lessons: namely, that poetry always resonates on two registers simultaneously, the register of meaning and that of sound (Jakobson 2006).

There is, however, another reason why poetry can be usefully compared to the symptomatic language of Fulvio and the other adolescent autistic members of Roi's group of patients. Poetry, at least in cultural societies that depend on the utterance of the spoken word, is generally recited in particular situations. Often, these are ritual situations where one collectively remembers experiences of great emotional intensity, whether they be painful or joyous, and where affect tends to take priority over representation. Often the very intensity of the ritual experience may make normal linguistic communication difficult or sometimes even impossible. As a result, in many cases the ritual action replaces speech in order to symbolize a mental and bodily state that it is not possible to symbolize directly. In this way, in so-called "traditional" societies poetry often takes the form of a ritual song, thereby becoming closer to sound and simultaneously linking itself strictly to the lived experience.

Here is an example. A remarkable Canadian linguist, Kevin Tuite, made a lengthy study of a body of Georgian traditional songs composed of both meaningful words and purely sonorous passages totally without meaning (Tuite 1992, 1993). The strictly linguistic part of these songs has a parallelist structure of the kind that is by now familiar to us: a series of repeated formulae with regular variations. In the utterance of the song, an organization guided by meaning is combined with a sonorous organization effected by the regular repetition of the same groups of words. In this connection, the song which ritually celebrates the birth of a boy in a family, where the sun is called "mother of the moon," nicely illustrates this point:

Sun inside and sun outside
Oh Sun, come inside!
The cock has crowed
Oh Sun, come inside!
Rise up in the sky, sun
Oh sun, come inside!
The sun has given birth to the moon
Oh sun, come inside!
A little boy is born
Oh sun, come inside!

As we have noted earlier, the interpenetration that we find here between a particular sonorous organization and a particular way of conveying a meaning (a process that in this case functions by alternation) is an aspect inherent to all poetry. In the Georgian case, however, sound tends to free itself from meaning. From being simply an implicit aspect in the utterance of speech, here sound acquires an autonomy of its own. Tuite has been able to show that, in this tradition, inarticulate sounds obey the same internal organization, the same formal design, as that which guides the order of words. Even noises, once inserted into a context of special communication, are organized into pairs of oppositions by the regular repetition of the same sounds and by an alternating interplay that appears to be carefully calculated. Beyond words, one is tempted to say, the discourse of the song continues, as in the following funerary song, which is strictly parallelist and in which not a single word appears:

oi owo iawa,
eio woiwowo ioi oi oy
oho io woi, iowo owda woy!
wo iwoi woi io iwo iwo iwo iwo ioi
o io owoy

So there are some communication situations in which something imposes order upon the communication act as a whole, by mobilizing aspects of the utterance that, at first sight, seem totally independent of the creation of meaning. Sound, the purely sonorous matter of language, may elude speech and acquire an autonomous existence. This dimension is neither chaotic nor meaningless. If we are capable of hearing them, certain *regular sonorous configurations* may emerge.

For an understanding of how they may do so, both in the consciousness of a patient and in a ritual context, and, above all, in order to understand into which aspects of psychic life their roots are plunged, the research work of Roi into communication between autistic patients is crucial. Once he had understood that the words pronounced by some patients were not modified in a haphazard way and that their squiffed utterance was directed by a systematic kind of deformation or obeyed a particular style of sonorous deformation, the therapist was at last able to catch a hidden discourse up until then concealed beneath the stereotyped behavior of an autistic adolescent or considered as such by those who lived alongside him. In our Georgian example, we have discovered an organization of sound operating alongside that of meaning. However, the sounds that Tuite registered still remain without meaning. Roi proceeds further: within the framework of communication with other autistic patients of his, within the dimension that he calls "their singing," sound maintains a profound relationship with meaning. He discovers that a meaning hidden in speech may not only coexist or alternate with some kind of music, as we have seen in the Georgian example; it may also be hidden within the song itself: in the very tone that the young patient adopts, for instance, in order to repeat words uttered by his teacher or by the therapist. Clearly, the force of this discovery lies in its radicalism. We are naturally aware of the fact that certain levels of communication, rooted, for instance, in the modalities of sounds, may profoundly affect the meaning of our utterances. A study of such turbulent factors affecting communication is, of course, one of the tasks of pragmatics. Nevertheless, examples of a true construction of meaning in situations in which linguistic exchange, speech itself, seems completely absent are extremely rare. It is here that the work of Roi, which reveals the degree to which such infralinguistic and semilinguistic communication may be intense and rich in resonances, should concern anthropologists of ritual and provide them with more to think about.

What I have in mind, of course, is the Kuna song *The Way of Mu* and the interpretation of it that Claude Lévi-Strauss produced in his essay on "The effectiveness of symbols" (1963). As we have seen, the Kuna song, formulated in language incomprehensible to the sick woman, can no longer be regarded as an effective symbolic interpretation of her pain. However, it is surely clear that the efficacy of ritual language reaches far beyond a study of the shamanistic tradition of the Kuna alone. The study of ritual based on speech manifestations has long since discovered particular cases of linguistic exchange in which the effect expected from a ritual interaction (a transference from one social space to another, or from one time to another in human life, or the recognition of a new social status or even a cure) seems to be confined totally to a particular utterance of certain key texts. But precisely in cases in which linguistic exchange seems so important, everything seems to be designed to ensure that normal communication encounters a mass of obstacles. In many cases, verbal ritual seems to wish to avoid a, so to speak, average and normal level of linguistic communication. Either the ritual simplifies the utterance to the point of creating infralinguistic phenomena composed purely of sounds or nonwords (as Tuite calls them); or else, as among the Kuna, it chooses an extreme degree of complication, esoteric metaphors, and a specialized lexicon. This facilitates the creation of a whole special language that is incomprehensible to ordinary people. In both cases the result is to render comprehension arduous or even impossible. So what is the explanation for this paradox provoked by communication that, on the one hand, is assiduously prepared and practiced and in many cases carefully described and, on the other, is rendered increasingly difficult to the point where, as we have seen, sound takes precedence over meaning? Why do some cultures define communication with such attention even when, as in the Georgian funerary song, communication is not effected through words? What is it that is being communicated in these specific contexts? And then, how is it possible to understand the fact that this kind of communication is, with impressive regularity, associated with an act of therapy and with belief in the efficacy of speech?

The fact is that the results of Roi's research into therapies confront us with a very rare situation in which the complementarity conceived by Devereux (1978) between individual psychology and a collective elaboration of beliefs becomes practicable. For the problem of the symbolic efficacy of primitive or shamanistic therapies and that of the particular form of communication decoded by Roi seem to present us with a way of elaborating language (and the particular form of communication that stems from it) that is very similar. To put that in Devereuxian terms, it is perhaps a matter of the same phenomenon described in two different languages, the one anthropological, the other psychoanalytical. We are faced with two problems, seemingly separate and quite different, that suddenly appear to illuminate each other, thereby enabling us to think of a solution formulated in new terms. To be more precise, those two problems require us to explore from two complementary points of view a communicational phenomenon of unimagined depth: that "other way of saying," the intensity of which one of Roi's patients one day discovered. Still following the path that we began to follow in our analysis of the Georgian example—that is to say, by comparing the symbolic phenomena linked with the creation of meaning through speech to situations of communication linked with the mere emission of sounds—we shall perhaps be able to recognize in "the other way of saying" a situation analogous to that in which communication is established, across a therapeutic field, between a shaman and his patient.

Let us return to the Kuna shamanistic therapy. Faced with the hammock in which the pregnant woman lies, the native specialist, in a monotone musical chant, sings marvelous songs, often very poetic, which generally trace a parallel between the experience of the woman about to give birth and a sudden turbulence that strikes the universe. Thus, in the song devoted to difficult confinement, the Kuna shaman evokes scenes in which rivers of blood appear and mountains seem to palpitate in rhythm with the spasms that shake the woman's body as she gives birth. As the Kuna see it, this journey through a land constructed like the patient's body makes it possible to enter upon an exploration of the patient's experience that will favor her recovery. As we know, a Kuna song is generally perceived by the patient simply as pure sound: just a voice. The Kuna situation thus radicalizes the Georgian one. No meaning is conveyed, at least not vocally and directly, between the two figures engaged in this ritual communication. But all the same, everyone agrees that this communication has an *effect*. Although it is incomprehensible—the Kuna people say—this speech that is ritually uttered has the power to heal.

So what happens while a Kuna song is recited? Let us consider the ritual scene as a long sequence of mostly incomprehensible words. In the presence of the patient, a complex kind of *sonorous image* is gradually created. As in the perspective introduced by Roi, who resorted to hearing musically what his patients were formulating, I should like to try to set up a kind of *iconic decoding* of the shamanistic song. So it will be necessary to consider the song uttered by the shaman purely as a sonorous image, quite independent of the meaning of the words of which it is composed. My aim is to study it *purely as an acoustic image,* so to speak.

Ernst Gombrich, in his great book on *Art and illusion* ([1960] 1984), pointed out that much of the perceptive process is due to a particular way of operating a visual projection. When we look at an image, we always perceive a number of features that the image does not contain materially, but simply suggests. This interplay with the part that is not visible, which seems inherent in all perception, is often exploited in art that we are accustomed to call primitive. In many cases (for example, in order to represent a spirit), this projective interplay is exploited in order to reveal a link between what, in the image, is materially present and what, without actually describing it, it encourages the eye to see. It is a way of bringing to mind what one wishes to remain invisible. In order to understand this process, typically brought about by a representation that I have been calling "chimerical" (Severi 1991, 1992a, 1992b), one has only to look at a very ordinary visual illusion, like that which encourages us to project, and thus see a square on the basis of no more than four dots separated by a white equivalent space (Figure 79).

Figure 79. The schema of a visual projection on a nonexistent square.

Now, if we return to the shamanistic song and focus our attention upon the ways in which it is uttered, without bothering about its content or meaning, we find a situation that is analogous to that illusion, although this time it is transposed into the field of sound. The scene of ritual utterance exploits the elementary coordinates of projection in exactly the same way. In fact it would be incomprehensible without the active intervention of projection. Let us see how Gombrich defines the elementary characteristics of the process that leads to setting off a projective response:

> There are obviously two conditions that must be fulfilled if the mechanism of projection is to be set in motion. One is that the beholder must be left in no doubt about the way to close the gap; secondly, that he must be given a "screen", an empty or ill-defined area onto which he can project the expected image. (Gombrich [1960] 1984: 208)

In *La memoria rituale* (Severi 1993c) I studied how very complex and rich in meaning the image of the Kuna ritual scene can be, as can that of the supernatural landscape that is progressively described in a shamanistic song. So I shall not be dwelling on that aspect here but shall instead formulate a different question, which concerns not the meaning but the perlocutionary aspect of the song. If we are willing to adopt the point of view of the suffering woman lying in the hammock, next to the shaman, how does this sonorous image seem to her? It is, of course, not possible to understand that experience in detail. However, one thing is clear: the image will above all seem to her to be *an incomplete sonorous image*, entirely entrusted to a voice that formulates incomprehensible words, in the darkness, an image in which it will be very difficult for her, here and there, to seize upon the few words the meaning of which she understands.

This is therefore a situation quite similar to that of the Georgian funerary song. The sounds uttered (apparently devoid of meaning)—thanks to the parallelist structure of the song that constrains the shaman regularly to repeat the same expressions and to vary them only in accordance with a quite rigid schema of alternation—always possesses a perceptible sonorous regularity. It is reasonable to conclude that those sounds orient the patient's listening, even if no precise meaning is associated with them.

From the listener's point of view, this "sung" utterance seems a kind of sonorous carpet, a—so to speak—auditive Rorschach mark, composed of sequences of words that never dissolve completely into disorder but are organized according to a minimal degree of order that is established by the musical chant (continuously scanned by the shaman), without ever relying on the meaning. On the other hand, we know that the patient is aware of what everyone knows about shamans: that the shaman goes off on a journey, seeking a soul that has fled from its body, and that he is engaged in a duel with animal spirits; all these are ideas with which she is familiar. Furthermore, as I noted when translating *The Song of the Demon*, even if it is true that a song is mainly composed of incomprehensible words, a limited lexicon derived from everyday language always filters through, albeit partially, into the language of the initiate (Severi and Gomez 1983).

Despite the mystery engendered by incomprehensible sounds, a kind of atmosphere that is more familiar is thus established, in which the suffering woman, or indeed any other patient, does not feel totally disoriented. At the same time, such a patient understands, albeit only occasionally, at least a few of the words pronounced by the celebrant: partially, almost by chance, the patient is struck by a few indicative words, the meaning of which she can grasp. The image constructed by the song in the ritual utterance scene could thus be described as a kind of thread, a regular and continuous line composed of uttered sounds. Alongside this thread, in a discontinuous and irregular way, the words the meaning of which the patient has understood appear as luminous points.

This situation (in which I am at this point noting only the utterance's formal features, not its meaning) implies the two conditions that Gombrich assigned to the engendering of a perceptive illusion, as it appears once a process of projection is under way: on the one hand, familiarity with certain features that are seized upon and understood; on the other, the presence of an empty screen, here constituted by sequences of incomprehensible sounds uttered in the dark. Those sounds, although inserted into a context of communication, are not words. So they remain without meaning. As in the case of Chonradt Stöcklin, the Benandante in Obertsdorf, and in that of the Beast of Gévaudan, an empty or latent space—a seemingly negligible gap—appears in the flow of uttered representations. That empty space (as in the case of an illusion or partial vision) gives rise to mental activity that strives, through projection, to complete the sonorous image activated by the uttered sounds.

If one seizes upon this ambiguous nature of the shamanistic text (revealed by an aspect that can only be understood if one decides to study, over and above the words, the particular emission of the sounds themselves), it is possible to begin to understand the kind of ritual communication that Claude Lévi-Strauss called *symbolic efficacy*. Such a perspective makes it possible to identify an intermediate term midway between an individual perception and a collective codification of the malady, which is regularly missed when one concentrates on the content of the songs. The fact is that, by going down this new path, we find that what might be called the work of verbal ritual is revealed in all its complexity. On the one hand, it becomes clear that, from the point of view of culture and the system of shared signs, the sounds emitted by the shaman present a recognizable representation of the existence of the supernatural world and, in particular, of the spirits, which by definition, in the Kuna world, cannot be perceived visually. It is well known that a Kuna spirit is constituted purely by sound.

On the other hand, though, from the point of view of individual experience, and particularly an experience that is as difficult to share as pain is, the meeting point with speech lies in the construction not of discourse nor of a system of signs, but of a *particular perceptive illusion*. In the course of the utterance of a shamanistic song, the basic canvas that is familiar to everyone (the journey into the beyond, the battle against the spirits, the search for a lost soul, etc.) emerges gradually and in scattered fragments, within a neutral space of sound that is incomprehensible and secret, in which there is room for the patient to project something. We ourselves, who have the means to read the text of the song, are able to see that a detailed account of the shamanistic journey is given, sometimes with a wealth of details that borders on obsession. But what the patient perceives of that image is no more than a sketch of that journey, constructed by hints: like the rare strokes of a paintbrush in a Chinese painting separated by vast blank spaces. Now, as the passage from the *Dao of painting* quoted at the head of this section declares, the existence of a blank space simply has the effect of adding precision to the brush stroke or, in the present case, the words uttered by the shaman. It is certainly thanks to such blank spaces that the elaboration of the patient's experience of pain, set in motion by the creation of a field of projection, becomes more intense. It is here that the link with belief, a link established, as we have seen, not by adherence to a new certainty but, precisely, through uncertainty, becomes at once most compelling and most effective. It is in this way that the song, as a sonorous image, touches the imagination of the patient. Or, rather, it is thus that a point of infralinguistic mutual penetration is established between the two parties: on the one hand, the rhythmically uttered song and, on the other, the flood of thoughts that accompanies the experience of pain. Despite the fact that the words pronounced by one party are not materially and literally understood by others, nevertheless, in this ritual therapy, the *form* of this communication is constructed *both* by the patient *and* by the therapist. The thoughts of the former can in this way insert themselves imaginatively into the partly meaningless words pronounced by the latter. A ritual song, a text that always tells a stereotyped story (the same for everyone), in this way becomes an amazingly faithful image of the personal experience and secret story of the patient. And that is simply because it is up to the patient herself to construct for herself its own symbolic efficacy and to play her part in the song sung by the therapist, thereby making it the same word-image for both of them. So the magic force or symbolic efficacy of *The Way of Mu*, the Kuna song designed as therapy for difficult childbirth, does not originate, as Lévi-Strauss thought, from an image produced by the therapist that "embodied" the story of the patient's experience. The magic came from the suffering woman herself, who conferred meaning upon the latent aspects of whatever the therapist said. Before believing, the suffering woman engaged in a process of projection.

The "music" of the words, the sequence of sounds, thus constituted no obstacle to communication between the shaman and his patient. On the contrary, even as it made direct linguistic exchange more difficult, it simultaneously opened on to a communicational level peculiar to ritual which, even as it carefully marked the limits of what was communicable within the context, managed to focus the act of communication precisely upon what ordinary language normally fails to symbolize. In the Kuna case as in that of Roi's patients, over and above their evident differences, there was one omnipresent feature, possibly the one that marks the deepest origin of "the other way of saying," whether this was used in a Kuna shamanistic tradition, the witchcraft of the Friuli region in the sixteenth century, or in a present-day therapeutic community. That common feature is one of the very rare experiences that threatens the very existence of language: namely, extreme pain.

A few reflections on the nature of belief have led us, first, to shift our attention from the content of representations to the actual act of believing. That act seems to establish a specific relation, an intense link, between a representation and a believer; and it seems to come to be established by a negative process, through the exercise of doubt. Once the projective nature of what I have called "belief" was recognized, I wondered how that "belief" emerges in the context of a veritable critical state of thought such as the experience of pain represents. This new perspective has enabled us to reconsider the evidence of the symbolic efficacy of Kuna shamanistic songs. The effect of the belief that is established in this tradition seemed to me to originate in a series of projective responses aimed not at its content but rather at its uncomprehended part expressed only by a few recognized verbal hints and that ends up becoming a sonorous screen available to a projective process. It is in that way that belief establishes a link between the sonorous image and the person, man or woman, who believes. The link emerges, apparently spontaneously, from the activation of the process of projection. The suffering woman in the Kuna ritual is engaged in the projective process even before belief becomes established.

So she is, quite literally, the true *author* of the symbolic efficacy of the song.

This long itinerary, which has led us from the techniques of the mnemonic codification of ritual songs to the decoding of the conditions of their utterance, has enabled us to explore a number of aspects of the type of communication and thereby also the memorization that is characteristic of the song-form in Amerindian shamanistic traditions. We may conclude from our analyses that a number of features are typical of the song-form and also of the type of memory that it implies. We should bear in mind the following:

- the relationship between images and language that I have called mnemonic, because it is based on a particular way of constructing salient images, thereby constituting so many keys to memorization;
- the definition of the image of a ritual locutor as a polythetic figure;
- the specific relationship that is established between the implicit and the explicit aspects of images. I have called this a relationship established through doubt, which turns out to be the origin of a type of belief engendered by the context of ritual communication.

In this chapter we have seen that parallelism affects not only the representation of the world (things that people speak about) but also that of locutors. From this we may conclude that in such a case, ritual communication, in order to construct memorable representations, does not simply use counterintuitive ones but furthermore inserts counterintuitive representations into counterintuitive contexts of utterance. In this way, a literature that seems entirely composed of almost incomprehensible words, esoteric images, and unusual ritual gestures attains a salience at least equivalent to that of narrative. I shall soon be returning to that theme. But for the moment let me observe that parallelism is not just a technique for preserving certain images that typify traditional knowledge, as, among the Kuna, the Tree-Woman, the Celestial Jaguar, and the plural and ambiguous image of the shamanistic singer. Parallelism is also a technique for generating new images. We shall see now that the polythetic figure of the shamanistic locutor may itself engender other creatures, following the technique of imagination that parallelism implies and that thereby gives rise to other forms of projective belief. That process of generating new memorable images will be the theme of the last chapter of this book, in which we shall see how this schema, which I have deduced from a morphological and comparative analysis of the formal conditions that orient certain Amerindian ritual traditions, acts and operates in cases of social change and conflict.

CHAPTER 4

Christ in America
Or, an antagonistic memory

Tende
le sue braccia fra i càrpini: l'oscuro
ne scancella lo sguardo. Senza voce,
disfatto dall'arsura, quasi esanime,
l'Idolo è in croce.

Eugenio Montale, "Costa San Giorgio"

Memory processes to which, progressively, increasingly complex mental operations were added, along with acts of sonorous and visual perception, classification, inference, and imagination, and, finally, projective elaboration and belief: that is the image of the Amerindian arts of memory that we have gradually enriched and that finds its place within a general view of an anthropology of thinking. The thinking of each one of us and perhaps even certain aspects of our perceptive processes all take place within a universe of shared ideas. Amerindian parallelism, whether verbal or visual and whether applied to the object or the subject of an utterance, constitutes one of the itineraries that point the way to the exercise of individual thinking. However, all too often when we speak of shared ideas, we have in mind a kind of indistinct fund of representations and thoughts on the basis of which (or despite which) the ideas and experiences of an individual are generated and then express that individual's inimitable profile—as if it were a matter of a form detaching itself from that general fund absolutely clearly and with no confusion possible.

It is of course undeniable that thought, in order to become discovery and inventiveness, must always react against a tradition composed of accepted ideas. All the same, as a description of the nature of a legacy of shared ideas, nothing could be more false than an image of an inert fund fixed for ever. Plenty of ideas are propagated within a social group and become part of a tradition, not through inertia or out of habit, but precisely wherever conflict is most intense; wherever an individual perceives the threat of limits being abolished; wherever uncertainty can come to dominate consciousness; wherever pain or vertigo suddenly appears.

Before we return to the ethnography of distant peoples, let us consider an example from our own tradition. One of the great myths of the twentieth century, the crowd as described and analyzed by Le Bon, Freud, and Canetti, provides an eloquent example of this aspect of the epidemiology of representations. This image of a throng rising up against an imaginary enemy or fleeing from a fire, the flames of which are no more than hearsay, results from a twofold process. On the one hand, the content of the mental image is dramatically simplified into just a few salient features: *us, the fire, the enemy.* On the other, that process of simplification sparks off a violent intensification of the link that unites the members of the group. Although it is confused and unstable, an *us* comes into being at that moment. Elias Canetti, far better in his novel *Auto-da-fé* ([1935] 1946) than in his *Crowds and power* ([1960] 2000), produced an admirable description of such a situation. In the lucid apocalyptic tone that characterizes so much of his writing, he proclaims that there is

> an impulsion that urges men collectively to attain to the state of a superior animal, a mass, and in it to lose themselves completely, as if the human individual had never existed. . . . Such a mass, like a monstrous, wild, ardent animal full of shifting passions, boils up in the depths of our being. But despite its age that mass is the youngest of all animals, the earth's essential creature, its goal, even its future. . . . Sometimes it falls upon us like a threatening storm or a roaring Ocean in which every drop of water lives in the same way and with the same goal as all the others. (Canetti [1935] 1946: 436–37)

This throng, in the guise of a monstrous animal, a threatening storm, or an immense Ocean, presents us with an initial eloquent image that is at the origin of the propagation of ideas in which the thoughts of each one of us should be included. The *mental contagion* that is thereby created is, as Freud's famous expression puts it, similar to an indefinitely iterated "hypnosis."[1] But it is, no doubt, perfectly possible that another illusion lurks in the idea that only such a throng can effectively provide support for a rapid and intense propagation of representations within a social group. In reality, every individual daily encounters both the support and at the same time the weight and constraints that stem from shared ideas. As we have seen in the course of earlier analyses, the celebration of a ritual is probably one of the most intense ways of constructing that which is memorable. But it is not possible to ignore an aspect that has so far been neglected: in traditional societies, as in others, what is memorable also rests upon conflict and pain, and this underpins an invariably fragile network of shared ideas. I have endeavored at some length to elaborate and enrich the current concept of memory, in the twofold sense of a codification of a mnemonic trace of its recollection, of classification and inference, and also of the invention of an iconography and the constitution of a context of ritualized communication. In this way, I have tried to present a sufficiently rich account of the conditions of what, as an antithesis to narrative memory, might be seen as a process of memorization of complex images: the kind of memory which, without representing the sounds of language, constructs around a mental representation a series of utterance conditions that in a new way preserve the trace left in the common memory. I have in mind, in particular, the ritual actions and iconographies that such a common memory implies; for that is precisely what composes the memory of numerous cultures that we have, for far too long, been calling merely "oral." Seen in this perspective, the concept of memory should be understood in its full sense, as *a craft of thought*, a context of reference, a domain of classification, a persistent schema of evocation and so of the construction of ideas and poetic imagination.

---

1.   The term "contagion" applied to mental phenomena was coined by Le Bon and is cited in Freud, "Group psychology and the analysis of the ego" (Freud 1985).

Memory "in the full sense," then. However, the space for that memory by no means conforms with the kind of order that a researcher is expected to work on. On the contrary, it looms up in the midst of conflict, pain, and confrontation with an enemy. We should never forget that in social life memory is never unitary: memories are all different and in many cases they are antagonistic. In this respect, traditional societies are no different from others. That is why I should like to bring this book to a close by studying one last case, one in which, precisely, conflict dominates. The last part of Chapter 2 referred to an Apache pictographic tradition. If we reconstruct its context in which a new world of shamanistic beliefs is taking shape, we find an eloquent example of social memory as operating in an open conflict. In this new context, we shall certainly not be abandoning either an examination of forms or an attempt to specify clearly the type of mental operations that are to be found in these new traditions. The techniques of memory in the fullest sense, which we have been considering so far, are much more resistant to cultural and political conflict than one might expect. Perhaps that is precisely how it is that they make it possible to focus on a few essential features even when, as we have just seen, a social memory develops through the establishment of a religious belief.

AN APACHE CHRIST

I now intend to undertake an analysis of the development of Apache shamanistic tradition, while bearing in mind the hypothesis of a study of the cognitive bases of culture. In the course of two Malinowski Lectures a few years apart, Dan Sperber and Pascal Boyer sketched in the profile of an epidemiology of representations (Sperber 1985; P. Boyer 2000), inscribing it within a new perspective as regards the definition of the object of anthropological research. They suggested that this should become a study of the way in which collections of representations are propagated in a society. So it would be a matter no longer of "visions of the world" but rather, in an undeniably more technical and interesting way, of the chains of representations that are produced by the propagation of ideas. Seen from this point of view, it is the constant exchange of representations in the course of daily communication that engenders the veritable phenomenon of contagion that we customarily call "culture."

Both Sperber and Boyer attribute the success of an idea essentially to its counterintuitive character, which makes it easier to remember. In fact—to be more precise—it is the transgression of a certain number of ontological features, which one assumes to be innate in the human mind, that confers upon a representation its own particular salience. And it is that salience that explains the persistence in time or the rapid propagation of a representation within a social group. There can be no doubt that this new approach, here summed up extremely succinctly, imparted a strong stimulus to anthropological research and at the same time suggested a new understanding of the relationship between culture and cognition. It is also unnecessary to underline the interest that this approach presents for an anthropology of memory. In my view, this theory still lacks specificity. In many situations—and we have already considered a number of them in our study not only of Amerindian pictography but also of the representation of names in Oceania—counterintuitiveness certainly does not suffice for the construction of a memorable representation. We all have dreams that are rich in salient representations that do not persist for long and that do not easily propagate themselves in the world of common knowledge.

Our study of specific techniques of memorization in America and Oceania and the type of communication and elaboration of speech that characterizes ritual recitation showed us, on the contrary, that, in order to construct memorable representations (the Tree-Woman, the Celestial Jaguar, and even the image of the singer-shaman surrounded by uncertainties), cultures often insert counterintuitive representations into the framework of counterintuitive contexts of propagation. In all the situations that we have examined in this book, ranging from the autobiographical song of the Plains warrior to the ritual therapies of the Kuna, a memorable or dominant representation is a counterintuitive one that is expressed within a counterintuitive situation of communication (P. Boyer and Severi 1997–99). We have noticed that, in order to construct a theory appropriate for cultural propagation, it is not sufficient to refer, as Sperber and Boyer do, to a general psychology of memory; it is also necessary to take into account the pragmatic aspect, that is to say, the specific conditions in which the cultural propagation of representations is taking place. So one must take into account not only the specific salience of certain religious or mythical notions but also, as I did in the analysis devoted to the Kuna recitation, the conditions in which those notions are being communicated. In short, one of the results of our study of these mnemonic techniques is that there exists not only a semantic counterintuitiveness but also a pragmatic counterintuitiveness, a salience that concerns the ways and conditions in which memorable speech is to be pronounced and interpreted. The existence of those two levels and the need to keep them distinct, which may pass unnoticed in homogeneous and static situations, becomes crucial when it comes to interpreting cultural conflict. One such situation of conflict is certainly represented in the Amerindian context by messianism. So let us now examine the Apache example in detail.

Messianic movements are particularly interesting for any anthropological theory based on the propagation of representations. Very often, these movements imply an extraordinary intensification of the process. These new religions, which in general possess a quite reduced body of doctrine, become propagated surprisingly rapidly and conquer whole peoples within very brief periods of time. The Ghost Dance, a messianic cult promising resurrection to all dead warriors and imminent victory over the Whites, which sprung up in northern America around the mid-nineteenth century, conquered almost all the Amerindian peoples in less than twenty years.

It is reasonable enough to wonder how it was that these cults were propagated so irresistibly and so rapidly. It has often been pointed out that prophetic movements are nearly always linked with situations of great turbulence and intense social conflict. In such cases, these religions become a veritable instrument of political battle, often enough launched against colonial intervention. The classic anthropological cases are, apart from the Amerindian Ghost Dance, the cargo cults of Melanesia and the Hauka movements of the Songhay of the Niger (Mooney 1896; Linton 1943; Worsley 1968; La Barre 1972; Stoller 1989). However, it is clear that the political role played by these movements does not fully explain their extraordinary efficacy. In theory, there is no reason to think that the traditional religions already well rooted in these societies could not have played a similar role and even been more effective in the struggle against the violent intrusion of the Whites. The intensification of the process of cultural propagation, which is typical of such prophetic phenomena, was no doubt due to a change in the traditional religious practices brought about by a new message proclaimed by a native prophet. In their discussion of the Apache dances known as *nial'do*, one of the most striking rituals linked with the Native Americans' Ghost Dance, Grenville Goodwin and Charles Kaut have written as follows: "The religious movements seem to have been successful only when an important medicine man has been able to capture the imagination of the Apache, and in each instance some innovation was necessary to do this" (Goodwin and Kaut 1954: 386). Why does a prophetic movement so often generate a change in traditional religions? And what kinds of changes are involved in these situations? In order to understand those changes, we first need to decide to suspend the usual explanations. It has often been customary to repeat that traditional religious beliefs are replaced in these situations because they either have been weakened by time or else have proved to be inadequate in the new situation. But such explanations are clearly circular since they use, *a posteriori*, what we already know. So they can tell us nothing about the process of propagation that is at the origin of a given situation. The answer to the problem is far less simple than it might appear.

One particularly interesting point concerns the *content* of representations of the messianic type. In a number of these movements, contacts between different beliefs (for example, Christianity and the local religion), regarded as a contagion or conflict, naturally play a central role. However, it is remarkable that the combination of different or even antagonistic religious features which, to the anthropologist, appear to be completely heterogeneous is usually presented by the new prophet as a harmonious and coherent vision of the world. A man or woman who joins the syncretistic Haitian movement, for example, will detect no contradiction between the Christian faith and the practices linked with Voodoo. As a faithful Voodooist once told Alfred Métraux, as they left the Port-au-Prince cathedral: one needs to be a good Christian to be a good Voodooist (Métraux [1959] 1972). Such an attitude was widespread among the Native Americans who joined the Ghost Dance messianic movement. Many perplexed observers at the time repeated that the new Apache, Sioux, or Paiute faithful detected no incoherence in practicing shamanism and Christianity both at the same time. In their eyes, Holy Mass (or a Protestant cult) in no way excluded recourse to shamanistic singing, nor, as we shall see, did a cult of the snake abolish that of Christ. So we have to concede that these messianic religions, although often described as "cultural hybrids," are in no way characterized by radical changes in the logic presiding over their doctrine.

As we shall see, what does change is something quite different. What emerges is a new phenomenon that in no way affects the semantics of the native religious discourse but that does exert a decisive influence upon the pragmatic process of cultural communication: namely, the appearance of what could be called a "paradoxical I," embodied by the native prophet. Let us consider an example. From the 1860s onward, among Native Noth Americans the figure of a shaman-prophet would arise, proclaiming a new religious message, seemingly interwoven with Christian references. However, in most cases this young Native American prophet did not claim to be analogous, similar, or comparable to Jesus Christ, the son and the incarnation of the God of the Whites; what he claimed was that he, and he alone, was the *true* son of the God of the Christians. In some cases, he also claimed to be the sole and unique Christ ever to have been sent to earth.

The most impressive case was probably that of the founder of the cult of the Ghost Dance. This was the Paiute prophet Wovoka, who lived in the Mason Valley in Nevada. In 1887 and 1889 Wovoka had received his first revelations, which were immediately propagated by many of his disciples, almost all of whom came from the tribes of the Plains Indians. In his vision, Wovoka had felt transported to the sky. There, he had met a supernatural being who had given him a message to take to his people. What he thereupon began to announce was that soon the day would come when all the Native American warriors killed by the Whites would return to earth, restored to the full flower of their youth. On that day, even the animals that constituted the most important hunted prey on which the Native Americans depended, and that were now becoming increasingly rare, would reappear. Also on that day, all the Whites would be vanquished (Mooney 1896: 771–74; Overholt 1974: 42). An important part of Wovoka's message concerned the very identity of the prophet. A document known as the "Messiah Letter" clearly stated that Wovoka and Jesus Christ were one and the same person: "Do not tell the White people about this, but Jesus is now upon the earth. He appears like a cloud. The dead are all alive again."

In a meticulous analysis of this document, Overholt (1974) has shown that when Wovoka tried to deny the above fact to James Mooney, who had been sent by the Bureau of American Ethnologists (Mooney 1896: 773), he was simply trying to conceal his new identity. Many of Wovoka's Indian disciples addressed him as "Christ." Some of them even claimed to have seen with their own eyes the stigmata on his hands and feet (Overholt 1974: 44). In a statement cited by Mooney, the new Indian Christ is explicitly identified with the Christ sent in the past to Israel:

> In the beginning, after God made the earth, they sent me back to teach the people, and when I came back on earth the people were afraid of me and treated me badly.... I found my children were bad, so went back to heaven and left them. I told them that in so many hundred years I would come back to see my children.... My father commanded me to visit the Indians on a purpose. I have came [*sic*] to the white people first but they are not good. They killed me, and you can see the marks of my wounds on my feet, my hands and on my back. (Mooney 1896: 796–97).

Wovoka, the messianic prophet, "is" Christ. Consequently, to become a faithful devotee of his new religion is, from the point of view of a Native American recently converted, by no means an abandonment of Christianity. On the contrary, as he sees it, it is a way of becoming a *true*, or even, in some cases, the *only* true, Christian. That was the view of the very many converted Native Americans who, in great numbers, joined the messianic movement in the late nineteenth century.

All the same, it was at the time manifestly clear, as it is today, that in the context of the Ghost Dance ritual, a declaration such as "I am a Christian" (or even "I am Christ") did not, of course, signify, "I belong to the religion of the Whites." The meaning of this statement had to be understood quite differently, that is to say, as: "It is precisely because I declare that I am a true Christian that I am a member [or even, in the case of the prophet, a founder] of a religion that is radically opposed to that of the Whites." "Being similar" in this case strictly implied "being different" or even "very different from the traditional Christian religion." In other words, what emerged here was a paradoxical situation in which "to resemble someone means to be very different from him, and vice-versa."

The transition from the traditional religion to a messianic cult entails a move from, on the one hand, a situation in which the traditional

shaman opposed Christianity because he held a profoundly different religious point of view to, on the other, a situation in which he (or rather
his disciple who had become a prophet) opposed Christianity because
he claimed to be even closer to true Christianity than a white missionary
was. The transformation here, often hastily called "inversion" by anthropologists, should be, more precisely, described as the constitution of a
paradox. The new prophet claims to be more powerful than the preceding one because he considers himself to be *both different from and similar
to* the god of the Christians. From a logical point of view, then, his message can be formulated as follows: "I oppose you, God of the Whites,
because I resemble you *and* because I am different from you."

One result of this process is a characteristic way of defining such
a new subject, a native Messiah, who embodies contradictory connotations. He can produce utterances that are typically contradictory or
indeed meaningless, such as: "To be me is the equivalent of being you."

Anthropologists and historians of religions have all too often described this process in a summary and excessively simplified manner. It
has been interpreted simply as an imitation of Western religion or else as
an inauthentic "invention of a tradition" (Hobsbawm and Ranger 1983).
An anthropologist's professional reaction was, in many cases, to concentrate on the inauthentic, nonindigenous, and therefore hybrid and non-
traditional character of the religious movement that had just come into
being. Whatever a shaman-messiah such as Wovoka presented as the
heritage of a tradition at the same time as he posed as a second Christ
now returned to earth was thus, with no more ado, identified as resulting
from some "modern" invention.

As for myself, I shall here adopt a diametrically opposed point of
view. I shall try to show that, in the Amerindian case that we shall be
considering in this chapter, but also in all cases that have come to my notice, the fact of producing paradoxical statements of this kind is in truth
equivalent to remaining perfectly faithful to the indigenous tradition, not
to the Christian tradition. I shall conclude that in the case of American
messianic shamanism it is totally erroneous to speak of "cultural hybrids."
However, it will not be possible to reach that conclusion and to see clearly
upon what it is founded unless we manage to attain the appropriate level
of abstraction that is implied here by the constitution of a social memory.
We shall therefore be taking into account not only the semantic content

of the messianic discourse, but also the practices of ritual utterance that constitute the pragmatic conditions for its propagation.

The starting point for our analysis is the public pronouncement of a new religion delivered by a young Apache who was born in 1887 in the Fort Apache reserve in Arizona. The name of this boy was Silas John. In 1916 Silas declared that he was the Messiah and began to preach. A few years later, he "attracted a sizeable crowd, and informed them that, although his rituals were to be performed on Sunday mornings, like the one of the local Lutheran Church, his religion did not require that he speak from the Bible. Holding up a cross on which was drawn the figure of a snake, he said that this was the image the Apache should follow"(Kessel 1976: 176).

By about 1920 it was clear to everyone that Silas had been accepted as the new prophet by the local Apache. At this point he chose twelve assistants who were sent out to preach to all the Apache tribes, praying for them and encouraging them to follow the new rituals (Basso and Anderson 1975). In the last period of his preaching, adopting what I have called a process of paradoxical self-definition, Silas John eventually told his disciples in New Mexico, who were still calling him Yusen, the name of the original creator of Apache mythology, "You have to accept Jesus. Call me Jesus, not Yusen" (R. M. Boyer and Gayton 1992: 294–95).

The movement founded by Silas John spread extremely rapidly among the Apache of San Carlos and of White Mountain, in Arizona. After 1920, it reached the Mescalero Apache of New Mexico and led to the foundation of a "New Prayer" that was adopted in many villages and soon became the signal of a general rebellion amongst the Apache, in particular those of White Mountain, against the Christianity of the missionaries. It was immediately clear, above all to the military authorities in the reserve to which the Native Americans were all at that time confined, that to declare "Call me Jesus" was certainly not a way of spreading the Christian message, but was, rather, a sacrilegious way of calling for a revolt. The military Superintendent forbade Silas from attending or taking part in any dances, and spelled out his reason very clearly: "I have told Silas and all the Indians here that I do not object to them keeping up to some extent their ancient rites and tribal teachings, but that I would not permit any of the young men to start new religions" (cited in Kessel 1976: 157).

The typical features of the birth of a messianic movement (troubled minds, intense political conflict, the announcement of a new religious message) were all present in the Apache situation during those years. However, as we shall see, Silas chose an unusual way to establish the opposition between the old and the new religions. His preaching constitutes precisely an example in which it was not enough to register the birth of new salient or counterintuitive representations, defined on the sole basis of their meaning, in order to explain the propagation of these new ideas. To understand the nature of that propagation and its intensity, we need to be aware of the pragmatic conditions in which Silas John's "counterintuitive" message was formulated. Only an interpretation of the new ritual introduced by Silas, a ritual involving a New Prayer and a specific sequence of ritual actions, will make that possible. But for the time being let us just briefly reconstruct the historical and ethnographic context of his message.

The succession of Apache shamanistic movements from the 1870s onward clearly show, within a period of less than forty years, the switch between what I have called an opposition to Christianity founded on difference, on the one hand, to an opposition founded upon analogy, on the other. In 1870, after a period of particularly violent warfare between the Apache and the US army, a number of Apache groups were confined in two reservations in Arizona: White Mountain and San Carlos. During this period of confinement there arose among the Apache four different religious movements, all led by shamans, which expressed their anger and resentment.

The first messianic movement started around 1880, when a shaman called Noch-ay-del-klinne celebrated a number of rituals designed "to raise the dead warriors and bring back the old leaders for a joint uprising with the Chiricahua against the United States army" (Goodwin and Kaut 1954: 387). Noch-ay-del-klinne was "an ascetic, slight medicine man . . . [whose] complexion was so pale as to seem almost white" (Thrapp 1988: 217). He had acquired a summary knowledge of Christianity but, after a period of doubt, he abandoned the Christian teachings. The story of his transfiguration into a Messiah is relatively brief. In 1871, the reservation authorities were still describing the twenty-six-year-old as "a kindly White Mountain herb doctor," "widely known as a dreamer and mystic, although not considered a dangerous one" (ibid.).

In the course of those years, Noch-ay-del-klinne was sent to Santa Fe, to attend school. There, "he absorbed but hardly understood the elements of the Christian religion. He was particularly impressed by the story of the Resurrection" (ibid.). Soon after his return to the reservation, this "rustic dreamed his way into the subconscious of his people, arousing them to a fervor of devotion and trust" (ibid.: 217–18). By June 1881, Noch-ay-del-klinne had become the central figure in a series of collective rituals celebrated in order to resurrect Apaches who had died in battle. The message was similar to that of all the religious movements that were, at that time, linked with the Native Americans' Ghost Dance. It focused exclusively upon the resurrection of warriors killed on the battlefield. The meaning of this return to life was neither ambiguous nor metaphorical: Noch-ay-del-klinne taught his faithful followers a new dance, a variation on the traditional Dance of the Wheel "in which all the performers face a central focus, aligned outwards like the spokes of a wheel, and dance a forward–backward time step, irregularly so that the wheel slowly revolves" (Haley 1981: 336). Noch-ay-del-klinne promised the faithful that celebrating this dance would bring the Apache chiefs back to life, in particular a certain Diablo (Haskedasila in the Apache language, meaning "constantly angry"), who had been killed shortly before. In this way, thanks to the aid of the resuscitated Diablo, the Whites would be chased out of the Apache territory. In a vision, Noch-ay-del-klinne had "dreamed that the white-eyes would be gone when the corn was ripe" (ibid.: 337). During one of these meetings, a journalist named Connell (cited in Kessel 1976: 63–64) recorded the words pronounced by the shaman:

> Are we not natives to the earth around us?
> Are we not part of the forest, the rocks, and the air?
> Do not the birds sing, for the Apache? Is not the deer part of our lives?
> [. . .]
> Do not the bodies of our ancestors lie beneath the earth that belongs to us?
> Why then do the Whites come hither? Why do they kill our game?

There was only one brave among the Apache who could keep the whites back, Diablo, the chief.

His spirit hovers amid the rustling pine; the fluttering leaves indicate his presence.

The wail of the mountain lion and the roar of the bear tell you that he is near. He will come again, not in spirit, but in the flesh, to deliver us from the hated whites.

Diablo guards our interests, Diablo seeks a remedy, and Diablo will live again. In the dance we seek an inspiration.

With rhythmical movements, we commune with the spirits. The dance inspires passion, faith, fury, bravery and strength.

Is it not I, who revives the message at the meeting place of the bones of Diablo?

According to an account collected in 1976 by William B. Kessel, an anthropologist who carried out particularly detailed research on these religious movements, Noch-ay-del-klinne tried several times to bring about the resurrection of Diablo by dancing directly on his tomb.

One White Mountain Apache woman who was born in 1908 learned from an eye-witness that a dance was held over the grave of one of the dead chiefs. The chief had been buried in a shallow grave covered with a blanket and a piece of canvas on which he had placed his personal belongings and a covering of rocks. Noch-ay-del-klinne removed the rocks, grave goods, and canvas until the blanket was exposed. The burial then became the centre of the dance. (Kessel 1976: 70)

That was the dance that the American army soldiers interrupted. Noch-ay-del-klinne's teachings had caused great excitement in the reservation. The intense fervor with which the Apache celebrated those rituals had made the American military nervous. The new dance spread rapidly from one village to another and, above all, had the alarming effect of fostering a new solidarity among the rival Apache groups who found themselves confined together in the same reservation. The army immediately perceived the political meaning and the possible consequences of the ritual taught by the young shaman. What alarmed the civilian and military authorities in particular and propelled them into action was the fact that many Apache "scouts" and even the Apache police agents were implicated in the movement and suddenly became hard to manage. The men sometimes became hostile, always ready to protest against the Whites' domination on Indian land (Haley 1981). This is not the place to trace the history of this first Apache movement. Suffice it to bear in mind that the movement launched by Noch-ay-del-klinne was considered as a threat serious enough to warrant violent repression by the US army. The soldiers killed the young shaman along with many of his disciples. Here is how Noch-ay-del-klinne's end was described by John Bourke, a military man who, like Hoffman, Mallery, and many others, was both an army officer and an ethnographer working for the Bureau of American Ethnology:

> This Apache medicine-man . . . exercised great influence over his people in Camp Apache, in 1881. He boasted of his power to raise the dead, and predicted that the whites should soon be driven from the land. He also drilled the savages in a peculiar dance. . . . This prophet or "doctor" was killed in the engagement in the Cibecue canyon, August 30, 1881. (Bourke [1892] 1993: 55)

Clearly, this first religious movement was still closely connected with the war between the Apache and the Whites, an extremely violent conflict that had ended only a few years earlier and was still a memory very much alive in the minds of all. The political implications of the return of the dead announced by Noch-ay-del-klinne did not escape any of those involved in this conflict. To "capture the imagination" of his disciples (as Goodwin put it), the first Apache prophet had used only very vague references to the history of the Christian Resurrection (and, no doubt, to the message propagated widely in the course of those years, which was launched by movements linked with the Ghost Dance founded by Wovoka). In truth, he never did imitate any of the Christian teaching and throughout his life remained a practicing shaman, absorbed by the utterance of his songs. In particular, he was very familiar with songs linked to the spirit of the Snake-Lightning and the therapeutic power derived from them (Goodwin 1969: 35; Kessel 1976: 59). The dance that he taught his disciples was a version that remained very close to the original traditional dance. The movement of ideas implanted by Noch-ay-del-klinne still expressed total opposition to Christianity. When he recounted his dreams or invited members of his tribe to accompany him in his new dance, he spoke in the name of the Apache tradition. Syncretism was virtually absent from his doctrine.

After the death of Noch-ay-del-klinne, a number of young Apache shamans, among whom Big John is particularly mentioned in the relevant sources (Goodwin and Kaut 1954; Ferg 1987), endeavored to keep his movement alive and to continue to follow his teaching. We possess evidence of the rapid diffusion, from village to village, of a new circular dance, between 1903 and 1906. The search for contact with the world of the dead, embodied by a village somewhere in the heavens and populated by the people of Lightning, held a central position in this ritual, known in the Apache language as Dahgodia ("they will arise again and be resuscitated"). For instance, Big John, who seems to have been one of Noch-ay-del-klinne's successors, declared to his disciples that, thanks to the new ritual, "you will be raised up from the earth in a cloud, and while you are gone the earth will be changed. Then you will be lowered on to it again and it will be all ready for you" (Goodwin and Kaut 1954: 393).

The obvious implication of this announcement was, of course, that the Whites would have vanished from the earth. The end of Noch-ay-del-klinne's movement and his attempt to resuscitate the old chiefs of the Apache war had been tragic. But the prophet's death had been full of dignity. This time, though, the result of this attempt to wipe the Whites off the face of the earth by means of a ritual was crueller. Daslahdn, one of the shamans involved in the movement, one day declared that he had become able to travel to the world of the dead and to come back alive, three days later. Once again, a Resurrection was to be performed. This time the return from the beyond directly involved the person of one of the prophets. Neil Buck, an Apache disciple of the movement that preached "the rise of the Native Americans into the sky," recounted his own version of the story of Daslahdn and the shamans who accompanied him:

> We have danced four or five years in this new way, but finally we quit it because all the medicine men who ran it died. Daslahdn was the first to die: he felt that he could return from the dead and had his followers cut

off his head so that he could prove it. But it never came true. They all died, so everybody got scared and quit. Big John was the only one left. (Cited in Goodwin and Kaut 1954: 393)

With Big John, some new customs were introduced. Some were already paradoxical: the disciples of the "new dance" movement had to dress in white, in accordance with the traditions of the Apache. But a new symbol appeared amid these white clothes: it combined the cross with a shape resembling a crescent moon (Figure 80).

Figure 80. The first variation on the theme of the cross: introduced by Big John.

Since Big John, like his predecessors, shared the knowledge and shamanistic power linked with the Snake-Lightning, in all probability this symbol was associated with the Snake. The sources that I have collected record that Big John sang, in particular, "the therapeutic lightning songs" and his new dance was widely perceived as a new "snake dance"

(Goodwin and Kaut 1954: 399 and 400). In Apache tradition, the power of the snake was strictly linked with the mythological image of the People of the Lightning, which, in its turn, was one way of designating the world of the dead. So it is by no means impossible that this association was already well established as early as the time of Noch-ay-del-klinne. Besides, as early as 1884, John Bourke had noticed, in Apache villages, crosses associated with an image of a snake:

> The sign of the cross appears in many places in Apache symbolism. . . . It is related to the cardinal points and the four winds, and is painted by warriors. . . . In October 1884, I saw a procession of Apache men and women, led by the medicine-men bearing two crosses. . . . They were decorated with blue polka dots upon the unpainted surface. A blue snake meandered down the longer arm. (Bourke [1892] 1993: 29)

In these two new versions of the movement linked with "the return of the dead warriors", some of the symbols had changed. But the identity of the prophets, for its part, had undergone no modification. Big John, like Daslahdn and the other young prophets, was an altogether traditional shaman. After the failure of Daslahdn's attempted resurrection, Big John withdrew to a distant village. He quite simply admitted the failure of his power and gave up his ambition to reach the sky and lead the Apache there.

When Silas John entered upon the scene and publicly announced his new prophetic message, he showed the crowd a cross upon which a snake was drawn. There can be no doubt that, in so doing, he was referring to the recent tradition established by the messianic movements that had preceded him. In particular, that gesture of his referred, with precision, back to the snake dances performed by Big John. Silas, too, was a shaman and he too, like Big John and Noch-ay-del-klinne, possessed the power and the knowledge of the Snake-Lightning. In his teachings, he made use of a typical range of elements linked to the tradition founded, forty years earlier, by Noch-ay-del-klinne: the snake, the cross, the dead warriors' return from the world of the dead, the travel to the clouds, the white robes, and the songs. His Mescalero disciples (some of whom were particularly close to him in the last years of his teaching) told one of the best anthropologists of the Apache culture, Ruth McDonald Boyer, the story of one of his miracles. In that case, the intervention of Silas John involved the transformation of a drum into a living being. This is how the story is, still today, told:

> "Silas converses with God."
> "He sees angels, angels with wings, dressed all in white."
> "Silas has thirty-two kinds of medicines [songs]."
> "Everything listens to Silas now, even the clouds."
> "He can bring a dead man back to life."
> "They say he has a drum. He just put his drum on the ground and it beats
> by itself when Silas talks to it." (R. M. Boyer and Gayton 1992: 152)

Clearly, in this text, although some elements of the messianic tradition recur, things have already changed a great deal. Silas John, instead of aiming to defend the old shamanistic tradition against the teaching of missionaries, is beginning, in some respects, to act as a typical "paradoxical I."

At first, when he began to preach publicly, he had strictly followed the traditional model of Apache initiation. His father, too, was a shaman and he had followed the latter's teaching. Silas went into the forest, ate no food, and tried to obtain a vision of the Gan, a traditional Apache animal spirit that constituted the animal double of a human person. From 1914 to 1916, Silas learnt, probably from the teaching offered by his father, all he could about the Snake spirit and the knowledge of Lightning. His first vision involved a meeting with one of the forest spirits. And it was Lightning, precisely, that taught him his personal songs. As we shall see, among the Apache, the source of a shaman's power lay in the knowledge of those songs.

> Silas was carried to a place . . . where the earth was made, and where
> time began. It was a white mountain with a black cloud over it. From
> the cloud a supernatural being came to Silas John and informed him
> he would become a prophet. . . . This being also taught him his prayers.
> (Kessel 1976: 163)

The supernatural spirit of Lightning, as the Apache saw it, was of course related to the Snake. Silas saw snakes in his vision and so became a specialist endowed with "the special power that is attributed to the snake."

> Silas John told me that a snake visited his house in 1913. It wouldn't go away. So Silas decided to put some beads on its neck. He did that, and the fourth time he did that, the snake left for good. . . . When Silas was in heaven, the Spirit said: "You had a visitor. I am going to show you this visitor." They went to a green spot where there were sixty-four snakes. They all stood up. "Pick out the one you put the beads on"—said the Spirit. (Cited in R. M. Boyer and Gayton 1992: 153–54)

The Gan dances are one of the most important rituals in Apache society. Founded on a ritual sequence of symbolic relations between the Snake and the Lightning, these dances maintain the relations that connect men with the animal spirits, which in return pass on a number of powers to them. The Gan can appear in dreams and in certain visions. They can talk to humans and teach them their powers. As Keith Basso has written, as a result of these relations with the spirits, a kind of code of conduct is established between a spirit and the person who is the recipient of its teaching and its power:

> Apache say that the surest way to maintain effective contact with a power is to accord it the same courtesies customarily extended to human beings. For example, instructions given by a power, however onerous, should be carried out without complaint or suppressed ill feeling. When making requests, the power should be addressed politely and spoken to in a low, unhurried key" (Basso 1970: 39).

However, here, too, Silas was determined to leave his mark on tradition. When he at last experienced a vision of one of the most powerful of the spirits and was admitted to the knowledge of a number of songs associated with the power wielded by snakes and lightning, he forbade his disciples to perform the rituals associated with the Gan. He said they should be replaced by his New Prayer. Old Man Arnold, one of his earliest Mescalero disciples, remembers a prayer in which it was no longer the Gan who were said to be the founders of the universe, but Jesus Christ himself: "When the earth was made, when the sky was made, in the very beginning, they walk around with Jesus" (cited in R. M. Boyer and Gayton 1992: 149). According to him, this new way of describing the origin of the world aroused a measure of perplexity among Silas' disciples:

> It troubles me that Silas doesn't like the Crown [= Gan] Dancers. He said their dances belong to the devil and do harm. That is hard to understand for me because I know their blessing has helped our people. But I guess we should follow the prophet. (Cited in R. M. Boyer and Gayton 1992: 149)

As we have seen, when Silas decided to present his God publicly, he showed a cross together with a painted image of a snake:

> The people from Campo Verde, Mescalero and both Arizona Apache Reservations gathered to be cured and to watch the much publicized snake medicine man at work. The dances were held on Sundays and between 500 and 600 Indians were in attendance. Silas John made a large cross from plywood, the vertical piece about five feet high. On this was painted a large serpent with its tail at the bottom and its head just below the point at which the crosspiece was attached. (Kessel 1976: 172)

In this representation, the snake was positioned very precisely in the place of the body of Christ, which was thus explicitly identified with the snake. Both were at once Apache and Christian. Later on, Silas took to declaring that God had, in reality, chosen the Apache, not the Jews, as the elect people. As Old Man Arnold, one of his closest disciples, declared: "The Silas cult is better for the Apaches than the Dutch Reformed service. Since the Jews crucified Jesus, the Apache have become God's favored people. That is what Silas has said" (cited in R. M. Boyer and Gayton 1992: 295).

Toward the end of Silas' life, when the ritual that he preached—which was explicitly hostile to the Christianity of the American soldiers and missionaries—had gained in prestige and was shared by many Native Americans, he began to demand to be called Christ. These apparent paradoxes, which were considered scandalous and aroused violent hostility around him, all point to one conclusion: in the eyes of his disciples and the Apache in general, Silas the shaman had become the new Christ.

The prophet is Silas John. . . . He started to preach about three years ago on the Fort Apache Indian reservation. Lots of those folks listen to him now. He is a great orator. He has power, just like the medicine men of the old times. And he tells the Indians to live good lives . . . he tells them to stop their fighting. . . . He knows all about Christianity and says we should listen to what it says in the Bible. He says our medicine men are no longer enough. We should turn to Jesus. (J. Henry [no date], cited in R. M. Boyer and Gayton 1992: 143)

From a superficial point of view, this "careful blend of Apache and Christian belief and symbolism" (Goodwin and Kaut 1954: 388) may seem absurd, even confused, or—worse still—to create the illusion of an Apache conversion to Christianity, a conversion that never, in truth, took place. Even today, the conversion of the Apache remains problematic, confused, and incomplete. Nevertheless, Silas John's message enjoyed great success among the Apache and at the same time became one of the weapons that helped them to resist external cultural pressure. In order to gain a better understanding of the religious movement that he founded and the remarkable mixture of traditional memories and renewal that characterized it, let us now make a closer study of the way in which he communicated his message through ritual action. We must analyze the particular modalities of this New Prayer and the new songs that Silas— the specialist of the Snake's Song but also the Messiah linked so closely with the figure of Christ as to seek to be identified with him—required his faithful followers to recite.

The cultural basis of the new ritual introduced by Silas naturally enough remained the tradition with which he was so familiar: shamanistic singing. As we have seen from the analysis of the Kuna case, this tradition is characterized by two distinct uses of the parallelist technique, understood as a way of engendering new images as well as purely a mnemotechnique for memorizing songs. The use of varied repetition creates transformed images of the external world. It is a process which, as we have seen, leads to the formulation of the great chimerical figures that are so characteristic of shamanistic literature in America. We should also bear in mind that these are figures constructed by combining contradictory ontological features, such as the Celestial Jaguar and the Tree-Woman from Kuna tradition, both of them good examples of the procedure. As we shall see, it will not be hard to find equivalent chimerical figures in other Amerindian traditions such as, precisely, the Apache. We have also already identified a second but less obvious way of using the parallelism so characteristic of the Amerindian shamanistic tradition: a reflexive use of the parallelist technique, which leads to focusing the same process of combining contradictory features in the image of the celebrant of the ritual or the locutor of a song. In the course of the song's celebration, that celebrant, as well as being a human being like any other, also becomes a "deer," a "monkey," a "boar," or even, as in the Kuna case that we have studied, the incarnation of his own supernatural adversary, the "Jaguar." The complex ritual identity of an American shaman is thus characterized by the progressive inclusion of a series of contradictory connotations, which turn him into a plural figure capable of arousing a lasting uncertainty. The specific tension between doubt and belief that surrounds the celebration of such rituals renders them memorable. It is worth emphasizing that the definition of the locutor is, in the technical sense, parallelist in this context. His image is defined in the same terms as those used to represent the supernatural chimeras evoked in the songs. In this way, the locutor himself becomes a chimerical figure composed of "canonical pairs" that represent opposed values (Fox 1988).

Now let us return to the Apache shamanistic tradition. For an Apache shaman, likewise, the act of formulating a song is a way of revealing the power of an animal spirit through a particular use of language. As Keith Basso has noted, the power of such a spirit is in many cases identified with his song:

> Chants and prayers are said to "belong" to a power; they are also described as being "part" of it. In fact, the relationship between the two is so close that the term *diyi* may be used either in reference to a power itself or to its associated chants. . . . This is especially true of medicine men, whose effectiveness in ceremonials rests squarely on their ability to "sing" to this power in such a way that it feels disposed to make diagnoses and aid in cures. (Basso 1970: 42)

Now let us consider the example of the Gan dances, the Gan being the animal spirits embodied by the famous Apache "masked dancers" (Figure 81).

Figure 81. Gan dancers.

The very rich documentation gathered by William B. Kessel and Alan Ferg relating to the collection of masks now to be found in the Arizona State Museum (Ferg 1987: 117–25) reveals that the spirit impersonated by the Gan dancers (sometimes referred to simply as "the Spirit of the Mountain") is a complex representation referring to a sequence of different supernatural beings. This sequence of supernatural spirits, which is often led by the Snake and closed by the Lightning, may include creatures that belong to the Sky as well as to the Earth. These creatures include the Cross, the indigenous representation of the four cardinal points of the earth, the Eagle, and the Rays, which may emanate from the Sun as well as from lightning itself (Figure 82).

In the Apache shamanistic tradition, the four cardinal points are constantly present. The dance of the Gan always takes place within an oriented space, in which the Cross, which represents the four cardinal points, is clearly marked by long thin tree-trunks. The trunks are painted in the colors that, according to Apache cosmology, correspond to the four cardinal points: black, white, yellow, and blue. The dancers have to kneel facing in each of the four directions and then "gyrate clockwise"

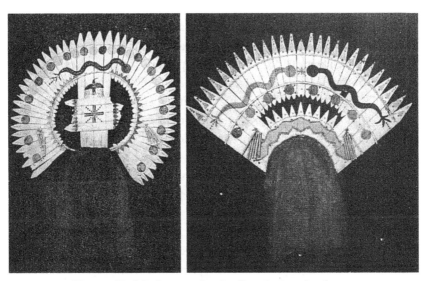

Figure 82. Masks worn by the Gan during the dance.

round the ritual space (Opler 1941: 107–8). When the celebrant sprin-kles a certain amount of pollen within the sacred space—pollen that is sacred matter always used in ritual actions in Apache tradition—he must also direct his gesture toward each of the cardinal points. Morris Opler has described this preparation of the ritual space in great detail (Opler 1941: 76–134); and John Bourke had already observed the ceremonies as early as 1887:

> I have seen this dance a number of times, but will confine my descrip-tion to one seen at Fort Marion (St Augustine, Fla.) in 1887, when the Chiricahua Apache were confined as prisoners. . . . The medicine man advanced to where a squaw was holding up a little baby in its cradle. . . . The baby was held so as to occupy each of the cardinal points, and face each power directly opposite: first on the east side, facing the west, then the north side, facing the south, then the west side, facing the east, then the south side, facing the north. (Bourke [1892] 1993: 133–34)

Now let us move on to the dancers who impersonate the Gan. In Apache tradition, a ritual dancer was most strictly obliged to regard his role with the greatest respect. The kind of fiction that the ritual staged was of such importance that no-one had the right to cast doubt upon it:

"No one may address or call the name of an impersonator whom he recognizes" (Opler 1941: 112). Women, in particular, were officially obliged to ignore the fact that the Gan who appeared in the dances were not really spirits, but men (Goodwin 1969: 535). An Apache dancer had to make himself a faithful image of a spirit, an image always considered utterly independent of his personal identity. If we now turn to Opler's splendid description of a Gan dance celebrated on the occasion of an Apache girl's initiation, we find that the entire ritual action is founded on a connection between the movements of the dancers and the chant sung by the shaman. We should note first that the shaman's song dictates the rhythm of the dance:

> The songs are classified in three groups, each related to one of three types of dance: the "free step," the "short step," and the "high step." The dancers, and especially their leader, must be able to recognise a song at once, and enter upon the proper step. (Opler 1941: 114)

So speech and the ritual action are synchronized. However, the relation established on the ritual stage between the singer and the dancers goes far beyond this. In this context, the dancer becomes the image of the spirit and the shaman becomes the latter's voice. Through the ritual action, a progressive identification is established, on the one hand, between the dancer and the spirit and, on the other, between the singer and the dancer. When the shaman sings, for example,

> In the middle of the Holy Mountain,
> In the middle of its body, stands a hut,
> Brush-built, for the Black Mountain Spirit.
> White lightning flashes in these moccasins;
> White lightning streaks in angular path,
> I am the lightning flashing and streaking! (Opler 1941: 108)

a complex identity is established both through the voice of the singer and through the image of the dancer. As we have seen, this image also combines the representation of a sequence of supernatural beings that may range from the Lightning to the Snake. A declaration such as "I am the lightning flashing and streaking!" thus, in this context, supposes a chain of identifications such as the following:

I am the lightning
I am the *Gan*
I am the snake
I am the one who possesses the power and the song of the Snake
I am the shaman.

In the utterance of this repeated "I," the voice of the one and the image of the other merge into a single presence. This new presence is that of an identity ritually constructed by the shaman singer. So, here too, the definition of the shaman is, as in the Kuna case, engendered through a reflexive application of parallelism. An analysis of the process of utterance shows that the Kuna and the Apache situations, although far from identical, are nevertheless comparable. In the Kuna case, the complex identity of the locutor is created out of a cumulative inclusion of features that is expressed or realized only through the utterance of songs. In the Apache case, this complex identity of the ritual locutor is, rather, constructed through the image of the Gan dancer, itself complex, which refers back to a sequence of supernatural beings.

Let us now return to Silas John, who must certainly have been familiar with this type of singing (and maybe with precisely the song devoted to the power of Snake-Lightning, which was the object of his earliest initiation, with his father). We should take a closer look at the new cult that he founded: the Prayer of the Holy Ground. As we know, the doctrine preached by Silas might have seemed, morally, very close to Christianity. But the difference of his religious message found expression elsewhere: in symbols and ritual. The memoirs published by some of his disciples today help us to gain a better understanding of this point. The first act of the New Prayer was to delimit a specific space that was to be strictly respected by celebrants. That space was named the Four Crosses Holy Ground; within that space, the four cardinal points were identified precisely: "The church consisted of a rectangle about six feet by four feet. Its sides faced the four sacred directions: the long sides were north and south, the short sides east and west. A five-foot Cross stood at each corner." There is an obvious analogy between those four crosses—"painted in black, white, yellow, and blue"(R. M. Boyer and Gayton 1992: 150)— and the long, thin, painted tree-trunks mentioned by Opler in his description of the Gan dances (Opler 1941: 107). But there is more to it: according to Silas John's disciples, those crosses acted exactly as if they themselves were Gan: they "talked to them in their dreams"(R. M. Boyer and Gayton 1992: 150).

Once an oriented space was thus established, the celebrant had to recite the New Prayer, at the same time performing a special dance. Silas himself was always the first to dance. The believer had to follow his movements exactly, slowly crossing the Holy Ground. Very precise instructions were given regarding the gestures to be performed while saying the prayer, the steps to be danced, the parts of the Holy Ground to be reached, and, finally, the sequence of the cardinal points to be touched (or, as Silas put it, honored). The description of a dance celebrated in the Mescalero village, in New Mexico, among the Chiricahua Apache during the recitation of Silas' New Prayer, and of the "blessing" made with pollen on the Four Crosses Holy Ground leave no room for doubt. The typical gestures of the Apache tradition were systematically associated with those of the Christian liturgy: "When the leader of the service approached the Holy Ground, he removed his hat, placing it to the east side of the plot. Then he walked to the west side of the rectangle and knelt, facing east." Those were precisely the movements prescribed for the Gan dancers, in Opler's description. Silas then immediately after made a kind of gesture that performed a sort of synthesis between the sign of the cross and the traditional shamanistic manipulation of the pollen. According to Ruth McDonald Boyer, "He took a pinch of pollen in his right hand, holding it to the east while his left hand, palm in, lay across his breast. He touched his right shoulder, the top of his head and his breast with the yellow powder, finishing by making two clockwise circles over his head." Then "he blessed each Cross with pollen"(R. M. Boyer and Gayton 1992: 151). This sequence of gestures was so important that all the participants in the ritual had to repeat the example set by the prophet, in the same order and with the same gestures.

Many commentators on the rituals founded by Silas John attribute the scandal provoked by the dances to the fact that he often resorted to the use of live snakes. As they saw it, this was his principal method for "capturing the imagination" of the Indians and thereby becoming a prestigious religious and political leader. But it is quite clear that there was nothing new about this practice from the point of view of the Apache tradition. All Silas' predecessors were shamans who specialized, precisely, in the cycle of songs associated with the power of the Snake-Lightning. His own father had specialized in this same cycle and had taught his son how to capture and use rattlesnakes without risk. A whole series of ethnographers, such as Albert Reagan (1930), mentioned the use of live snakes in the traditional shamanistic practices of the Apache. Despite appearances, the explanation for the scandal and hence the success of the rituals founded and taught by Silas John is to be found elsewhere.

A comparison between the ritual recitation taught by the prophet and the traditional rituals of the Apache reveals that while he was reciting and singing of the glory of the new Christ, the faithful follower of Silas John's cult was actually simultaneously performing something very similar to a Gan dance—the very dance that Silas had forbidden. When the believer, imitating the behavior of the prophet, uttered his prayer, he behaved as a perfect Christian. But when he used the sacred Apache pollen, when he knelt before a cross bearing the image of the Snake-Lightning, which represented the East, or when he left the Holy Ground, turning clockwise, he was performing the very gestures that characterized a Gan dancer before his dance.

We have seen that the traditional dance of the Gan implied a progressive identification of the shaman with an animal spirit, the Gan. Next, the singer actually identified himself with the dancer, who had become an image of the spirit. During the Prayer of the Four Crosses, a similar process took place: the person who prays like a Christian becomes identified with Silas John, the prophet, by copying the latter's gestures, and also, simultaneously, with the spirit of the Mountain, the Gan, whose dance the shaman was showing him. What the shaman was doing as he performed the appropriate dance steps ("I am celebrating the Gan") contradicted what he was saying when he uttered his prayer ("I am addressing my prayer to Jesus Christ"). There, in the ritual space of the Holy Ground, the man who was praying to Christ at the same time became someone celebrating the dance of the Gan. An analysis of the ritual action, based on the identification of the pragmatic context of the enunciation of Silas John's New Prayer, shows that the ritual actions taught by Silas contradicted his doctrine. The so-called "new religion" was *also* the traditional religion: the New Prayer included the traditional dance that Silas had forbidden.

Nevertheless, the cult of the Holy Ground, founded by Silas, is neither absurd nor contradictory. It was a ritual way to engender complexity by means of paradox. For the most remarkable result of this distinct use of speech and gestures within the ritual context was the construction of a complex identity. Silas John *speaks* as a Christian and *acts* as an Apache shaman: once he enters the ritual space, he becomes both, simultaneously. An analysis of the counterintuitive conditions of communication that he imposed upon his disciples in order to found his New Prayer thus shows that the solution to the problem of interpretation posed by a messianic utterance such as "I am Jesus because I am a shaman" is to be found not in the usual contradiction established between the predicates, but rather in the ritually created complexity of the "I" who utters it.

This conclusion, which I have drawn by using the analysis of the shamanistic song-form in a new context, has a general consequence that concerns both the concept of religious syncretism and that of cultural contact. Despite appearances, the ritual definition of Silas John as Jesus, the Apache shaman founder of the Prayer of the Holy Ground of the Four Crosses, is not the result of a cultural exchange of beliefs. On the contrary, that definition represents a further application of the parallelistic logic that we have seen operating in both the case of the Kuna singer and that of the traditional Apache shaman. So we may conclude that, when Silas John claimed that he had become Jesus, he was certainly not adhering to Christianity: he was still opposing it and doing so on the basis of a perfectly traditional attitude. The "I" who asked his disciples thenceforth to call him "Jesus" was not simply the product of the mixture of cultural traditions. This "I" should be seen as a paradoxical, but still parallelistic, enunciator, made of "canonical pairs of contradictory connotations." The case of Silas John helps us to see clearly that, in the tradition, this series of connotations remained an *open series* that was always ready to include a new term.

It is thus reasonable to conclude that there is no trace of syncretism in the Apache messianic movements. Given that, ever since the first attempts to "resuscitate" the chiefs killed by the Whites by dancing on their tombs, the term "Christ" became one of the basic terms of the

Apache shamanistic world, it was bound to become incorporated into the series of canonical couples that defined the locutor of a song (jaguar and bird, woman and tree, snake and lightning, voice and image). So calling Silas John "Christ" was not a way of betraying the shamanistic tradition but, on the contrary, a new way to be faithful to it.

Now let us finally return to the formal analysis, which has proved effective, even in the case of an exploration of cultural conflict as violent as that of the Apache. Let us look for a formal explanation to account for the intense and rapid character of the propagation of the Apache messianic message. If we accept the thesis of Dan Sperber and Pascal Boyer, both traditional shamanism and the preaching of the missionaries had equal chances to prevail in this context. What the story of the cult introduced by Silas John shows us is that the two religions, the one local, the other Christian, which already existed before the prophet's arrival, were seriously weakened by his message; and the cult that won out was the messianic one. Nevertheless, from a doctrinal point of view, Silas John's religious message contained nothing really new.

What was new was *the manner in which the message was propagated*: through a ritual that prescribed the paradoxical use of speech within a context of ritual actions that implicitly contradicted its content. What was new here was neither the dance nor the prayer. Rather it was the strict and obligatory relationship between a prayer and a dance that was manifested yet apparently forbidden. That relationship (which was certainly not conscious and probably resulted from a sudden intuition on the part of the prophet) was a means of establishing a new, counterintuitive way of propagating a message that itself contained nothing new. In this way, Apache messianism prevailed, not because it founded a new religion, but because it established a paradoxical relationship between two religions that already existed. So it was not the new representations or symbols that explained the extremely rapid propagation of the new ritual, but the unexpected relation that Silas John established between two contradictory religious messages. The Christian cross that exhibited the Apache snake condensed that process into a single image of formidable intensity. The conflict between two rival cultures is here successfully interpreted by recourse to paradox, for, in the messianic view, all the components of this image represent God in a succession of parallelistic "canonic pairs," but not a synthesis of enemy figures: Christ and the Snake, the dancing Gan and the prophet.

LADY SEBASTIANA

Perhaps we can pursue this line a little further. Let us now consider another religious movement, which originated in southwestern America at roughly the same time as the birth of Apache messianism and was also, in different ways, linked with a ritual reelaboration of the image of Christ.

In a vast region situated between present-day Arizona and New Mexico, between 1616 and 1629, the Franciscans embarked upon an initial campaign to Christianize the Native American peoples; and this led to the conversion of several tribes (Zuni, Pueblo, Hopi, Tiwa, Keres of Rio Grande, Taos, etc.). By 1628 the missionaries had already built fifty churches. However, this rapid conversion turned out to be fragile. By 1635, the Zuni, followed by other communities, were refusing to have anything to do with the missions and returned to their own territory. That first reaction was followed by a general movement of revolt and led, in 1680, to the great revolt of the Pueblo, who took control of Santa Fe for twelve years. It was not until 1692 that General de Vargas managed to regain control of the town. But the region remained extremely unstable; fires, attacks against the missions (often led by the Apache), and revolts were very common. The example of the towns of the Salinas region, all of which were abandoned between 1672 and 1676, spoke for itself.

The historical situation was thus similar to that which I have briefly noted in the case of Apache messianism: violent conflict, incessant Indian attacks on isolated and very poor neo-Hispanic communities, ripostes on the part of the defenders of the missions that were sometimes bloody but always discontinued. One point, nevertheless, needs to be underlined: with the gradual extinction of Franciscan preaching, from the late eighteenth century onward, the region found itself the victim of a scarcity of ecclesiastical personnel that was universally recognized. As soon as the Independence of Mexico was declared, in 1821, the neo-Mexican clergy withdrew from the region and tended to return to Spain (Stark 1971: 304). Now a truly exceptional situation arose, one that threatened the very survival of the Spanish-speaking communities, in which it became impossible to celebrate the essential rituals of the life-cycle of a Christian: baptism, the Eucharist, marriages, and funerary rituals. Antonio Barreiro, a jurist who went to New Mexico in 1831, wrote as follows in one of his letters:

> The spiritual administration is in a truly lamentable state. Nothing is more common than the sight of many sick people dying deprived of confession or the Last Sacrament. Nothing is more rare than the sight of the administration of the Eucharist. Corpses remain without burial for many days. The newborn are seldom baptized and only at the price of great sacrifices. Many unfortunate people here have to forgo attending mass for much of the year. Almost all the churches are destroyed and most of them are certainly not worthy to be called the temples of God. (Cited in Escudero [1849] 1972)

The figures, established by the historical research of Marta Weigle (1976), speak for themselves. In the whole region of New Mexico, which in 1850 contained about sixty thousand inhabitants, one third of whom were Native Americans, twenty-two Franciscans and two priests were working in 1812. In 1826, there were nine Franciscans and four priests. By 1828 only two Franciscans remained. When the French bishop of Santa Fe, recently appointed, arrived in his town, he could count on only a dozen priests for his work of spiritual reconquest in the region.

In this way, a new religious tradition that practically eluded ecclesiastical control sprang up out of the need to celebrate the essential rituals in a situation defined not only by isolation but also by contact and constant conflicts with the Native Americans. This was a situation that favoured the emergence of the principal religious organization of the neo-Mexican communities; it was an association which, without ever proclaiming itself to be a new church, was to introduce remarkable and radical changes into the cult of Christ and jealously defend its autonomy in relation to the religious hierarchy. This organization was the Cofradía de los Hermanos del Santo Sangre, also known as the Hermandad de los Penitentes, a rural brotherhood for mutual help. Already by possibly the second half of the eighteenth century, it was spreading extremely rapidly throughout a vast region stretching from the present-day Mexico–United

States frontier to north of the Rio Grande (New Mexico). At the heart of these religious societies, for which there is trustworthy evidence from around 1810 onward, new churches that were not consecrated by the clergy sprang up. They were known as *moradas*. It was in these that new religious images as well as new rituals became established. The cults of the *moradas* celebrated by the *Penitentes* enjoyed such success that, throughout the entire nineteenth century and well into the 1950s (Weigle 1976: 11), the Catholic Church struggled to impose on the neo-Mexican communities statutes that were closer to the orthodoxy of Rome and rituals that respected the Catholic tradition (Figure 83).

Figure 83. A *morada* in New Mexico.

The neo-Mexican brotherhood appeared to be organized along the lines of a classic European brotherhood, with strong Andalusian features. Like other similar associations, it was above all initiatory and, from a sociological point of view, was founded on a distinction between the *Hermanos de Sangre*, the Brothers of Blood, who were veritable Penitents, and the *Hermanos de la Luz*, the Brothers of Light, whose role was more that of organization and spiritual leadership (Weigle and Lyons 1982). As in the Brotherhood of our Father Jesus of Seville, in which Fray Chavez (1954) and Dorothy Woodward ([1935] 1974) have identified one of the probable models for the American *Penitentes*, the religious life of the community was centered on the exercise of penitence and on an imitation of Christ. In particular, a penitent member of the brotherhood was always expected to practice self-flagellation when taking part in the processions of Holy Week. However, differences between the neo-Mexican cults and European practices soon began to appear, much to the alarm of the church. There were essentially two major new aspects. The first consisted in a ritual cycle devoted to a celebration of the Passion, which among the *Penitentes* took the violent form of a simulated crucifixion. The second aspect that troubled the church consisted in a curious representation of death as an old woman, which soon began to appear on the altars of the secret chapels of the Cofradía that were reserved solely for its own members. These innovations were definitely different from the Mexican and Spanish Catholic traditions. They aroused among the peasants a respect mixed with a degree of fear, while the clergy, for its part, was definitely scandalized. They also provoked open hostility in the ecclesiastical hierarchy, which took to speaking not only of excess and sin, but also of veritable crimes and heretical beliefs that they even judged to be comparable to those of the Native Americans (Rieupeyrout 1987: 52–53). In the course of the campaign tenaciously conducted against the *Penitentes*, it was even claimed that, during their processions, they "worshiped death as do the Indians." It would also be said that in their intended simulations of the crucifixion during Holy Week, they subjected young members of the brotherhood to veritable tortures: for instance, it was said that they forced those young men to walk carrying enormous wooden crosses on their backs; then they tied or even nailed them to their crosses, in an imitation of the martyrdom of Jesus Christ. Already in 1833, the bishop of Durango, José Antonio Laureano de Zubiría, was sounding the alarm, and in a very severe pastoral letter forbade the exercise of such rituals. Zubiría's tone was solemn, almost threatening:

> I prohibit these brotherhoods of penance, or rather, of carnage, which have grown in the shelter of an unlawful tolerance. . . . That nowhere is [there to be] a storehouse for those large crosses. . . . with which some

half-murder their bodies, at the same time forgetting their souls, which they leave for whole years in sin. (Cited in Weigle 1976: 195–96)

But such admonitions were ignored. In 1879, the new French bishop of Santa Fe, Jean-Baptiste Lamy, who had made an inspection of the entire territory and followed it up with threats of excommunication, recorded that these excessive rituals still continued and even that some of the young men chosen for the ritual had died in the course of them:

Unfortunately, the chiefs of these societies do not obey our orders. In the past they have carried out cruel practices and customs in out-of-the-way places, at night, inflicting on themselves whip lashes so terrible that in consequence of these penances not only have many of them fallen ill but some have even died. (Cited in Weigle 1976: 206)

"*Costumbres crueles en partes retiradas*": penitential excesses, secret rituals and prayers not approved by the hierarchy; simulations, sometimes of a cruel nature, of the crucifixion of Jesus Christ. And then the appearance on altars of new ritual figures dedicated to death itself. The certainly justified alarm of the bishops was swiftly followed up by the scandal-oriented newspapers established in the eastern states of America, which tended to be of Protestant inspiration. Authors of every kind, of both the Catholic and the Protestant faiths (Darley [1893] 1968; Lummis [1893] 1906; Chavez 1954; Steele 1974), constructed around the American *Penitentes* a vast literature composed of polemics and shocking stories, exaggerations and pleas. From the 1930s onward, when the *Penitentes* came to the notice of American public opinion, many of these works concentrated on, for example, the question of whether the instruments used to "crucify the young man chosen to be the ritual incarnations of Christ" were in fact nails or simply ropes; or whether there had ever existed among the *Penitentes* any ritual proceedings devoted in particular to death, which was referred to as *comrade death* or "friendly death"; or else whether the exercise of penitence testified to sadism on the part of the initiators of the cult or simply to their exalted faith. More recently a more balanced view has emerged, tending to refute the legends and silence the polemics. But all too often it has been accompanied by a defense of dogma and censure of embarrassing testimonies and sources, to the point that, even recently, there have been demands to the ecclesiastical authorities to authorize the publication of studies on this matter (Wallis 1994).

I myself have no religious faith to defend or condemn. I shall thus limit myself to returning to the question that I raised concerning Apache messianism: What is it that makes these new rituals and the representations that they imply so memorable? Can one detect in the tradition of the *Penitentes* any coherent memory or configuration of mnemonic traces that can cast light upon the nature of this particular type of imagination, which constitutes such an essential part of the neo-Mexican ritual memory and the images that it engenders? Let us take a closer look at the rituals celebrated within the Hermandad del Santo Sangre and try to identify the features that distinguish them from a simple imitation of the ceremonies practiced by Spanish and European brotherhoods.

We have already considered the situation, characterized by both contacts and cultural conflict, in which the Indian and neo-Mexican peoples found themselves in this period. Some authors have tried to shed light upon a direct exchange between the Native Americans and the Spaniards of New Mexico. There has, for example, been talk of flagellation rituals among the Pueblo (Benavides, in Weigle 1976: 35) and of certain Native Americans who may have become active members of the Cofradías de Penitentes (ibid.: 28) or even, conversely, of certain *Penitentes* taking part in rituals celebrated among the Pueblo (Rodriguez 1996). But if one refers to the present-day state of research, that approach does not seem to get us very far. The culture of the Spaniards of New Mexico, in particular their religious traditions (with the sole possible exception of the architecture of the *moradas*, which often seems to adopt certain hybrid forms typical of the earliest churches constructed by the Franciscans, with the aid of Pueblo people), does not seem to have reacted to that cultural contact by seeking compromises or mediations. On the contrary, all the signs appear to suggest that the Spanish tradition adopted quite the reverse policy, constantly seeking to magnify the differences. The efforts of such rural communities were always aimed at clearly setting up a frontier to separate the two communities. That frontier, at once physical and cultural, was designed to maintain a rigorous distinction between the Catholic tradition of European origin and the traditions of the Native American tribes with whom the neo-Mexicans entered into contact (McCoy in

Darley [1893] 1968; Woodward [1935] 1974; Rael 1951). That process continued for a long time, in fact almost down to the present day. And the first thing that strikes an observer about these "scandalous new ceremonies" invented and practiced by the *Penitentes* is the direct link with the conflict that for a long time set the neo-Mexicans and the Native Americans in opposition. Central to this tradition are numerous legends in which the image of an unconverted Indian warrior (who may, depending on the regions, be a Comanche, a Pawnee, a Tepehuan, or, in many cases, an Apache) constitutes a threat not only to the farms but also to the churches founded by the Hispanic settlers. An Indian warrior was a direct threat to the figure of a missionary, who, in many cases, became a martyr in the course of the attacks regularly made by the Indian tribes of these regions. Sometimes the Native American warriors went so far as to attack the very image of Christ. This may have given rise to one of the recurrent themes of the religious rituals and representations linked with the traditions of the neo-Mexican *Penitentes*: that of the *Cristo flechado*, the image of Christ on the altar pierced by the arrows of the Native Americans. This was an early and persistent theme typical of the oral tradition of the *Penitentes*. It was, for example, said of the Mapimi Christ (a crucifix still revered in the *moradas* of the *Penitentes* at the beginning of the twentieth century) that he had miraculously survived an attack by the Tepehuans upon a Catholic sanctuary in northern Mexico (Rael 1951: 72–75). In one of the versions of this legend collected in the 1930s, the image of Christ on the cross seems to have been the direct target of the Tepehuans' attack, which aimed directly for the altar.

> It was a sculptured image of the Holy Christ, of the size of a man, and below the knees it had a bleeding wound. The image was very much venerated. The wound below the knee had been caused by an Indian arrow during an attack on the town of Mapimi, causing the miraculous flow of blood. (Saravia in Rael 1951: 74)

Many stories in the *Penitentes'* tradition contain direct or indirect echoes of this theme, in which the real presence of Christ (and, in particular, his blood) seems suddenly revealed by these images. Another legend, studied by William Wroth, tells the story of Father Juan, a Franciscan killed by the Pueblo at the time of the 1680 rebellion. On the point of death, Father Juan prophesied the return of Christ and his triumph in New Mexico. As soon as he was struck by an arrow, the sky turned a dark red color, which, still today and throughout the region, is known as the "*sangre de Cristo*" (the blood of Christ). On that particular occasion, Father Juan is supposed to have declared,

> My body only has thou killed
> Blood of Christ over mountains spread
> Shall preach to you when I am dead. (Wroth 1983: 283–84)

So hidden behind the Franciscan's body was the presence of Christ: it was his blood, not just that of Father Juan, that the Native Americans had shed, as was testified by the red color that appeared in the sky. The theme of Christ pierced by arrows did not appear solely in stories about supernatural miracles and occurrences. Indeed, it was so common that, when New Mexico was annexed by the United States, it was even taken up by the press. In 1891, the *Las Vegas Daily Optic* published an article telling how Apache warriors had attacked *Penitentes* who were celebrating a simulated crucifixion; on this occasion, "the Cristo, who was left tied on the cross, was shot full of arrows"(Weigle 1976: 64).

These stories, and the theme of Christ pierced by arrows around which they were organized, direct us toward a specific tradition that elaborated a quite particular image of the Passion. During Holy Week, the *Penitentes* organized processions in the course of which the members of the brotherhood had to imitate the Via Crucis (the Stations of the Cross), carrying on their shoulders huge crosses, or *maderos*, all the way along the path that led from the *morada* to a place called Calvary. The brotherhood had also devised, no doubt on the basis of representations of the Passion of Christ that were connected with the popular religious theater in Europe, a sequence of ceremonial actions in the course of which the Passion was deliberately mimed. At the end of the procession, a young penitent, his head hidden in a hood, was bound to the cross. It was an action that could at any moment be seen as scandalous, for these ritual actions, which—it should be remembered—eluded the control of the church, involved many spontaneous interpretations, several of which were suspect or unorthodox. For example, it was sometimes suggested and repeated in the *alabados*—the praises or prayers recited by the *Penitentes* during their ceremonies—that the sacred wood of the *madero* and the very person of Christ became one and the same thing in the course of the ritual. Or people might believe and suggest that Christ himself, during the procession, was hidden in the wood of the cross, which, in turn, was identified with a tree that could grow and produce fruits—as in one of the *alabados* collected by Rael:

> My Redeemer's body was nailed to the cross by three nails
> That was how my Jesus' body was nailed,
> Emprisoned by the enemy and guilt
> That is how Christ is eternally hidden within the sacred wood. (Rael 1951: 204–6)

Another potentially dangerous aspect of the crucifixion as celebrated by members of the brotherhood was certainly the excessive suffering inflicted upon the young penitent who embodied the Savior on the occasion of the Passion simulated during Holy Week. The *Penitentes'* ritual undeniably tended to intensify the young boy's identification with the Christ of the Gospel to an unimaginable degree. One of the very rare first-hand descriptions that we possess of the celebrations of Holy Week in a *morada* underlines this aspect:

> During the night of La Porciuncula, a single Penitente, his arms and body tightly bound with a chain to a cross, would make a visit to the church. As the cross to which he was bound was a little less in length than his own height, the progress of this Penitente would be slow. . . . This type of penance used to be one of the most severe, as, after a few minutes of being bound in this manner, the retardation of the circulation of the blood would cause the veins on the arms to stand out like cords, and the trunk of the body to assume a purplish-blue color. Sometimes the hermano would fall in a faint to the ground. (Cited in Wroth 1991: 58–59)

The body of the *Penitente*, in this extreme suffering, took on the blue color that is typical of the image of Christ in the iconography of the tradition connected with the brotherhood (Figure 84). Other direct testimonies, such as that recorded in 1893 by Charles F. Lummis, one of the rare witnesses who managed to photograph one of these crucifixions (Figure 85) make it possible to complete this description and convey even more deeply the sense of scandal provoked by the excesses of these acts of penitence:

Figure 84. Crucifixion linked to the iconographic tradition of the *Penitentes*.

I effected a modus with the Hermano Mayor [Chief Brother], and the next day, Good Friday, March 30, 1888, I photographed . . . the procession of the self-whippers and the men bearing crosses thicker than their own bodies and three times as long. Then, forcing the hostile mob of onlookers back, the Hermano Mayor marked a spot . . . where I might stand (with my camera): there, from a few yards' distance, I photographed the crucifixion of an American citizen. . . . And now the Hermano Mayor went into the *morada* with two of his assistants. In a few moments they emerged leading the allotted victim, a stalwart young fellow dressed only in his white drawers and black head-bag. . . . He walked firmly to the prostrate cross, and laid himself at full length upon it. . . . A long, new, half-inch rope was brought and the Hermano de la Luz [Brother of Light] began to lash him to the great timbers . . . the stiff rope sank deep into his flesh and prohibited the throbbing blood. In less than three minutes his arms and legs were black. . . . A clean white sheet was now wound about him from head to foot, leaving exposed only his purpling arms and muffled head. (Lummis [1893] 1906: 97–99)

Figure 85. Simulated crucifixion during a *Penitentes* ritual in 1893.

The simulation of the crucifixion was but one of the inhumane sufferings that members of the brotherhood inflicted upon themselves. There were others: on that same occasion, Lummis describes other *Penitentes* who, at the foot of the cross, bound cacti to their bodies or even pulled along heavy carts filled with stones on top of which lay sinister representations of death. We shall later be considering what one should think of these strange representations. But for the moment let us concentrate on the aspect of these ceremonies that was the most shocking: physical pain. The *Hermano de Sangre* (the brother of blood), who was a faithful member of the brotherhood, overstepped the boundaries of theatrical fiction by which the representation of the martyrdom of Christ ought to have been limited. His suffering was *real*; and in the eyes of the *Penitentes* it was this that made that representation a veritable ritual from which one could expect redemption and salvation. However, in the eyes of the church and also of Protestants such as Lummis, it was precisely this that transformed it into a truly scandalous spectacle.

But there may have been other reasons why the church was so scandalized. The exaggeration of the ritual, by insisting on the identification of the young *Penitente* with Christ himself, ended up by identifying the young sufferer not only with the image of Christ, but also with a veritable representation of death. Sometimes the *Penitente* would turn into a skeleton or a corpse returned from the world of the dead. Here, chosen from a large number of possible examples, are three traditional images that clearly illustrate such identifications adopted by the *Penitentes*. The first is an image of the flagellation of Christ (now preserved in the Bunker collection) that comes from northern Mexico and that Robert Shalkop (1970) has linked with the *Penitentes* tradition and dated to the late eighteenth century (Figure 86). According to him, the theme of flagellation, very common in America, reached an intensity in Mexico that puts one in mind of surrealism. In this *Flagellation*, an image of a veritable skeleton appears beneath the lacerated skin of the Savior.

Another illustration of this tendency to identify penitents with Christ and death comes directly from a neo-Mexican *morada*. Here the crucifix is superposed upon the image of a *velorio* (Figure 87), one of the main instruments used in the funerary night-watches organized by the *Penitentes*. In the course of this ritual, the candles on the triangular-shaped candelabra were each extinguished until only the one at the very top remained alight. That candle, which symbolized Christ, was then taken away to an adjoining room, while the *morada* was plunged in total darkness. At that moment, the sound of maracas and pitos (flutes) was heard coming from the room, together with other loud noises that symbolized the earthquake and general disorder that had engulfed the whole world

Figure 86. Popular Mexican art, *The Flagellation of Christ*, late eighteenth century.

on the night of Good Friday, when Christ died. It is worth noting that this ritual was reserved exclusively for funerary ceremonies designed to consecrate the deaths of members of the brotherhood.

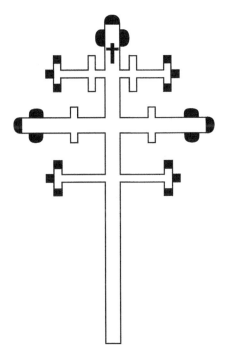

Figure 87. A *Calvario* used in a *morada*. The image of the crucifix is superposed upon that of the *velorio*.

The belief according to which the *Penitentes* sustained a particular relationship with Death, which they called their "friend" or *comadre*, was certainly one of the essential themes of the religious tradition of neo-Mexican brotherhoods. Marta Weigle has published a number of stories featuring the recurrent theme of a deceased *Penitente* reappearing among the living to take part in the rites of Holy Week. The dead man returning to celebrate a ritual always had his head covered by a hood, just like the one worn by the brotherhood's Christ in his simulated crucifixion. He could therefore not be distinguished from the rest of those taking part in the ritual. His presence could only be detected by counting the celebrants, whose number miraculously increased in the course of the ceremony:

In those days [the late nineteenth century], a strong belief existed among the people of the small villages that the souls of departed penitentes used to assume human form and come to this world to accompany processions, taking their places in the rows of penitentes. . . . An Arroyo Hondo woman was to carry the Muerte from the morada to the church on Holy Thursday. . . . Two rows of nine Brothers accompanied her. However, she counted twenty in all, with the last in each row seeming "to possess a translucency of the flesh that showed the outline of his skeleton, the ribs especially seemed to show more prominently." (Weigle 1976: 182–89)

In other stories, a hooded *Penitente*, pursued by some unbelievers, unexpectedly removed his hood, thereby revealing his skull. This was the source of representations of a *Penitente* in the guise of a self-flagellating skeleton. Such an image is strikingly illustrated by our third example, a small sculpture published by Weigle (1977), today preserved in the Denver Museum (Figure 88). A figurine representing a skeleton kneels before a cross; in between the cross and the praying skeleton, a small skull is placed.

Figure 88. A devotional skeleton linked with the iconographical tradition of the *Penitentes*.

In times of crisis, such as in 1886, when the winter was so harsh that many shepherds and peasants literally died of the cold, it was said that whole groups of dead *Penitentes* joined the living to celebrate the rituals of Holy Week and to pray with them for help from heaven. The *morada* itself, now seen in a different light, appeared as the residence of brothers from the other world (*Hermanos del Otro Mundo*). It is perhaps this particular theme that most likens the *Penitentes* to the Apache shamans, such as Noch-ay-del-klinne, Big John, and Daslahdn, who, in reaction to their defeat and the invasion of the Whites, tried desperately, at the tomb of the Native American chiefs who had just died, to reestablish a ritual contact with their dead. In Hispanic villages such as Cordova and Arroyo Hondo, the *tinieblas*, the funerary rituals that the *Penitentes* celebrated in the dark *morada*, were designed for precisely the same purpose: "Penitentes Brothers and villagers literally huddle together, in the din-filled, disorienting darkness, while symbolically taking a stand in the face of this chaos by calling out the names of their beloved departed, those who built their community" (Wroth 1991: 62).

Seen in this perspective, the *morada* built and cared for by the brotherhood of the Hermanos seems very different from a church, precisely because it turns into a "house of the dead." Another *alabado*, collected by Alice Corbin Henderson in 1937, in which the person reciting it embodied the voice of one of the dead, confirms this essential aspect of the beliefs of the *Penitentes:*

Farewell for the last time
That I may be seen on earth
I am given a tomb
That is my true home
Farewell to all present
To all those who accompany me. (Cited in Boyd 1991)

As we have seen, the Catholic Church's reaction to the diffusion of these rituals and beliefs—a reaction the reasons for which we are now beginning to understand—was swift and energetic. Already, Bishop Zubiría was speaking of *carnicerias* ("carnages"). However, it was not solely the very heavy physical effort demanded by cruel penitence that led the church to speak of "excesses"; there were facts and actions of an even graver nature. Among the rituals celebrated in the *moradas*, which included quite traditional processions commemorating the encounter (*Encuentro*) between the Holy Virgin and Christ, there were also celebrations that were less acceptable and stories about the dead and their hooded skeletons. One of these ceremonies featured the transportation of a strange representative of death called Lady Sebastiana (Doña Sebastiana), who, amid an atmosphere of great piety (Weigle 1977: 144), was carried to the *morada* altar, where she took her place alongside images of the saints, the Virgin, and Jesus Christ himself (Figures 89 and 90). On other occasions, but particularly on Good Friday evening, this figure, placed on a little cart filled with stones, was pulled by one of the faithful right up to the Cross. At this point, the ritual action, albeit swift and rudimentary, almost took on the form of a triumph. Indeed, this enigmatic figure and her actions gave rise to a number of beliefs.

Figure 89. A representation of Lady Sebastiana.

One of these beliefs definitely recalled the theme of Christ pierced by arrows: it was believed and said that Lady Sebastiana (exactly like the Apache, according to a report in the Las Vegas *Daily Optic*) had once killed one of the *Penitentes* while he was on the cross, by shooting an

Figure 90. A representation of Lady Sebastiana.

arrow into him. The figure of Death in this way indicated, on the one hand, its terrifying efficacy and, on the other, the fact that, behind the sculpture representing it, Death itself was really present. This legend, which linked this figure with the story of the Mapimi Christ and others too, mentioned above, reflected an extremely eloquent ritual. In one of the most secret rituals celebrated in the *morada*, it was Lady Sebastiana who selected the youth who was ritually to embody Christ on the Cross; it was said that it was the statue itself, sometimes representing a blind old woman, sometimes—on the contrary—one with a threatening look in her eyes, made of fragments of glass or metal, who, from her place at the altar, shot an arrow at the boy. That act confirmed him to be worthy of the name that he would bear for a whole year: so it was thanks to the action of Lady Sebastiana that he became the brotherhood's " Cristo."

Behind this representation, which was intimately linked with the image of Christ but, at the same time, with that of the Native American aggressor, there lurked a complex logic that implied both the form taken by the iconography and also that of the ritual action. Let us first consider what may be the oldest example of a representation of Lady Sebastiana. This is a sculpture commissioned from Nazario Lopez de Cordova by the *morada* of Las Trampas, which was almost certainly completed in 1860 (Boyd 1991). Today, this sculpture, known as *Muerte en su carreta*, is preserved in the Museum of New Mexico, Albuquerque (Figure 91). John Bourke, the US army officer who, as we saw earlier, was present both at Apache rituals devoted to the veneration of crosses bearing the image of a snake and also at Gan dances and so was able to provide a description of them, first set eyes on the *Muerte en su carreta* in 1881. The disapproval, at once Protestant, secular, and rationalist, that fueled the reaction of the young Bourke was similar to that which he manifested a few years later, in 1891, when faced with the dances of the Apache:

> In a room, to the right of the door, which corresponded to our church vestry, there was a hideous statue, dressed in black, with pallid face and monkish cowl, which held in his hands a bow with arrows drawn in position. It was seated upon a wooden wagon, something similar in shape to an artillery limber, but made in the crudest way of wood, fastened with pins of the same material. The wheels were sections of a pine trunk, ungreased axles and ungreased pole made an unearthly music and to add to the difficulty of hauling such a vehicle, the box seat upon which Death sat as grim charioteer was filled with smooth-worn and heavy boulders. (Bourke 2005: 154–55)

This representation was exhibited, up until the 1960s, in the church of San José, along with three skulls said to be those of three missionaries who had been killed by the Native Americans. In Nazario Lopez's sculpture, directly linked with ceremonies conducted by the brotherhood, the head of Lady Sebastiana is a skull; her body is composed of tree branches and is covered by a cloak. She holds a bow and some arrows. The whole figure is placed on a roughly shaped little cart that resembles the cart that appears in representations of the Triumphs of Death that were popular in Hispanic lands and Europe in the Middle Ages.

Figure 91. Nazario Lopez, Lady Sebastiana of the "Sangre de Cristo" type.

This early iconographic model was reproduced in two ways, throughout the nineteenth century, in the area bounded by northern New Mexico and southern Colorado. The historian of art Louisa Stark has distinguished between two types of representations of Lady Sebastiana: the "Sangre de Cristo" type and the "San Luis Valley" type. The original New Mexico representations are generally "seated or kneeling skeletons" carrying a bow and arrows. These "Sangre de Cristo" figures, as in Figure 91, are characterized by their

> large hands, tiny head . . . and grotesque appearance; gray and white horsehair is often attached to the crown with animal glue. . . . Occasionally eyes of obsidian are added, although the sockets are usually left empty. . . . A great deal of attention is paid to the anatomy of the body. The ribs are prominently displayed and the limbs seem to billow at the joints. (Stark 1971: 305)

The representations produced in the San Luis alley (Figure 92) are rather different:

> The San Luis figure assumes a crouching position in the cart, while holding a bow and arrow. The figure is usually made of wooden blocks which are later covered with outer garments. . . . In the case of the head, only the face is covered, the rest of the block is covered with a hood. . . . The expression of the face is achieved by a hood which, when placed on the head, shades the eyes and gives them a menacing expression. (Stark 1971: 305)

The small group of Hispano-American sculptors close to the tradition of the *Penitentes*, working in completely new conditions and within a context of popular art, thus renovated an iconographical theme of medieval origin.

The theme developed in Europe in various forms, ranging from the Dance of the Dead, popular in central Europe, to the different manifestations adopted by the *Carreta de a Muerte* (the cart of death), which was typical of the Spanish tradition. Of course, it is not possible, here, to follow the whole history of the American survival of this famous European iconographic theme (though see Frugoni 1988; Camille 1996). But let us briefly consider a few of its features so as to gain some understanding of its development within the framework of this veritable iconographic

Figure 92. Lady Sebastiana: the "San Luis Valley" type.

renaissance that flourished in the popular art of New Mexico throughout the nineteenth century. Lady Sebastiana certainly stemmed from a
new tradition, the origins of which can, with a degree of precision, be
identified in New Mexico. But she was also a result of a late return to a
very ancient Christian iconographic tradition that was a source of reference for the neo-Mexican group of sculptors and painters who were directly linked with the construction and decoration of the *moradas*. These
artists were at the origin of a tradition known as "the art of the *santeros*." As George Kubler (1964) perceived, these *santeros* of New Mexico,
with the conservative attitude typical of isolated populations, in general
took over the traditional iconography of the Catholic Church, despite
knowing hardly anything about their illustrious sources. In the work of
an artist such as the anonymous creator of the picture preserved in the
Taylor Museum of Alice Springs, we find, for example, a representation
of the Trinity executed by means of a replica of three simply sketched
but identical figures. This iconographic theme, of Byzantine origin, had
been forbidden as early as 1745 by Pope Benedict XIV. The figurative
tradition of the *santeros* was thus full of provincial archaisms and rep-
licas. However, as Kubler pointed out, the conservative attitude of the
neo-Mexican *santeros* was accompanied by new procedures: in particular
the fusion of different iconographic themes into a single image. We have,
in fact, already come across one example of this process: the image of the
Calvario, created by the superposition of a *velorio* (the triangular candelabra used in a funerary vigil) upon a crucifix. A similar process is to be
found in the case of a representation of Nuestra Señora de los Dolores
(Our Lady of Suffering), where the image is merged with one of Saint
Veronica (Wroth 1991).

This iconic contamination certainly took place following the principles that Warburg has called a polarization of images. In this tradition,
ritual actions confer a new dynamic upon the iconography and from this
there emerge new meanings and new connections between the various
images. This can be seen particularly clearly in the ritual use of sculpted
representations of the saints and the Virgin. Let us consider another example. The fact that Lady Sebastiana is clad in a voluminous black over-
coat, particularly in the "San Luis Valley" type of representation, may
suggest a possible contamination from the iconic theme of Our Lady of
Suffering. Both images are associated with the function of representing

mourning. The difference between the two figures may seem obvious: whereas Our Lady of Suffering actually suffers, Lady Sebastiana, as seen in the *Penitentes'* procession in Holy Week, is there to inflict suffering upon others. Carrying her image on one's shoulders in many cases indicated a desire to expiate one's sins. However, the ritual use of an image may well change its meaning, transforming a passive representation into an active one. In the context of penitence, such a switch involves the figure of Our Lady of Suffering, thereby revealing its ambiguity. Laurence F. Lee, one of the earliest to witness the rituals of the brotherhood, describes one of the ceremonies as follows:

> We find mention made of the Figure of Our Lady of Sorrows being used at times as a means of penance in the nineteenth century. A brother is reported to have carried this figure above his head, with his arms upraised. Should the brother at any time lower his arms, the blades of two long knives which were inserted at the base of the figure . . . would enter his flesh. (Lee 1920: 10)

However, there are further aspects to this logic of contamination between different and contradictory images within a single representation, which is particularly intense in the case of Lady Sebastiana. The process that seems to determine the survival of the European theme of the Triumph of Death in the shape of Lady Sebastiana in America implies at least three aspects: an iconographic contamination, a polarization of ritual meanings (active–passive), and finally, resulting from those two operations, a great intensification of the image, which thus becomes particularly salient. This point, which makes the image at once unexpected and complex, may well account for its diffusion and persistence. Here (as in the case of Silas John, who, from being a shaman, proclaimed himself to be the "new Christ"), the contamination directly springs from social conflict. In the *Penitentes' morada* Lady Sebastiana does, to be sure, represent Death; however, she does not carry a scythe with which to reap souls, as do other European or Mexican representations that probably constitute the immediate sources for this figure. On the contrary, she holds a bow and arrows, an iconographic theme quite unknown in the lands where the neo-Mexican culture originated, that is to say, Mexico and Spain. Those attributes of Death, which are rare in Europe, are altogether in keeping with the American theme that is linked with the Franciscan preaching about a Christ pierced by arrows. So this menacing crone is not simply "one of the dead," as are her Mexican and Spanish sisters. For the *Penitentes* of New Mexico, she is also "old Goodwife Sebastiana," as she is called by them. One of the iconographic and religious models with which this strange representation is indirectly associated is certainly Saint Sebastian (and, perhaps—as we shall see—behind Saint Sebastian, a Christ undergoing flagellation at the column). This remarkable connection with the figure of Sebastian the martyr, which some authors have, overhastily, attributed purely and simply to a "confusion" (Stark 1971; Weigle 1976; Boyd 1991), certainly calls for an explanation. In a detailed and fascinating essay, William Wroth (1991) meticulously reconstructs the origins of the *Penitentes'* funerary images and the ritual objects that accompany them. His conclusion as to Lady Sebastiana is that she is certainly derived from Catholic Mexican iconography: such *Muertes* (female incarnations of Death) came from Europe and constituted a natural enough ultimate manifestation of a series that originated in the Triumphs of the Middle Ages. At one stage in this process of the metamorphosis of a Triumphal Death, the representation on Tarot cards may or may not have been involved.[2] However that may be, this Triumphal Death figure eventually reached the cult of the Holy Week Passion of Christ, as practiced in New Mexico by the Brotherhood of Holy Blood. According to Wroth, the traditional Catholic rite to which this representation refers is the ceremony that enacted the burial of Christ on the evening of Good Friday, in which he was represented as ritually triumphing over Death. Death is pictured seated at the foot of the Cross, accompanied by expressions such as "Death, where is thy sting?" or "Death, I shall be the death of thee." Louisa Stark has reconstructed a most convincing series showing the iconographic transformations leading from Seville to New Mexico and passing by way of Mexican iconographies such as that linked with the funerary Paso, in use in the town of Mexico already in the sixteenth century (Figures 93 and 94).

---

2.   According to a thesis dear to Boyd, which has recently been challenged by Weigle (1976: 169, and 271 n. 48).

Figures 93 and 94. Two traditional representations of Death: one belongs to
the Brotherhood of the Buried Christ of Seville (seventeenth century), the
other to a church in Mexico (sixteenth century).

In short, a number of heterogeneous elements turn Lady Sebastiana into a very singular figure and greatly alter her traditional meaning. First, we should note that, riding in triumph on her little cart painfully pulled along by a *Penitente*, Lady Sebastiana represents an inversion of the triumph devoted to Jesus Christ. Within a *morada*, by following the logic of the ritual action, it is thus not Christ who triumphs over death. Rather, it is she, Sebastiana, who, by shooting her arrows at Christ, triumphs over the *Penitente*, who is identified with the figure of the Savior; it is she whom the *Penitente* is obliged to drag along in a cart laden with stones. The other surprising aspect concerns the iconography. In an overwhelming majority of cases, in place of the traditional scythe, we find a bow equipped with arrows, which immediately links the representation of death with the menacing image of the Indian of the *Penitentes'* legends that are woven around the theme of a Christ pierced by an arrow. The same effect is produced by the renaming of this figure. Actually in Spanish popular culture and in Mexico, this kind of representation used to be known simply as *Muerte en su carreta* (Death on Its Cart), as it was still called in Cervantes' *Don Quixote*. In New Mexico, she becomes Lady Sebastiana.

As a result of this new name, the representation of Death becomes symbolically linked with a Saint Sebastian pierced by arrows, a representation that here remains, so to speak, in the background, evoked but not actually present.

This metamorphosis also implies a second inversion: Lady Sebastiana shoots her arrows rather than being shot by them, as is the saint tied to the pillar. Furthermore, the evocation of Saint Sebastian opens on to another series of similar connotations that lead to Christ bound, like the saint, to a pillar. In the hymn sung by the *Penitentes* as they walk in procession, such a figure appears as follows:

Onto a pillar
The King of Heaven was tied
Wounded and bloody
He was dragged on the ground. (Weigle, in Wroth 1991: 61)

In the Gospel, Christ, like Sebastian, is bound to a pillar. In the simulated image of his martyrdom, as it appears in the ritual enacted by the

Penitentes, he, like Sebastian, is struck by an arrow, but this is shot by Lady Sebastiana. Actually the sequence of images reveals a series of partial ritual identifications (Christ, Sebastian, the dead . . .) that designates the complex figure that is embodied, in the ritual, by a *Penitente*. On the one hand, he is wounded by an arrow, like Sebastian; on the other, like Christ, he sheds his blood as a martyr. We should remember that, as a *Hermano de sangre* (brother of blood), it is to the blood of Christ that he has promised his devotion. In the ritual of the simulated crucifixion the blood that he sheds in his self-flagellation becomes the blood of Christ himself. The *Penitente* even pushes the identification so far as to carry the weighty cross on his shoulders, like Christ, and, over and above that, to ascend the cross of martyrdom.

Lady Sebastiana can only be understood if she is inserted into two series of representations. On the one hand, she refers back to a complex series of partial identifications with the figure of her ritual victim, the brotherhood's "Christ." On the other, through the arrow that she lets fly, she also refers to the presence of the Native American enemy . In this way, the part that she plays simultaneously effects two specific operations in the ritual. The first reverses the traditional rite by turning Christ's triumph over death into the triumph of death over a Christ ritually represented by the *Penitente*; the second, by evoking the Indian's arrow as a means of symbolic aggression against Christ, inserts into the new ritual a trace of the conflict between different cultures.

Opposite the Christ embodied by the *Penitente* (and identified partly with Sebastian but also, as we have seen, with a member of the community of the dead), there is this apparently traditional figure constructed to a large degree out of preexisting symbolic elements. Yet this figure entails such a new, contradictory, and paradoxical use of those elements that she becomes a means of indicating a presence quite alien to the traditional system of representation: the figure of the Native American .

We should also bear in mind that Sebastiana, although a part of the traditional cult of Holy Week, also introduces an inversion of that ritual. If we examine the series of partial identifications of which she is composed (an operation that the believers are careful not to undertake), we can see that it is in fact she who triumphs over Christ, rather than the other way round, as the official tradition would have it. This last aspect makes the representation of her particularly disquieting, for it introduces an alien, partially uncontrollable presence into the Catholic ritual. Lady Sebastiana has a role of her own to play within these ceremonies. It is through her that the Native American warrior, a very real presence and a daily threat, finds a way into the symbolic lexicon of the religious community of the *Penitentes*. It may be this that, among external observers with a different culture, such as Bishop Lamy and the Anglo-Protestants, gave rise to a vague sense of sacrilege and, above all, to the accusation, which may at first sight seem strange, that the *Penitentes shared* with the Native Americans a mysterious cult of death. The Native American warrior is not depicted as such, but he gains access to the church through his bow and his arrows.

This implicit presence of the death-bearing Native American turns Lady Sebastiana into an intense image of an unresolved conflict and a collective vector of something forgotten: a double forgetting, so to speak. On the one hand, this is a forgetting of the original meaning of the Christian ritual of Holy Week, in which Christ triumphs over death, which is first forgotten, then reversed; and, on the other, it is a forgetting that equals a denial of the existing conflict with the Native Americans, which is linked with a rejection of contact and an exasperation at the cultural differences that permeate the entire religious tradition of the *Penitentes*. What the statue of Lady Sebastiana seems to be declaring is: "It is not they, the aliens, who are threatening our lives; but our death does arrive through them. It is death which we recognize, just as the church has always represented it." Except that, precisely, one detail has changed: that arrow that is shot, which plunges the entire representation into ambivalence and turns it into an extreme image of the fragile relationship that may be established at the very heart of the ritual action—the relationship between remembering and forgetting.

IMAGE, CONFLICT, AND PARADOX

To conclude our analysis of antagonistic memories, we must now adopt a more general perspective and try to understand the logic that guides the process of transforming the religious representations, both Amerindian and Hispanic, that we have been considering. In our analysis of the sequence of iconographic transformations that, in New Mexico created the figure of Lady Sebastiana, we have identified a number of aspects of the logic that guides what might be called the posthumous life, or the American survival, of a number of the crucial themes in the figurative tradition of European Christianity that are linked with the representation of death. Sebastiana takes on an enigmatic aspect and acquires her visual intensity as a result of the contamination of different iconographic themes and the polarization of their ritual meanings. Adopting a Warburgian point of view, we may now see her as the extreme outcome of a series of iconographic variations. In this popular and transgressive context, she results from the "reuse" of preexisting materials in order to invent a new image. This is altogether consistent with the aims of Warburg, whose ambition it was to extend the concept of *Nachleben* beyond the limits of the history of European art. However, when Warburg seeks the iconic precedents for an image, he never limits them to formal affinities. His reading of iconographies, as we have noticed many times in this book, may always imply a reconstruction of a morphological series, but it equally aims to go beyond a formal analysis. In his work, an analysis of iconographic models, and in particular of *Pathosformeln*, implies the idea of a posthumous life not only of forms themselves but also of their impact, in particular their ability to inspire belief. In his essay on the Warburgian concept of "reuse," Settis (1997b) makes this point with great clarity. When Nicola Pisano sculpted an angel, taking as his model an image of the young Hercules found on a Roman sarcophagus (Figure 95), he was not simply referring to an iconographic precedent, but also wished to capture the pathos and persuasive force that the image of the young Hercules conveyed, in order to transfer them to a new representation of the Christian angel. The artist thus strives to polarize the force of a preexisting image to transform it into a new representation. Seen in the perspective that I have progressively developed in the present book, this notion of "the force of an image" was conveyed by the idea of the ritual impact of religious representations. In this sense it is quite true that Lady Sebastiana partly owes her pathos to her way of transforming and thereby evoking a whole series of iconographic precedents at the same time as inserting them into a new context. However, the specific visual intensity of this representation (which, we should remember, immediately made her the object of particular devotion among the *Penitentes*, who called her "Goodwife," "friend", etc.) did not result solely from an accumulation of explicit or implicit iconographic precedents. Rather, this representation of her evoked contradictory features and a kind of iconographic dissonance that made her far more complex. In the case of the reuse studied by Settis (and, before him, by Panofsky), the persuasive force of the Roman Hercules is transferred, as a kind of echo, to the figure of the angel: its force is transferred to the representation of the angel, thereby rendering it all the more effective. However, the logic that creates Lady Sebastiana is different. She is the result of a sudden transgression, an invention intended to confront a situation that is both unexpected and dramatic. Hercules confirms and strengthens the Christian angel. Lady Sebastiana contradicts her tradition in an almost sacrilegious way, thereby signaling a crisis in the traditional cult and the birth of a new belief. In her case, the reuse of iconographic features eludes the context of Western tradition. Its purpose is at least in part to contradict a tradition, rather than solely ensure its survival. So what is at stake here is not simply cultural continuity, but also the representation of a split, a confrontation between two opposed fields. In this case, the series of transformations undergone by traditional iconography thus implies a negation of certain features, an allusion to images that are not represented, and an enrichment of those implicit aspects. In this respect, Lady Sebastiana, too, is, in her own way, a chimera.

Let us further explore this point. One of the objections often raised against any attempt to attribute to images a particular function amid the instruments used by tradition consists in declaring that images are too weak and too variable a vector to be really able to transmit knowledge. Even Franz Boas (1927) often expressed his perplexity when faced with this so to speak "semiotically fragile" nature of an image. Perhaps the most widespread illustration of this prejudice is the idea, frequently repeated, that iconographic language cannot express negation. A particularly clear formulation of this notion is to be found expressed in Wittgenstein's 1914–16 *Notebooks*:

> Can one negate a *picture*? No. And in this lies the difference between picture and proposition. The picture can serve as a proposition. But in that case something gets added to it which brings it about that now it *says* something. In short: I can only deny that the picture is right, but the *picture* I cannot deny. *By* my correlating the components of the picture with objects, it comes to represent a situation and to be right or wrong. (Wittgenstein 1961: 33e–34e)

These remarks by Wittgenstein are, as always, very illuminating. For him, it is the logical nature of the image that rules out a discursive treatment that might imply the use of negation, to which, in contrast, we

Figure 95. Nicola Pisano, Pulpit of the Baptistery, Pisa (1257–60), detail.

do often resort when we consider a proposition expressed in linguistic terms. Seen from this point of view, an image can only account for a particular state of things in the world in an inadequate or erroneous manner. To borrow the terms used in the *Tractatus* (Wittgenstein 1922), it is possible to affirm that the internal structure of an image is typical of the act of showing, as opposed to a linguistic proposition's way of engendering a meaning. So an image cannot be denied, since it is not a part of language; it can only convey a meaning if one adds to it a proposition or a commentary. Wittgenstein declares that, on the basis of the articulation of its constitutive parts, an image may correctly reflect the state of things; nevertheless, in the logical sense of the term, an iconic representation cannot predicate. Consequently, it may be false or inadequate to cope with the state of things in the world, but it can never deny or contradict it.

Wittgenstein neglects here two essential aspects of the question. The first is what one might call the connotative complexity of the image. In a brief but extremely dense essay, Michael Baxandall (1993) has, with great precision, analyzed this aspect of an image and its own specific way of engendering meaning, which differentiates it from a linguistic statement. In his comparison between, on the one hand, a text in the Bible describing the annunciation to Mary and, on the other, the visual transposition that Fra Angelico produced in a famous fresco, Baxandall pointed out that transferring a verbal description into an iconic one always involves a very remarkable process. When an artist has to transpose a text into images, not only must he transfer into his representation what the text contains literally (here, for example, an angel, a kneeling young woman, a garden, and so on), but he must also add *other details*. The simple fact of having to transpose a statement into an iconic register obliges the artist to reconstruct a coherence in the image, which, although not without references to the original text, cannot be reduced solely to that. In this way the image always increases the number of the connotations already present in the text. The image, because it is an image, demands a different complexity. That which can be expressed in a linear manner and a sequential form in a text must be transposed, in an image, according to a different syntax, one that organizes a space by means of introducing simultaneous elements. So, when moving from the announcement made to Mary, as the Gospel describes it, to the iconic theme of the Annunciation, Fra Angelico has to imagine (Figure 96) a space entirely

Figure 96. Fra Angelico, *Annunciation*, fresco, 1438, Florence, San Marco Museum.

independent of the text of the Gospel. Baxandall suggested using the term *pictorial enforcement* for this process of creating a meaning strictly linked with the very nature of the image, which leads to limiting the connotations of the text. This basic feature of iconic representation, which consists in always playing upon a plurality of connotations, is certainly present in the religious Hispanic and Apache iconic series that we have studied above. Indeed, that plurality even seems to be one of the essential conditions of the series of transformations that lead from a traditional iconographic schema to a new representation.

The other aspect that Wittgenstein's text neglects is the fact that an image may be related not only to a particular state of things in external reality, but also to other images or other series of images. As we have seen in the case of Lady Sebastiana—but the same could be said of the paradoxical figure interpreted by Silas John in his sacred song—an image may *confirm*, that is to say, correctly imitate, or, on the contrary, *contradict* another image. Both the figure of the Apache shaman-prophet Silas John, and likewise the threatening representation of death invented by the *Penitentes* of New Mexico, may associate within themselves features that are totally contradictory. The presence of a negation expressed in visual terms is thus clearly, in both cases, a common factor in ritual iconography. One might even say that, in all those cases of iconographic transformation, this visual negation presupposes the complex connotations peculiar to the image. Indeed, one important feature of this process lies in the fact that one image may partially contradict another. In such a case, it may both refer to another image yet, at the same time, negate or contradict some feature of it.

It is clear that, at least insofar as the *relations* established *between images* are concerned, it is perfectly possible to make use of negation in an iconic context. The representation of the Apache Christ and that of Lady Sebastiana both illustrate this particular complexity that is peculiar to an image and enables it to include negations of its own, or, rather, to condense contradictory features within itself. We may conclude that even if an image is unable to use negation in the way any proposition does, it can efficiently represent a paradox: the coexistence, often within the context of unresolved conflict, of contradictory elements.

A study of these two cases—the one Amerindian, the other Hispanic—of a transformation of the religious tradition leads one to conclude that an image is able to take on a negative meaning by establishing a paradoxical relation between themes both iconographic and ritual within a tradition. The function of Lady Sebastiana, like that of the Apache shaman who transforms himself into a new Christ, is to use the representation of a paradox to capture an image of the enemy within an already established ritual. In this respect, the two cultural worlds the transformation of which we have reconstructed—that of the Apache and that of the Hispanics of New Mexico—turn out, despite their manifest differences, to be comparable. We have seen that, in the context of the new rituals instituted by Apache messianism, saying that the shaman Silas John was *also* Christ was not a way of betraying the shamanistic tradition, but rather a new way of remaining faithful to it. So it was not entirely new symbols created by the prophet's imagination or his visions that accounted for the rapid propagation of his new ritual. Rather, it was the unexpected relationship that the prophet managed to establish between two contradictory religious messages. The Christian cross that showed the snake (and, behind it, the Gan dancer, the cardinal points, the eagle, the lightning . . .) condensed that process into a single image. In this way the clash between the two rival cultures was interpreted by a visual paradox.

Like the Apache Christ, Lady Sebastiana confronted her enemy at the same time as embodying it. Through this representation, the threat exerted by the presence of the Native American, excluded from explicit discourse, became an aspect of the ritual representation of the Passion in Holy Week. The same image, that of Christ, was thus shot through by not only two different cultures but also two different modalities of a visual interpretation of the conflict through a paradox. Two antagonistic memories confront each other in a single image. You could say that two different silhouettes appear in the representation of Christ on the cross. The iconographic elements (the cross) and even certain ritual features (linked with the relation to the dead) may seem similar. However, the two traditions project upon the image of Christ profoundly different lights and shadows. Like two differently structured crystals, they reflect the light in accordance with incompatible sets of symmetry. The confrontation between two opposed cultures thus gives rise to something resembling a visual illusion, an ambiguous image that can be interpreted in incompatible ways. The process that produces such conflicting images and makes them so effective is still, for the most part, unexplored. The dynamics and logic of it still require further study, and the analysis of different ethnographic examples. But our study of these two religious renaissances, the one in Arizona and the other in New Mexico, leads for the time being to the conclusion that, at the heart of the contact between antagonistic cultures, conflict and contagion, far from being mutually exclusive, can in fact coexist.

Conclusion

Why should traditions and cultures that make a constant and articulate use of images be called simply "oral"? That is the apparently technical question that has prompted this research. It concealed a purely theoretical perplexity. The qualifying term "oral," when applied to the concept of a tradition that presupposes the establishment of a shared knowledge and then a common memory, is not strictly false, but it is misleading on two counts: the first is that it covers a whole family of different uses of language, in particular the two functions, each with its own logic, of narration and ritual activity through the medium of speech. At a textual level, to say that a ritual song and a fairy story or myth are both "oral" reveals neither the resemblances nor the differences between them. It also seems to me that such a description fails to account for one essential aspect, namely, the type of relation established through the use of speech in such different contexts: on the one hand, the expectation implicit in a narrative and, on the other, the progressive construction of an image in which whoever is listening to the ritual song projects his or her own image.

The second reason why I was led to question the concept of orality is that the exclusive distinction between "oral" and "written" masks a third feature, namely the image, despite the fact that, as we have seen, this plays a crucial role in many of the traditions that we have become accustomed simply to call "oral." That is how I came to conceive the notion of tracing the profile of a new concept, that of an iconographic tradition, which is what I set out to do in this book.

Of course, my attempt to venture beyond a distinction so deeply rooted and so familiar in a number of domains of anthropological research right from the start implied a risk of regression into disorder. A taxonomy, even a rudimentary one, always remains a reassuring reference. How can one establish new criteria when those to which we are accustomed turn out to be deeply unsatisfactory? The purpose of much of my work recorded in this book has been to encompass within a unitary but vast geographic area, such as that of Amerindian shamanism, a coherent investigation consisting of what might be called a series of exemplary cases.

My studies of the cultures of the Iatmul, Bahinemo, Kuna, and Apache, but also those of the Dakota, Ojibwa, Cheyenne, Inuit, and New Mexicans, has progressively constituted a series of new criteria and distinctions which, I hope, will be of use in the study of other oral and iconographic traditions. It has led to opening up a new horizon which, in the present Conclusion, I should like to set out in full.

Faced with the perplexity aroused by the distinction between "oral" and "written," my first reaction was to seek some intellectual precedent, a field in which my new research work might discover for itself an intellectual genealogy or—more modestly—a set of premises that would be of use in this new investigation. I discovered such an intellectual precedent in the biology of images, as conceived by the young Warburg. Warburg had a very clear vision of the necessity of images and of their extremely close relationship to thought in any culture. That relationship, although without coinciding with the arts of our own culture, nevertheless does share one of its roots: the manner in which an image orients visual inferences.

This field of the biology of images also suggested a basic methodological move so characteristic of the morphological tradition since the scientific work of Goethe. We might sum it up as follows: when faced with a seemingly infinite multiplicity of phenomena, seek out the most simple example and carefully evaluate its complexity. For me, this turned out to be a study of the mnemonic iconographies of the Sepik (Papua New Guinea): a series of apparently simple images that enabled one to discern a configuration which, although minimal, displayed a number of phenomena constitutive of any cultural memory. This minimal configuration (which one might almost call an *Urphenomenon* of cultural memory) revealed two primary features. On the one hand, it enabled me to identify the linguistic materials that tend to become the subject of the shared knowledge of a tradition, thanks to some visual record; and I noticed that this generally consisted of lists of names of a toponymic or anthroponymic nature. On the other hand, the example of the Sepik enabled the detection of a possible perceptual dynamic, constructed on the basis of a chimerical interaction between heterogeneous visual features that made it possible to represent these names in order to memorize them. I concluded that there are two formal features that organize the most simple techniques for exercising a memory founded upon images. The first is salience, based upon the mobilization of aspects implicit in the image. The second consists in the imposition of an order that organizes images and names in ordered linear sequences, thereby providing the memory with an elementary organization of mental representations. My analysis of the Sepik traditions thus marked my first step toward a concept of cultural tradition founded no longer on the semiotic means (pure speech, either written or spoken) by which representations of knowledge are expressed, but instead upon the *simple but recurrent relations* that are established between different means of expression in a particular culture. That has been the case in the multiple relations that become established, in different ways, in the various traditions that I have analyzed, between images and words. If it is founded upon an analysis of salience and order, the concept of a tradition in this way reaches beyond means of expression and rests, more profoundly and solidly, upon the cognitive functions and the mental operations that are mobilized by the establishment of a common memory. By following up such an approach, an anthropology of memory can evolve toward an anthropology of the exercise of thought.

Initially, I had been concentrating on salience and order. But those two characteristics by no means apply solely to the Oceanic case, for they provide primary elements that define a configuration that can develop and adopt other, more complex, forms. Such is the case of Amerindian pictographs, which we examined in Chapter 2. On the basis of those features, it has been possible to reveal the efficacy and internal coherence of the great Amerindian arts of memory. These arts underwent an original evolution very different from that which, in the traditional view of many historians of writing, leads from pictograms to the invention of writing.

According to that traditional schema, drawings led to signs, a symbolism that was supposed to cover the entire field of words pronounced in some language and, in general, in one language only. In this view a pictogram had to lead to a complete syllabic or alphabetic representation of the sounds made by a language. However, Native American pictography, as I have managed to reconstruct it, has for several centuries followed a quite different path. In an early phase it was linked, in the form of an organized and recognizable iconography (what Mooney [1898], before Warburg, called a "heraldry"), to a specific domain of the tradition, namely the biographical song of a warrior, and so to a very limited linguistic lexicon. The Plains Indians' drawings could, therefore, register only specific features and certain episodes linked to a form of narration and possibly ritual songs that are perfectly identifiable. This lexicon of forms or specifically oriented iconography, although independent of any sound or speech, nevertheless spread throughout the entire family of languages spoken by the Plains Indians, all the way from Alaska to northern Mexico at the very least. In this way, a pictographic notation became, in principle, accessible to locutors who had no knowledge of the language spoken by its author.

From one point of view, an Amerindian pictogram seems more limited than a system of writing. But if we adopt a different perspective, we discover that this system may, on the contrary, be richer, since it ensures communication that spreads beyond the frontiers that separate different languages. But the evolution of the Amerindian pictograph is also unexpected for other reasons. The invention of writing, at least in the form in which it is usually presented, refers to an autonomous symbolism which, as it is applied to the use of daily language, is said to inaugurate a new universe constituted by its own mental operations. In the traditional view, writing is therefore considered to be a means of replacing oral tradition.

Actually, the evolution of pictography presupposes an evolution that runs parallel to that of the oral tradition: it follows the development of the latter or, in certain cases, anticipates that development. Its history is that of the relation between organized speech and iconography. For that reason, a study of the Amerindian pictogram makes it possible to sketch in, in a new and far richer manner, the history of one of the textual forms that, at least since Albert B. Lord's work ([1960] 2000), has been seen as a constitutive element in so-called "oral" traditions: namely, parallelism.

The trajectory of this parallel evolution of pictography and the oral tradition led me to identify a crucial development: the introduction of the use of pictography in the context of ritual utterance. In all the cases that I have studied, the relation between pictographic images and ritualized language is very close. We find it among the Indian warriors of the Plains, the Kuna shamans, and the Apache prophets. In this respect, the pictogram seems to be the crystallized form of a particular type of utterance that possesses the symbolism peculiar to ritual singing—a genre that Native Americans (this book has mentioned several examples) have developed in an unexpected and fascinating manner.

It was precisely through the establishment of this connection between images and ritual speech that there emerged a second order of facts, linked to cultural memory: the elaboration of a conventional image of the locutor. Pictograms not only are used within a well-defined semantic field but also involve a particular type of locutor. So the use of pictography is characterized not only by a particular link with the object but equally by a crucial link with the subject. We have seen how parallelism, one of the ways of organizing salience and order so as to memorize phenomena more complex than mere lists of names, underpins the memorization of ritual songs in Amerindian traditions. But parallelism is not just an instrument of mnemonic codification; it is also a means of orienting evocation and even the type of imagination that evocation implies. Thus, the use of parallelist mnemotechniques gives rise to chimerical creatures: the Celestial Jaguar, the Tree-Woman, the Lightning-Snake, all of which really are creatures engendered by a parallelist imagination. I have called this type of parallelism *objective*, because it is applied to the interpretation of the external world. And, as we have seen, it is particularly highly developed in Amerindian ritual traditions.

However, in these traditions, parallelism does more than influence a vision of the world; it also constitutes an essential instrument for defining the locutor of that vision, the shaman. I have proposed calling the parallelism that is used to define the locutor of ritual utterance *reflexive* parallelism. The development of my study of the pictogram thus led me to study the emergence of a figure who is central to shamanistic singing: an I-memory, a complex locutor described in ritual singing, a number of examples of whom we have studied in the Kuna and Apache shamanistic traditions. That analysis led me to sketch in, through Amerindian shamanism, the general characteristics of a process of communication that is played out in the relations between figures and memory, a process that seemed to me typical of the exercise of ritual speech.

When we speak of non-Western traditions, what fascinate readers and usually researchers too are the new, sometimes astonishing themes around which the beliefs of far-distant or little-known peoples are organized. We find an anaconda that embodies a shaman in Amazonia; a path in the Australian desert marked into the far distance by traces of a life of dreaming; a Yoruba god who is at once a blacksmith and a spirit of lightning and who, in more recent times and in Brazil, has been transformed into a general in command of guards armed with rifles and shining bayonets. Clad in white trousers and a blue jacket and equipped with a gleaming sword, this figure may eventually have been established as a replacement for Saint John on the altar of a Baroque church. The *form* taken by such transmissions of knowledge usually attracts less interest, eliciting no more than a hasty mention of the fact that the transmission of such beliefs from one generation to the next is effected orally. Such an attitude makes it hard to understand or even to notice the considerable differences that, within traditions without writing, distinguish specific modes of transmission. In contrast, empirical research shows that it is only possible to understand how a tradition functions if we study the type of communication that it uses. In the present book we have noted at least two ways of constructing memories. The first, entirely confined to the narrative mode, may seem commonplace: it relies on legends, myths, and stories that are always based upon a linear sequence of episodes that follow on from one another in what is basically a preestablished order. The second mode, in contrast, is linked to ritual and to an iconic formulation of knowledge. The ritual may presuppose a narrative sequence but hardly ever presents it directly. What ritual action, for its part, does is construct complex images that take a form that is not linear but instead is based on simultaneity and a condensation of different aspects, *the commonplaces* that are then transmitted by the tradition. Those who are present at the celebration of a ritual do not follow a storyline as it is recounted; rather, they find themselves in the position of people seeking answers in images that are in many cases allusive or contradictory and that are never immediately understood.

Another formal difference between the narrative and the ritual forms concerns the use of language and, in particular, the definition of the locutor. Anyone can tell a story: its narration seems to flow along spontaneously, encountering no obstacles. Within a culture, we all know a number of stories; and each of us can recount them. In contrast, the locutor of a ritual text is, in most cases, hemmed in by many precautions. His or her identity is complex; it does not go without saying and has to be redefined in the context of any particular instance of communication.

This series of formal features entails important consequences with respect both to the construction of the content of the mental representation and to its interpretation and the type of believing or of heeding that it may imply. The switch from a narrative form to an imagistic one and the definition of a special pragmatics for the locutor in fact define the context of communication and therefore the *type of fiction* that the complex images engendered by the ritual establish and perpetuate in time. The Amerindian shamanistic traditions provide a good model for this process since they construct what is memorable by inserting counterintuitive representations (of fairy-tale yet very familiar creatures) into contexts of utterance and styles of formulation that are themselves counterintuitive. This makes it possible to shed light upon certain aspects of belief that can then be regarded as an exercise of imagination analogous to that which comes into play in a mnemonic evocation. Memory and belief are thus linked through the very exercise of imagination—through an exercise of projection that is oriented by ritual action.

The last chapter in this book tries to establish how this model, which, as we have seen, encompasses both uncertainty and doubt, reacts to cultural conflict. The analysis presented above shows how, in a new context, the anthropological concept of contact and syncretism turns out, in situations of intense conflict, to be both incomplete and overhasty. I tried, first, to see how the logic that led the Apache culture to commandeer certain features of the Whites' culture functioned internally. We have seen the appearance of the figure of Christ undergoing a full metamorphosis prompted by ritual action within a shamanistic context which, for its part, remains completely unchanged. This process engenders a paradoxical figure, a new chimera: a figure doubly defined, both as the son of God sent long ago to Palestine and also, simultaneously as a young Indian who proclaims himself to be the new Messiah. He is not only Christ on the cross but also Lightning and Snake; and possibly also Gan, an ancestral animal. The memories of conflict engender not just a cultural hybrid but, well and truly, a paradox.

That interpretation of conflict, using a visual paradox only made possible by a ritual image, was not embraced solely by Native Americans. Even the European Christian tradition, as dispersed and transformed within the isolated communities of Spanish *Penitentes* who were enemies close to those very Native Americans, displays clear traces of the same process at work. Lady Sebastiana, like the Apache Christ, embodies and at the same time confronts her enemy. The rituals and images on both sides are transformed and encompass new realities. But the conflict, for its part, remains open and the memories on both sides remain resolutely antagonistic.

Christ on the cross in this way becomes an ambiguous idol—an inexhaustible source of scandal and of a new faith.

Bibliography

Agamben, Giorgio. 1998. *Image et mémoire*. Paris: Hoëbeke.

Aristotle. 1972. "De memoria et reminiscentia." In *Aristotle on memory*, edited by Richard Sorabji, 47–60. London: Duckworth.

Austin, John. 1962. *How to do things with words*. Oxford: Oxford University Press.

Balfour, Henry. 1899. *The natural history of the musical bow: A chapter in the developmental history of stringed instruments of music, primitive types*. Oxford: Clarendon Press.

Barasch, Moshe. 1994. *Imago hominis: Studies in the language of art*. New York: New York University Press.

Bartlett, Frederic C. 1932. *Remembering: A study in experimental and social psychology*. Cambridge: Cambridge University Press.

Basile, Bruno. 1979. "Tasso egittologo: Geroglifici, obelischi e faraoni." *Filologia e critica* 4 (1): 21–72.

Basso, Keith. 1970. *The Cibecue Apache*. New York: Holt, Rinehart & Winston.

Basso, Keith, and Ned Anderson. 1975. "A Western Apache writing system." In *Linguistics and anthropology: In honor of C. F. Voegelin*, edited by D. Kinkade and K. Hale, 27–52. Lisse: The Peter de Ridder Press.

Bateson, Gregory. 1932. "Social structure of the Iatmul People of the Sepik River." *Oceania* 2 (3): 245–89; 2 (4): 401–53.

———. (1936) 1958. *Naven: A survey of the problems suggested by a composite picture of the culture of a New Guinea tribe drawn from three points of view*. Stanford: Stanford University Press.

————. 1979. *Mind and nature: A necessary unity.* New York: Dutton.

Bax, Dirk. 1979. *Hieronymus Bosch: His picture-writing deciphered.* Rotterdam: Balkema.

Baxandall, Michael. 1985. *Patterns of intention: On the historical explanation of pictures.* New Haven, CT: Yale University Press.

————. 1993. "Pictorially enforced signification: St. Antonius, Fra Angelico and the Annunciation." In *Hülle und Fülle: Festschrift für T. Buddensieg,* edited by Andreas Beyer, Vittorio Lampugnani, and Gunther Schweikhart, 31–39. Alfter: VDG Verlag.

Berlo, Janet. 1996. *Plains Indian drawings 1865–1935: Pages of a visual history.* New York: Abrams.

Berlo, Janet, and Ruth Phillips. 1998. *Native North American Indian art.* Oxford: Oxford University Press.

Bertozzi, Marco. (1985) 1999. *La tirannia degli astir: Aby Warburg e l'astrologia di Palazzo Schifanoia.* Livorno: Sillabe.

Boas, Franz. 1927. *Primitive art.* Oslo: Aschehoug.

Boissel, Josiane. 1990. "Quand les enfants se mirent à dessiner 1880–1914: Un fragment de l'histoire des idées." *Les Cahiers du Musée National de l'Art Moderne* 31: 15–43.

Bolz, Peter. 1988. "Die Berliner *Dakota-Bibler*: Ein frühes zeugnis des Ledger-Kunst bei den Lakota." *Baessler-Archiv* (Neue Folge) 36: 1–59.

Bolzoni, Lina. (1995) 2001. *The gallery of memory: Literary and iconographic models in the age of the printing press.* Translated by Jeremy Parzen. Toronto: University of Toronto Press.

Bourke, John. (1892) 1993. *The medicine-men of the Apache.* New York: Dover.

————. 2005. *The diaries of John Gregory Bourke,* Vol. 5. Denton: University of North Texas Press.

Bowden, Mark. 1991. *Pitt-Rivers: The life and archaeological work.* Cambridge: Cambridge University Press.

Boyd, Elizabeth. 1991. *Popular arts of Spanish New Mexico.* Santa Fe: Museum of New Mexico Press.

Boyer, Pascal. 1990. *Tradition as truth and communication.* Cambridge: Cambridge University Press.

————. 1994. *The naturalness of religious ideas: A cognitive theory of religion.* Berkeley: University of California Press.

————. 2000. "Functional origins of religious concepts: Ontological and strategic selection (Malinowski Lecture)," *Journal of the Royal Anthropological Institute* (N.S.) 6 (2): 95–214.

Boyer, Pascal, and Carlo Severi. 1997–99. "Cognition, culture et communication: Acquisition et effects culturels des catégories ontologiques intuitives." Research project report. Paris: Ministère de la Recherche.

Boyer, Ruth McDonald, and Narcissus Duffy Gayton. 1992. *Apache mothers and daughters: Four generations of a family*. Norman: University of Oklahoma Press.

Brincard, Marie-Thérèse. 1990. *Afrique: Formes sonores*. Catalogue de l'exposition. Paris: Musée des Arts Africains et Océaniens.

Browne, Alison. 1981. "Dreams and picture-writing: Some examples of this comparison from the sixteenth to the eighteenth century." *Journal of the Warburg and Courtauld Institutes* 24: 90–100.

Bruner, Jerome. 1990. *Acts of meaning*. Cambridge, MA: Harvard University Press.

Camille, Michael. 1996. *The master of death*. Oxford: Oxford University Press.

Canetti, Elias. (1935) 1946. *Auto-da-fé*. Translated by C. V. Wedgewood. London: Cape.

————. (1960) 2000. *Crowds and power*. Translated by Carol Stewart. London: Phoenix.

Carneiro de Cunha, Manuela. 1998. "Pontos de vista sobre a floresta amazonica: Xamanismo e tradução." *Mana: Estudos de Antropologia Social* 4 (1): 7–18.

Carruthers, Mary. (1990) 2008. *The book of memory: A study of memory in medieval culture*. Second edition. Cambridge: Cambridge University Press.

Cassirer, Ernest. 1970. *Philosophy of symbolic forms*, 3 vols. Translated by Ralph Mannheim. New Haven, CT: Yale University Press.

Chadwick, H. Munro. 1926. *The heroic age*. Cambridge: Cambridge University Press.

Chapin, Marc. 1970. *Pap Igala: Historias de la mitologia kuna*. Panama: Universidad Nacional.

————. 1983. "Curing among the Kuna Indians." Ph.D dissertation, University of Arizona.

Chapin, Marc, James Howe, and Joel Sherzer. 1980. *Cantos del congreso kuna*. Panama: Universidad de Panama.

Chavez, Fray A. 1954. "The Penitentes of New Mexico." *The New Mexico Historical Review* 29: 97–123.

Clark, Andy, and David J. Chalmers. 1998. "The extended mind." *Analysis* 58: 7–19.

Cohen, Marcel. 1958. *La grande invention de l'écriture*, 2 vols. Paris: CNRS.

Colley March, Henry. 1889. "The meaning of ornament: Its archaeology and its psychology." *Transactions of the Lancashire Antiquarian Society* 7: 160–91.

———. 1896 "Evolution and psychology in art." *Mind* 20: 442–63.

Crocker, Christopher. 1985. *Vital souls*. Tucson: University of Arizona Press.

Curtius, E. R. 1953. *European literature in the Latin Middle Ages*. Princeton, NJ: Princeton University Press.

Cushing, Frank Hamilton. 1886. "A study in Pueblo pottery as illustrative of Zuñi culture growth." *Fourth Annual Report of the American Bureau of Ethnology, 1882–1883*, 473–521. Washington, DC: Government Printing Office.

Dampierre, Eric de. 1992. *Harpes Zandé*. Paris: Klincksieck.

Darley, Alex M. (1893) 1968. *The Passionists of the South West, or the Holy Brotherhood*. Glorieta, NM: Rio Grande Press.

Darwin, Charles. (1872) 1993. "The expressions of emotions in man and animals." In *The portable Darwin*, 364–93. London: Penguin.

DeFrancis, John. 1990. *Visible speech: The diverse oneness of writing*. Hawaii: University of Hawaii Press.

Descola, Philippe. 1996. *The spears of twilight*. Translated by Janet Lloyd. London: HarperCollins.

Descola, Philippe, and Anne C. Taylor. 1993. "La remontée de l'Amazone." Special issue, *L'Homme* 33 (126–28).

Detienne, Marcel. 1966. *The creation of mythology*. Translated by Margaret Cook. Chicago: University of Chicago Press.

———, ed. 1994. *Transcrire les mythologies*. Paris: Albin Michel.

Devereux, George. 1978. *Ethnopsychoanalysis: Psychoanalysis and anthropology as complementary frames of reference*. Berkeley: University of California Press.

Didi-Hubermann, Georges. 1999. "L'image survivante: Aby Warburg et l'anthropologie tylorienne." *L'Inactuel* 3: 39–59.

Diringer, David. 1937. *L'alfabeto nella storia della civiltà*. Florence: Barbera.

Donato, Maria Monica. 1993. "Archeologia dell'arte: E. Loewy all'università di Roma 1889–1915." Special issue, "L'archeologia italiana dall'unità al novecento," *Ricerche di storia dell'arte* 50: 62–77.

Einstein, Carl. 1992. *Negerplastik*. Berlin: Fannei & Walz.

Eliade, Mircea. (1951) 1989. *Shamanism*. Translated by William R. Trask. London: Arkana.

Ellemberger, Henry. 1970. *The discovery of the unconscious: The history and evolution of dynamic psychiatry*. New York: Basic Books.

Enciso, Martín Fernández de. (1519) 1857. *Descripción de las islas occidentales*. Santiago, Chile.

Errington, Susan, and Donald Gewertz. 1983. *Sepik River societies*. New Haven, CT: Yale University Press.

Escudero, José Agustín de, ed. (1849) 1972. *Noticias históricas y estadísticas de la antigua provincial del Nuevo Mexico*. West Las Vegas, NM: Our Lady of Sorrows Church.

Ewers, John C. (1939) 1979. *Plains Indian painting: A description of an aboriginal American art*. New York: AMS Press.

Fausto, Carlos. (2001) 2012. *War and shamanism in Amazonia*. Cambridge: Cambridge University Press.

Ferg, Alan, ed. 1987. *Western Apache material culture: The Goodwin and Guenther collections*. Tucson: Arizona University Press.

Ferguson, Adam. (1767) 1971. *An essay on the history of civil society*. New York: Garland Publishing.

Fewkes, Jesse Walter. 1892. "A few summer ceremonials at the Tusayan Pueblos." *Journal of American Archaeology and Ethnology* 2: 1–160.

Fiedler, Konrad. (1878) 1994. "Observations on the nature and history of architecture." In *Empathy, form and space: Problems in German aesthetics, 1873–1893*, edited by Harry Francis Mallgrave and Eleftherios Ikonomou, 125–46. Los Angeles: Getty Research Institute Publications.

Forster, Kurt. 1999. "Introduction." In *The renewal of pagan antiquity: Contributions to the cultural history of European Renaissance*, edited by Aby Warburg, 1–76. Los Angeles: Getty Research Institute Publications.

Fox, James J. 1988. *To speak in pairs: Essays in the ritual languages of Eastern Indonesia*. Cambridge: Cambridge University Press.

Foucault, Michel. 1970. *The order of things: An archaeology of the human sciences*. London: Tavistock.

Freud, Sigmund. (1900) 1976. *The interpretation of dreams*. Translated by James Strachey. Harmondsworth: Penguin.

———. 1985. *Civilization, society and religion: Group psychology, civilization and its discontents and other works*. Translated by James Strachey, edited by Albert Dickson. Harmondsworth: Penguin.

Frugoni, Chiara. 1988. "Altri luoghi, cercando il paradiso: Il ciclo di Buffalmacco nel camposanto di Pisa."*Annali della Scuola normale superiore* 18 (4): 1557–643.

Galilei, Galileo. (1610) 1989. *Sidereus nuncius or the sidereal messenger*. Translated by Albert van Helden. Chicago: University of Chicago Press.

———. (1632) 1953. *Dialogue on the great world systems*. Translated by Thomas Salusbury, revised by Giorgio di Santillana. Chicago: University of Chicago Press.

Gassó, Leonardo. 1910–14. "La misión de San José de Narganá entre los Karibes." *Las Misiones Católicas*, Vols. 27–32. Barcelona.

Gelb, Ignace J. 1952. *A study of writing*. Chicago: University of Chicago Press.

Ginzburg, Carlo (1966). 1983. *The night battles: Witchcraft and agrarian cults in the sixteenth and seventeenth centuries*. Translated by John and Anne Tedeschi. London: Routledge & Kegan Paul.

———. (1989) 1991. *Ecstasies: Deciphering the witches' Sabbath*. Translated by Raymond Rosenthal. Harmondsworth: Penguin.

———. 1990a. "From Aby Warburg to E. H. Gombrich: A problem of method." In *Myths, emblems, clues*, 17–59. Translated by John and Anne Tedeschi. London: Hutchinson Radius.

———. 1990b. "Clues: Roots of an evidential paradigm." In *Myths, emblems, clues*, 96–125. Translated by John and Anne Tedeschi. London: Hutchinson Radius.

Gombrich, Ernst. (1960) 1984. *Art and illusion*. Princeton, NJ: Princeton University Press.

———.1970. *Aby Warburg: An intellectual biography*. London: Warburg Institute.

————.1984. "Art history and psychology in Vienna fifty years ago." *Art Journal* 44 (2): 162–64.

————. 1999. "Aby Warburg: his aims and methods: An anniversary lecture." *Journal of the Warburg Institute* 62: 268–82.

Goodwin, Grenville. 1969. *The social organization of the Western Apache.* Tucson: University of Arizona Press.

Goodwin, Grenville, and Charles Kaut. 1954. "A native religious movement among the White Mountain and Cibecue Apache." *Southwestern Journal of Anthropology* 10: 385–404.

Goody, Jack, ed. 1968. *Literacy in traditional societies.* Cambridge: Cambridge University Press.

————. 1987. "Memory and apprenticeship in oral and literate cultures: The reproduction of the Bagre." In *The interface between the oral and the written,* 167–90. Cambridge: Cambridge University Press.

Gozzano, Guido. 1996. *Fiabe e novelline.* Turin: L'Unità/Einaudi.

Graeber, David. 2013. "Culture as creative refusal." *Cambridge Anthropology* 31 (2): 1–19.

Greub, Susan. 1985. *Authority and ornament: Art of the Sepik River.* Basel: Tribal Art Center.

Guidi, Benedetta, and Nicolas Mann. 1998. *Photographs at the frontier: Aby Warburg in America, 1895–1896.* London: Warburg Institute.

Haberland, Eike, and Siegfried Seyfarth. 1974. *Die Yimar am oberen Korowari (Neuguinea).* Wiesbaden: Steiner.

Haddon, Alfred. 1894. *Decorative art of British New Guinea: A study in Papuan ethnography.* Dublin: Academy House.

————. (1895) 1979. *Evolution in art, as illustrated by the life-histories of designs.* New York: AMS Press.

————. 1910. *History of anthropology.* London: Watts & Co.

Haley, James L. 1981. *Apache: A history and culture portrait.* Norman: University of Oklahoma Press.

Harrison, Simon. 1990. *Stealing people's names.* Cambridge: Cambridge University Press.

Hauser-Schäublin, Brigitta. 1983. "The Mwai masks of the Iatmul." *Oral History, Institute of Papua New Guinea Studies* 9 (2): 1–54.

Hays, Hoffman Reynolds. 1958. *From ape to angel: An informal history of social anthropology.* New York: Knopf.

Helms, Mary. 1979. *Ancient Panama.* Austin: University of Texas Press.

Henderson, Alice C. 1937. *Brothers of light: The Penitentes of the South West*. New York: Harcourt Brace.

Henry, Jules. n.d. "The cult of Silas John." Unpublished manuscript.

Herrera, Leonor, and Marianne Cardale y de Schrimpff. 1974. "Mitologia kuna: Los kalu." *Revista Colombiana de Antropologia* 17: 201–48.

Hildebrand, Adolf. (1893) 1994. "The problem of form in the fine arts." In *Empathy, form and space: Problems in German aesthetics, 1873–1893*, edited by Harry Francis Mallgrave and Eleftherios Ikonomou, 227–80. Los Angeles: Getty Research Institute Publications.

Hinsley, Curtis. 1994. *Savages and scientists: A history of the Smithsonian Institute*. Washington, DC: Smithsonian Institution Press.

Hobsbawm, Eric, and Terence Ranger. 1983. *The invention of tradition*. Cambridge: Cambridge University Press.

Hoffman, Walter. (1891) 1975. *Graphic art of the Eskimo*. Washington, DC: AMS Press.

———. 1895. *The Mide-wiwin, or grand society of the Ojibwa. Seventh Annual Report of the Bureau of American Ethnology*. Washington, DC:

———. 1898. "Comparison between Eskimo and other pictographs of the American Indians." Miscellaneous Papers. Washington: Bureau of American Ethnology.

Højbjerg, Christian Kordt, Cecilie Rubow, and Inger Sjørslev. 1999. "Introductory paper." Paper presented at the Institute of Anthropology conference on Religious Reflexivity: Anthropological Approaches to Ambivalent Attitudes to Religious Ideas and Practice, University of Copenhagen, September 15–17.

Holmer, Nils. 1947. *Critical and comparative grammar of the Kuna language*. Göteborg: Etnografiska Museet.

———. 1951. *Kuna crestomathy*. Göteborg: Etnografiska Museet.

———. 1952. *Kuna ethnolinguistic dictionary*. Göteborg: Etnografiska Museet.

Holmer, Nils, and Henry Wassén. (1947) 1953. *The complete Mu-Igala*. Göteborg: Etnografiska Museet.

———. 1958. *Nia ikala: Canto magico para curar la locura*. Göteborg: Etnografiska Museet.

———. 1963. *Dos cantos chamanisticos de los Indios Kuna*. Göteborg: Etnografiska Museet.

Holmes, Richard. 1984. "In Stevenson's footsteps." Special issue, "Travel writing," *Granta* 10: 130–51.

Holmes, William Henry. 1886. "Origin and development of form and ornament in ceramic art." *Fourth Annual Report of the American Bureau of Ethnology 1882–1883*, 443–66. Washington, DC: Government Printing Office.

Houseman, Michael, and Carlo Severi. 1998. *Naven or the other self: A relational approach to ritual action.* Translated by Michael Fineberg. Leiden: Brill.

————. 2001. "Rituel interaktion og illusion." *Tidsskriftet Antropologi* 41: 83–98.

Howe, James. 1976. "Communal land tenure and the origin descent groups among the San Blas Kuna." In *Frontier adaptations in Lower Central America*, edited by Mary W. Helms and Franklin O. Loveland, 151–63. Philadelphia: ISHI.

————. 1986. *The Kuna gathering.* Austin: University of Texas Press.

Howe, James, Joel Sherzer, and Marc Chapin. 1980. *Cantos y oraciones del congreso kuna.* Panama: Editorial Universitaria.

Hugh-Jones, Christine. 1978. *From the Milk River: Spatial and temporal processes in Northwest Amazonia.* Cambridge: Cambridge University Press.

Hugh-Jones, Stephen. 1979. *The palm and the Pleiades: Initiation and cosmology in Northwest Amazonia.* Cambridge: Cambridge University Press.

Humphrey, Caroline. 1996. *Shamans and elders: Experience, knowledge and power among the Daur Mongols.* Oxford: Oxford University Press.

Humphrey, Caroline and James Laidlaw. 1995. *The archetypal actions of ritual.* Oxford: Clarendon Press.

Jakobson, Roman. 1973. *Questions de poétique.* Paris: Le Seuil.

————. 1968. *Six lectures on sound and meaning.* Translated by John Mepham. Hassocks: Harvester.

Kandinsky, Wassily. (1912) 1982. "On the question of form." In *Wassily Kandinsky, complete writings on art*, edited by Kenneth C. Lindsay and Peter Vergo, 235–57. London: Faber.

Karadimas, Dimitri. 1999. "La constellation des quatre singes." *Journal de la Société des Américanistes* 85: 115–46.

Kessel, William B. 1976. "White Mountain Apache religious cult movements: A study in ethnohistory." Ph.D. dissertation, University of Arizona, Flagstaff.

Keyser, James D. 2000. *The Five Crows Ledger: Biographic warrior art of the Flathead Indians.* Salt Lake City: University of Utah Press.

Kramer, Fritz. 1970. *Literature among the Kuna Indians.* Göteborg: Etnografiska Museet.

Kubler, George. 1940. *The religious architecture of New Mexico in the colonial period and the American occupation.* Colorado Springs: The Taylor Museum.

———. 1964. "Introductory essay." In *Santos: An exhibition of the religious folk art of New Mexico,* 1–9. Fort Worth, TX: Amon Carter Museum.

———. 1988. "W. H. Holmes (1846–1933): Geology as panoramic vision." *Res: Anthropology and Aesthetics* 15: 157–62.

La Barre, Weston. 1972. "Materials for a history of studies of crisis cult." *Current Anthropology* 12: 3–44.

Laude, Silvia de. 1992. "Curtius and Warburg." *Strumenti critici* 2: 291–307.

Laurenty, Jean-Sebastien. 1960. *Les cordophones du Congo belge et du Ruanda-Burundi.* Brussels: Tervuren Museum.

Leach, Edmund. 1966. "Ritualization in man in relation to conceptual and social development." *Philosophical Transactions of the Royal Society of London,* series B, 251 (722): 403–8.

Lee, Laurence F. 1920. "Los hermanos Penitentes." *El Palacio* 8 (1).

Lehmann, Walter. 1920. *Zentral-Amerika,* Vol. 1, Part 1. Berlin.

Lévi-Strauss, Claude. 1963. "The effectiveness of symbols." In *Structural anthropology.* Translated by Claire Jacobson and Brooke Grunfest Schoepf, 186–205. Harmondsworth: Penguin.

———. (1964) 1983. *The raw and the cooked.* Translated by John and Doreen Weightman. Chicago: University of Chicago Press.

———. 1982. *The way of the masks.* Translated by Silvia Modelski. London: Cape.

Linton, Ralph. 1943. "Nativistic movements." *American Anthropologist* 43: 230–40.

Lord, Albert B. (1960) 2000. *The singer of tales.* Cambridge, MA: Harvard University Press.

Lovejoy, Arthur O. 1936. *The great chain of being*. Cambridge, MA: Harvard University Press.

Löwy, Emanuel. (1900) 1907. *The rendering of nature in early Greek art*. Translated by John Fothergill. London: Duckworth.

Lummis, Charles F. (1893) 1906. *The land of poco tiempo*. New York: Scribner.

Luria, Aleksandr. 1987. *The mind of a mnemonist: A little book about a vast memory*. Cambridge, MA: Harvard University Press.

Mallery, Garrick. (1893) 1972. *Picture-writings of the American Indians*, Vols. 1 and 2. New York: Dover.

Mallgrave, Henry Francis and Eliftherios Ikonomou, eds. 1994. *Empathy, form and space: Problems in German aesthetics, 1873–1893*. Los Angeles: Getty Research Institute Publications.

Marlowe, Christopher. (1590) 1950. "Tamburlaine the Great." In *Plays*, edited by Edward Thomas. London: Dent & Sons.

Martire, Pietro. 1577. *De rebus oceanicis et novo orbe, decades tres*. Cologne.

Maurer, Evan M., ed. 1992. *Visions of the people: A pictorial history of the Plains Indian life*. Catalogue of the exhibition. Minneapolis: Institute of Arts.

Mercati, Michele. 1598. *De gli obelischi di Roma*. Rome.

Métraux, Alfred. (1959) 1972. *Voodoo in Haiti*. Translated by Hugo Charteris. New York: Schocken.

Michaud, Philippe-Alain. 2007. *Aby Warburg and the image in motion*. Translated by Sophie Hawkes. New York: Zone Books.

Momigliano, Arnaldo, ed. 1982. *Hermann Usener: Filologo della religion*. Seminar at the Pisa Scuola Normale, Giardini.

Mooney, James. 1896. "The *Ghost Dance* religion and the Sioux outbreak of 1890." *Annual Report of the Bureau of American Ethnology* 14 (2): 635–1136.

———.1898. "Calendar history of the Kiowa Indians." *Annual Report of the Bureau of American Ethnology* 17: 141–468.

Morison, Samuel Eliot. 1942. *Admiral of the ocean sea: A life of Christopher Columbus*. Boston: Little Brown.

Napier, A. David. 1987. *Masks, transformation, and paradox*. Berkeley: University of California Press.

———. 1996. *Foreign bodies: Performance, art, and symbolic anthropology*. Berkeley: University of California Press.

Needham, Rodney. 1972 *Belief, language, and experience*. Oxford: Blackwell.

Newton, Douglas. 1971. *Crocodile and cassowary: Religious art of the Upper Sepik River*. New York: Museum of Primitive Art.

Nordenskiöld, Erland. 1928. "Picture-writings and other documents." *Comparative Ethnographical Studies* 7 (2).

———. 1930. "Karl von den Steinen." *Journal de la Société des Américanistes* 22.

———. 1938. *An historical and ethnological survey of the Kuna Indians*. Göteborg: Etnografiska Museet.

Novalis. (1797–98) 1984. "Vermischte bemerkungen (und blüthenstaub)." In *Fragmente und studien: Die Christenheit oder Europa*, edited by Carl Paschek. Stuttgart: Reclam.

Opler, Morris. 1941. *An Apache life-way: The economic, social, and religious institutions of the Chiricahua Indians*. Chicago: University of Chicago Press.

Overholt, Thomas W. 1974. "The *Ghost Dance* of 1890 and the nature of the prophetic process." *Ethnohistory* 21: 37–63.

Oviedo y Valdes, Gonzalo F. de. 1851–55. *Historia general y natural de las Indias*, Vol. 4. Madrid.

Pagden, Anthony. 1982. *The fall of natural man: The American Indian and the origins of comparative ethnology*. Cambridge: Cambridge University Press.

Palomera, Esteban. 1963. *Fray Diego Valades: Evangelizador humanista de la Nueva España*. Mexico: Editorial Jus.

Panofsky, Erwin. 1955. *The life and art of Albrecht Dürer*. Revised 2nd edition. Princeton, NJ: Princeton University Press.

Parry, Milman. 1930. "Studies in the epic technique of oral verse-making. I. Homer and Homeric style." *Harvard Studies in Classical Philology* 41: 73–148.

Patterson, Alex. 1994. *Hopi pottery symbols*. Illustrated by Alexander M. Stephen, William Henry Holmes, and Alex Patterson. Based on the *Pottery of Tusayan*. Catalogue of the Keam Collection, 1890. Boulder, CO: Johnson Books.

Perrin, Michel. 1976. *Le chemin des indiens morts*. Paris: Payot.

Petersen, Karen D. 1971. *Plains Indian art from Fort Marion.* Norman: Oklahoma University Press.

———. 1988. *American pictographic images: Historical works on paper by the Plains Indians.* New York: Alexander Gallery.

Piggott, Glyne, and Ann Grafstein. 1983. *An Ojibwa lexicon.* Ottawa: National Museums of Canada.

Pitt-Rivers, Augustus H. (1874) 1979. "Principles of classification." In *The evolution of culture and other essays*, 1–19. New York: AMS Press.

———. (1875) 1979. "On the evolution of culture." In *The evolution of culture and other essays*, 20–44. New York: AMS Press..

Pomian, Krzysztof. 1999. *Sur l'histoire.* Paris: Gallimard.

Pouillon, Jean. 1983. *Le cru et le su.* Paris: Seuil.

Prestan, Amulfo. 1975. *El uso de la chicha y la sociedad kuna.* Mexico: Instituto indigenista interamericano.

Propp, Vladimir. (1946) 1983. *Les racines historiques du conte merveilleux.* Paris: Gallimard.

Prosperi, Adriano. 2000. *L'eresia del Libro Grande.* Milan: Feltrinelli.

Rael, Juan B. 1951. *The New Mexican alabado.* Stanford: Stanford University Press.

Ramusio, G. B. 1985. *Navigazioni e viaggi*, Vol. 5. Turin: Einaudi.

Raulff, Ulrich. 1998. "The seven skins of the snake: Oraibi, Kreuzlingen, and back; stations on a journey into light." In *Photographs at the frontier: Aby Warburg in America, 1895–1896*, edited by Benedetta Cestelli Guidi and Nicholas Mann, 64–74. London: Warburg Institute.

Reagan, Albert. 1930. "Notes on the Indians of the Apache region." *Anthropological Papers of the American Museum of Natural History*, Vol. 31.

Ricci, Corrado. 1887. *Arte dei bambini.* Bologna: Zanichelli.

Ricoeur, Paul. 1988. *Time and narrative*, Vol. 3. Translated by Kathleen McLaughlin and David Pellauer. Chicago: University of Chicago Press.

Riegl, Alois. 1992. *Problems of style: Foundations for a history of ornament.* Translated by Evelyn Kain. Princeton, NJ: Princeton University Press.

Rieupeyrout, Jean-Louis. 1987. *Histoire des Apache.* Paris: Albin Michel.

Rodriguez, Sylvia. 1996. *The Matachines Dance: Ritual, symbolism, and interethnic relations in the Upper Rio Grande Valley.* Albuquerque: University of New Mexico Press.

Roi, Gaetano. 1998. *La bellezza dell'invisibile: L'ombra poetica del sintomo.* Milan: F. Angeli.

Rossi, Paolo. 1969. *Le sterminate antichità: Studi Vichiani.* Pisa: Nistri-Lichi.

———. 1983. *Clavis universalis.* Bologna: Il Mulino.

———. 1991. *Il passato, la memoria, l'oblio.* Bologna: Il Mulino.

Rubin, William. 1984. *Twentieth-century art primitivism,* Vol. 1. New York: Museum of Modern Art.

Sales, Anne de. 1991. *"Je suis né de tes coups de tambour": Sur le chamanisme magar (Nepal).* Paris: Société d'Ethnologie.

Sangro, Raimondo di. 1982. "Parole maestre." *Tauma* 3.

Sassi, Maria Michela. 1982. "Dalla scienza delle religioni di Hermann Usener ad Aby Warburg." In *Hermann Usener: Filologo della religion,* edited by A. Momigliano, 65–91. Seminar at the Scuola Normale. Pisa: Giardini.

Saxl, Fritz. 1957. "Warburg's visit to New Mexico." In *Lectures,* Vol. 1, 325–30. London: Warburg Institute.

Schegloff, Emmanuel. 1992. "To Searle on conversation: A note in return." In *(On) Searle on conversation,* edited by John Searle, Herman Parret, and Jef Verschueren, 113–28. Amsterdam: John Benjamins.

Scherner, Karl A. 1861. *Das Leben des Traumes* Berlin.

Schoell-Glass, Charlotte. 1998. *Aby Warburg und der antisemitismus.* Frankfur on Main: Fischer.

Schoolcraft, Henry G. 1851. *Historical and statistical information respecting the history, condition, and prospects of the Indian tribes of the United States, collected and prepared under the direction of the Bureau of Indian Affairs.* Philadelphia: Lippincott.

Schuster, Carl. 1993. "Comparative studies of certain motifs in cotton embroideries from Western China." *Res: Anthropology and Aesthetics* 24: 45–54.

Schuster, Meinhardt. 1965. "Hakenfiguren der bahinemo." In *Festchrift für Alfred Bühler,* edited by Carl A. Schmitz and Robert Wildhaber, 628–803. Basel: Pharos Verlag.

Searle, John R. 1969. *Speech acts.* Cambridge: Cambridge University Press.

Semper, Gottfried. 1989. *The four elements of architecture and other writings.* Cambridge: Cambridge University Press.

Settis, Salvatore. 1985. "Warburg continuatus: Descrizione di una biblioteca" *Quaderni Storici* 58: 5–38.

———. 1990. *Giorgione's tempest: Interpreting the hidden subject.* Translated by Ellen Bianchini. Cambridge: Polity.

———. 1993. "Kunstgeschicte als vergleichende kulturwissenschaft: Aby Warburg, die Pueblo-Indianer und das nachleben der antike." In *Kunstlerischer Austausch/artistic exchange, Akten des XXVII Internationalen Kongresses für Kunstgeschichte*, Berlin, July 15–20, 1992, edited by Thomas W. Gaehtgens, 139–58. Berlin: Akademie Verlag.

———. 1997a. "Pathos und Ethos: Morphologie und Funktion." In *Vorträge aus dem Warburg Haus*, 33–73. Berlin: Akademie Verlag.

———. 1997b. "Les remplois." In *Patrimoine, temps, espace: Actes des entretiens du patrimoine*, edited by François Furet. Paris: Fayard.

Severi, Carlo. 1982. "Le chemin des metamorphoses: Un modèle de connaissance de la folie dans un chant chamanique kuna." *Res: Anthropology and Aesthetics* 3: 32–67.

———. 1987. "The invisible path: Ritual representation of suffering in Cuna traditional thought." *Res: Anthropology and Aesthetics* 14: 66–85.

———. 1988. "Structure et forme originaire." In *Les idées de l'anthropologie*, edited by Philippe Descola, Gérard Lenclud, Carlo Severi, and Anne-Christine Taylor, 117–50. Paris: Armand Colin.

———. 1990. "L'io testimone: Biografia e autobiografia in antropologia." *Quaderni storici* 75, 15 (3): 896–918.

———. 1991. "Una stanza vuota: Antropologia della forma onirica." In *Il sogno rivela la natura delle cose.* Exhibition catalogue, 226–74. Bolzano: Mazzotta.

———. 1992a. "Présence du primitive: Masques et chimères dans l'oeuvre de Joseph Beuys." *Cahiers du Musée National d'Art Moderne* 42: 31–47.

———. 1992b. "Le chamanisme et la dame du Bon Jeu: À propos d'un livre de C. Ginzburg." *L'Homme* 121, 32 (1): 165–77.

———. 1993a. "Protée ou la propagation d'une forme: Art primitif et mémoire." In *Künstlerischer Austausch/artistic exchange, Akten des XXVII Internationalen Kongresses für Kunstgeschichte*, edited by Thomas W. Gaehtgens, 121–38. Berlin: Akademie Verlag.

———. 1993b. "Talking about souls: The pragmatic construction of meaning in Kuna shamanistic chants." In *Cognitive aspects of religious symbolism*, edited by Pascal Boyer, 165–81. Cambridge: Cambridge University Press.

———. 1993c. *La memoria rituale: Follia e imagine del Bianco in una tradizione sciamanica amerindiana.* Florence: La Nuova Italia.

———. 1994. "Paroles durables et écritures perdues: Réflexions sur la pictographie kuna." In *Transcrire les mythologies*, edited by Marcel Detienne, 45–73. Paris: Albin Michel.

———. 1997. "The Kuna picture-writing: A study in iconography and memory." In *The art of being Kuna: Layers of meaning among the Kuna of Panama*, edited by Mari Lyn Salvador, 245–73. Exhibition catalogue. Los Angeles: Fowler Museum.

———. 1999a. "Scritture figurate e arti della memoria nel nuovo mondo: Valades, Schoolcraft, Löwy." In *Memoria e memorie*, edited by Lina Bolzoni, 29–65. Rome: Accademia dei Lincei; Florence: Olschki.

———. 1999b. "Les ratés de la coutume: Folies chrétiennes et rituels de guérison." A critique of *Folie, marriage et mort: Pratiques de la folie en Occident* by G. Charuty. *L'Homme* 150: 235–42.

———. 2001a. "Cosmology, crisis, and paradox: On the White Spirit in the Kuna shamanistic tradition." In *Disturbing remains: Memory, history, and crisis in the twentieth century*, edited by Michael S. Roth and Charles G. Salas, 178–206. Los Angeles: Getty Institute for the History of Art and the Humanities Publications.

———. 2001b. "La parola-percorso: Ordine e salienza nella tradizione orale." *Quaderni della Società Italiana di Antropologia del Mondo Antico* 4: 107–37.

———. 2002a. "Memory, reflexivity and belief: Reflections on the ritual use of language." Special issue, *Social Anthropology* 10 (1): 23–40.

———. 2002b. "Here and there: Supernatural landscapes in Kuna shamanistic tradition." In *Tod, jenseits und identität: Perspektiven einer kulturwissenschaftlichen thanatologie*, edited by Jan Assmann and Rolf Trauzettel, 587–612. Munich: Karl Alber Verlag.

———. 2003. "Warburg anthropologue, ou le déchiffrement d'une utopie: De la biologie des images à l'anthropologie de la mémoire." In *Image et anthropologie*, edited by Carlo Severi. *L'Homme* 65: 77–129.

———. 2009. "L'empathie primitiviste: Intensification de l'image et déchiffrement de l'espace." In *Traditions et temporalités des images*, edited by Carlo Severi, Giovanni Careri, François Lissarrague, and

Jean-Claude Schmitt, 165–88. Paris: Éditions de l'École des Hautes Études en Sciences Sociales.

Severi, Carlo, and Enrique Gomez. 1983. "Nia Ikala, los pueblos del camino de la locura: Texto kuna y traducción espanola." *Amerindia: Revue d'Ethnolinguistique Amérindienne* 8: 129–79.

Shalkop, Robert. 1970. *Spanish colonial painting.* Colorado Springs: The Taylor Museum.

Sherzer, Joel. 1983. *Kuna ways of speaking.* Austin: University of Texas Press.

———. 1990. *Verbal art in San Blas.* Cambridge: Cambridge University Press.

———. 1990. "The grammar of poetry and the poetry of magic: How to grab a snake in the Darién." In *Verbal art in San Blas: Kuna culture through its discourse,* edited by Joel Sherzer, 239–65. Cambridge: Cambridge University Press.

Silverman, Eric. 1993. *Tambunum: New perspectives on Eastern Iatmul (Sepik River, Papua New Guinea), kinship, marriage, and society.* Minneapolis: University of Minnesota Press.

Simón, Pedro. 1882. *Noticias historiales de las conquistas de tierra firme.* Bogota.

Smith, Pierre. (1979) 1982. "Aspects of the organization of rites." In *Between belief and transgression: Structuralist essays in religion, history, and myth,* edited by Michel Izard and Pierre Smith. Translated by John Leavitt, 103–28. Chicago: University of Chicago Press.

Spence, Jonathan. 1985. *The memory palace of Matteo Ricci.* New York: Penguin.

Spencer, Herbert. 1855. *Principles of psychology.* London: Longman, Brown, Green, and Longmans.

Sperber, Dan. 1975. *Rethinking symbolism.* Translated by Alice L. Morton. Cambridge: Cambridge University Press.

———. 1985. "Anthropology and psychology: Toward an epidemiology of representations." *Man* (N.S.) 20: 73–89.

———. 1996. *Explaining culture: A naturalistic approach.* Oxford: Blackwell.

Sperber, Dan, and Deirdre Wilson. 2012. *Relevance: Communication and cognition.* Oxford: Blackwell.

Spinelli, Italo, and Roberto Venuti, eds. 1998. *Mnemosyne: L'Atlante della memoria di Aby Warburg*. Rome: Artemide.

Stanek, Milan. 1983. *Sozialordnung und Mythik in Palimbe: Bausteine zur ganzheitliche Beschreibung einer Dorfgemeinschaft der Iatmul, East Sepik Province, Papua New Guinea*. Ethnologisches Seminar der Universität-Museum fur Völkerkunde-Wepf, Basel. *Basler Beiträge zur Ethnologie* 23.

Stark, Louisa. 1971. "The origin of the Penitente Death Cart." *Journal of American Folklore* 84: 304–11.

Steele, Thomas. 1974. *Santos and saints*. Albuquerque: Calvin Horn.

Stevenson, Robert L. (1879) 2004. *Travels with a donkey in the Cévennes and The amateur emigrant*. London: Penguin.

Stirling, Matthew. 1938. "Three pictographic autobiographies of Sitting Bull." *Smithsonian Miscellaneous Collections* 97 (5): 1–56.

Stoller, Paul. 1989. *Fusion of the worlds: An ethnography of possession among the Songhay of Niger*. Chicago: University of Chicago Press.

Stolpe, Hjalmar. 1927. *Collected essays in ornamental art*. Stockholm: Aftonbladets Tryckeri.

Stout, David. 1947. *San Blas Cuna acculturation: An introduction*. New York: Viking Fund Publications in Anthropology.

Szabo, Joyce M. 1994. *Howling Wolf and the history of ledger art*. Albuquerque: University of New Mexico Press.

Tambiah, Stanley J. 1985. *Culture, thought, and social action: An anthropological perspective*. Cambridge, MA: Harvard University Press.

Taylor, Andrew. 1987. *El arte de la memoria en el Nuevo Mundo*. San Lorenzo del Escorial: Swan Editorial.

Tedlock, Dennis. 1983. *The spoken word and the work of interpretation*. Philadelphia: University of Pennsylvania Press.

Telban, Borut. 1998. *Dancing through time: A Sepik cosmology*. Oxford: Oxford University Press.

Thomas, Nicholas. 1995. *Oceanic art*. London: Thames & Hudson.

Thompson, Michael W. 1977. *General Pitt-Rivers: Evolution and archaeology in the nineteenth century*. Bradford-on-Avon: Moonraker.

Thrapp, Dan. 1988. *The conquest of Apacheria*. Norman: University of Oklahoma Press.

Townsley, Graham. 1993. "Song paths. The ways and means of Yaminahua shamanic knowledge." *L'Homme* 33 (126–128): 449–68.

Triana, Miguel. 1921. *La civilizacion chibcha*. Bogota.

Tuite, Kevin. 1992. "Towards a typology of words and non-words in South-Caucasian Literature." Address to the congress of the Canadian Society of Anthropology, Montreal.

———— 1993. "Relations between the sexes in SouthCaucasian folk poetry," *Annual of the Society for the Study of Caucasia* 4–5: 3–32.

Urban, Greg. 1986. "Ceremonial dialogues in South America." *American Anthropology* 88 (2): 385–400.

Urry, James. 1993. "From zoology to ethnology: A. C. Haddon's conversion to anthropology." In *Before social anthropology: Essays in the history of British anthropology*, 61–82. Philadelphia: Harwood Academic Publishers.

Valadés, Diego. (1579) 1983. *Rhetorica Christiana ad concionandi et orandi usum accommodata, utriusque facultatis exemplis suo loco insertis; quae quidem, ex indorum maxime deprompta sunt historiis. Unde praeter doctrinam, summa quoque delectatio comparabitur.* . . . Translated and edited by Esteban J. Palomera. Mexico: Fondo de Cultura Economica, Universidad Nacional Autónoma de México.

Valeriano, Pier. 1556. *Hieroglyphica seu de sacris Aegyptiorum literis*. Basel.

Velasquez, Ronny. 1992. "El canto chamanico de los indigenas Kuna de Panama." Ph.D. dissertation, Universidad central de Venezuela, Caracas.

Vernant, Jean-Pierre. 1980. "The myth of Prometheus in Hesiod." In *Myth and society in Ancient Greece*, translated by Janet Lloyd, 183–201. New York: Zone Books.

Vignoli, Tito. 1879. *Mito e scienza*. Milan: Fratelli Dumolard.

Vischer, Robert. (1873) 1994. "On the optical sense of form: A contribution to aesthetics." In *Empathy, form and space: Problems in German aesthetics, 1873–1893*, edited by Harry Francis Mallgrave and Eleftherios Ikonomou, 89–124. Los Angeles: Getty Research Institute Publications.

Viveiros de Castro, Eduardo. 1989. *From the enemy's point of view*. Chicago: University of Chicago Press.

————. 1991. "Spirits of being, spirits of becoming: Bororo shamanism as ontological theatre." *Reviews in Anthropology* 16: 77–92.

————. 1996. "Os pronomes cosmologicos e o perspectivismo amerindio." *Mana: Estudos de Antropologia Social* 2 (2): 115–44.

Voltaire. 1794. *Zadig, or the book of fate: an oriental history*. No translator given. London: Cook.

von den Steinen, Karl. (1894) 1940. *Unter den natturvölkern Zentral-Brasiliens*. Published in Brazil as "Entre os aborigenes do Brasil Central." *Revista do Arquivo*, 34–57. São Paolo: Departamento de Cultura.

Walker, Paul. 1958. *Spiritual and demonic magic: From Fucino to Campanella*. London: Warburg Institute.

Wallis, Michael. 1994. *En divina luz: The Penitente moradas of New Mexico*. Albuquerque: University of New Mexico Press.

Warburg, Aby. (1923) 2007. "Memories of a journey through the Pueblo region." In *Aby Warburg and the image in motion*, Philippe-Alain Michaud. Translated by Sophie Hawkes, 293–330. New York: Zone Books.

———. (1927) 2007. "On planned American visit." In *Aby Warburg and the image in motion*, Phillipe-Alain Michaud, 331–35. Translated by Sophie Hawkes. New York: Zone Books.

———. (1929) 1998. "Introduzione." In *Mnemosyne: L'Atlante della memoria di Aby Warburg*, edited by Italo Spinelli and Roberto Venuti, 37–43. Rome: Artemide.

———. (1932) 1999. *The renewal of pagan antiquity: Contributions to the cultural history of the European Renaissance*. Los Angeles: Getty Research Institute Publications.

———. (1939)1988. *Schlangenritual: Ein reisebericht*. Berlin: Verlag Klaus Wagenbach. English translation, 1939 "A lecture on serpent ritual." *Journal of the Warburg Institute* 2: 277–92.

Wassman, Jürg. (1982) 1991. *The song to the flying fox: The public and esoteric knowledge of the important men of Kandingei about totemic songs, names, and knotted cords (Middle Sepik, Papua New Guinea)*. Boroko, Papua New Guinea: Cultural Studies Division, National Research Institute.

———. 1988. *Der Gesang an das Krokodil: Die rituellen Gesänge des Dorfes Kandingei an Land und Meer, Pflanzen und Tiere (Mittelespik, Papua New Guinea)*. Ethnologisches Seminar der Universität-Museum für Völkerkunde-Wepf, Basel.

Weigle, Marta. 1976. *Brothers of light, brothers of blood: The Penitentes of the South West*. Albuquerque: University of New Mexico Press.

———. 1977. "Ghostly flagellants and Doña Sebastiana: Two legends of the Penitente brotherhood." *Western Folklore* 36 (2): 135–47.

———. 1983. *Hispanic arts and ethnohistory*. Albuquerque: University of New Mexico Press.

Weigle, Marta, and Thomas R. Lyons. 1982. "Brothers and neighbors: The celebration of community in Penitente villages." In *Celebration: Studies in festivity and ritual*, edited by Victor Turner, 231–54. Washington, DC: Smithsonian Institution Press.

Wengrow, David. 2011. "'Archival' and 'sacrificial' economies in Bronze Age Eurasia: An interactionist approach to the hoarding of metals." In: *Interweaving worlds: Systemic interactions in Eurasia, 7th to the 1st millennia BC*, edited by Toby C. Wilkinson, Susan Sherratt, and John Bennet, 135–44. Oxford: Oxbow.

Whitehouse, Harvey. 1992. "Memorable religions: Transmission, codification and change in divergent Melanesian context." *Man* (N.S.) 27: 777–97.

———. 2000. *Arguments and icons: Divergent modes of religiosity*. Oxford: Oxford University Press.

Wied, Maximilian zu. (1833–34) 1976. *People of the first man: Life among the Plains Indians in the final days of glory. The first account of Prince Maximilian's expedition up the Missouri River, 1833–1834*. New York: Dutton.

Wiesel, Elie. 1972. *Célébration hassidique*. Paris: Seuil.

Wilbert, Johannes. 1993. *Mystic endowment: Religious ethnography of the Warao Indians*. Cambridge, MA: Harvard University Press.

Wind, Edgar. 1964. *Art and anarchy*. New York: Knopf.

———. 1980. *Pagan mysteries of the Renaissance*. Oxford: Oxford University Press.

———. 1983. "On a recent biography of Warburg." In *The eloquence of symbols: Studies in humanist art*, edited by Edgar Wind, 106–13. Oxford: Clarendon Press.

———. 1983. "Warburg's conception of *Kulturwissenschaft* and its meaning for aesthetics." In *The eloquence of symbols: Studies in humanist art*, edited by Edgar Wind, 21–35. Oxford: Clarendon Press.

Wittgenstein, Ludwig. 1922. *Tractatus logico-philosophicus*. Translated by David Francis Pears and Brian McGuinness. London: Routledge & Kegan Paul.

———. 1961. *Notebooks 1914–1916.* Translated by G. E. M. Anscombe. Oxford: Blackwell.

———. 1963. *Philosophical investigations.* Translated by G. E. M. Anscombe. Oxford: Blackwell.

Wittkower, Rudolf. (1972) 1977. "Hieroglyphics in the early Renaissance." In *Allegory and the migration of symbols*, 114–28. London: Thames & Hudson.

Wölfflin, Heinrich. (1886) 1994. "Prolegomena toward a psychology of architecture." In *Empathy, form and space: Problems in German aesthetics, 1873–1893*, edited by Harry Francis Mallgrave and Eleftherios Ikonomou, 150–93. Los Angeles: Getty Research Institute Publications.

Wong, Hertha Dawn. 1992. *Sending my heart back across the years.* Oxford: Oxford University Press.

Woodward, Dorothy. (1935) 1974. *The Penitentes of New Mexico.* New York: Arno Press.

Worsley, Peter. 1968. *The trumpets shall sound: A study of cargo cults in Melanesia.* New York: Schocken Books.

Wroth, William. 1983. "La sangre de Cristo: History and symbolism." In *Hispanic arts and ethnohistory*, edited by Marta Weigle, 283–92. Albuquerque: University of New Mexico Press.

———. 1991. *Images of penance, images of mercy: Southwestern santos in the late nineteenth century.* Norman: University of Oklahoma Press.

Wundt, Wilhelm. (1896) 2014. *Lectures on human and animal psychology.* Hove: Routledge.

Yates, Frances. 1966 *The art of memory.* London: Faber.

Zempleni, Andras. 1987. "Des êtres sacrificiels." In *Sous le masque de l'animal: Essais sur le sacrifice en Afrique noire*, edited by Michel Cartry, 267–317. Paris: Presses Universitaires de France.

Index

HAU Books is committed to publishing the most distinguished texts in classic and advanced anthropological theory. The titles aim to situate ethnography as the prime heuristic of anthropology, and return it to the forefront of conceptual developments in the discipline. HAU Books is sponsored by some of the world's most distinguished anthropology departments and research institutions, and releases its titles in both print editions and open-access formats.

www.haubooks.com

Supported by
Hau-N. E. T.
Network of Ethnographic Theory

University of Aarhus – EPICENTER (DK)
University of Amsterdam (NL)
University of Bergen (NO)
Brown University (US)
California Institute of Integral Studies (US)
University of Canterbury (NZ)
University of Chicago (US)
University of Colorado Boulder Libraries (US)
CNRS – Centre d'Études Himalayennes (FR)
Cornell University (US)
University of Edinburgh (UK)
The Graduate Institute, Geneva Library (CH)
University of Helsinki (FL)
Johns Hopkins University (US)
University of Kent (UK)
Lafayette College Library (US)
Institute of Social Sciences of the University of Lisbon (PL)
University of Manchester (UK)
The University of Manchester Library (UK)
Museu Nacional – UFRJ (BR)
Norwegian Museum of Cultural History (NO)
University of Oslo (NO)
University of Oslo Library (NO)
Pontificia Universidad Católica de Chile (CL)
Princeton University (US)
University of Queensland (AU)
University of Rochester (US)
Universidad Autónoma de San Luis Potosi (MX)
University of Sydney (AU)

www.haujournal.org/haunet

Printed and bound by CPI Group (UK) Ltd, Croydon, CR0 4YY

09/06/2025

14685765-0001